MICROCOMPUTER PRIMER

by

Mitchell Waite
and Michael Pardee

Howard W. Sams & Co., Inc.
4300 WEST 62ND ST. INDIANAPOLIS, INDIANA 46268 USA

Preface

This new expanded second edition of *Microcomputer Primer* marks a major turning point in the brief but exciting history of the microcomputer. In the five years since its birth, microprocessor technology has managed to spread into just about every imaginable area of commerce. Consequently, there has been an "explosion" of new innovative methods for working with micros, and, as to be expected, there is an even greater need for understanding how these magic "slices" of electronic intelligence actually work.

This new edition has been revised, updated, and broadened to cover the most recent advances in microprocessor technology. One of the most important of these advances is the new breed of supermicroprocessor, a micro with vastly increased computing power—so much power that this new breed rivals the largest mainframe computers, like the giants from IBM. These are supermicroprocessors that handle 8, 16, 32, and even 64 bit data, and manipulate megabytes of memory. These new devices are a result of further perfections in microminiaturization, and the first of the new VLSI chips . . . *Very Large Scale Integration*. VLSI promises the world a new surge of intelligent products with more capability, efficiency, and reliability than was previously possible. We have expanded the book to include these devices in the MPU Comparison section: the 16-bit micros—8086, Z8000, and 68000; an assortment of new 8-bit micros—2650, 1802, and Z80; and the new "enhanced" 8-bit microprocessors that work internally like 16-bit machines—6809 and 8089. For those wishing to compare this second edition with the first edition, by far the greatest changes have occurred in the realm of hardware, and this is reflected in the added new text and drawings in Chapters 3,

4, and 5. For example, it is no longer a pain to work and construct circuits around 40-pin chips thanks to new tools and construction aids. Consequently we have added information on new ribbon cable interconnect devices, bus-organized prototyping boards, solderless breadboards, and a new innovation in wire wrapping called "slit-n-wrap." For those who do not wish to "reinvent the wheel," a new section on the commercial single-board prototyping computers is provided. These devices which are already set up to interface to the real world are completely tested by the manufacturer, and are a terrific way to learn how to use microprocessors. Besides improvements in the microprocessor itself, many new interface devices have been developed, including Tri-State buffers, latches, and byte-wide transceivers; these are included in all places where they would be useful. More importance has been placed on the microcomputer interface. The new intelligent programmable support chips made especially for input/output, such as the PIA, are explained, and a super low parts count interface to a display and keyboard using a PIA is examined. Another area affected is the memory of the microcomputer. New low-cost "dynamic" RAM chips are explained and a complete schematic of a 64K byte dynamic RAM memory is presented.

There is also tutorial information provided on these new hardware subjects: single instruction stepping, I/O interfacing, buses, switching power supplies, memory-mapped video methods, and EPROM programmers.

The software front is one area where microcomputers have really "grown-up," particularly in the utilization of mass-storage devices, like the floppy disk. As a result of the floppies, microcomputers of today have the ability to store and to make vast amounts of information accessible in super fast time. With such information control, the microcomputer has evolved an overall group of management, utility, and development programs that, among other things, help to write other programs, and are properly referred to as the "operating system" of the computer. In Chapter 7 we have attempted to give the reader a brief picture of the various software aids such as assemblers, compilers, and interpreters, and to show how they are used in concert on a typical system.

Until recently, few people have had the opportunity to really get involved with computer hardware and software. However, with the development of the microprocessor, relatively inexpensive, high-quality computers are within the financial reach of almost everyone. With this new, expanded

CONTENTS

CHAPTER 1

PERSPECTIVES 9

What Is a Microcomputer?—Where Did Microcomputers Come
From?—What Are They Capable of Doing?—How Hard Is It
to Get Into Microcomputing?—What Do I Do With a Computer?—Microcomputer Buzz Words

CHAPTER 2

BASIC COMPUTER CONCEPTS 25

Central Processing Unit—Memory—Input/Output Devices—
Input/Output Interfaces—Software

CHAPTER 3

CENTRAL PROCESSING UNIT 66

Microprocessor—MPU Viewed Through Its Pins—The Two
Major Types of Microprocessors—Power, Timing, and Loading
Rules—Construction, Prototyping and Breadboard Techniques
—Input/Output Control—MPU Comparison—The Future of
Microprocessors

CHAPTER 4

MEMORIES 180

Addressing—Memory Page and Line Organization—Speed—
Volatility—System Memory–Big RAMs—PROMs and ROMs

CHAPTER 5

I/O INTERFACING 218

    Elements of the I/O Interface—Minimum I/O Interface—
Alphanumeric Interface—Serial Data Transmission

CHAPTER 6

PROGRAMMING 258

    Execution of a Program—Instruction Set—Addressing Memory—Programming Techniques—Writing a Program

CHAPTER 7

OPERATING SYSTEMS 304

    What Is an Operating System?—Anatomy of an Operating System—Operating Modes—Advanced Operating Systems

APPENDIX A

NUMBERING SYSTEMS 329

    The Binary System—Octal Number Systems—The Hexadecimal System

APPENDIX B

MEMORIES 347

    Read/Write Memories—Read-Only Memories

APPENDIX C

RAM SELECTION AID 368

APPENDIX D

MOS PROM SELECTION AIDS AND PINOUTS 371

APPENDIX E

MICROCOMPUTER MATH TABLES 375

INDEX 379

chapter 1

PERSPECTIVES

Few technological developments have affected us as much as the computer. Perhaps only the automobile could come close to being compared with the computer, considering the latter's impact on our daily lives. The evolution of the computer in the last ten years has been even more rapid than was first expected. We had just become used to seeing the computer as a room full of hard-working tape drives and flashing lights when we were told that state-of-the-art electronics had put a computer on a chip! Just how far this technology will continue to evolve seems beyond our comprehension.

For now, we will discuss some questions regarding the microcomputer, on a general level. We will begin with the most basic question of all:

WHAT IS A MICROCOMPUTER?

"Microcomputer" is the name given to a computer that utilizes an integrated-circuit processor. As we shall discover, the processor is the heart of any computer. Consisting of several different types of electronic circuits, the processor controls the overall operation of the computer. A *microprocessor* is a processor that is contained on one IC chip.

There is, however, more to a computer than simply a processor. As we shall learn, other components are also necessary to make a microprocessor behave like a computer.

WHERE DID MICROPROCESSORS COME FROM?

The early electronic computers were developed at a time in history when the vacuum tube was the prevalent electronic device. Although faster than relays, vacuum tubes had one major drawback. They operated on the principle of "burning themselves out," requiring significant amounts of power in the process. Early computers occupied entire buildings, and demanded heavy-duty cooling apparatus to keep the operating temperature within the specified tolerance.

The arrival of the transistor in the electronics world can be hailed as the turning point in the design of many electronic devices, including the computer. Being an obviously superior replacement for the vacuum tube, the transistor was quickly incorporated into the design of the computer. This led to faster, smaller, and cooler computers. However, computers were still composed of discrete parts. Transistors, diodes, resistors, and capacitors were connected together on printed-circuit boards, and plugged into their respective sockets within the computer.

A few years later, the technology developed that allowed us to build solid-state devices containing several components, all on the same "chip." This was an excellent development for the computer industry, since the large number of switching circuits formerly constructed from discrete components could now be found in a few "integrated circuits." These ICs became the foundation for the pocket calculator. In less than two years the price for an 8-digit electronic calculator was cut in half. The evolution of solid-state technology skyrocketed as

more and more types of integrated-circuit devices became available. The inevitable combining of the computer circuits into one IC chip was to produce the first of the so-called microprocessors in the early 1970s.

WHAT ARE THEY CAPABLE OF DOING?

The first of the microprocessors was not really what you would call a computer. It was programmable, however, within a limited range, and therefore had all the attributes of the larger machines. Within one year these first models were already obsoleted by the development of even more sophisticated versions of microprocessors. The present-day microprocessor is quite capable of being used as the heart of a

general-purpose computing system. The fact that it is entirely self-contained is of little consequence to the programmer, but it means ease of maintenance and repair.

Aside from the general-purpose computing type application, the microcomputer lends itself to many special types of processing. Its physical size will allow it to be included within some other machine, without much physical modification. The continuing decrease in microcomputer cost will lead to many consumer applications which until now have been unrealistic in terms of expense. In short, the world had better get ready for the onrush of the microcomputer. For as sure as $E = IR$, the microcomputer will find its way into the everyday lives of most of us.

HOW HARD IS IT TO GET INTO MICROCOMPUTING?

If you are thinking that you would like to have a microcomputer, there are certainly many opportunities to do so. Several companies manufacture ready to use computers that you simply plug in, and they work. There is a great variety of these computers, ranging from those which have been designed primarily for home entertainment and games, to those which are quite capable of doing business data processing.

There are all kinds of accessories that can be connected to a computer. There are printers, cassette tape recorders, and computer terminals, to name but a few. As each year goes by, there are more and more of these devices available at lower and lower cost.

At this time, programming of the computer is by far the most significant factor. The hardware can be procured and made to work with little effort. The programming on the other hand requires many man hours of time to develop and to get running smoothly. Although there are many programs that can be purchased today, there is still a great need for people who can write good programs. If you are going to be a computer experimenter, then you will most likely need to know how to program the particular computer that you get.

WHAT DO I DO WITH A COMPUTER?

Perhaps this question could have been asked first. A computer without some computing to be done is a rather woeful sight. Granted, the experimenter will undoubtedly learn a lot while assembling the parts of a microcomputer, and perhaps this in itself is sufficient justification for building the computer. Usually, the builder eventually plans to use the computer for some worthwhile purpose. Many times, the worthwhile purpose may develop only after the computer has been built and has been holding down a shelf in the workshop.

Your imagination is the limit. Program the computer to play games such as tic-tac-toe, blackjack, or poker. Maybe there is some application such as checkbook balancing or kitchen inventory control for which you could program it. For clubs or other groups, a microcomputer lends itself well to the management of membership lists and other record-keeping chores. As the heart of a home security system, a microcomputer could be programmed to react to different situations according to predetermined criteria.

Most important of all, remember that the microcomputer has evolved in a relatively short time, and will probably continue to evolve. As time goes by, the accepted ways of dealing with certain electronic circuits may become obsolete, and techniques yet to be discovered will become commonplace.

MICROCOMPUTER BUZZ WORDS

The following glossary is designed to familiarize you with the language of the small computer community. The best way to use it is to read the entire glossary from A to X. Each buzz word is defined in simple terms and used in a short sentence to illustrate its meaning.

A

A/D Conversion—An A/D (Analog/Digital) conversion measures an input voltage level, and then outputs a digitally encoded number corresponding to the voltage. This provides a relatively simple way to get signals from the outside world to the inside of a computer. "That's the fastest *A/D conversion* I've ever seen."

Algorithm—The sequence of steps to be followed to arrive at a solution to a problem. It is usually a programming procedure that uses "iteration" to produce the desired result. Frequently algorithms are named after their originators. "The *Widro-Hoff LMS algorithm* is a programming procedure that removes 'noise' from a signal."

Alphanumeric—The set of symbols containing the letters A–Z (alpha) and the numbers 0–9 (numeric), as well as special punctuation characters. "Most computers use *alphanumeric* characters."

Applications Program—A program that actually solves a specific problem, as opposed to the programs that perform system functions, such as assemblers, etc. "The *applications program* is rather long."

Assembler—A system program that allows programming in the mnemonic codes of assembly language. Assembler programs are one step above binary machine-language programming. "Many computer hobbyists use *assemblers*."

Assembly Language—A low-level symbolic programming language, that uses mnemonic codes such as ADD, LDA, SUB, etc. Historically the first programming aid. "What is the *assembly language* format for add?"

ASCII Character—Short for *A*merican *S*tandard *C*ode for *I*nformation *I*nterchange, ASCII is the most widely recognized 8-bit code for representing alphanumerics of the English language. Pronounced "*ask-ee*." "The *ASCII* code for 7 is 00110111."

B

BASIC—Stands for *B*eginners *A*ll purpose *S*ymbolic *I*nstruction *C*ode. BASIC is a widely used beginners high-level programming language. Like most high-level languages, it uses powerful statements like "10 PRINT X/Y + 1" rather than machine codes or mnemonics. "Hobbyists love *BASIC* because it's so much like English."

Baud Rate—The number of bits per second a computer is capable of sending or receiving. Baud rate usually varies from 300 (teletypewriter speed) to 9600. "The *baud rate* of a typical computer is 300."

Binary—The base-two number system which uses the digits 0 and 1. The first four numbers in binary are 00, 01, 10, 11. Computers use binary because electronic components can be made cheaply to switch between two states such as $+5$ volts and ground. "To get a feeling for how computers calculate, try counting in *binary*."

Bit—A contraction of the words *B*inary dig*IT*, a bit is the smallest unit of computer information. Several bits together make up a letter, number, or word. "Eight *bits* is a byte."

Bootstrap—The general technique of using one thing to aid in the start of another thing. In computers, a short program that allows a larger program to be entered into the computer. "First load the *bootstrap* loader, then load the program."

Branch—The process of taking a departure from the normal sequence of operations in a computer program. Also a programmed jump based on continuous testing in the computer program. "Computers make good use of *branch* instructions, such as BNE (branch on not equal)."

Bug—Something which causes the computer program to malfunction. Usually, but not always, due to an error in the logic of the program. "Not another *bug!*"

Byte—A group of adjacent bits. A specific portion of a binary word. The most common size byte is 8 bits, although 16 is also used, as well as 4 and 12. "I always think of a *byte* as 8 bits."

Buffer—A temporary storage location for holding a number of bits. For instance a keyboard buffer may hold several ASCII characters, each of which is 8 bits long. "Your *buffer* overflowed."

C

Chip—Another word for "integrated circuit," this is a technique where thousands of electronic semiconductor components can be mass produced on a tiny piece of silicon (sand). "Did you know there's a *chip* in your telephone, and one in your car, and one in your watch?"

Collate—To compare or merge two things into one thing. Usually refers to files in the computer. "Lets *collate* the data."

Compiler—A compiler is a computer program. Its purpose is to convert high-level language statements typed in at a keyboard to machine code for the computer. "*Compilers* are more efficient than 'Interpreters' when it comes to saving memory space."

Complement—The number produced by performing a basic operation on the original number. In binary the complement of a number is found by reversing all the digits, i.e. 101 complemented is 010. "Certain computer instruction codes *complement* a number in a register."

Core Memory—The early computers used little doughnuts of ferrite material to store bits. Because ferrite is a magnetic material a core memory doesn't forget its contents. Bubble memory may revive the concept of core memory. "Time to do a *core* dump, and find out what's in it."

Console—The part of a computer system that is used for communication between the operator and the system. The console usually contains switches, lights, and keyboards specifically for man-machine communication. "As usual the *console* is dead."

CRT Display—A type of computer terminal that displays information on a television-like screen. This screen is the face of a cathode ray tube (CRT). "That's really a fast *CRT*, but I don't like the green characters."

D

Debug—The art of removing errors, or "bugs," from a computer program. Usually the crucial stage in developing a good program. Unfortunately, not all bugs are always found. "Always allow at least 10 minutes per BASIC statement, for *debugging*."

Disk—A type of mass storage technique that stores information on magnetically sensitive surfaces, about the size of a 45-rpm record. "The cheapest form of mass storage in 1977 was the floppy *disk*."

DOS—Stands for *D*isc *O*perating *S*ystem. A computer system that uses a magnetic disc to contain all the routines and programs that run the computer. An FDOS is a floppy disk-based DOS. "Soon there will be Bubble Operating Systems, and the *DOS* will be obsolete."

Dump—The action of causing the pattern of binary bits in a computer to be displayed on an output device. "By doing a *dump* we'll determine the bad bit."

Dynamic Memory—A type of memory arrangement where all the various memory cells must be refreshed every so often so they keep their proper state. Although a less-power-consuming form of memory than static memory, dynamic memory requires complex addressing circuits. "Sometimes you hear about pseudo-*dynamic* memory."

E

Editor—A special computer program that allows changing, moving, and general editing of statements. Editing is a simple form of word processing, but is often reserved for changing assembly statements. "An *editor* is a fantastic tool for fixing computer programs."

EPROM—Stands for *E*lectrically *P*rogrammable *R*ead *O*nly *M*emory. A type of memory that can hold data forever. EPROMs are programmed by an electrical process that establishes each bit as a 1 or a 0. EPROMs are often used to hold the monitor or operating system programs. "You can buy special *EPROM* programmers, but they are expensive."

F

File—A sequence of related records, frequently found in floppy disc, cassette, or mass storage systems. A file is an abstract name for an aggregation of data sets in the form of a series of characters or bits which together may describe some quantity or numeric value. "The disc has fanstastic *file* commands."

Firmware—Software or programs that are permanently stored in ROM or EPROM. Also any microprogram that causes a machine to emulate a certain instruction set. "The nice thing about firmware is that you can easily change it (compared to changing hardware)."

Floppy Disk—Disc storage where the magnetic medium is located on small flexible discs, which are encased in a protective cardboard container. Floppies are somewhat slower than "hard" disks, they wear faster, but are less costly. "Wait till they make a micro-*floppy* disk."

Flowchart—A diagram that represents the logic and reasoning behind a program or a circuit. "Programmers are always forgetting to *flowchart* their programs."

FORTRAN—Stands for *FOR*mula *TRAN*slation, and refers to a computer language that is used for computational-type programming, especially when involving algebraic problems. A compiler language. "*FORTRAN* is almost as easy as BASIC, but much more mathematical."

H

Handshaking Logic—A type of computer interface design where the computer sends a signal, and waits until the interface sends a signal back signifying it is done. The back and forth communication is like shaking hands. "*Handshaking Logic* makes troubleshooting easy."

Hex—Short for hexadecimal, the base-16 number-system is commonly used in computers because it is easier to remember FF than 11111111. "Compared to binary, *hex* is much easier to work with."

Heuristic—A special program that has the ability to alter itself to improve itself. Often associated with artificial intelligence (AI), heuristics are used in many non-AI computer programs. "I really enjoy chess playing *heuristics*."

I

IC—Stands for *I*ntegrated *C*ircuit. *See* Chip.

Instruction Set—The "menu" of instructions a computer can execute. Unless computers have identical instruction sets, they cannot run the same programs. "The XYZ-80 has over 180 instructions."

Interface—A circuit that allows one type of electronic unit to communicate with another electronic or mechanical device. Chiefly used as a buffer between computers and mechanical devices. "Better check the serial *interface*."

Interpreter—A computer program that converts high-level-language statements to "machine" code for direct computer operation. Unlike a compiler, however, it executes the statements immediately, instead of later. BASIC is an interpreter language. "Most *interpreter* languages are slow."

Interrupt—An external event that overrides any current computer action and causes a certain special program to be run. Frequently "priorities" are established among interrupts so that several devices can interrupt a computer. "Do computers mind being *interrupted?*"

I/O—Stands for *I*nput/*O*utput. A generalized expression for the action of sending information into a computer (I or Input) and getting it out of the computer (O or Output). "Try wiggling the *i/o* cable."

L

Looping—A programming technique where a portion of a program is repeated over and over, until a certain result is obtained. "Try *looping* until the bit goes high."

LSI—Stands for *L*arge *S*cale *I*ntegration. A way of making denser and more complex integrated circuits. Eventually LSI will be replaced by VLSI (*V*ery *L*arge *S*cale *I*ntegration), and VLSI by ELSI (*E*xtremely *L*arge *S*cale *I*ntegration). "General Motors uses advanced *LSI*-hybrid circuits in fuel regulators."

Line Printer—A very high speed printer output device that can type text at several hundred lines per minute. A very expensive computer peripheral, but also a very powerful one. "I would buy a *line printer* if I could sell some service and make a profit to pay it off."

M

Machine Language—The lowest level of computer programming; this is the only language the computer can understand without the aid of another program. Looks like: .... FF FF FF FF B8 C9 D9 C0 .... "Programming in *machine language* isn't quite so bad."

Macro—Short for macroinstruction. An instruction that generates a larger sequence of instructions. "Good assemblers have many *macros*."

Microprocessor—All the essential electronics of a computer miniaturized to a single chip the size of a pin head. Contained usually in an IC package with 18 to 40 leads. "*Microprocessors* keep getting smaller."

Mnemonic—Pronounced "new-monic." A short word or group of letters that stands for another word, and is easy to remember. For instance, "Add X to the Accumulator" might be abbreviated "ADDX." "This computer has elegant *mnemonics*."

Modem—Stands for *MO*dulator *DEM*odulator. Usually connects between the computer and telephone line and converts digital signals to audio tones and vice-versa. "A good *modem* is simple to use."

MPU—Stands for *M*icro *P*rocessor *U*nit. Another way to say microprocessor. "Motorola makes an *MPU* called the 6800."

N

Nanosecond—One billionth of a second, or 1/1000 of a microsecond. "Some of today's faster personal computers operate in the *nanosecond* range."

Nested Program—A program which is contained as a part of another larger program. "The printing subroutine is *nested* within the main program."

Network—An interconnected group of computers, terminals, or even telephones. "Computer *networks* are becoming more and more popular."

NOP Instruction—A computer instruction which has no effect on computer operation, and is therefore called a no-op. These are often used to reserve space within a program for possible future expansion. "Leave a *NOP instruction* after the last byte of the program."

Nonvolatile Memory—A form of computer memory that will store information for an indefinite period of time with no power applied. "Magnetic core is *nonvolatile memory*, as are ROMs and EPROMS."

O

Object Program—A program that is in machine executable form. This means that the program is most likely to be in some sort of a binary pattern, ready to be used by the computer. "Object programs are very difficult for the average person to understand."

Octal—A number system based upon the number 8. There are eight digits in the octal system—0 through 7. "The use of the *octal* system makes programming easier than when using binary."

Off-Line—Refers to computer equipment which is not at the time directly connected to the computer. "Take the printer *off-line* for a minute."

On-Line—Describes the condition of a piece of computer equipment which is directly connected to the computer. "This system has 5 megabytes of *on-line* disc storage."

Operand—The object or "target" of some program operation, usually a number or variable that is involved in some arithmetic operation. "The *operand* of that instruction has not been defined."

Operating System—A group of special programs that are used in various combinations to make a computer easier to use. "Some computers have very flexible *operating systems*."

Operation Code—Sometimes referred to as "Op-code" this is the electronic binary pattern that directs the computer circuits to perform some particular operation. "The *Op-code* for an ADD instruction is 11000101."

Overflow—The result of performing an arithmetic operation within the computer which yields an answer that is too large to be contained in the MPU. "Adding two large numbers together may cause an *overflow* to occur."

P

Page—A term often used in conjunction with computer memory. A memory page contains some fixed number of bytes. "The keyboard input buffer occupies one *page* of memory."

Paper-Tape—A means of storing binary information by punching small holes in a continuous strip of paper. This is most common in teletypewriter-related equipment. "Many programs are available on *paper-tape*."

Parallel—Pertaining to events that occur simultaneously. Most commonly used in conjunction with the transmission of binary information, where all the bits of a given byte are sent at the same time. "The ASCII keyboard is a *parallel* device."

Parameter—A special element of data that is to be used as a condition for some type of processing. "There are several *parameters* involved in processing this data."

Parity—A means of determining the validity of computer data stored in binary. "A *parity* error occurred while reading the data."

Patch—A quick change to an existing program to cause it to operate differently. "Let's *patch* in a jump instruction at a key point."

Peripheral—A device which is connected to the computer in order to provide communication with the real world. "There are many different kinds of *peripherals* available for your personal computer."

Photoelectric—Pertaining to the use of light to detect the presence or absence of holes in paper tape, or punched cards. "*Photoelectric* readers are faster than mechanical ones."

Picosecond—One-millionth of a microsecond, or 1/1000th of a nanosecond. "A *picosecond* is almost too small an interval of time to conceive."

PL-1—A very powerful high-level programming language, generally found in use on large computer systems, but which will inevitably be used with the personal computer. "Programming in *PL-1* is a snap."

R

Random Access—Pertains to the storage of data in memory of some sort. Random access means being able to access any location of memory individually, as opposed to "serial access" memory which requires that the memory locations be accessed in sequence. "Floppy discs are *random access* devices."

Read—To sense, or obtain the state of the data either in memory, or from an input device. "*Read* in the program from cassette tape."

Real-Time—An expression used in discussing a type of computer operation in which the computer is interacting with events in the world of people, rather than of circuits. Generally speaking, the interaction must take place in a fast enough time so as to be able to influence or react to the particular "people" event in progress. "The computer can monitor the apparatus in *real-time*."

Record—An assemblage of several data elements that are all in some way related, and are handled as a unit. "How many *records* can the disc file contain?"

Register—An electronic circuit within the microprocessing unit that is capable of storing one or more bytes of information. The most common register is the accumulator register, in which all of the arithmetic operations are performed. "When the operation is complete, the result will be in the A register."

Routine—A group of program instructions which accomplishes a particular task that needs to be done frequently. A group of instructions can be used over and over again, simply by referring to it from another part of the program. "Write a *routine* that finds the largest of five numbers."

S

Seek-Time—The length of time required to find a record of data, generally with reference to disc files. "The average *seek-time* for a good floppy disc is in the millisecond range."

Sequence—Pertaining to the order that things (bits, bytes, records, or files) are arranged. "It may be important to maintain alphabetic *sequence* in some applications."

Serial—An arrangement where one element of data is linked to the next so that progress must start at the beginning and proceed from the first element through the next, and on to the finish, never skipping any. "Cassette tape files are stored in *serial* form on the tape."

Software—A nickname given to computer programs, which, of course, are not composed of electronic circuits, or hardware. "There is a lot of *software* available for some personal computers."

Statement—Often used when discussing high-level languages such as BASIC. A BASIC statement is a single unit of program command, of which there are many making up the entire program. "The PRINT *statement* causes the data to be displayed on the video display."

Storage—Sometimes used as a synonym for memory. This might be "core storage" or "disc storage" or any other form of computer memory. "There is a lot of space for program *storage* on a floppy disk."

Store—The act of saving some data in a computer memory. The data can then later be "retrieved" or "read" and used in further operations. "*Store* the results of the test in memory."

Subroutine—*See* Routine.

System—A group of programs and subroutines that are all related to processing for a particular application area. "There are good general ledger *systems* available for CPAs."

T

Terminal—An Input/Output device that can be connected to a computer in order to communicate with it and control processing. "A common *terminal* consists of an ASCII keyboard and a video display."

Time-Sharing—A process in which a single computer divides its time among several tasks to be done. This makes it appear as if all the tasks were being processed simultaneously. "The cost of *time-sharing* on a large computer decreases as the number of people sharing the time increases."

U

Update—To make current. As with programs that have been modified to comply with some change in circumstances. Or, any form of data, such as a disc file record, might be renewed with more current information. "It is important to *update* your system as new features become available."

V

Video Display—A computer output device which presents the data to the user in the form of a television picture. This picture can either be in the form of printed characters, or as a video image of some sort. "One drawback of *video displays* is that there is no hard copy."

Volatile—Pertaining to the characteristic of certain types of computer memory which lose their contents when power is removed. "All of the application programs can be stored in *volatile* memory."

W

Word—A term used for years in the computer world to describe a logical group of bits. "The term 'byte' has become dominant for the term *word* in personal computing."

Write—Often used synonymously with "store," this word means to deposit data into some form of computer memory. This might be magnetic memory, or disc memory, or writing information onto magnetic tape. "Data can be read back after we *write* it onto the disk."

chapter 2

BASIC COMPUTER CONCEPTS

Perhaps the computers of tomorrow will operate in a way that we have yet to discover. Breakthroughs are being made nearly every day. In the meantime, if we examine the microcomputers of today, we see that, although they are in a different physical form from their full-sized counterparts, much the same design architecture has been employed in both types. This architecture is mainly due to the fact that digital computers operate by using the binary number system, which demands a certain type of logical approach to performing various types of computer operations. We see, therefore, a kind of mimicking of the full-sized computers by this new breed of machine. This leads us to believe that there are some basic concepts about computers in general that can be applied to the microcomputer as well. Of course, there are exceptions to, and variations on, these basic concepts, but generally the processing objectives are the same, and the user of the microcomputer can analyze the different types in order to choose the one best suited for the intended application.

As shown in Fig. 2-1, there are five main parts to a computer. These five parts are found, in one form or another, in every digital computer, whether it is the massive system used by an insurance company to keep track of its premiums, or a microcomputer that is used to control a model railroad. These five main ingredients are:

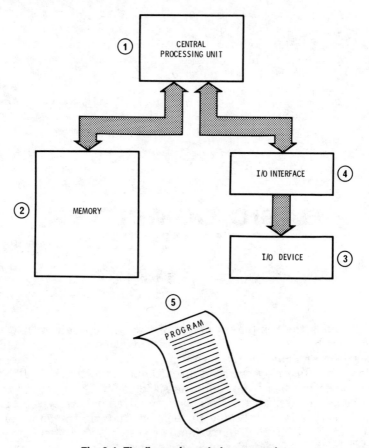

Fig. 2-1. The five main parts to a computer.

1. Central processing unit.
2. Memory.
3. Input/output devices.
4. Input/output interfaces.
5. Program.

1. *Central processing unit* (CPU).
   The "brain" of the computer—this is where the actual computing is done. The CPU usually controls all the operations of the computer.
2. *Memory.*
   An electronic storage medium used to hold the program which instructs the CPU and other components of the computer.

3. *Input/output devices.*
   These are the link between man and machine. They vary in type and complexity according to the processing requirements. Input/output devices include keyboards, teletypewriters, video displays, and so on.
4. *Input/output interfaces.*
   These are the "middlemen" between the CPU and the I/O device. They provide the actual hard-wired control of the I/O device, according to the commands that are issued by the CPU.
5. *Program.*
   Without the program, a computer is no more than a handful of parts that sits there and draws current. The program coordinates the operations of the computer in order to perform some desired process.

Each of these five main ingredients will be explored in more detail in this chapter. The emphasis will be on the logical operation of these elements within the computer. Chapter 3 will deal with these five elements from a "hardware" viewpoint, discussing the various electronic aspects of each.

CENTRAL PROCESSING UNIT (CPU)

Every computer has some sort of central processing unit (CPU), which is the "brain" of the computing machine. The CPU is a combination of several "parts," interconnected in such a way as to permit certain logical operations to be performed. Computers of ten years ago required a fairly large enclosure to house the components of their CPUs. Swing-out logic gates holding rows of pc boards, interconnected by garden-hose-sized cable, were not an uncommon sight. Today, the microcomputer uses a CPU that is contained in an LSI chip. This is the *microprocessor*, which, by itself, is not a computer but is the main component in any microcomputer.

Simple Binary Information—the Bit

Microprocessors are digital devices using digital logic concepts to accomplish some processing goal. This digital logic, or binary logic, as it is sometimes called, is based on the fact that certain electronic circuits can be either *on* or *off*, the state being determined by their operating characteristics. These provide a means of defining two "states" or "conditions."

If we have a single circuit, which is to be used to indicate one or the other of two possible conditions, this circuit is said to contain a *binary digit*, or *bit* of information. This bit can designate "on" or "off." Another frequent expression is that the bit is a "1" or a "0." This terminology corresponds to the only two numerals in the binary number system. The binary and other number systems are described in further detail in Appendix A.

When we have only one bit, it's plain to see that we can represent only one of two situations. As in Fig. 2-2, this would be sufficient to tell us whether we had left the front porchlight on or off, but for any serious computing, it simply will not do.

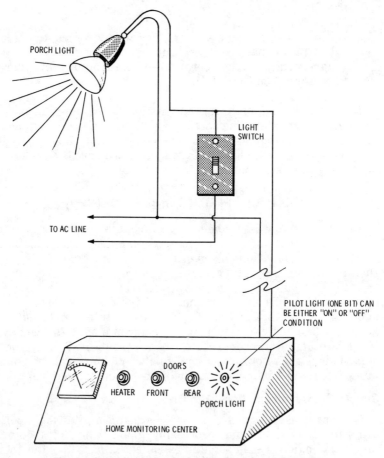

PORCH LIGHT

LIGHT SWITCH

TO AC LINE

PILOT LIGHT (ONE BIT) CAN BE EITHER "ON" OR "OFF" CONDITION

DOORS

HEATER   FRONT   REAR

PORCH LIGHT

HOME MONITORING CENTER

Fig. 2-2. Porchlight circuit yielding one bit of information.

Combining Bits to Make Words

To be able to represent more than two conditions with binary logic, several bits may be connected in such a way as to provide a more usable logical unit called the *word*. A word may have any number of bits, depending on several factors to be discussed later. Also, it is convenient if the number of bits in a word is some exact power of 2 (4, 8, 16, and so on). Each word can then be used to represent many different conditions, depending on how many bits are used to make up the word. For example, with 4 bits, we can represent 16 different conditions, by choosing various combinations of "bit patterns," or 1's and 0's. With 8 bits, we can represent 256 different conditions. Thus, we can see that the total number of different combinations of the bits in a word is 2^n, where n is the number of bits.

When a microprocessor manufacturer decides to use a certain "word length" (number of bits in a word), the requirements of the CPU are directly involved. If, for example, it is decided to use 8-bit words, then all of the information with which the CPU is to work will be in the form of 8-bit words. This implies that the CPU must be built to process 8-bit words, and that some other word length, say 4 bits, would be meaningless. There are processors that are built to handle variable-length words, but this requires a significant amount of consideration on the part of the programmer, in order to keep everything straight. For the most part, microprocessors of today are fixed word length machines. The most common word length of 8 bits is known as a "byte" (pronounced "bite"). There are some 16-bit machines, and these are considerably more powerful, since approximately 65,000 different conditions can be represented with 16 bits, as compared to only 256 combinations for an 8-bit word length. Other microprocessors use 4-bit words. These are not as powerful as higher-bit computers in the sense that they cannot represent as many different conditions. However, they are adequate for many of the simple applications.

Using Words to Define Instructions

Perhaps the one single attribute that differentiates the microprocessor from other machines is that it can be "told" what to do. This is accomplished by using words which contain a bit pattern that is meaningful to the processor. This meaningfulness is determined by the manufacturer. One bit pattern may be used to tell the processor to add two numbers. Another bit pattern may be used to tell it to print a character on a teletypewriter. Another bit pattern may have no meaning to the processor at all.

The group of bit patterns that the manufacturer decides will have some meaning is called the *instruction set*. These instructions will tell the processor what operation it is to perform and, in many cases, how the operation is to be modified due to the bit pattern contained in some other word. The variety of different operations defined by the instruction set is determined by the manufacturer, in order to fulfill some design criteria. Most instruction sets include some standard arithmetic operations, e.g., addition and subtraction. Also, some "bit manipulation" instructions are usually provided, as well as the frequently used logical operations AND, OR, and EOR (or XOR). Other than these, different instruction sets contain various sorts of operations depending upon the intended application of the processor. Some will be prolific in input/output instructions, if the application demands complicated input or output procedures. Others offer more sophisticated arithmetic instructions in order to process mathematically oriented problems with greater precision.

As shown in Fig. 2-3, the processor cannot distinguish between bit patterns that are instructions and those that are not instructions. If the processor should accidentally try to execute "data" instead of an instruction, usually an error is created. Some processors contain circuitry that can tell if an invalid instruction is being executed, and will halt the process.

Most processing objectives will require that a certain sequence of steps be performed. For example, suppose that we want to compute the area of a circle using the simple formula

$$\text{area} = \pi \times (\text{radius})^2$$

Since we know that the value of π is a constant, we can rewrite the equation as follows:

$$\text{area} = (3.14) \times (\text{radius})^2$$

Now, suppose that we can somehow "input" the radius of the circle into the computer, and that the computer, after calculating the area, will "output" the answer. The sequence of operations involved here would be:

1. INPUT the radius.
2. SQUARE the radius.
3. MULTIPLY the radius by the value of π.
4. OUTPUT the answer.

(A) Binary representation of the number 22, in an 8-bit word.

(B) The bit pattern representing an instruction to add two numbers.

Fig. 2-3. Bit patterns for a data element and for an instruction.

We can appreciate that we would not obtain the correct answer if the operations were not executed in this sequence. For example, if we were to reverse the order of steps 2 and 3, we would be multiplying the radius by the value of π before we squared it, which would yield a totally different answer.

The Instruction Register

Only one instruction can be executed by the processor at any given time. The result of executing one instruction may set up

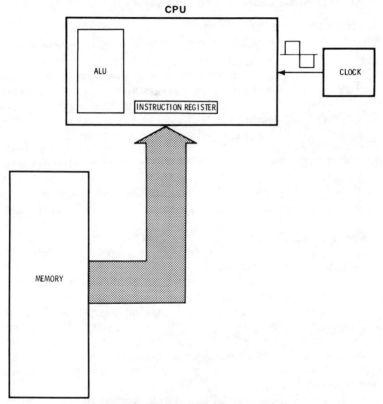

Fig. 2-4. Simplified CPU configuration.

certain conditions that are required for the execution of the next instruction. The sequence of instructions that is to be performed by the processor is usually stored in memory of some kind, which will be discussed in further detail later in this chapter. As each instruction is needed, it is fetched from the memory and put into the instruction register (Fig. 2-4), which is a circuit that can electronically hold one word.

Electronic circuits in the processor "decode" the word in the instruction register and, based on the bit pattern of that word, determine what operation is to be performed. The 1 and 0 bits in the word contained by the instruction register can be thought of as "connections," each one being used to shape the circuitry in the processor to enable it to execute the desired operation. The instruction register will contain the instruction all during the time that it is being executed. When it is finished with one instruction, the next instruction in the sequence is fetched from the memory, and loaded into it.

Synchronizing the Operations

We can see that there must be some sort of synchronization of the various operations of the processor. For example, it can not be fetching an instruction from the memory at the same time that it is executing an instruction already in the instruction register. Also, we must consider that the various operations of the processor will not necessarily require the same amount of time. For example, operations requiring accessing of the memory will take longer to execute than those that do not use the memory. Likewise, operations that involve the activating of some I/O device will initiate some external action of another machine. This may take a million times as much time as is required to execute some instruction that does not use any external I/O device.

For these reasons, there must be a way of getting everything to happen in reference to the same time frame. This can be accomplished in several ways. Some processors use a quartz crystal "clock" to establish a universal time pulse for the coordination of the events that occur internally. Other processors use a simple type of oscillator circuit to provide this periodic signal.

The clock will have a great deal to do with the ultimate speed of the processor, since all the functions are performed in step with it. In general, the processor with the faster clock will perform operations more quickly than the processor with the slower clock.

We might think of the CPU clock as similar to the crank on the old organ grinder. The faster the crank is turned, the faster the mechanism inside produces the music.

Arithmetic/Logic Unit (ALU)

The arithmetic/logic unit (ALU) is the part of the CPU used to perform the arithmetic and logical operations that are defined by the instruction set. The ALU contains electronic circuits that perform binary arithmetic as described in Appendix A of this book.

There are various binary arithmetic operations that the ALU circuits can perform. The circuits are directly controlled by a part of the CPU that decodes the instruction in the instruction register and sets up the ALU for the desired function. Most binary arithmetic is based on the "addition" algorithm, or procedure. Subtraction is carried out as a kind of "negative addition." Multiplication and division are generally not performed as discrete instructions, but rather as chains of additions or subtractions under program control. ALUs found in the more powerful microprocessors do offer multiplication and division, as well as other arithmetic operations, in the form of "hardware" circuits which are accessible through one machine instruction.

Arithmetic Modes

There are several types of arithmetic modes used in the microprocessors of today. The most commonly encountered are *signed binary* and *unsigned binary.*

Signed binary arithmetic uses the "leftmost," or most significant, bit (MSB) of the word to indicate the sign (positive or negative) of the number that is represented by the remainder of the bits in the word. The usual convention here is that, in a negative number, the sign bit will be *set* (equal to 1), and in a positive number, the sign bit will be *cleared* (equal to 0). Generally, negative numbers are stored in a "complemented" form which, as described in Appendix A, makes the binary subtraction operation a negative addition. It is important to note that using one of the bits in each word to indicate the sign of a number stored in the word reduces the range (or absolute value) of the number that can be stored in the remaining bits of the word. Thus, in an 8-bit word, using signed binary arithmetic, we can represent numbers from -128 to $+127$, and of course zero. This is still 256 total different combinations, but even when unsigned numbers are represented, their maximum size is also limited. As we will see in Chapter 4 on programming, this word size limitation can cause the programmer some serious problems in the generation of memory location addresses.

The unsigned binary arithmetic mode, as its name implies, does not offer the ability to represent positive and negative numbers. The MSB of each word is *not* used to indicate the sign of the number that is stored in the word. Therefore, the entire word can be used to store the number. This allows us to store a larger number in each word, but we must be sure that this number will never have to be negative, in order for the operations using it to have some meaning.

The ALU in most microprocessors is capable of handling both these kinds of arithmetic, and of distinguishing between them. Different instructions are used by the CPU to direct the ALU to perform the desired mode of arithmetic. Some microprocessors have ALUs that are capable of doing arithmetic operations on much larger numbers, which may be stored by using more than one word. This ability is another indicator of the amount of processing power that any given microprocessor

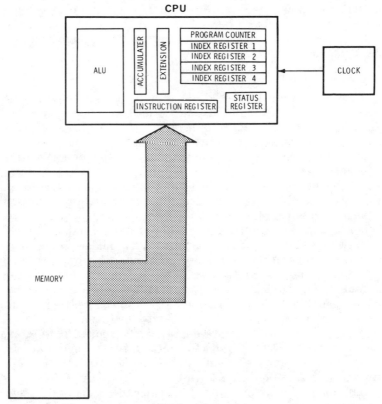

Fig. 2-5. CPU registers.

may have. For some applications, the simple combination of signed and unsigned arithmetic is more than adequate, and therefore the user must evaluate his processing needs to determine what criteria to use when selecting a microprocessor.

Accumulator and Other Internal Registers

Generally, a number of hardware registers are contained within the CPU. These are used for several purposes by the

CPU itself or by the ALU. All microprocessors contain some combination of registers.

The register most commonly associated with the microprocessor is called the *accumulator* (see Fig. 2-5). This register is the primary register used during many of the operations that are defined by the instruction set. It is used by the ALU to hold one element of data during an arithmetic operation. It is also directly accessible to the CPU as a working area for many nonarithmetic operations. The accumulator generally has the same number of bits as the defined word length of the particular microprocessor. It is used many times during the execution of a program as the threshold to the memory. The instruction set usually includes some kind of "load" operation, during which the contents of some memory location are loaded into the accumulator. Also, the instruction sets usually include a "store" operation, which causes the contents of the accumulator to be stored at some prescribed memory location.

Probably the next most common internal register found in microprocessors is the *program counter* (PC). This is used to hold the memory location address of the word of memory with which the CPU is concerned at any given time. As we will see in Chapter 4, a "program" is a sequence of instructions that are stored in the memory in the order that they are to be executed. Each time that an instruction has completed execution, the next instruction must be fetched from the memory. The program counter is used by the CPU to keep track of where in the program the current operation is located. Each time that a new instruction is fetched from the memory, the program counter is modified to contain the memory address of that instruction. The program counter is usually accessible by the program, which means that as a result of processing certain instructions, the PC itself may be changed, thereby forcing the program execution to be taken up at some other point.

The CPU usually has one or more *index registers* available for the storage of information that is going to be used by the program many times. Index registers are also used to hold addresses of areas of the memory that are to be "stepped through," such as tables of numbers. Chapter 4, on programming, shows several examples of how index registers are used by the program. Other uses are hardware type features that the manufacturer has built into the CPU, such as special "interrupt vectors," and these features will be described in more detail in the discussion of I/O interfaces.

In general, the number and size of the hardware registers is another parameter in determining the computing power of a given microprocessor—the more registers, the better, in most cases. As we shall learn in the chapter on programming, these registers can get used up quickly, leaving the programmer with no option but to use a word of memory for a job that really should be done by a register.

Another register generally found in a CPU is the *extension register*. The extension register is normally used in conjunction with the accumulator for performing "double-precision" arithmetic. This is an arithmetic mode in which each number is represented by two words of memory, both of which must be involved in any operation by the ALU. The extension register is normally used to hold the least significant bits (LSBs) of the number, while the accumulator is used to hold the most significant bits (MSBs) of the number. In this way, the two registers are connected together to form one large arithmetic register. The extension register is also used for other purposes depending upon the manufacturer's objectives in designing the microprocessor. One microprocessor uses this register as a "serial I/O port," where the input data are fed into the extension register's MSB, and the output data are fed out of the LSB of the register.

Another hardware register common to all computers is the *status register*. This is usually a one-word register that is used to keep track of various conditions within the computer. Each bit in the status register word may be assigned a certain meaning by the manufacturer. For example, a certain bit may be "set" if an arithmetic carry occurs as a result of performing some operation in the ALU. A carry occurs when the result of the arithmetic is too large to be represented by the particular word length of the CPU. Another example of the use of this register might be a bit that is used to indicate whether or not some I/O device is requesting service. Perhaps a bit is used by the I/O device to tell the CPU that it has finished the last operation that it was commanded to perform, and is ready to perform the next operation.

Here is another way to determine just how much computing power a particular microprocessor can offer. The complexity of the status register will give the user a pretty good idea of the "smartness" of the microprocessor.

A *storage address register* is found in various microprocessors. This register is used in conjunction with memory accessing. The storage address register is used to hold the memory address of the data that are being either "loaded" from memory or "stored" into memory.

Microprocessors may or may not have a *storage buffer register*. This is simply a hardware device that holds an image of the contents of the memory location addressed in the storage address register. In some microprocessors, all data that are transferred to and from the memory are routed through this register. This pertains to instructions as well as data, the instructions being routed to the CPU decoding logic, and the data being normally bound for the accumulator or one of the other registers.

Communicating With the CPU

In the previous paragraphs, we have learned about the insides of a typical CPU. We know that CPUs can do various types of arithmetic, that they can interpret certain bit patterns as instructions, and that they have several hardware registers that are used in various ways to aid in the processing. However, the CPU must be given all the information that is pertinent to the operation that is desired. We must furnish the CPU with the instruction and also tell it where to get the data to be operated upon and where to put the result after the operation has been completed. For this purpose, there are communication lines into, and out of, the CPU. These lines are usually a parallel to the binary format that the CPU uses for all of its operations. Therefore, if the word length is eight bits, there will be eight lines connected to the CPU in order to transmit data in or out. This group of lines is called a *bus*, and there are three different types of busses leading into, and out of, the CPU (Fig. 2-6):

1. Data bus.
2. Address bus.
3. Control bus.

We will examine each of these busses individually.

Data Bus—The data bus is used for the transmission of data in or out of the CPU. There are as many lines in this bus as there are bits in the data words for the particular microprocessor. The most common use of the data bus is in transferring information from memory into the CPU, and from the CPU into the memory.

There are some CPUs that have a separate data bus for *reading*, or transferring data from memory to the CPU, and for *writing*, or transferring data from the CPU into the memory. For the most part, this architecture has been avoided since it requires twice as many lines as the read/write combination bus method. In the latter method, the same bus is used for both reading and writing data.

Address Bus—This group of lines is used to select the individual location to or from which the transfer of data is to be made. The most common usage of the address bus is in conjunction with the memory. This bus will carry the address of the location in memory that is being accessed by the CPU at any given time.

Some manufacturers have combined the data and address busses into one, shared bus. This is accomplished by multiplexing data and addresses on the same lines. As we might imagine, this requires some sort of synchronization so that, at any time, the CPU can tell whether the bus is carrying data or addresses.

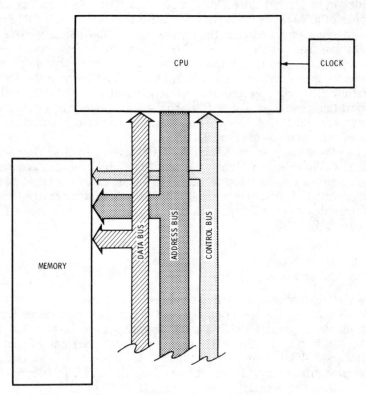

Fig. 2-6. Communicating with the CPU.

It is also possible to address I/O devices as though they were memory locations. This is done by several microprocessors currently on the market. As long as the I/O device does not interfere with the other uses of the bus, the CPU won't be able to tell the difference.

As we will see in the next section of this chapter, there are many addresses of memory, and perhaps many addresses of I/O devices that need to be represented on the address bus.

Therefore, in most processors, we will find that the address bus is wider (greater number of bits) than the word length of the machine.

Control Bus—The control bus is not quite the same kind of group of lines as are the data bus and the address bus. Rather, it is a group of several "dedicated" lines that are each used for some special purpose. Most processors have some sort of a control bus, some more complex and offering more control than others. One of the things that the control bus is used for is to *reset* the processor. This reset function clears the registers in the CPU to all 0's and prepares the processor for the beginning of some program. The reset is normally accomplished by some sort of a front-panel control which is connected to the reset line on the control bus. Likewise, once the processor is operating and actually executing instructions, we would probably desire to have some means to stop everything. Most processors have a separate line that, when switched, causes the processor to stop after completion of the instruction currently being executed.

There are a multitude of other control functions that various manufacturers employ in the design of their processors. Some are used when more than one CPU is to be using the same memory or I/O devices. Others are used to change the CPU operations during execution.

Here is another area for comparing the various microprocessors that are available. How many user control functions are provided for on the control bus?

There is one "bus" that we have not discussed. This is the *internal bus* inside the CPU chip which is used to connect all of the various registers and to connect the ALU with the instruction decoding logic. This is not a concept that is peculiar to the microprocessor. However, since it is contained within the chip itself, it is not really available to the user's program. We will take a closer look at this bus in the next chapter as we compare some of the microprocessors' hardware features.

MEMORY

As we have seen in the previous paragraphs, the CPU executes a sequence of instructions, which we call a program, in order to fulfill some processing goal. Since the CPU can deal with only one instruction at any given time, there must be a place to store all of the instructions of the program, and to fetch them, one at a time, for execution. This is the primary use of memory by the computer—to store the program instructions. The memory may also hold data (for example, a constant such as the value of π). In some cases, large tables of data are stored in the memory in order that they may be used as a reference by some program during execution. Whether used for instructions or data, the memory is utilized in the same way for both.

Types of Memory

Although the basic reasons for memory, and the ways that memory is utilized, are the same for both instructions and data, there are several different types of memory, each offering a special feature for the user. We will discuss five of these most common types:

1. *Core*—magnetic core memory.
2. *RAM*—random-access monolithic memory.
3. *ROM*—read-only memory.
4. *PROM*—programmable ROM.
5. *EPROM*—erasable programmable ROM.

Core Memory—Magnetic core memory has been the most popular form of computer memory for quite a few years. This type of memory is known as *nonvolatile* because it will retain the information that is stored in it for an indefinite length of time, and it need not have power applied or be refreshed. Over the years, this form of memory has become reasonably priced. However, the drawbacks of its use with a microprocessor are twofold. First of all, magnetic core does require quite a bit of power in order to write into it. Secondly, its physical size is just not compatible with the LSI technology of microprocessor chips. So, it looks as though the use of magnetic core memory may be waning. At least in the microprocessor fields, the alternatives are much more desirable.

RAM Memory—This memory actually should be called "monolithic random-access memory," but since it has become the most popular type of memory associated with the microprocessor, its name has been shortened simply to RAM. The term *random access* means that any word in the memory may be accessed, without having to go through all the other words to get to it. This memory, being monolithic (that is, being contained in an integrated-circuit chip), is much more suitable to the microprocessor. The power requirement for these memory chips is very similar to that of the microprocessor itself. The signal level necessary to write into this memory is relatively small. The only drawback of RAM memory is that it is a *volatile* form of memory. This means that when the power is removed from the chip, all the memory content is lost. When the power is returned, the content of memory will be unknown. On the other hand, the power consumption of these memory chips is so small that it is feasible to leave them "powered up" all the time. The only eventuality to contend with then would be the occasional power failure or brownout that might cause the loss of the content of memory.

ROM Memory—Read-only memory is very similar to RAM except for one thing. It is not possible to write into ROM memory the way it is to write into RAM. This type of memory is useful, then, only as a source of information, and it cannot be used by the program to store any data or instructions. When purchasing a ROM, the user must specify to the manufacturer exactly what the user wants to be in the memory. The manufacturer, using special equipment, prepares the ROM with the information that the user requests. This information may then be read as many times as desired, and ROM does not require that the power be supplied continuously in order that the information be retained. So ROM memory is also nonvolatile, as is core memory. The ROM memory is useful for such things as the storing of a table of information that is only referred to and never changed. Also, some programs that are required frequently can be stored in ROM and then read into a RAM memory to be executed. Some programs can be executed directly from the ROM, since each instruction is fetched from the memory, and passed on to the CPU instruction decoding logic. If, however, there are any parts of the program that are altered during execution, they cannot be left in the ROM, and they must be read into the RAM memory in order to be executed properly.

PROM Memory—PROM, or programmable ROM, is very much like simple ROM memory, except that it can be programmed by the user in the field. The PROM chips can be purchased blank and then be programmed by using a special machine. Once programmed, this memory behaves the same as the ROM. That is, it can be read as many times as desired but cannot be written into. Also, it is not necessary to supply power continuously to PROM memory in order to preserve the information. In other words, it is nonvolatile memory.

EPROM Memory—This is one of the latest types of monolithic memory. It is called erasable programmable ROM. It can be programmed in the field by the user, and it can also be erased and reprogrammed with different information. Once it has been programmed, the EPROM memory acts just the same as ROM. Again, this is a memory that cannot be written into, but it can be read as many times as necessary.

One way of combining memory types is shown in the block diagram of Fig. 2-7.

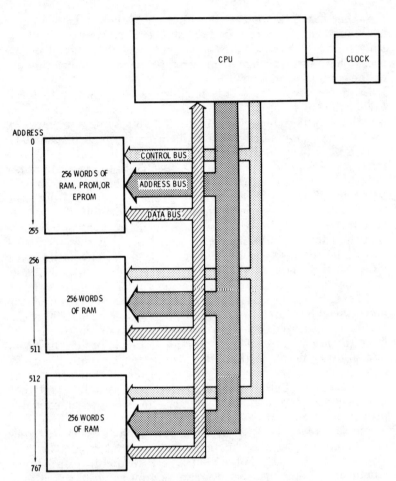

Fig. 2-7. Combining RAM and ROM memories.

Organization and Addressing of Memory

In organizing and addressing memory, the first fact that we should remember is that memory for a digital computer will have to be in binary form, because all information in a digital computer is stored in binary. Second, we must remember that each microprocessor has a word length that is determined by the manufacturer. This word length is the number of binary "bits" that are grouped together into one logical unit of information in binary. From these two facts, we can see that memory must be able to store information in binary words of the same length as the microprocessor word.

All the types of memory that were described in the last section are constructed so that they fulfill the requirements of binary memory. They are subdivided into words, each of which contains a bit pattern representing an instruction in the program or perhaps data which is to be operated upon by the computer program.

The next question is: How much memory is needed by the computer? This is a totally variable number which is dependent on several conditions. The complexity of the application for which the computer is going to be used is the first criterion for determining how much memory is needed. If there is going to be a need to store large amounts of data in memory, then the requirements may be determined by this fact. Certainly a program that would compute the area of circles would not require as much memory as a program to play chess, since program size is mainly a function of the number of instructions that are contained in the program.

Monolithic memory comes in very convenient IC packages, and, generally speaking, each chip contains some fixed number of words of memory. These chips may be grouped together to form however much memory is required.

Consider the addressing of memory. This is the ability to select any one of the many words of memory that we are likely to have available. When using the memory, the CPU must know where in the memory to find the next instruction, or possibly where to find some data that are to be used in the execution of an instruction. Therefore, the memory (already arranged in groups of bits to form words) is given numbered addresses for each word, much the same as all the people living on the same street have different addresses. This system of addressing makes it possible to store information at a specific memory address, and then later come back to exactly the right place to find it.

A number is assigned each word in memory, starting with 0 and continuing as high as need be for the amount of memory that is available. Then, any time that a particular word of information is to be referred to, its address may be used. The CPU can keep track of where it is in the program during execution, by storing the address of the location in the program counter. Each time that an instruction has completed execution, the program counter is incremented to contain the address of the next word in the memory, in which the next program instruction will be stored. (See Fig. 2-8.) In most cases, the program is stored in ascending sequence in the memory; that is, the beginning of the program is at a lower memory address than the end of the program.

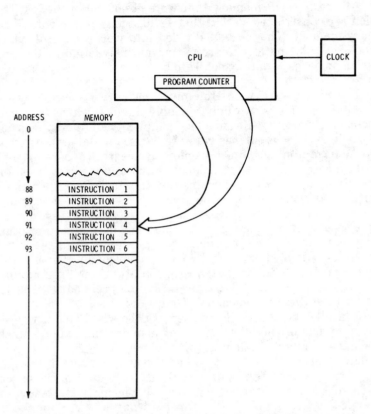

Fig. 2-8. Program counter "points" to the instruction being executed.

Reading From Memory

Reading from memory is the act of getting the information that is stored in the memory out of the memory and into some other place where it can be used. This is why earlier in this chapter we referred to this process as "loading" the contents of a memory location into a register. The contents of the memory location are not changed by the operation of reading from that memory location.

Writing Into Memory

Writing into memory is the process of putting some information into the memory for storage. Earlier in this chapter, we referred to this process as "storing" the contents of a register into a memory location. Of course, the writing process destroys the previous contents of the memory location and replaces them with the new information. This writing cannot be done with

44

any kind of ROM memory, since there are no circuits in the ROM chip to receive the information.

INPUT/OUTPUT DEVICES

In this chapter about basic computer concepts, we started at the center with the CPU and worked our way to the "outside world." For it is in the outside world that the ultimate effect of the processing inside the computer will be felt. The computer's function will have significance for whoever will use this powerful instrument. Since humans are not equipped with address and data busses that can be connected directly to the computer, we must have some other way of communicating with it.

Many forms of information may be entered into the computer. Depending upon the application and the volume of information that is likely to be involved, there are several machines that can be connected to a computer. These machines are constructed so that they can be operated by humans. The machine translates the operations into signals that can be interpreted by the computer. Some of these devices translate the signals generated by the computer into a "human language." These machines are called *input/output devices*, or more simply, *I/O devices*.

It is not always necessary that the computer be connected to some "human" interface. In many applications, the computer is used as a controller of other machines. Some applications involve several computers communicating with each other. In all cases, however, some kind of an interface with the world is necessary. It may be as simple as two wires used to turn something on and off, or it may be as complex as several dozen video monitors giving flight information to passengers at the airport.

Simple Devices

Many computer applications, especially those suitable for microcomputer use, may not require the complex I/O devices found in the big commercial data processing installations. The processing objective may be as simple as that of a typical four-function calculator. In this case, we can see that there probably won't be a need for a high-speed printer. Going a step further in simplicity, sometimes it is desirable to be able to see what is going on in the computer at any given moment. Likewise, it is desirable to be able to change something in the computer at will. These are operations that a programmer would be concerned with if he had just executed his new program for the first time, and found that it wasn't working right.

Front-Panel Switches and Lights—These are the simplest form of I/O devices. (See Fig. 2-9.) They provide the user with the "switches and lights" necessary to determine what is going on inside the computer, and to change it if so desired. Fundamental to this form of I/O device is the fact that the user must deal with the computer in its own language—binary. This seems awkward at first, but after a little practice it becomes more natural. This device usually has one or more rows of toggle switches, each switch representing a bit in some register. Each row of switches then represents the bit pattern in the register. Corresponding to the switches is usually one or more rows of lights. (For obvious reasons, LEDs are more popularly used here than incandescent bulbs.) Each light also represents a bit in some register, and the row of lights represents the bit pattern in some register.

A typical use of this type of I/O device might be as follows. Suppose you are the programmer, and your new program isn't working. You think you might know what's wrong, but in order to verify your suspicions, you need to find out what bit pattern is stored at some particular memory address. You must enter the memory address of the location as a binary number. You do this by setting the bit pattern that represents that number into the switches. You turn the switches on that correspond to 1 bits, and turn off the switches that correspond to 0 bits. Then you press the button that is labeled LOAD ADDRESS REGISTER. This loads the address register with the memory address that is represented by the switches. Next, you press the button labeled EXAMINE. This causes the contents of the memory location that was selected to be displayed as a binary bit pattern in the row of lights. An "on" light corresponds to a 1 bit; an "off" light corresponds to a 0 bit. Now you can interpret the binary bit pattern and determine if your guess was right or if you must look further for the answer to the problem.

The drawbacks to this type of I/O device are self-evident. The operator must resort to using the computer's binary language in order to do what is desired. The chance of making an error while doing this is great, even for one who is quite familiar with binary. Entering one bit in the wrong position in the word will cause an error. However, if this type of operation is required only once in a while, the user can take his time, and make sure that everything is done correctly.

Hex Keyboard and Seven-Segment Display—Here is a slightly more sophisticated I/O device. It lightens the load on the user as far as having to think in binary. With this type of I/O device, the same kinds of operations can be accomplished as with the switches and lights. The main difference here is

(A) Switch array.

(B) Front panel.

Fig. 2-9. Front-panel switches and lights.

47

that this device makes the computer do some of the work. It converts the information back and forth between binary and another form of notation called *hexadecimal*.

The hexadecimal number system is described in more detail in Appendix A, but, briefly, it is a kind of abbreviated binary format. "Hex" is a base-16 number system, which means that 16 different numerals are used. This is certainly convenient, as sixteen is an integral power of 2 ($16 = 2^4$). This means that a group of four bits in a word can be grouped together and represented by one hex digit.

The hex keyboard looks much like a regular calculator-type keyboard, except that we see that there are a few more keys (Fig. 2-10). Now, instead of having to set the position of each of several switches to enter a bit pattern, the user need only press the key that represents each four-bit group in the bit pattern.

The seven-segment display takes the place of the row of lights that represented the bit pattern being "examined." Here again, the binary information to be displayed is converted to the hexadecimal form and is then used to turn on the correct combination of the "segments" in order to produce the visual display.

We can see that this form of I/O device would make debugging a program much easier to achieve than in the previous example. This flexibility does not come free. In order to make this type of I/O device function, significantly more electronics is needed than was necessary with the switch and light approach. Many such I/O devices require special programs inside the computer to make them work. In any case, the difference in complexity between the switches and lights and the hex keyboard and seven-segment display is quite noticeable.

Moderately Complex Devices

Beyond the two examples of simple I/O devices given in the last section is a whole variety of devices used for every conceivable means of communicating with the computer. We will take a brief look at three of the most popular types of I/O devices that offer the user a lot of flexibility in various applications.

ASCII Keyboard—First of all, the word *ASCII* is an acronym for *American Standard Code for Information Interchange*. ASCII is pronounced "ass-key." ASCII is a binary code that is used to represent other forms of information. For example, the characters of the alphabet can be represented in ASCII, each as a distinct bit pattern. Likewise, the numerals of the regular decimal number system (0–9) as well as various

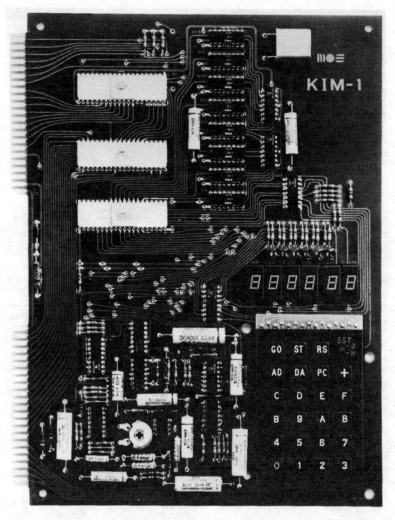

Fig. 2-10. Hex keyboard and seven-segment display.

special characters such as periods, commas, hyphens, and so on, can all be represented using this code.

An ASCII keyboard looks very much like a regular typewriter keyboard (Fig. 2-11). It has keys for each of the characters in the alphabet, as well as for the special characters, laid out in the familiar pattern for operation by both hands. Each key is simply a switch that, when pressed, causes the special electronic circuits connected to it to produce the ASCII bit pattern for that character. This bit pattern, then, can be sent along to the computer with ease since it is in a form that the computer recognizes.

The ASCII keyboard is an "input" device only. There is no way that it can be hooked up in reverse to serve as an "output" device. As an input device, it is considered quite flexible, since the human operator can easily operate the keys, and the computer can easily accept the ASCII coded character that it produces. There are other considerations, however, since the electronic circuits that are used in conjunction with the keyboard are themselves quite complex. One most obvious problem arises when the operator presses more than one key at a time. So, although this device offers ease of operation, it also requires "babysitting" hardware in order for it to be utilized fully.

Courtesy Stackpole Components Co.

Fig. 2-11. ASCII keyboard.

Teletype—The Teletype has long been a favorite I/O device for small computers and large ones too. Its main attributes are that it has a typewriterlike keyboard and it also has a printing unit which can provide "hard copy" output if desired. (See Fig. 2-12.) Although we usually find that the keyboard and the printer are physically in the same cabinet, it is important to note that they are two distinctly separate devices, and are not mechanically interconnected as in a regular typewriter. They may be connected, if so desired, so that when a key is pressed on the keyboard, the corresponding character will be printed by the printer.

The Teletype is more of a mechanical device than the ASCII keyboard, which is mainly an electronic device with the only mechanics being in the key switches. Pressing a key on the Teletype keyboard causes the mechanics inside to set up a series of switch contacts, making a binary representation of the character selected. In some machines, this binary representation is in the same ASCII code that the previous keyboard device produced. In other machines, the particular code

Fig. 2-12. Teletype console with paper tape.

that is used may be different. Any code can be used, as long as the computer that is to receive the coded information is programmed to recognize it.

The Teletype printer, used as an output device, operates in a similar mechanical fashion. The characters to be printed are sent to the printer in whatever binary code the printer is designed to operate with. As each bit pattern is sent to the printer, it is used to set up a series of selector solenoids which cause the desired type bar to strike the paper.

We can see why this particular I/O device is so popular, since it is both an input device and an output device in one unit. It also requires some external electronic circuits in order to be able to "talk" to the computer, but the usefulness of the system is increased considerably in most cases.

Paper Tape—Paper tape itself is not an I/O device. Rather, it is a storage medium making use of tape made out of paper. The tape is about one inch (2.54 centimeters) in width and of normal paper thickness, and comes in large rolls of several hundred feet (meters). Holes can be punched into this tape to form bit patterns of binary coded information. This information may be coded in ASCII or some other code, depending on the user's application.

A *paper-tape reader* is a machine used to detect the holes that are punched into the tape, and to create an electronic bit pattern to be sent to the computer. These machines can run at a fairly fast speed, depending on the model, and they make it possible for the user to reload the same information many times into the computer with very little effort. Tapes containing programs that are used often can be punched and stored in a small area and then read into the computer when they are to be executed.

There is also a machine called a *paper-tape punch*. This machine does as its name implies. Information, represented as an electronic bit pattern, is sent to the paper-tape punch from the computer. The bit pattern is used to set up the correct combination of punch dies so that the holes will be punched into the tape in the same pattern. As each bit pattern (or word) is punched into the tape, the machine pulls the tape through the punch dies so that they form a continuous series of words of information encoded in the holes in paper tape.

Many Teletype machines have paper-tape equipment attached to them. This is a very convenient arrangement. In such cases, the user has four I/O devices in one unit: a keyboard, a printer, a paper-tape reader, and a paper-tape punch. This makes a very simple yet flexible computer system.

Complex Devices

Any means of speeding up the rate at which information is transferred between the computer and the "real world" will result in the greater usefulness of the computer. Obviously, the more complex the information to be transferred, the more complex the I/O device must be. In this section, we will take a look at some of these complex devices. Only a few are represented here, since there are so many devices created for special applications.

Magnetic Tape—Magnetic tape is similar in many respects to paper tape, which was previously discussed. It, too, is a storage medium, and consists of the same kind of magnetic tape as that used for the recording of audio signals by a tape recorder. There are several different sizes of tape which are used for this purpose. The most common magnetic tape format (Fig. 2-13) in use with microcomputers is the familiar cassette cartridge.

Fig. 2-13. Magnetic tape I/O device.

The basic idea here is the same as that in the recording of music, except that instead of music we are recording binary information (1's and 0's) in a magnetic format that can later be read to re-create the binary information and feed it back into the computer. Although the cassette storage devices are quite a bit more sophisticated than the regular garden-variety cassette recorders (Fig. 2-14), they are also more expensive. Many microcomputer systems operate quite well using a $20.00 cassette tape recorder as an I/O device. This provides a convenient media for storing programs and data without spending a fortune.

An important thing to remember about magnetic tape is that, due to the fact that the tape is wound onto reels, the information is available only in a sequential manner. That is, if the desired information is somewhere near the end of the tape, the machine must read through all the information that precedes it on the tape, until the sought-after information is found. There is no way that the machine can go directly to the information.

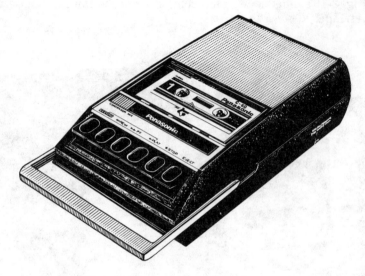

Fig. 2-14. Cassette tape recorder mass storage device.

Magnetic Disk—Magnetic disk (Fig. 2-15) is also a form of "secondary memory" used by the computer to store information which would take up too much room to store in RAM feasibly. The disk can be likened to a phonograph record, except that there are no grooves. Instead, the information is recorded magnetically, just as it is on magnetic tape.

The major difference between disk and tape storage is that the "head," which is used to read or write the information onto the magnetic disk, can be positioned so that any information is accessible, regardless of where it may be stored physically on the surface of the disk, without having to go through all the surface. This means information in any location on the disk can be accessed in any order. Contrast this with the cassette

Fig. 2-15. Floppy disk mass storage device.

tape, where it may be required to go through all the information to get to one bit. This ability to randomly access
information gives the floppy disk much greater access speed
than magnetic tape, and programs can be almost instantly
loaded into the computer. In fact, "floppies" are used in personal computer systems just like an electronic file of very
large proportions. This means you can have many programs
stored on a single disk.

Floppy disks come in several sizes (Fig. 2-16), usually the
smaller the floppy, the less total information that can be

Fig. 2-16. Microfloppy disk mass storage device.

recorded, and the lower the cost of the drive mechanism. The major problem with the floppy is its cost, which usually runs ten times that of the cassette recorder. However, one could argue that with a floppy disk, a computer's power increases by ten times.

Video Display Modules (*VDMs*)—A video display module is an output device that uses a televisionlike screen to display information to the user. (See Figs. 2-17 and 2-18.) This information may be in the form of the characters of the alphabet and other symbols meaningful to the user. It may also be presented as a picture, graph, map, or whatever the particular application may dictate.

This device is quite a complex one. We can well imagine that the process necessary to display a screen full of printed information involves some sophisticated electronics. Some video display units incorporate large amounts of their own memory to store the information to be displayed on the screen. Others even have a microprocessor inside them to manage the display operation.

Optical Scanners—An optical scanner is a device that can "see" certain things. It works mainly on the ability of various photoelectric components to distinguish between light and dark.

Fig. 2-17. ASCII keyboard/video display.

Fig. 2-18. Video display module with keyboard.

Optical scanners are very special-purpose input devices which are being used by industry for all kinds of functions, including measurement taking, recognition of various symbols, and, most recently, the Universal Product Coding system that we see printed on almost everything we buy at the store today. In this system, each product is marked with a bar code consisting of several dark lines of various widths, printed on a light background (Fig. 2-19). The scanner detects these lines and sends the product code along to the computer in binary. The computer then uses the code as a key to locate the information stored in memory regarding the particular product. The computer uses this information to operate the cash register, adding the value of the goods just scanned to the total for the given customer.

Modems—The word *modem* is a contraction of two words: "*mo*dulator," which is a device that encodes information into some form of transmittable code, and "*dem*odulator," which is a device that decodes incoming information. Thus, a modem is a device used in conjunction with the sending and receiving of information, to and from a computer.

The main purpose of a modem is to access a computer from a remote location, via the telephone lines. It converts the information to be transmitted into a series of audio tones. These

Fig. 2-19. UPC symbol.

tones are sent over the telephone line and must be "demodulated" at the receiving end by another modem. In some cases, these modems are simply "black boxes" that perform their function with little or no attention from the user. Other applications enhance the modem, perhaps adding some memory in order to store a simple program which will direct the operation of the modem or to provide an area to "buffer" the transmission of the information. Some modems even have a microprocessor inside them and could almost be called a computer.

INPUT/OUTPUT INTERFACES

In the previous section, we have discussed various kinds of I/O devices, from the simple front-panel switches and lights to the complex optical scanner. We have seen that these are the interface between man and machine. These I/O devices, however, cannot simply be "plugged in" to the computer and be expected to work. There is a significant amount of interfacing that must be done between machine and machine. Fig. 2-20 shows one kind of interface.

Control Lines

One of the most essential parts of I/O interfacing is that of controlling the device. For example, if we are using a magnetic-tape storage device with the computer, we will want to be able to start and stop the tape transport mechanism at will,

Fig. 2-20. I/O interface for cassette tape.

usually under control of the program. In general, control lines are used to operate a mechanical device, at the will of the program.

Status Lines

Closely associated with the control lines, these lines are used so that the computer can determine the condition of an I/O device. This is necessary, for example, if the program is ready to issue a command to the Teletype to print a character, and the machine is still in the process of printing the previous character. A status line will tell the computer that the printer is busy and is not ready to receive the next character yet. When the printing operation is completed, the status line will indicate to the computer that the printer is ready to perform the next operation.

Another example of the use of a status line is in the operation of the ASCII keyboard. When a key is depressed, a status line will indicate to the computer that someone has pressed the key and that there is information ready to be entered. Sometimes another line is used to tell the computer that more than one key is being pressed at the moment, and to ignore the data.

Data Lines and Buffers

Of course, there must be some means of actually getting the information into, or out of, the computer. This is the purpose of the data lines. In most cases, the processor's data bus is used for this purpose (Fig. 2-21). Some processors treat I/O functions as though they were simply references to memory.

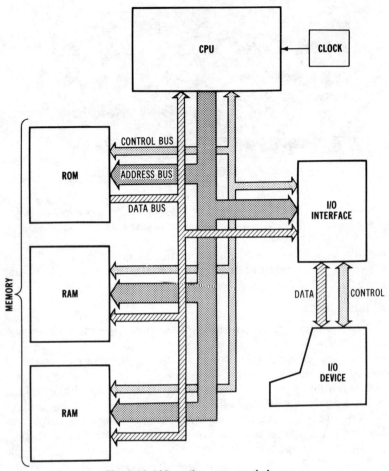

Fig. 2-21. I/O on the processor's buses.

Usually the computer has a limited ability to send and receive information on the data lines. In this case, the I/O interface must also contain circuitry that can buffer or temporarily store the information sent from the computer so that it can be modified in some way to make it usable by the device. In the case of the video display module, the buffer may be large enough to hold several "lines" of information to be displayed.

Synchronizing and Timing

When some types of I/O devices are used, the transfer of information between the computer and the device must take place under very close timing specifications. This is especially true for devices that communicate with the computer by using only two wires. These are called *serial* devices, since they send, or receive, information as a string of bits. The bits are sent one after the other at a very precise rate. This mode of transmission is useful when the I/O device is a long distance from the processor, and telephone lines are used to connect them. However, when the distance between the device and the computer is relatively short, the information can be transmitted as a complete word of data; all the bits in the word are sent simultaneously, with several wires being used to facilitate the transfer. This is called *parallel* I/O, because all the bits are transferred on several parallel lines simultaneously. An example of a parallel I/O device is the ASCII keyboard. When a key is pressed, the electronic circuitry associated with the keyboard interface generates the proper bit pattern for the character selected and puts it into a buffer as one word of binary data. The computer must then be notified that a key has been pressed and that there is a word of data in the buffer. Then, under the control of the program, the computer will read the word from the buffer and proceed to process it.

We can see that, in this case, there is very little need for synchronizing and timing, as compared with the previous examples of serial devices.

Interrupt Processing

As was discussed, there are many times when it is necessary to communicate with the computer, and each one of these cases requires the attention of the computer at some time or other in order to accomplish the transfer of information. In almost all cases, the information must be transferred under the control of the program. This would lead us to believe that the computer would always be tied up trying to determine if some device was trying to send or receive information. This would be the case if it were not for the ability of almost every microprocessor to be very carefully interrupted.

One of the control lines leading into the CPU is used to interrupt the normal flow of the program being executed. (See Fig. 2-22.) When a signal is put on this line, the CPU will complete the particular instruction being executed. It will then be forced into a special section of the program which will make a note of the place where the interruption occurred and will analyze the various conditions of the system to determine what caused the interrupt. In this way, the computer can be working on some part of the program, and will process I/O only when the

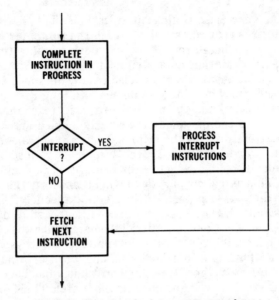

Fig. 2-22. Flowchart for interrupt processing.

need arises and when a device causes an interrupt in the processing.

Direct Memory Access (DMA)

Most I/O devices require the attention of the CPU in order to communicate with the memory. For instance, if there is some information in the memory that we wish to be printed on the Teletype, the program must take care of transmitting every character to the I/O device. This will require many instructions each time a character is to be printed.

A *direct memory access* (DMA) device, on the other hand, is one that can communicate with the memory of the computer without having to go through the CPU. This means that the I/O interface for this device must be capable of generating memory addresses, as well as providing the data transfer. These devices usually use the system address and data buses, just as the CPU itself does. As discussed in the section on the CPU, these buses are greatly used by the CPU, and if they are to be used by other parts of the system, there must be provision for control of the bus. Therefore, the DMA device interface must also be able to share the buses with the CPU and to coordinate their use.

A magnetic disk storage device is an example of a DMA device. The data transmitted between the computer and the disk are usually formatted in large blocks consisting of several hundred words. Generally speaking, the computer must specify the memory location of the data to be transmitted and the number of words to be transmitted to the disk I/O interface. The interface will then take over and access the memory directly in order to accomplish the transfer.

SOFTWARE

One fact that cannot be overstressed is that, regardless of the complexity of the various electronic devices that the computer comprises, the computer is nothing more than an expensive toy unless there is a purpose for its existence and a program that will cause the purpose to be realized. It is the program, consisting of the individual instructions arranged in the order that they are to be performed, that will make the computer a useful tool to many.

There are many different types of programs and programming systems, all of which are referred to as *software,* as opposed to the electronic and mechanical elements of the computer, or the *hardware.* Some of these programs are used to accomplish a particular computing goal, such as to balance a checkbook or compute the area of circles. Other programs are used to operate the many I/O devices that we have discussed. The mechanical operation, as well as the transfer of the information between the computer and the device, is controlled directly by the program. Still other programs are used for special-purpose types of computing, for example, computing the square root of a number or doing any other arithmetic that the hardware (ALU) does not do itself. Sometimes these types of programs are referred to as *subroutines* because they are usually part of some larger program. For some given computer system, many programs may be collected, and all stored on magnetic disk. Then, one program is used to selectively "call in" any of these many programs that are to be used. Such a collection of programs is called an *operating system,* and if it happens to be stored on a magnetic disk, it is called a *disk operating system.*

Start-up Programs

The first consideration for the new computer user will be, "How do I get this thing to start?" Just applying the power to the computer will not cause it to immediately begin processing in the way that the user desires. There must be a program that initializes the system and then determines what the user's processing goals are. Once this is established, there must be a program that will set up the computer to perform the desired processing. A most convenient method of accomplishing this "start-up" is to have a program such as that described here, stored in read-only memory (ROM), which will automatically be executed when the computer is turned on.

Writing Programs

There are many ways to program a computer. But, before you sit down and begin, you should always make a thorough evaluation of just what it is that you want the computer to do. Once this step has been done, you can then embark on your programming mission. Perhaps you want the computer to activate a loudspeaker, creating sounds as part of a computer game. This kind of task is probably best handled by a small "machine language" program that can be "called" by the game program when a sound is necessary. On the other hand, if you want the computer to balance your checkbook, machine language will not be a very good approach.

Most microcomputers that are available today include a package of programs known as an "operating system." This package usually includes features that allow the computer to be programmed using one of the "high-level" programming languages. These languages incorporate powerful commands like "PRINT" which causes the computer to output something, and "INPUT" which does the obvious opposite. With these kinds of high-level programming languages, it is quite easy to write programs to balance your checkbook, or to take care of inventory control problems, and the like.

Since this area is so important, we have devoted two entire chapters to a discussion of programming and operating systems.

Buying Programs

With the tremendous impact of the microcomputer on the consumer market, there have been many companies that have sprung up which provide various kinds of "canned programs" for the general application areas. There is a myriad of game programs that will operate on many different kinds of computers. Some of these are available on cassette tape at a relatively low cost. These are programs that some programmer has written and tested and then "dumped" onto the cassette in a standard form so that other computers, equipped with cassette tape I/O, can easily read them and run them.

There are also several software companies that are developing general business systems that will operate on a microcomputer. These are usually available on a floppy disk since they are generally much more complicated than the game programs. There are general ledger programs, accounts receivable programs, inventory control programs, to name but a few. Most of these come complete with operating instructions, and sample reports. These are very useful programs for small businesses that have never used a computer before and, therefore, do not have prejudices about how the system is supposed to work. If a company has had any previous experience with a computerized accounting system, then there will probably have to be some "modifications" made to the programs in the canned system.

chapter **3**

Central Processing Unit

Since the introduction of the first LSI microprocessor chip, the nature of hardware and of hardware logic design of digital systems has undergone vast and exciting changes. Although the design of digital systems has traditionally utilized large numbers of MSI (medium-scale integration) integrated circuits, such as counters, shift registers, gates, flip-flops, and multiplexers, connecting these chips together and debugging the design has remained a fairly complex and time-consuming practice. This problem is mainly due to the extremely large number of parallel interconnections between the MSI chips. For example an elevator controller might require 32 TTL chips, a traffic light controller 64 chips, a general purpose home computer programmable in BASIC over 128 discrete MSI packages! With each IC pin a potential trouble spot, it seems almost natural that the IC manufacturers would try to figure out a way to eliminate all these pins. The answer to this vast interconnection problem—the microprocessor . . . a 40-pin integrated circuit package about the size of a stick of gum and costing less than $20.00, that forms the brain (and digestive track) of a powerful computerlike design element.

Fig. 3-1 shows the physical size of the microprocessor; the microprocessor itself is a silicon chip about the size of a pin head that is installed by the IC manufacturer in a 40-pin DIP package. To build a product such as the devices we mentioned

THIS IS MADE OF
SILICON AND IS
ABOUT THE SIZE
OF A PINHEAD

MICROCOMPUTER
CHIP

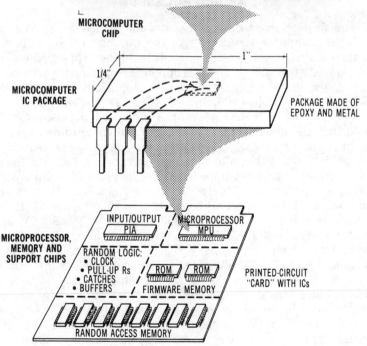

MICROCOMPUTER
IC PACKAGE

1/4"

1"

PACKAGE MADE OF
EPOXY AND METAL

MICROPROCESSOR,
MEMORY AND
SUPPORT CHIPS

INPUT/OUTPUT
PIA

MICROPROCESSOR
MPU

RANDOM LOGIC:
• CLOCK
• PULL-UP Rs
• CATCHES
• BUFFERS

ROM   ROM

FIRMWARE MEMORY

PRINTED-CIRCUIT
"CARD" WITH ICs

RANDOM ACCESS MEMORY

Fig. 3-1. How microprocessors are made.

above using microprocessor technology, you would expect to find the following elements on the printed circuit board: the microprocessor or MPU; a bank of RAM memory; one or more ROMs or EPROMs containing a program; and one or more input/output support chips which are also in a 40-pin package and are used for interfacing the MPU to the outside world. In addition, there will be a small assortment of MSI chips, and of course the usual collection of resistors and capacitors. The board which holds these parts usually has edge connectors for external devices, power supplies, and so on to connect to. The point is that the MPU approach compacts the design into just a very few but very complex integrated circuits. Yet, integrating MSI functions into one complex IC poses some interesting questions. For example, what type of computer structure should the chip emulate? The answer to this relatively simple question has produced a rich variety of microprocessor architectures, which has made the user's selection process complex.

MICROPROCESSOR

The first microprocessor was a 4-bit device with a rather indirect computer structure. As the microprocessor industry matured a wide assortment of 8-bit machines appeared on the market. A few of these microprocessors became extremely popular with the designer, and these included the Intel 8080, Zilog Z80, Motorola 6800, and the MOS Technology 6502.

Today there is a new generation of microprocessors available that claims to be at least an order of magnitude superior to previous processors. These new microprocessors feature a 16-bit data word that allows more accurate results with fewer instructions, and most importantly, a larger address bus that extends the number of bytes of memory that can be accessed as compared to the older 8-bit devices. Examples of 16-bit machines are from Intel (the 8086), Zilog (the Z8000), and Motorola (the 68000). All these micros can access over a million bytes of on-line memory. The Z8000 can access up to 8 megabytes of RAM. There are also enhanced 8-bit microprocessors, such as the 6809 from Motorola that have 8-bit buses, but inside deal in 16-bit data. Most of the new processors include instructions for on-chip multiply and divide. Then there are new 16-bit micros that use an 8-bit bus so they can easily upgrade older processors without causing a hardware redesign and board change (the 8088 from Intel). In addition to these new processors the more established 8-bit machines are steadily increasing execution speeds as new faster versions are born each month. At the same time versions of the popular 8-bit processors are becoming available in low-power CMOS, allowing applications in battery-powered equipment. Although there is no doubt that microprocessor technology will continue to improve, there will always remain the problem of interfacing these devices to the real world. Such an undertaking requires a working knowledge of these kinds of subjects: the microprocessor's pin functions, power, timing, and loading rules, the instruction set, bus systems, transceivers, serial and parallel transmission of data, interrupts, random access and read only memory, I/O interfacing, etc. Our goal is to give you a firm understanding of the concepts necessary to proceed with selecting a micro and designing a system around it.

Fig. 3-2 illustrates the internal structure of a general-purpose microprocessor. Shown is the popular and easy to use 6502, a memory-oriented* microprocessor. Inside the processor are the various registers described in Chapter 2. These registers are not really available to the hardware interface but rather are controlled by the software program. The wide arrows in the drawing indicate the fact that data flow inside the processor involves a large number of parallel lines. The various registers send and receive information over these lines (or internal buses) under control of the box labeled "instruction decode logic." The internal buses in turn connect to the chip pins through internal buffers. The address bus comes out on 16 pins and the data bus on eight. Not all microprocessors follow this exact arrangement. Some combine the address and data pins, some have up to 20 address pins, others have only 12 address pins. The single line arrows that connect to the chip pins are control and interface lines that allow the designer to control the chip with external circuits. These lines consist of voltage and ground for powering the IC, clock inputs for generating the master timing, and interrupt pins which cause the internal hardware to transfer program control to a new location. There is also a "start-up" or reset pin for clearing all internal registers to zero and beginning the program execution, "continue" or "ready" inputs for freezing the microprocessor in mid-operation so another device can claim control of the buses, and bus control pins that control the direction of data flow between the MPU and external circuits. In addition, some MPUs include "sense" pins which allow the software to sense

---

*We will have more to say about "memory-oriented" architecture later.

external logic levels and enter them into the program, "sync" pins that indicate what phase of an instruction is executing so the hardware can single step the program, "hold" inputs for inserting do-nothing wait cycles into the MPU's state flow, and now the new microprocessors are using "strapping" pins which switch a group of pins between two or more functions!

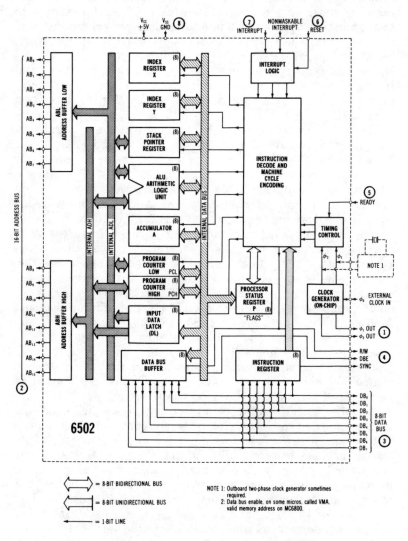

Fig. 3-2. Internal electronic structure of the 6502, a typical 8-bit microprocessor.

MPU VIEWED THROUGH ITS PINS

Like any IC the microprocessor is utilized by properly connecting its pins to external hardware. Viewed through its pins the microprocessor's operation appears quite simple. Each pin performs a single specific function, such as zeroing all internal registers (RESET), or a group of pins work together to perform a function, like the 16 address pins for addressing memory. As seen in Fig. 3-2 the 40 pins on the MPU have been organized into eight groups as follows:

1. clock
2. address bus
3. data bus
4. bus control
5. ready
6. reset
7. interrupt
8. power and ground

Every microprocessor that accesses external memory has pins that fall into this grouping. However, the exact naming of pin functions varies widely among manufacturers. The definitions used in this book mainly refer to the 6500 and 6800 family of microprocessors.* This is because these two devices are much alike in conventions and they are both easy to conceptualize as compared to the 8080 family. However, when the 8080 handles a concept in a radically different way than the 6500 or 6800 we will say so. We will now examine each of these pin signal groups in detail. Refer to Fig. 3-2 as you read.

The Clock (Phase 1 and Phase 2)

The timing of all microprocessor operations is controlled by the system clock. The clock of the microprocessor is what "turns the crank" and steps the MPU logic through its various operations.

Most microprocessors require a two-phase clock signal which consists of two nonoverlapping square waves as shown in simplified form in Fig. 3-3. The clock can be seen as two alternating positive-going pulses, referred to as phase 1 and phase 2. The importance of this is that during the phase 1 clock pulse the address lines of the MPU can change, while during the

---

*The 6502 is manufactured by MOS Technology, Rockwell and Synertek, the 6800 by Motorola and AMI, the 8080 by Intel and the Z80 by Zilog.

phase 2 clock pulse data can be transferred on the data bus. Fig. 3-3 also indicates how the program counter (PC) is put out on the address bus during the rising edge of phase 1, and incremented on the falling edge. The combination of the phase 1 and phase 2 clocks is called the machine cycle time and varies from about ½ to 2 microseconds. In most microprocessors one to five machine cycles make a so-called "machine-language instruction." In the case of microprocessors such as the 8080, a machine cycle is made up of 3 to 5 clock periods making timing more complex to follow.

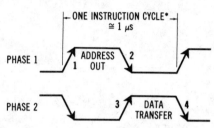

1 PROGRAM COUNTER (PC) PLACED ON ADDRESS BUS
2 PROGRAM COUNTER INCREMENTED
3 DATA FROM LOCATION ADDRESSED PLACED ON DATA BUS
4 CONTENTS OF DATA BUS LATCHED INTO MPU

* 6500 and 6800 family of microprocessors.

Fig. 3-3. Two-phase clock controls the overall timing of data transfers.

Fig. 3-4 illustrates the waveforms for signals going into and coming out of the 6502. Note that all are referenced to the system clock. Table 3-1 lists the timing requirements for these signals.

Not all microprocessors require that the clock signals be generated externally. The trend is to have the clock circuitry contained on the chip itself and the user installs a crystal or RC network to control the overall frequency of operation. However, phase 1 and 2 clock signals are still required by external hardware and are, therefore, available as outputs on the pins of the MPU.

The Address Pins (AB$_0$-AB$_{15}$)

The address pins output memory addresses and sometimes, as in the case of the 8080, I/O addresses. Sixteen pins are used and these are usually Tri-State outputs, which let the pins enter a "floating state," and allow other devices to grab control of the address bus itself (DMA or direct memory devices need to do this). The address pins are connected to push-pull type

Table 3-1. Timing Requirements for the 6502

Characteristic	Symbol	Min.	Typ.	Max.	Unit
Cycle Time	T_{CYC}	1.0 μs	—	—	μs
Clock Pulse Width $\phi 1$ (Measured at Vcc- 0.2V $\phi 2$	PWH $\phi 1$ PWH $\phi 2$	430 430	—	—	ns
Rise and Fall Times (Measured from 0.2V to Vcc- 0.2V)	T_F, T_R	—	—	25	ns
Delay time between Clocks (Measured at 0.2V)	T_D	0	—	—	ns
Read/Write Setup Time from MCS650X	T_{RWS}	—	100	300	ns
Address Setup Time from MCS650X	T_{ADS}	—	200	300	ns
Memory Read Access Time T_R T_{CYC} — (T_{ADS} — T_{DSU} — tr)	T_{ACC}	—	—	500	ns
Data Stability Time Period	T_{DSU}	100	—	—	ns
Data Hold Time	T_H	10	30	—	ns
Enable High Time for DBE Input	T_{EH}	430	—	—	ns
Data Setup Time from MCS650X	T_{MDS}		150	200	ns

MOS drivers and can drive at least 130 pF and one standard TTL load. We will cover this subject in more detail later. When an address is placed on the address bus it is only valid for a certain minimum time (usually about 300 nanoseconds). With 16 address pins the MPU can access 2 raised to the 16th power memory locations which is 65,536* locations. The newer 16-bit processors have additional address pins called segment outputs which allow the processor to access over 2 raised to the 20th power, or over one million locations!

---

*This is commonly referred to as 64K bytes because 1K = 1024 bytes, so 64 $\times$ 1024 = 65,536.

Data Bus Pins (DB₀-DB₇)

All instructions and data transfers between the processor and memory I/O devices take place over the 8-bit data bus. Each data bus pin is connected to an input buffer and an output buffer connected in parallel so the combined buffer is bidirectional and can send or receive data. The output buffer remains in the high impedance floating state until the processor transfers data to memory or to support chips in a "write" operation. The data bus switches between the floating and the active state during each clock cycle. Like the address drivers, the data bus drivers can handle one TTL load and 130 pF of

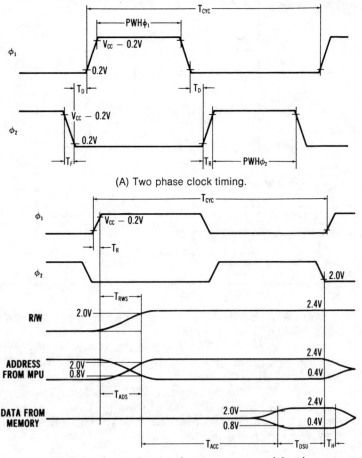

(A) Two phase clock timing.

(B) Timing for reading data from memory or peripherals.

Fig. 3-4. Timing

capacitance. Data that is being returned to the MPU from memory or a support chip must be stable at least 100 nanoseconds before the end of the phase 2 clock cycle on the data bus.

Read/Write (R/W)

The read/write line is an output used to control the direction of data transfers between the MPU and memory or support chips. The R/W line is normally high, except when the processor is writing to memory or to a peripheral device. Normally R/W connects to all chips that can receive as well as send data and enables the write operation when it goes low. All R/W transitions occur during the phase 1 clock pulse. R/W forms the "direction" input to all bus transceivers.

Data Bus Enable (DBE)

This is an input to the MPU which allows an external device to turn on the data bus for a period longer than the phase 2 clock period. DBE is rarely used.

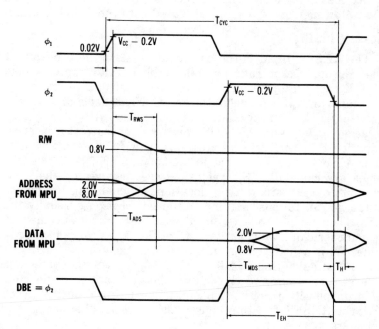

(C) Timing for wiring data to memory or peripherals.

waveforms for the 6502.

Sync (SYNC)

The sync output provides a signal that indicates when the processor is doing an OP CODE fetch (the first byte of an instruction). With some external logic the SYNC and the READY line can work together to cause single instruction execution.

Ready (READY)

Ready is an input to the MPU that when pulled low makes the processor enter a waiting mode, freezing the address on the address bus as well as the contents of all internal registers. The MPU does this by inserting a stream of "do-nothing" clock cycles into the normal MPU timing. This happens after completion of the current instruction. When the ready input goes high again the processor continues with the next instruction as if nothing happened. The ready input is generally used by external devices which cannot respond to an MPU access request within the allocated time (500 nanoseconds for the 6502). By having the external device hold the READY input low, the address will stay on the bus until the slower device can respond to it. Slow memories are typically used with the READY input.

Reset (RESET)

The RESET input is the basic way to start the program of the microprocessor running. When the RESET input is held high it causes all internal registers to be set to zero, including the important program counter or PC. Next, depending on the type of MPU, the program either begins executing at memory location 0000 (as in the 8080), or it will execute at a location specified by two RESET bytes stored in ROM memory locations FFFC and FFFD* (as in the 6502 and 6800). These two bytes are called RESET vectors, since they vector the computer into a certain starting location. By changing the vector bytes we can force start-up at different locations. Usually the RESET input is connected to a push button on the computer so the user can manually start or restart the program at anytime. With a little extra circuitry it is possible to have the RESET input automatically pulled high when the processor is first turned on, and thus cause the program to begin running on power-up without pushing the RESET button. Note that the RESET function is used also to clear all support chip registers to zero.

---

*Hexadecimal notation used here. See Appendix A.

Interrupt Request (IRQ)

When the IRQ input is brought low by an external signal it causes the processor to cease operating its current program and transfers control to a new program at a new memory location. When the old program stops, the MPU neatly stores the PC and the status register (P) on the "stack" (the stack is a place used to save important processing information in a special order). Later these two registers will be restored so we can restart processing as if nothing changed. Next a special interrupt mask bit is set. This blocks other interrupts from affecting the processor. Finally, the processor fetches a set of IRQ vectors which point to the new interrupt program. Like the reset vectors the IRQ vectors are stored usually in a high memory location. The MPU makes these the new PC and execution begins at the new address. When the interrupt program intercepts a return from interrupt instruction (RTI in the 6502), it causes a reversal of the above steps, the PC is restored from the stack along with the program counter P and the processor resumes execution at the old program location. The IRQ input is level sensitive, meaning the input must stay low until the processor sets the mask bit. If the mask bit was not set, the processor would respond to the same interrupt repeatedly.

Nonmaskable Interrupt (NMI)

This is another interrupt which is like IRQ, except NMI is an edge-triggered interrupt. Because there is no masking bit, it cannot be disabled like the IRQ can.

Power and Ground (V_{cc} and V_{ss})

For the 6500 and 6800 families of MPUs supply voltage V_{cc} is +5.0 V dc, plus or minus 5%. The absolute limit on V_{cc} is 7.0 V dc. The 8080 requires +12, +5, and −5 V dc for power. The 8085 (a similar processor to the 8080) needs only +5 V dc.

THE TWO MAJOR TYPES OF MICROPROCESSORS

In general, microprocessors fit into one of two types, memory-oriented micros (6800/6500), and the register-oriented micros (8080/Z80). Fig. 3-5 illustrates the 8080 type of micro for comparison with the 6502 in Fig. 3-2. The 8080 differs from the 6502 and 6800 in that it contains a larger complement of internal registers that can be manipulated by the programmer. However, timing and control are more complex, and three

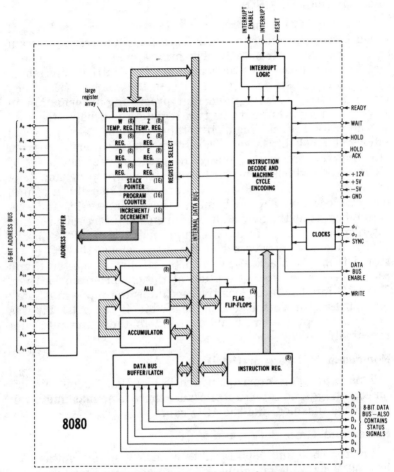

Fig. 3-5. The 8080 register-oriented microprocessor.

power supplies are required. There are eight 8-bit registers, arranged in pairs so a high byte and a low byte can be stored for dealing in 16-bit quantities. This makes the 8080 register-oriented because most operations occur in these registers. The 6502 on the other hand has only two internal registers (other than the accumulator) called the X and the Y register. However, the 6502 uses memory for representing registers, and has instructions that can do things to memory locations that the 8080 can only do to registers, so the 6502 is considered memory-oriented.

POWER, TIMING, AND LOADING RULES

Let's examine the microprocessor rules mentioned previously in more detail, one at a time.

Power

The power requirements of most microprocessors are quite easy to meet. The usual voltage requirement is a 5-volt logic supply regulated to ±5 percent. Some of the earlier processors and some of the more cost-effective designs require a −7- to −12-volt bias supply, also regulated to within 5 percent. Some MPUs also require a +12-volt supply. Power dissipation of the microprocessor IC itself is relatively low, due to the fact that the monolithic structure is usually made of n- or p-channel MOS (metal-oxide semiconductor). A typical chip may dissipate a maximum of 1.2 watts, and typically produce only ¼ to ½ watt of power. The designer can find the actual numbers on the "common characteristics" data sheet for the particular microprocessor being examined. Usually, however, this amount of power is simply added to a list of system power requirements, which consist of the I/O device requirements, the interface dissipation, and the memory requirements. Typically the microprocessor will consume less than 20 percent of the total dissipation. (See Chart 3-1.) A good example of a small microcomputer power supply suitable for handling 512 words of RAM memory, 256 words of PROM, the processor, and miscellaneous interfaces is shown in Fig. 3-6.

In addition to the system power-supply requirements, the designer may often opt to have his system run off a less-regulated supply (say 10 percent) and have a postregulator on each pc card in the system. (See Fig. 3-7.) These regulators can be simple three-terminal devices with no large filter capacitors required (except, of course, in the main supply). The advantage to this approach is that the main power supply can be much cheaper, and additional regulators are required only as the system grows.

Some of the more efficient computer supplies use switching regulators instead of the static series pass-type of regulator and the heavily filtered transformer supply. The switching power supply is more complex to build, as it converts the input voltage to a moderately high frequency signal, regulates it (which is easier now since it's ac), and then rectifies it back to dc. The problem, however, with these supplies is the transient switching pulses which can get into the memory or CPU and interfere with normal operation. Careful shielding can usually avoid this, but at a high cost. Since the series pass regulator is simple to use and troubleshoot, it makes good sense to utilize it in a microprocessor-based system where more complexity is not needed.

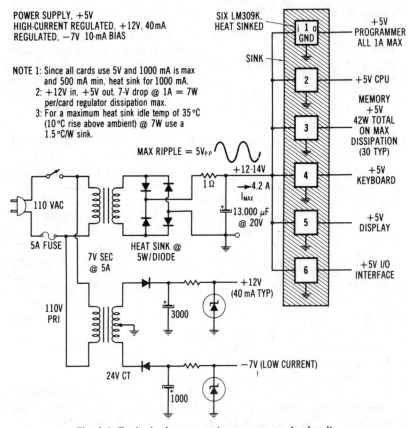

POWER SUPPLY, +5V
HIGH-CURRENT REGULATED, +12V, 40mA
REGULATED, −7V 10-mA BIAS

NOTE 1: Since all cards use 5V and 1000 mA is max and 500 mA min, heat sink for 1000 mA.
2: +12V in, +5V out. 7-V drop @ 1A = 7W per/card regulator dissipation max.
3: For a maximum heat sink idle temp of 35 °C (10 °C rise above ambient) @ 7W use a 1.5 °C/W sink.

MAX RIPPLE = 5V$_{P-P}$

SIX LM309K, HEAT SINKED

1 GND
2
3
4
5
6

+5V PROGRAMMER ALL 1A MAX

+5V CPU

MEMORY +5V 42W TOTAL ON MAX DISSIPATION (30 TYP)

+5V KEYBOARD

+5V DISPLAY

+5V I/O INTERFACE

SINK

110 VAC

5A FUSE

7V SEC @ 5A

HEAT SINK @ 5W/DIODE

1 Ω

+12-14V

→4.2 A I$_{MAX}$

13,000 µF @ 20V

110V PRI

24V CT

+12V (40 mA TYP)

3000

−7V (LOW CURRENT)

1000

Fig. 3-6. Typical microcomputer power-supply circuit.

Good power-supply layout is extremely important here, and classic design rules should be followed to the tee. Ground traces should be made large and thick, and filter capacitors should be carefully distributed on the board to avoid contact with the heat developed by the regulator elements. Fuses are a must, and it will be well to fuse each individual pc board. Burning out an expensive microprocessor chip can be a terrible experience, especially when it represents more than 25 percent of the system cost. It would be good practice to check your ac outlet for improper voltage levels or noisy operation. Not all

Chart 3-1. Typical Microcomputer Power Supply Current Requirements (Single-Board Computer Assumed)

PROM Programmer: 575 mA @ 5 V, 40 mA @ 12 V

3 7447	70 mA ea.	= 210 mA
3 Displays	84 mA ea.	= 252 mA
Balance		100 mA
		562 mA

CPU: 500 mA @ 5 V, 10 mA @ −7 V

SC/MP	200 mA
Balance	300 mA
	500 mA

Memory: 1 A @ 5 V

ROM 8 8223	77 mA ea.	= 616 mA
RAM 4 2101	70 mA ea.	= 280 mA
Balance		100 mA
		996 mA

DMA Keyboard/Bus Multiplexers: 625 mA @ 5 V
9 TTL MSI 70 mA = 630 mA

DMA Keyboard Display: 1 A @ 5 V

5 8223	77 mA ea.	385 mA
5 Displays	84 mA ea.	420 mA
2 TTL	77 mA ea.	154 mA
		959 mA

I/O Interface: 500 mA @ 5 V; 50 mA @ 12 V; 20 mA @ −7 V

Summary:

	+5 V	+12 V	−7 V
Programmer (mA)	575	40	
CPU (mA)	500		10
Memory (mA)	1000		
DMA Keyboard/Bus (mA)	625		
DMA Keyboard/Display (mA)	1000		
I/O Interface (mA)	500	50	20
Totals (mA)	4200	90	30

regulator designs can cope with large voltage spikes on the ac line. Monitoring the line for a couple of days with an oscilloscope will give some idea of the variations to expect. A digital voltmeter (dvm) would be excellent, and the numbers could be recorded for reference when you are choosing the regulator power supply. Fig. 3-8 illustrates some commercial microprocessor power supplies, including epoxy ±15-V modules; open-frame +5-V, 3-A supplies; and hefty autotransformer preregulators for transient protection.

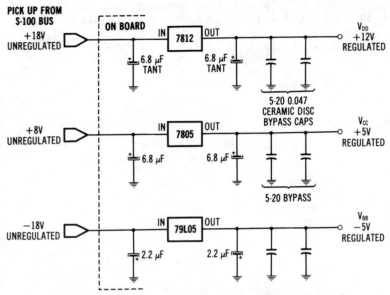

Fig. 3-7. Typical regulation and filtering on 5100 circuit board.

Quasi-Switching Power Supplies

A new kind of switching power supply that is much better suited to the vast majority of microprocessor applications is the *quasi-switcher*. A *pure* switching power supply uses a special and expensive ferrite transformer to meet the isolation requirement, and because of this, pure switchers are not price competitive with the old linear supply at power levels of under 200 watts. However, the new quasi-switcher (shown in Fig. 3-9) pioneered by Conver Corporation, eliminates the pure switchers expensive ferrite transformer (replacing it with a 60-Hz transformer on the input) and thereby becomes competitive with *linear* supplies at a power level of only 27 watts!

The trick of the quasi-switcher is to do the switching at lower voltages (90 Vac) than is normally done on a pure switcher (300-400 Vac). This relaxes the demands on the main transistor switch, the main storage/filter capacitor and eliminates the need for opto-isolating the feedback circuit.

By allowing the use of lower cost high volume components, the quasi-switcher can deliver 4 amps at 5 volts for the main TTL supply in a space one-third the size of a conventional linear supply. The auxiliary outputs of the quasi-switcher (+12, −12, −5) are achieved with conventional linear regulators, because of less demanding power requirements (less than 7 watts).

Diagrams of the pure switcher and the quasi-switcher are shown for comparison in Figs. 3-9B and 3-9C.

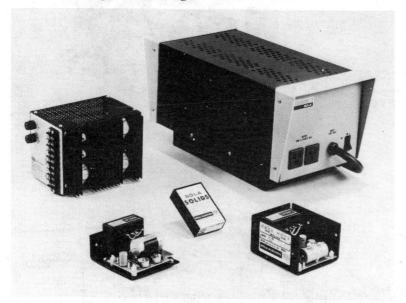

Fig. 3-8. Microprocessor power supplies.

Protecting MPUs from Voltage Transients

With a single microprocessor chip costing (in "sample" quantities) as much as $150, it is necessary for the designer to protect the delicate MOS structure of the processor (and the slightly stronger structure of the TTL) from being zapped in-circuit by dangerous, unexpected, and overly large voltage pulses, or so called "transients." A transient voltage spike can be caused by electromechanical switching or coupling, by switching large capacitive or inductive loads, by voltage reversals, or by electrostatic charge. A typical example would be the interference and inductive glitches appearing on the data bus of a microprocessor controlling a bank of high-power incandescent lights. Another example would be the huge inductive kick of a starting motor, or the static discharge into a CMOS gate.

One solution to this problem is to use a special device called a "Transzorb" by its manufacturer, General Semiconductor

Courtesy Conver Corp.

(A) Switching supply with 4 amp current capability.

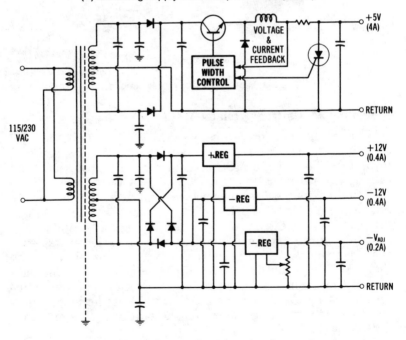

(B) Quasi-switching power supply.

Fig. 3-9. Switching

Industries. A Transzorb is a single diode device that provides a "crowbar" or clamping response to voltage spikes. When the voltage across a Transzorb exceeds its specified breakdown voltage, it literally absorbs the extra current (heating up in the process), thereby clamping the voltage and keeping the current flow from harming any TTL or MOS circuits. (Keep

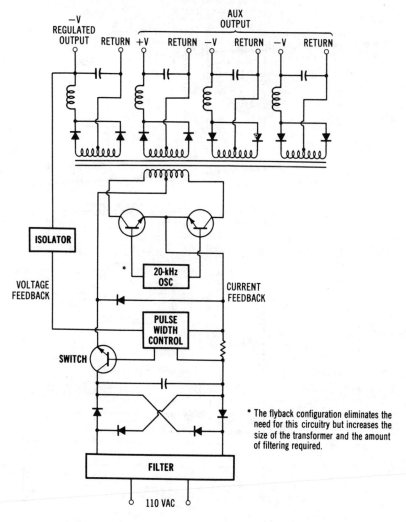

(C) Typical pure switching power supply with multiple outputs.

power supplies.

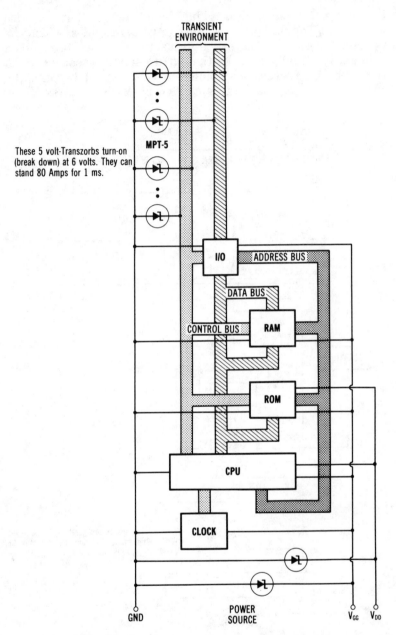

These 5 volt-Transzorbs turn-on (break down) at 6 volts. They can stand 80 Amps for 1 ms.

Courtesy General Semiconductor Industries, Inc.

Fig. 3-10. Transient voltage spikes on buses are absorbed by Transzorb clamping devices.

in mind that 10 volts applied to a TTL circuit for 30 nanoseconds will cause total destruction of the device.)

Fig. 3-10 shows a typical application of several Transzorbs used on a microprocessor system power lines, data and control buses. The address buses do not usually need transient protection because they do not normally extend into the transient environment.

The Transzorb can respond and clamp an overvoltage spike in less than 10^{-12} seconds (1 picosecond). They can also be used on the input, power, and control lines of a peripheral I/O interface.

The Clock

The clock requirements of various microprocessors range from as simple as a single capacitor and resistor (6502 and 6802) connected to the chip pins, to dual-phase, nonoverlapping, controlled–fall-time, transistor driver circuits. The particular design depends on the way the manufacturer decides to implement the signals. In the more cost-effective designs, the clock should be extremely simple. In this case, the ideal clock is no clock (at least no external clock), and the manufacturer will either allow a capacitor to be connected to cause an internal circuit to oscillate at the desired frequency or use an external crystal which does the same thing but has a stability at least 1000 times that of standard-grade capacitors. Fig. 3-11 illustrates the simple RC and optional crystal clock circuitry for the 6502. The choice depends on how much stability is really needed; complex timing requirements are usually associated with complex high-speed interfaces. So, if the system is fairly simple, a crystal may not be necessary. Since all the various components in the microprocessor system use the clock as a reference, everything will drift at the same rate and only the overall time will vary. As soon as the microprocessor must

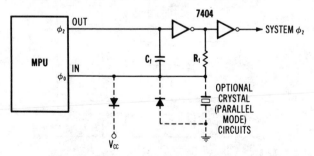

Fig. 3-11. The 6502 clock using external RC network.

interface with a device having its own clock circuit, using a capacitor for timing is asking for trouble.

The next level up in clock circuits is the simple crystal-controlled two-phase clock shown in Fig. 3-12A which is suitable for running an 8080 microprocessor. A crystal in the feedback loop of two NAND gates causes stable oscillation at 4 MHz. A dual flip-flop divides the oscillator signal by four, producing a stable 1-MHz clock. The final flip-flop works with two NAND gates to produce two nonoverlapping complementary waveforms. Fig. 3-12B shows the timing diagram for these signals.

At the other extreme of the spectrum are the requirements of the more complex microprocessors. Fig. 3-13 shows the typical clock waveforms for an n-channel MC6800 microprocessor. The two clock signals are the $\phi1$ and the $\phi2$ clocks. These signals come from the same oscillator and are complementary and nonoverlapping. Since the inputs to the CPU chip are primarily capacitive (typically 110 to 160 pF maximum), the

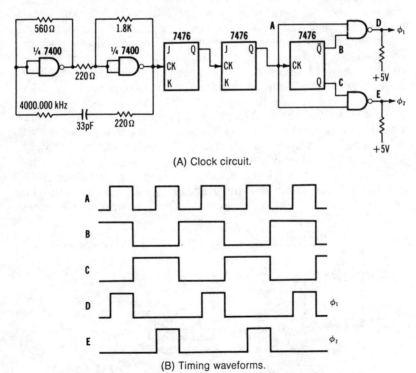

(A) Clock circuit.

(B) Timing waveforms.

Fig. 3-12. Crystal-controlled two phase, 1-MHz clock circuit.

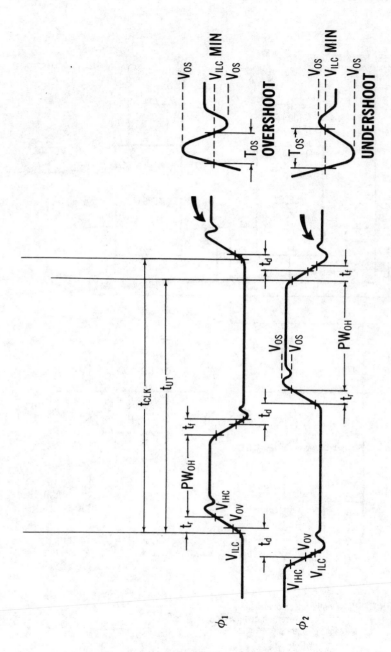

Fig. 3-13. Clock waveforms for the MC6800.

89

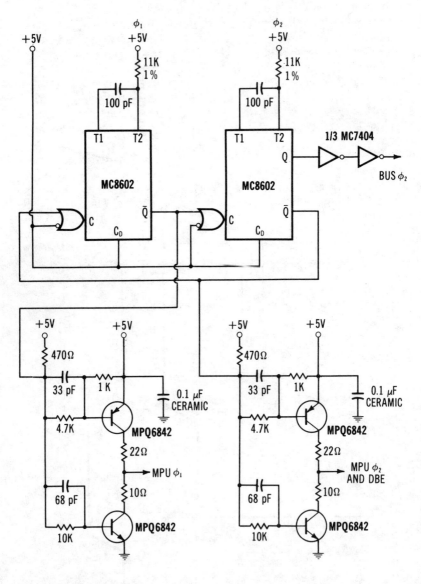

Fig. 3-14. Typical clock circuit for driving the MC6800.

NOTE: Unless otherwise noted
All resistors are carbon composition ¼ W, ±5%
All capacitors are dipped mica ±2%

spec sheet is designed to handle the overshoot and undershoot produced from driving such a capacitance load. The clock specifications that constrain the clock the most are: the rise and fall times required to meet the pulse widths at the maximum operating frequency of 1 MHz, the nonoverlapping requirement, and the logic level requirements of $V_{ss} + 0.3$ volt and $V_{cc} - 0.3$ volt. The clock buffer circuit must handle the logic levels and the rise and fall time needs. The nonoverlapping requirement can be met by the design of control logic to drive the buffers. But in many systems, especially in the breadboard and evaluation stage, it may be desirable to have the flexibility to vary the system clock to test the effects on data throughput, to check real-time operation with interrupts, or to help diagnose a system timing problem. In these applications, a pair of crosscoupled monostable multivibrators with individual pulse width control, like the one shown in Fig. 3-14, can be used as the oscillator with the previously described driver circuits. The nonoverlapping clock is generated by the propagation delays through the multivibrators. Very small variations in pulse width will occur as the circuit elements are varied in this type of circuit. Since it will probably be necessary to drive other devices with the clock signal, it is good practice to buffer the master oscillator signal and provide a "clock out" signal on the clock circuit.

Today, manufacturers of those MPUs with external clocks

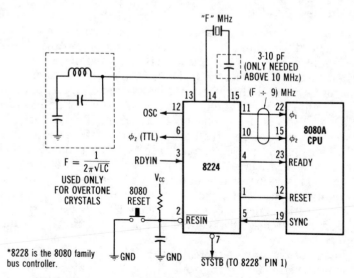

Fig. 3-15. Single chip 8224 clock circuit for the 8080 MPU.

also provide a single IC that contains all the discrete clock circuitry. Fig. 3-15 is an example of a single chip clock for driving the 8080 microprocessor. It also provides several important system control features as shown in the figure.

One final consideration for the clock circuit is the problem of cross talk from one clock line to another. This may occur with high-speed clocks and can be reduced by isolating the clock lines with ground l nes and placing series damping resistors close to the drivers. The actual value of damping resistors should be on the order of 30 to 60 ohms and will depend on the particular circuit board layout. Rise time will be reduced with increasing resistance, and the ultimate value should not reduce this below the recommended values on the data sheet.

How is the top frequency of the microprocessor clock selected? Usually this is set by the application the MPU is used in. For example, in the case of an MPU used to interface with a television, the clock will have to be synchronized with the horizontal scanning rate of the tv circuits, usually 15,750 Hz. If the MPU is to work with a color tv display, then the clock will often be derived from the high-frequency color burst frequency which is exactly 3.579545 MHz.

In other applications the exact clock frequency may not need to lock to any external signal and so the clock itself will set the overall timing for the rest of the devices connected to the microprocessor.

Fan-In and Fan-Out

Since most microprocessors are monolithic n- or p-channel MOS (mostly n-channel), it is necessary to carefully examine the signal buffering required to drive any particular load connected to the processor chip. MOS is a fairly high-impedance type of logic and therefore has restricted drive capabilities. This loading is designated as the chip's *fan-out* and is available as a specification on the data sheet. The cost-effective processors tend to require no buffering unless more than one TTL load or 130 pF of capacitance is to be connected to the chip's pins. Translated into current, one TTL load is equal to 1.6 mA. This value of current may be exceeded by connecting too many devices to the processor. In many minimum systems, it is perfectly logical to have only one TTL load to drive; but in larger systems, it is quite likely that buffering will be required.

On the other side of the coin, the MOS high impedance is a blessing when used as an input. Since MOS gates draw in the microampere range (less than 2.5 μA typically), the limiting factor without buffering will be the loading that these inputs create on the bus. This is referred to as *fan-in* and is a measure of the leakage of the input transistors. It should be made clear that not all the pins on the processor have the same requirements. For example, the clock inputs require a TTL driver or special transistor drive circuit. The halt and continue outputs may be capable of driving low-power TTL or CMOS directly. If we are driving MOS inputs, not more than 10 such inputs may be driven simultaneously by a MOS output. This is because the maximum leakage of a MOS gate is a rather large variable and may be 10 to 100 μA. Thus, the typical fan-out when using MOS devices that are from the same family is on the order of 10 gates.

A third type of logic level found on most microprocessors is Tri-State. Developed initially by National Semiconductor, Tri-State has become a powerful tool for any application where many logic gates have to "talk" to each other over a common party line. In the regular mode, Tri-State acts identical with TTL; that is, a gate is one TTL load in, and can drive 10 TTL loads out. In the third state, the logic reverts to an open circuit. It is not a level halfway up but is physically disconnected from whatever line it was driving. This is accomplished by applying a logic signal to the gate's *output enable control.* Since the gate assumes a high-impedance state, it draws no current from the bus when it is not being used.

Most microprocessors' address and data pins are Tri-State gate outputs and are idle in the high-impedance open-circuit state. When the device is ready to transmit valid information to these pins, the outputs are selected by the processor and assume the desired TTL levels; when the information has been picked up by a receiving device, the output goes back to the high-impedance "off" state. Bus receivers, transmitters, and transceivers will be described in more detail when we consider the circuit organization for data transfers.

CONSTRUCTION, PROTOTYPING AND BREADBOARD TECHNIQUES

The number of ways to approach the efficient and creative use of microprocessor hardware and software covers a very wide spectrum. At one extreme is building your own microcomputer system from scratch (acquiring the chips, wiring them together, designing programs, burning PROMs, etc.). At the other (more costly) extreme is purchasing a full-blown microprocessor development system (including dual

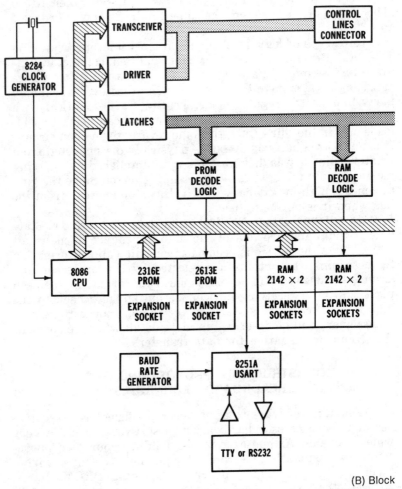

(B) Block

Fig. 3-16. The SDK-86

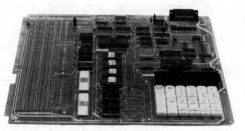

(A) Photo of board.

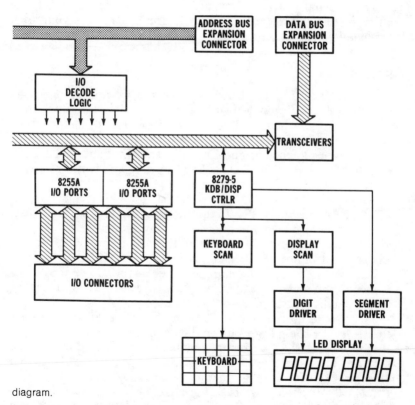

diagram.

Courtesy Intel Corp.

16-bit system design kit.

floppy disks, crt terminal, lots of RAM, development languages, and so on).

In between these two extremes are a number of very helpful and powerful single-board development prototyping microcomputer products. A few of these are in kit form, but most are preassembled, due to the high density and complexity of the pc layouts. These single-board prototyping microcomputers range in price from $200 to $500. Basically, almost all the single board development micros have a microprocessor, a system monitor (with system utility programs) usually in ROM, a moderate amount of RAM (1K to 4K), an operator's front panel (or equivalent interactive display/keyboard), an interface to an audio cassette or paper tape punch-reader for permanent storage of programs, a serial interface to a crt or tty, and often a wire wrap area for adding your own circuits.

There usually are one or more "user-dedicated" interface chips on the board, with I/O ports for controlling your own external circuitry or devices. A description of four single board prototyping computers follows.

SDK-86

This is Intel's single board prototyping computer based on the 16-bit 8086 microprocessor. Intel calls it the SDK for *System Design Kit;* you have to build it yourself, but it goes together in less than 10 hours. The SDK-86, as shown in Fig. 3-16A, has a 24-key keyboard and an 8-digit LED display. There is a 110-4800 baud serial I/O port for a crt or tty, while program storage is designed for a paper tape punch.

Although the SDK-86 provides a powerful 8086 16-bit microprocessor, only 2K bytes of user RAM are provided; sockets are provided for another 2K bytes, but Intel expects you to use the expansion area for more than 4K of RAM. There are 48 lines of parallel user I/O (two 8255s).

The system monitor is made to reside at the top of the 8086's 1 megabyte address range, FE000 to FFFFF. RAM is at 0-7FF, and to FFF if 4K option is used.

The people at Intel have designed the SDK-86 to be easily connected to their high power development system computer, the Intellec, so that programs may be uploaded, or downloaded, between these two systems. A program would be developed on the $10,000 Intellec using a high-level language like PL/M-86 and then downloaded and run on the SDK-86 for test.

Still, without the Intellec, the SDK-86 8K byte monitor has 10 commands to insert, examine, and alter memory or registers, single-step or run a program, and relocate a block of program.

A block diagram of the SDK-86 is shown in Fig. 3-16B.

SYM-1

The SYM-1 shown in Fig. 3-17A is based on the most popular 8-bit microprocessor in the world (in terms of volume, that is)—the 6502. Synertek second sources the 6500 family of parts, and put together the SYM-1 to help users quickly learn about designing with the 6502 family. (The SYM-1 is the second generation of an earlier similar product called the KIM-1, put out by MOS Technology, and now available through Commodore Business Machines.)

Unlike the SDK-86, the SYM-1 is made to expand via low cost ROMs, to give you an 8K microsoft BASIC programming language and a resident assembler and editor. Synertek offers a crt/tv-Keyboard-Terminal interface also. The board comes with 1K byte of static RAM, a 4K byte ROM monitor, 6 digit LED display, a 28 double-function keypad, and interfaces including serial tty, crt, RS-232, an audio cassette recorder interface (with capability for 135 baud KIM-1 format tapes, or "Hi-Speed" 1500 baud format), a user expansion port bus/interface with 15 bidirection I/O lines (note the SDK-86 has 48 I/O lines), and a user expansion connector that brings out 51 system bus and control lines.

SYM-1 has a very compact but powerful monitor called SUPERMON, which allows a formidable array of utility commands to move, delete, deposit, examine, and alter register or memory contents. Single-step is also provided. The most amazing thing about the SYM-1, besides how easy it is to use, is the cost—only $270 with manuals. A block diagram of the SYM-1 is shown in Fig. 3-17B.

The SYM-1 also has a neat single-line oscilloscope display driver function, which allows a long line of 32 characters to be displayed on an ordinary oscilloscope. An interface module allows an ASCII keyboard to be used for input to the SYM-1, and a television to be used as a multiline character output display. There are three on-board programmable interval timers on the SYM-1.

AIM 65

Here is another 6502-based single board prototyping microcomputer, but this one comes with a built-in 54-key ASCII alphanumeric keyboard, a 20-character alphanumeric LED display, and a 20-character alphanumeric thermal printer, all

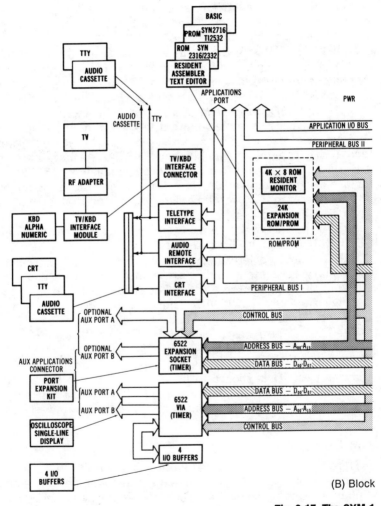

(B) Block

Fig. 3-17. The SYM-1

(A) Photo of board.

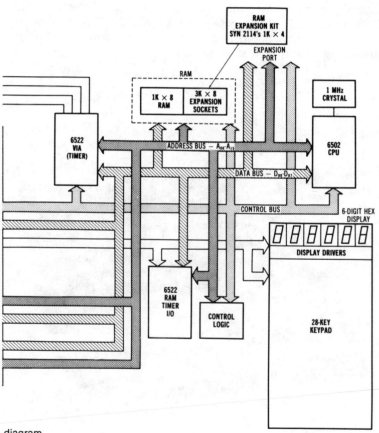

diagram.

Courtesy Synertek Systems Corp.

8-bit microprocessor.

for only $375. (See Fig. 3-18A.) The AIM 65, is made by Rockwell, Inc., and naturally uses Rockwell's 6500 chips. Like the SYM-1, the AIM 65 offers upward expansion to BASIC and a 2-pass assembly language via low cost plug-in ROMs. (A more sophisticated 6502 development system, called SYSTEM 65, is also available from Rockwell, and although AIM 65 programs can run on it, the cost of $5000 makes it attractive mainly for larger organizations and companies.)

The AIM 65 has an incredibly advanced system monitor which allows you to enter BASIC, the assembler, editor, or monitor; allows instruction entry by mnemonic, disassembly of instructions by op-codes, alteration memory or registers, and manipulation of break-points. There is also capability to control program trace mode, control peripheral devices (turn them on and off, dump code), call user defined functions, and over 10 powerful line-oriented text entry commands for manipulating program text in memory.

(A) Photo of board.

Fig. 3-18. The AIM 65

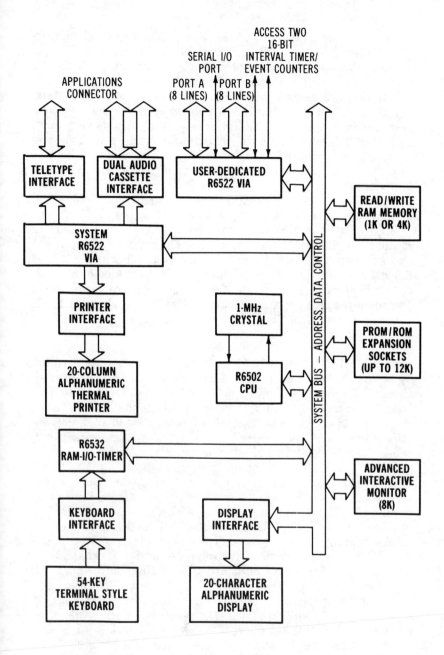

(B) Block diagram.

8-bit microcomputer.

Also like the SYM-1, the AIM 65 provides two 8-bit bidirectional user ports, and it can control two audio cassette recorders through built-in motor control transistors. There is also a serial line and access to the on-chip timers of the VIA.

The thermal printer with the AIM uses a 5×7 dot matrix, prints out 64 ASCII characters (no lower case) per line at a fast 120 lines per minute (2 lines per second), and is very quiet and very reliable. By having a printout, your programs can be very long and still be easy to "debug." You will also be able to permanently document your programs. This is an invaluable accessory.

The LED display uses special 16-segment characters and displays the same 64 ASCII characters as on the printer.

Both of the 44-pin connectors on the AIM 65 are KIM-1 compatible. The AIM 65 comes with 1K bytes of static RAM and can expand to 4K bytes with two more Rockwell RZ114 RAMs. For simple custom packaging the AIM keyboard module pc board can be removed from the main processor board and mounted in a separate location. Fig. 3-18B shows a block diagram of the AIM 65.

MMD-2

The MMD-2 (Fig. 3-19A) is a development system called by its manufacturer (E & L Instruments) a "minimicro designer." Besides being based on the 8080, the MMD-2 is unique from other development microcomputers in that its software monitor and its various interfaces are explained in great detail in special "courseware" texts from the manufacturer, called "Bugbooks." The MMD-2 is especially designed for the educator and student. It has a large breadboard area with all important system, port, and bus signals connected to a solderless socket device. System firmware provided in a 2K byte ROM is called KEX, and is made to tie in with the Bugbook tutorials provided with the MMD-2. A full editor/debugger allows single-stepping, examine/modify memory, display status and flags, contains calculator functions (+ and −), and allows the programming of an on-board 2708 EPROM in under $2\frac{1}{2}$ minutes.

Like other systems, the MMD-2 comes with 1K bytes of static RAM and can expand to 4K bytes. But unlike the other computers, the MMD-2 offers a Real Time Clock, and 8-level priority interrupt interface (5 levels available to user), 24 LEDs for address bus binary readouts, *a display that can switch between hex and octal* (very important for a learning aid), and the EPROM programmer.

Parallel I/O consists of one 8-bit input port and three 8-bit output ports. Serial I/O consists of a 75 to 2400 baud RS232 interface, a 20 mA current loop for connecting a tty, and an audio cassette interface that uses the Kansas City Standard and runs at 300 or 1200 baud.

Another valuable feature of the MMD-2 is that the expansion bus is based on the 56-pin "STD" (for STanDard) bus backed by Prolog, Mostek, and Analog Devices. This means the MMD-2 can take advantage of the large number of microprocessor peripheral boards and devices made by these companies.

Built-in power supplies provide all current needed for the MMD-2, with plenty juice left for your breadboarded circuits. The two-set data and function keyboards accept both octal and hex input.

A 2K byte "tiny" BASIC is available on cassette tape for expanding the MMD-2 to high-level language programming. Fig. 3-19B shows a block diagram of the MMD-2.

There are several ways to breadboard your prototype system, including solderless breadboards, wire-wrap (the most popular), and expensive matrix plug boards. Solderless breadboards (which go by other names including EL strips, protoboards, and distribution strips) are a universal .1″ × .1″ matrix of tiny socket pins located on a strong nylon insulator (Fig. 3-20). The pins are arranged so an IC can easily be plugged into the matrix. Each pin of the IC will then have four tiny solderless sockets that can readily accept wire, resistor leads, etc.

Solderless Breadboards

One of the major tasks facing the microprocessor builders user is how to connect and disconnect these devices in a real circuit. With high-density 40-pin chips, buses with 16 lines, and 8-wire I/O ports, it is obvious that the old techniques of solder and wire just won't do.

The universal solderless breadboard can accept component leads up to 0.032 inch in diameter. There are several size and matrix configurations available so that the user can expand the design *ad-infinitum*. There are also hundreds of components that use the tenth-inch universal spacing of solderless breadboards.

Fig. 3-21 shows jumper ribbon cables, in-line ribbon cable splitters, and in-line ribbon cable switches that can be used with solderless breadboards. Fig. 3-21 shows a group of solderless strips organized on a board, with power and ground

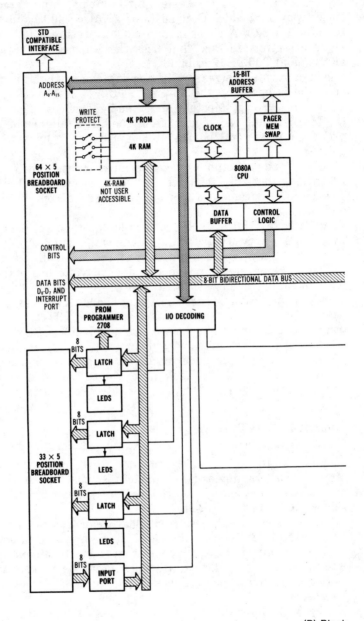

(B) Block

Fig. 3-19. MMD-2, an

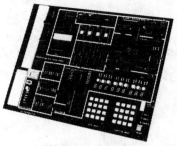

(A) Photo of board.

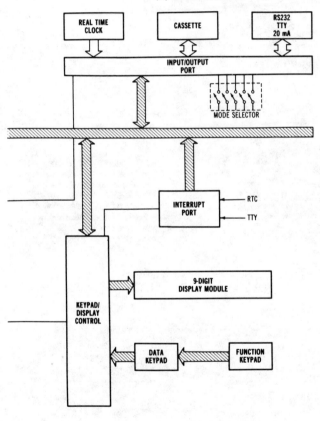

diagram.

Courtesy E & L Instruments, Inc.

8080-based minimicro designer.

(A) Typical size unit.

(B) Internal connection details.

(C) Holding digital MSI ICs.

Courtesy E & L Instruments, Inc.

Fig. 3-20. Solderless breadboard.

terminals, that is called an All-Circuit Evaluator by its manufacturer, AP Products.

The only drawback to the solderless strip is that, when used with digital logic of any complexity, the possibility of bad connections becomes a serious problem. Wires not properly inserted in the solderless strip can come loose and go unnoticed. This can cause some strange results when the system is first fired up, and one can very well appreciate the use of carefully inserted connections.

Wire-Wrapping

The other popular approach to a maximum flexibility system is the wire-wrap technique. In this case, special wire-wrap sockets are used with a Wire-Wrap gun (Fig. 3-22) that spins a wire around the posts of an IC socket. Such a "wrap" is solid and reliable, and if the wire isn't nicked in the process, it can take quite a bit of flexing without breaking. A thin, solid, sol-derplated (tinned) wire with thin Teflon insulation is usually used for making the wrap.

Wire-wrapping can be done manually with a tool like the one shown in Fig. 3-23. Available from Vector Electronic Company, the tool wraps and at the same time "slits" the insulation off special Tefzel (teflon nylon) coated wire. The slit occurs where the wire touches the corners of the post. Thus no separate time-consuming removal of insulation is required, and wraps can proceed at a quick rate.

If manual wire-wrapping is too tedious, and the pneumatic wrap guns are too expensive, then you will want to investigate the battery powered "hobby-wrap" tool, like the one shown in Fig. 3-24, made by OK Machine and Tool Company. This wire wrapping tool can handle 26 and 28 AWG wire, and with a special bit, 30 AWG wire. A special bit and sleeve produces "modified" or "regular" wrapping, and an overwrap protection device is included to prevent bad wraps. The tool weighs just 11 ounces and uses two alkaline "C" size batteries.

Vector Boards

Wire-wrap sockets are usually used in an epoxy pc board (Fig. 3-25) with holes punched in it every one-tenth of an inch and with edge connectors etched on one end of the card. This type of breadboard is often referred to as vector board. The edge connectors may be soldered to, and in turn connected to, an edge connector receptacle. This brings the various connections on the board to the pins of the edge connector receptacle, and serves to anchor the board mechanically in place.

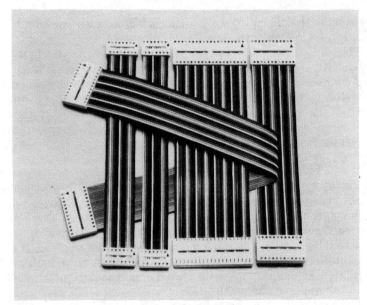

(A) Ribbon-cable jumpers.

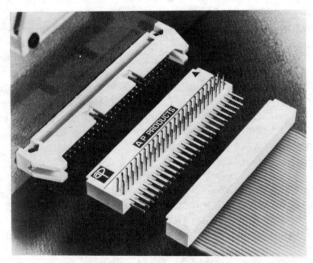

(B) In-line ribbon cable splitter.

Fig. 3-21. Solderless

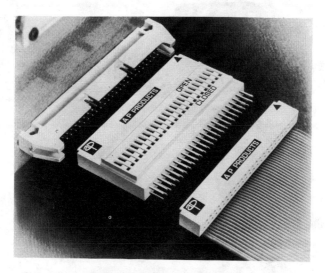

(C) In-line ribbon cable switches.

(D) Large array of breadboards on a board.

breadboard accessories.

Fig. 3-22. Wire-Wrap gun.

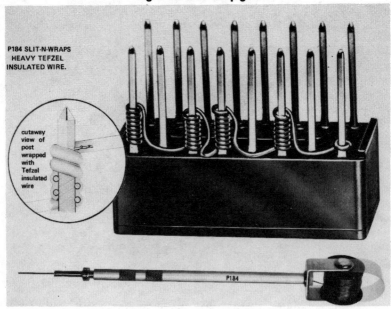

P184 SLIT-N-WRAPS
HEAVY TEFZEL
INSULATED WIRE.

cutaway
view of
post
wrapped
with
Tefzel
insulated
wire

P184

Fig. 3-23. Manual wire-wrapping tool.

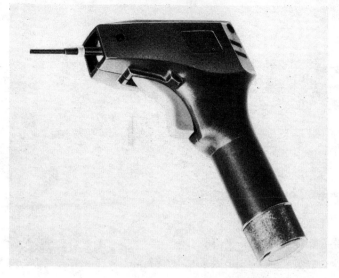

Fig. 3-24. Battery-powered wire-wrapping tool.

A question that often arises when selecting a vector board for microprocessor work is how many pins to use on the edge connector for the various bus signals. One very popular configuration, called the S100 bus, uses 100-pin edge connectors, and is shown in Fig. 3-26A. Another bus configuration gaining attention is the 56-pin STD bus.

The attraction of the S100 prototyping board is that it is a self-supporting system. Fig. 3-26B shows how an S100 motherboard is used. Thirteen 100-pin receptacles are mounted on the motherboard and are physically interconnected by pc traces on the motherboard. This pc network is called the system's *back-plane*.

Card Cages

Microcomputer projects can easily grow to requiring several boards, a large power supply, a front panel with LED displays, keyboard, etc. A card-cage is a pc board holder that allows the project to be mechanically stable, electrically shielded, packaged for protection, and moved about. Fig. 3-27 shows several examples of pc card-cages. Fig. 3-28 shows a card-cage for holding S100 circuit boards. Room for a large power supply is provided.

Wire-Wrap Techniques

If wire-wrap sockets are to be used, the builder should be acquainted with some of the techniques involved in building

111

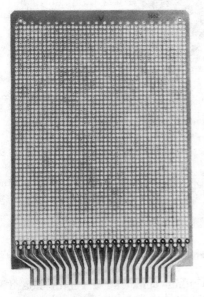

(A) Simple universal vector board.

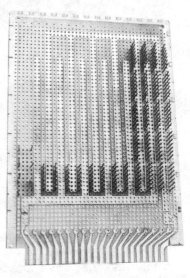

(B) Vector board with etched ground and V_{ee} traces.

(C) Microprocessor vector board accommodates 14-, 16-, 24- and 90-pin LSI DIPs.

Fig. 3-25. Epoxy pc boards for wire-wrap sockets.

circuits with them. One of the first subtle problems with wire-wrap breadboards is the problem of connecting components that are not in a dual in-line (DIP) package. A resistor, for example, poses an interesting insertion problem. If we try to squeeze it into a DIP socket, it will probably not fit too well (unless it's a small resistor). In other words, most of the discrete parts must be either made to fit into the DIP socket or soldered to a "header" pin which serves no other useful pur-

(A) S100 bus system prototype board.

(B) S100 motherboard holds 13 S100 edge connectors.

Courtesy Vector Electronic Co., Inc.

Fig. 3-26. S100 bus system prototyping.

(A) Simple vertical pc card holder.

(B) Card cage for vector boards.

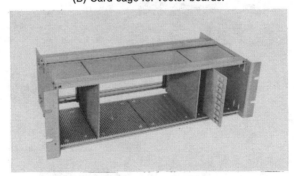

(C) Card cage with flexible card spacing.

Courtesy Vector Electronic Co., Inc.

Fig. 3-27. Commercially available card cages.

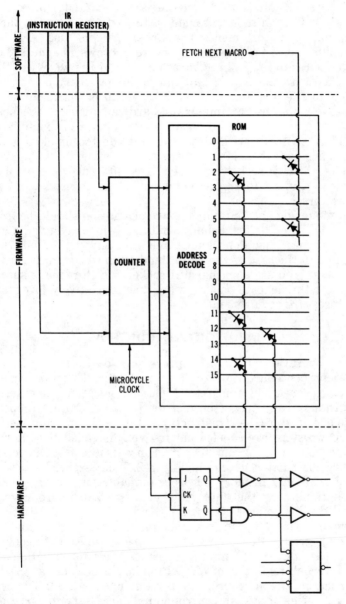

Fig. 3-28. Microprogram instruction decoder.

pose than to provide a place to wire-wrap to. However, most good digital design at the prototype level will minimize the number of discrete parts. After all, the main reason for digital integrated circuits is to reduce the parts count. Of course, some circuits will require larger solid-state parts, such as the three-terminal regulators mentioned earlier. In this case, it is best to mount these parts with hardware (screws and nuts) and solder wires to their pins. The other ends of the wires are then attached with the Wire-Wrap gun to the necessary points.

One of the nice things about wire-wrap is the fact that an increasing number of important hardware devices are being made to plug into a 16- or 14-pin DIP socket. For example, all kinds of switches with tiny penpoint- or toothpick-actuated levers are available. Many of the seven-segment LEDs can fit in a 14-pin DIP socket, and there are different types of plugs that can connect to 16-conductor cable and be used as 16-pin connectors.

In mounting the LSI chips, extreme caution should be exercised. These chips are usually contained in fairly fragile ceramic or epoxy plastic packages, and have anywhere from 16 to 64 pins. In the case of the 64-pin and 40-pin LSI processors, it is advisable to use a special LSI socket, which is made specifically for the delicate packages and has a relatively low insertion pressure requirement.

INPUT/OUTPUT CONTROL

The operation of all microprocessors basically consists of the same procedure repeated over and over. The procedure is to access repeatedly for "fetch" instructions from the external program storage area (the memory) then execute the operations specified by these instructions. Inside the microprocessor these two steps are carried out by what is called the internal hardware microprogram. The microprogram exists in the box labeled instruction decode in Fig. 3-2. It is essentially a dedicated read-only memory or programmable logic array which the designers of the chip have created. The microprogram takes the incoming bytes from the instruction register and converts them to specific control signals. Sprinkled around the microprogram's PLA or ROM are various gates and decoding logic that convert the microprogram signals to operations on the internal registers of the chip, i.e., executing a specific instruction. The microprogram is similar to a state table specifying a series of system control signals necessary to carry out each instruction.

The Input/Output Cycle

Referring back to Fig. 3-2, which illustrates our general-purpose microprocessor, the fetch routine causes an instruction address to be transferred from the program counter register to the address bus, and initiates an input data operation. Various strobe signals occur, signaling the memory to provide the data at this address. When the instruction is provided on the data bus, the fetch routine causes it to be loaded into the instruction register (IR). The instruction operation code is now transformed into the address of the appropriate instruction-execution routine by the address generation logic. As a last step in the fetch routine, this address is loaded into the "microprogrammed" address register in the decoder, causing a branch to the appropriate instruction/execution routine.

The execution routine consists of one or more "microinstructions" to implement the functions required by the instruction. The number of microinstructions varies with the instruction. For example, the routine for a register ADD instruction would access the two registers to be added over the data bus (or operand bus if the architecture were different), cause the ALU to perform the ADD operation, load the carry and overflow flags from the ALU into the status register, and store the result in the specified register. The control logic interprets the microinstructions to carry out these operations.

The number of times the MPU must perform a fetch operation depends directly on the type of instruction that is being executed. For example, an immediate mode instruction (such as load the accumulator with data) will only require two machine cycles, one cycle to fetch the OP CODE for the instruction, and one cycle to fetch the one byte of data to be loaded. On the other hand an instruction such as load the accumulator with data from an absolute two-byte address would require four cycles to complete, the first to fetch the OP CODE, the second to fetch the low byte of the effective address, the third to fetch the high byte of the effective address, and finally a fourth cycle to fetch the actual data using the two effective address bytes. Usually the hardware manual supplied with the MPU will specify the cycles for every instruction in great detail. In general the more cycles in an instruction the slower its execution will be.

Microprogram

The internal instruction decoders in a microprocessor chip are designed around ROMs or PLAs. This way the manufacturer can program the ROM and thus the instruction set. Fig. 3-28 shows how the ROM (in this case a diode ROM for simplicity) interprets the instruction code into a hardware address that causes certain flip-flops and gates to operate (execute). This inner level of programming is called *microprogramming*, while the regular level of programming is referred to now as *macroprogramming*. These terms should not be confused with the terms used to describe the physical size of computers, as in minicomputers and microcomputers. Rather, this definition is useful only in illustrating the nature of the internal processor operation.

The internal clock is called a *microcycle clock* because it is used for driving the microsteps in an instruction. In this case it drives a counter that compares the incoming instruction from the IR to the count. When the value of the count reaches the address of the instruction, the counter stops and the ROM enables one particular set of diodes connected to that address. This, in turn, causes the hardware inside the chip to operate so as to complete the desired number of cycles for that particular instruction, and then to fetch the next macroinstruction into the IR.

The only way the designer can change the microprogram is to use MPUs that are designed to have their microprogram changed. Custom and Bit Slice microprocessors usually have sections of ROM that the user can customize to create specialized instructions. But in general the set of instructions provided by the manufacturers is more than enough for most applications.

Bus Access

The standard type of *data* transfer among modern microprocessors is over a single 8- or 16-line I/O bus. This is usually a two-way type of bus system (called *bidirectional*). Most microprocessors use special control signals to allow many electronic devices to use the I/O bus without conflicts. Since the number of signal lines would double if *separate* data-in and data-out buses were used, the two-way system saves on wires and connections. Another refinement of microprocessor bus systems is a "shared" type of operation where, as shown in Fig. 3-29, digital I/O devices "hang" on a continuous eight-wire data bus. What makes such a bus system possible is the use of Three-State* bus transceivers. In the illustration, these are shown as switches which completely isolate all de-

---

*You may also find Three-State logic referred to as 3-State or Tri-State.

vices from the bus unless they are involved in a data transfer. For example, data from a keyboard may be entered directly into the processor, without the memory outputs interfering. Since the memory data pins are also Three-State, it will not

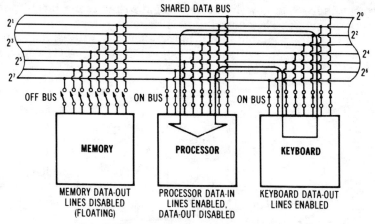

Fig. 3-29. Shared data bus.

affect the bus unless it is actively sending out information. The processor and keyboard thus share the bus, and the memory is disconnected electrically.

Bus Transceivers

Since the system data bus is bidirectional, and the processor may sometimes be sending data and other times receiving data, some means of controlling the direction of the data on the bus is required. For example, consider a memory read (LOAD). The CPU addresses a word in memory and transfers it into the accumulator. In this operation, the memory will be "sending" and the CPU will be "receiving." To accomplish this the memory data output pins (connected to the low-impedance output stage of a MOS transistor) may be connected directly to the processor high-impedance data input pins. Now consider the opposite case, when the operation is a memory write (STORE). The CPU addresses a word in memory and transfers the contents of the accumulator into that location. Here, the processor will be sending and the memory receiving. The CPU chip will be presenting its low-impedance output transistor to the memory, but the memory still has its low-impedance output stage hooked up. This is bad news, and according to Ohm's law the two stages will try to burn each other out. The answer is to "float" the memory's output stage (disconnect it) during the time the memory data inputs are used.

Figs. 3-30A and B show the internals of a low power Schottky 3-State noninverting buffer/driver and its symbolic logic diagram. A 3-State gate is much like a regular TTL gate except there is a new input to the gate that turns its output stage on or off. This new input is usually referred to as the control, gate, or enable input, here called $\overline{G1}$. Figs. 3-30C and D show the purpose of the logic signal sent to the $\overline{G1}$ control

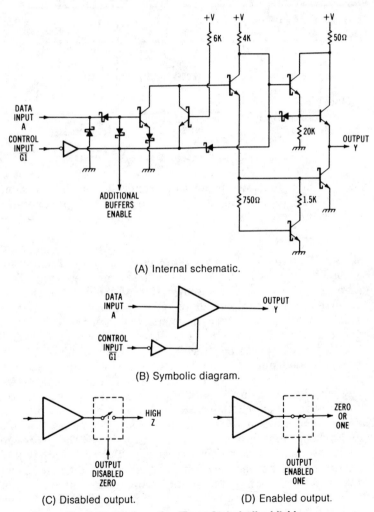

(A) Internal schematic.

(B) Symbolic diagram.

(C) Disabled output.   (D) Enabled output.

Fig. 3-30. Noninverting Three-State buffer/divider.

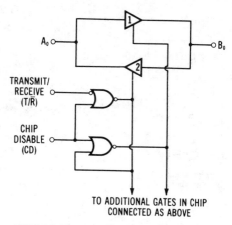

NOTES 1: If CD is logic ONE both gates become floating.
        2: If CD is logic ZERO, then the logic of T/R̄
           controls which gates output is enabled.
           If T/R̄ = 0 → A_{OUTPUT}, B_{INPUT}
           If T/R̄ = 1 → A_{INPUT}, B_{OUTPUT}

Fig. 3-31. Two-state gates and some direction logic make a single line transceiver.

input is to disable the output (make it high impedance) or to enable it (allow the logic input to be transferred or passed to the output). In an IC package the same control input controls several gates. If two 3-State gates are connected back to back, as shown in Fig. 3-31, and some additional logic is tied to the control inputs, we get what is called a bus transceiver, a gate arrangement that allows the direction of the data transfer on the data bus to be reversed by CPU control.

There are now two inputs to the transceiver, the direction input called transmit/receive (T/R), and the chip disable* input called C̄D̄. Normally the chip disable input would be connected to the chip select bus. Applying a logic 1 to C̄D̄ keeps both gates in the floating mode, when the transceivers are not needed. When C̄D̄ becomes logic 0 the direction input controls which of the gates has its output turned on. If T/R is a logic 1 then gate No. 1 is enabled, gate No. 2 is disabled, and information goes from A to B. If T/R is a logic 0 then information flows from B to A.

Fig. 3-32 shows a single IC package that contains eight bus transceivers. This device comes in a special narrow (0.3 inch) 20-pin epoxy package. When MPUs first came out, ICs with only four transceivers were available.

---

*This control input is also referred to as Output Enable, or Chip Select.

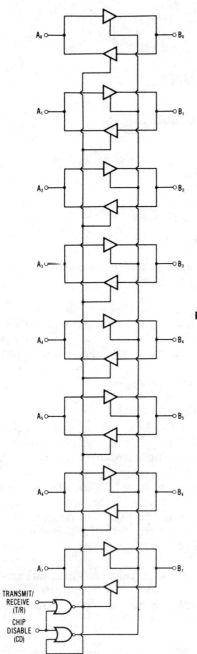

Fig. 3-32. The 74LS245 octal 3-State bidirectional transceiver.

Now as far as the address bus is concerned the MPU is normally always the sender and it would seem buffers or Three-State drivers would be unnecessary. However, as we saw evidence of earlier there are many cases where it is desirable to

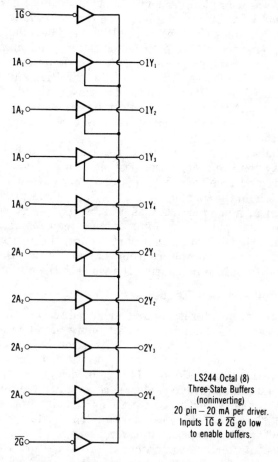

LS244 Octal (8)
Three-State Buffers
(noninverting)
20 pin — 20 mA per driver.
Inputs $\overline{1G}$ & $\overline{2G}$ go low
to enable buffers.

Fig. 3-33. Address buffer.

have the MPU disconnected from the address bus so that another device can send information to the memory directly, without going through the MPU. This is called Direct Memory Access or DMA for short. To accomplish disconnecting the MPU from the address bus we can use the device shown in Fig. 3-33 on the address lines of the MPU. For 16 address lines we would need two packages as each package handles 8 lines. The IC is divided into two quad sections so the designer could connect the device up as a four line transceiver, if desired.

Fig. 3-34 illustrates a typical bus system for a modern microcomputer. Here we can see that the address and data bus of the processor are buffered and drawn as heavy lines to indicate several wires are in the bus. The drawing shows a popular 40-pin interface chip called the PIA (for Peripheral Interface Adapter) we will learn more about later, that implements two 8-bit input/output ports. A 16K to 64K byte random access memory is also shown. Note that the PIA and memory both contain Three-State output drivers on the data bus so there is no conflict. The chip select bus is simply a decoder that uses the high order address lines to enable one of several PIAs or the memory.

Note that this type of design is for a flexible, many-module-capacity system. In a processor designed for an "end product," the drivers and receivers may be absent or replaced with some type of latch on the memory or I/O device. In end-product low-cost design, as much hardware as possible is replaced with software. For example, if the input device requires that all its data be inverted for minimum parts count, the software program can include a simple routine that inverts all the bits in the data word before presenting the word to the output device.

Bus Control and Bus Request

One of the most interesting and advanced features of modern microprocessors is the ability to have more than one processor working on a single application. With several chips working on the same job, the overall time required to complete the job is shortened. An example of this type of design is a processor fitted with a mass storage device, such as a flexible disk. Since the disk requires a complex formatting circuit to organize the storage of data, the logic designer may choose to use a microprocessor for this purpose, to lower package count. But since the disk is to interface to another microprocessor, how do we effectively share the system bus between these two?

The solution is to use what is known as *bus request* and *enable input* and *enable output* functions on each microprocessor. Let's consider the flexible disk when data are to be read directly into the microprocessor's memory. Fig. 3-35 shows three control signals: bus request (BREQ), enable out (ENOUT), and enable in (ENIN). These signals appear on pins on each microprocessor. BREQ is actually an input and output type of circuit; ENIN is an input that stops all processor activity; and ENOUT is an output that indicates the processor is active.

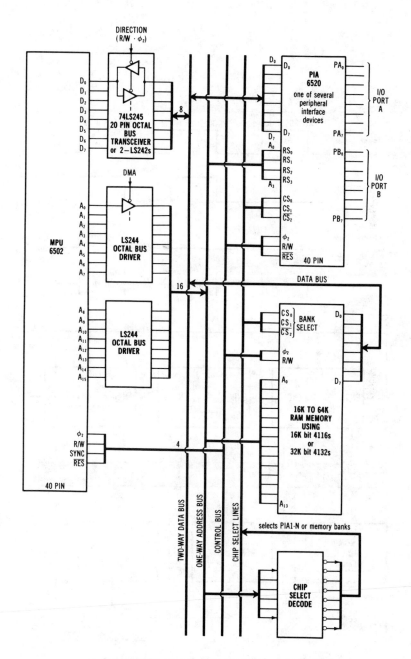

Fig. 3-34. Complete 3-State system buses.

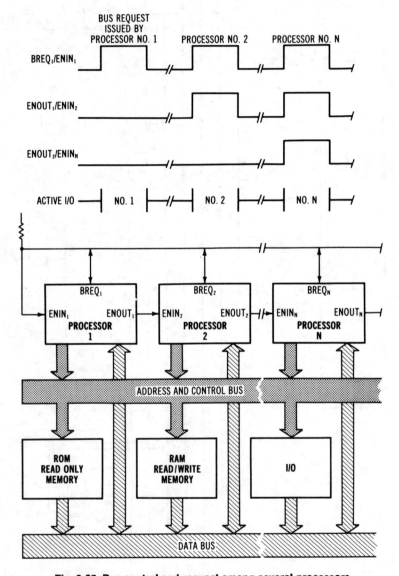

Fig. 3-35. Bus control and request among several processors.

Bus request (BREQ) is used as a bus-busy and bus-request signal. When processor No. 1 is ready to use the bus (for example, if a memory fetch is to be executed), its BREQ line goes high. If the ENIN line on this processor is *not* low (lockout condition), its ENOUT line will go low, signaling the other processors that this processor now has control of the bus. When the fetch cycle is complete, the BREQ input/output line on the processor will go low. Since BREQ is tied back to the ENIN line, processor No. 1 ENOUT line will go high, freeing processor No. 2 to issue a bus request. If this processor needs the bus, its BREQ line will go high. Since its ENIN input is high, its ENOUT line is forced low, locking out any other processors down the line from it. Now processor No. 2 has control of the bus. If all processors issue a bus request simultaneously, the string is served on a priority-select basis—processor No. 1 first, No. 2 second, and so on. However, if processor number N issues a bus request and there are no others awaiting service, ENIN is high and the request is granted. Thus, any one of the processors can be a DMA controller. For example, suppose that processor No. 1 has just finished an instruction and now requires that a special program on the floppy disk be loaded into the processor's read/write memory. If we hook up the second processor as the DMA controller, then as soon as the No. 1 instruction is finished, the No. 2 processor will take control of the bus and begin to execute a search for the desired program on the disk. Since this may take many milliseconds (a very long time in CPU terms), the DMA controller has the bus only when the first processor is "in-between" instructions, that is, when it is doing an internal calculation or when it is waiting for an input. During this period the first processor is not using the bus, and the data on the floppy disk are transferred directly into the read/write memory, one word at a time.

Flags and Sense Bits

CPU flags are output gates that can be controlled by the program. For instance, suppose the programmer wanted to turn on a light at the end of the program. In this case, an LED is connected to the flag pin. The program reaches the end, puts a logic 1 on the flag bit, and the LED glows. When the program is started again it first turns off the LED by putting a logic 0 on the flag. Other uses of flags include turning I/O devices on and off, locking out interrupt signals, and any application where timing pulses are needed. A microprocessor may have from none to eight flags to manipulate.

"Sense" bits can be used to determine when an external device has completed an operation, such as when a printer has finished printing one character. These bits are nothing more than flip-flop states inside the CPU, which can be set, or reset, by signals applied to the CPU pins and then used by the program. For example, suppose an output device such as a printer has completed a print operation. It sends a logic signal to a sense pin on the CPU, setting the internal flip-flop. The CPU keeps checking this bit in a programmed loop (i.e., it checks it over and over). When it finds that the bit has been set, the CPU branches to a routine that resets the flip-flop (so that the next time the event occurs it will be ready) and completes a series of instructions to send another character to the printer.

Of course, sense information must be checked constantly by the processor to see if it has changed, which can easily tie up the entire processing time. Often it is desirable to have the external event actually signal to the processor when it occurs, freeing the CPU to operate on another job. This technique is known as interrupting the processor, or more commonly as an *interrupt* driven system.

Interrupts

The classical form of interrupt uses a pin on the CPU usually called the interrupt request input (labeled INT on the 8080 and IRQ on the 6800 and 6502). The pin is connected to an internal hardware circuit which performs a rather complex but extremely useful purpose when activated. Assume the microprocessor is running a program and an external device puts a logic 0 on the 6800's interrupt input (normally IRQ is held high by a 3K ohm pull-up).

What happens to the processor after the IRQ input is brought to logic 0 is illustrated in flowchart form in Fig. 3-36A. First the program checks if an internal interrupt mask bit is set. If the mask bit is set, it means another interrupt is already in progress so it will block the current interrupt as shown in the flowchart. If the bit is not set, then the MPU is free to execute the interrupt procedure. First the current instruction is completed. Next the mask bit is set to block all other interrupts. Next if the MPU is a 6800, it automatically saves all important registers on the stack, including the current program counter, accumulator, index registers and status registers. In the case of the 8080 or 6502, the programmer must save these registers with instructions in the program (this is both good and bad). Next the processor jumps to the program whose beginning address is stored in locations FFF8 and FFF9 (assuming the programmer has stuffed these locations with the proper starting address). The interrupt program begins executing. The interrupt program most likely now communicates with the interrupt device. Perhaps a keyboard caused the interrupt. The interrupt program might read a byte in the port of the keyboard. Or perhaps the interrupting device was the vertical sync pulse from a video display device. The interrupt program might refresh the display memory with new data. The interrupt program will hum along until a return from interrupt instruction is executed (RTI) signalling the interrupt routine's end. This will cause the processor to restore all the registers that were saved on the stack at the time the interrupt first occurred. The old program counter will be restored and the interrupt mask bit turned off. Finally the processor will return control to the original program and continue executing its instructions where it left off.

Because of the masking bit of the IRQ, the signal to the pin must remain at a logic 0 for a certain minimum time while the IRQ mask bit is checked. Therefore, the IRQ is level sensitive, meaning we must hold the logic level at 0 for a certain time (a one-shot would work here). In some cases we want the processor to respond instantly to an interrupt and in some cases unconditionally with no masking bit to block the interrupt. The 6800 and 6502 have an additional pin called the nonmaskable interrupt, or NMI. NMI is an edge-triggered interrupt that reacts to the logic change, i.e., when the logic goes from a 1 to a 0. There is no mask bit so the NMI interrupt is faster than the IRQ. The NMI procedure is much like the IRQ procedure, except the vector addresses for the interrupt program are stored at FFFC and FFFD. Fig. 3-36B shows the complete flowchart for the way the 6800 and 6500 processors handle interrupts.

The NMI interrupt is best used when you want the interrupt to occur regardless of the processing task in progress. A power failure might be such a condition, where you would have a fast NMI interrupt program that saved all important registers, the state of the real time clock (if one is equipped), and so on.

The logic in the flowchart labeled HALT is the way the processor handles an external signal applied to the HALT pin.

In the case of the 8080 the interrupt program must contain instructions to save all the important registers, including the program counter, and it must restore these registers when the program ends. This requires use of the stack PUSH and PULL instructions. Although this makes the programmers

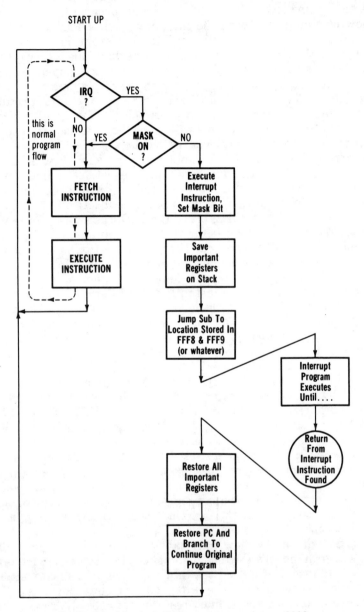

START UP

IRQ?
YES
NO

this is normal program flow

MASK ON?
YES
NO

FETCH INSTRUCTION

EXECUTE INSTRUCTION

Execute Interrupt Instruction, Set Mask Bit

Save Important Registers on Stack

Jump Sub To Location Stored In FFF8 & FFF9 (or whatever)

Interrupt Program Executes Until....

Return From Interrupt Instruction Found

Restore All Important Registers

Restore PC And Branch To Continue Original Program

(A) Flowchart for typical interrupt processing on 6800.

Fig. 3-36. Interrupt

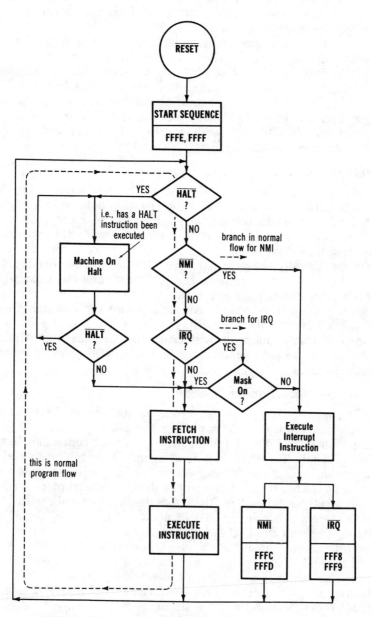

(B) 6802 MPU flowchart showing normal program flow and two possible interrupt branches.

flowcharts.

job more complex, it allows saving only those registers that actually need saving, which may speed up the interrupt response, when compared with the 6800.

Another strangeness of the 8080 is that it expects the interrupting device to provide the address of the interrupt program. This is done by having the interrupt device "jam" a restart N (RST n) single byte instruction on the data bus. The N specifies one of 8 possible memory locations that contain three byte CALL subroutine instructions. Although this may seem overly complicated the 8080 interrupt structure actually is more flexible than the 6800 and 6500 allow.

Polled Interrupts

Because the IRQ and NMI pins are high-impedance inputs it is possible to connect several interrupting devices in a wired OR configuration to the inputs. In the case of more than one interrupting device, the processor must "poll" the external interrupting devices to determine which device caused the interrupt. Usually the external device has a flip-flop that it sets to indicate it is interrupting the processor, and the processor checks this flip-flop on every device one at a time. Unfortunately polling is very time consuming and the reaction time of the interrupt will be slowed. Further what does the processor do if two or more devices interrupt it at the same time? The answer to both problems is to use special priority interrupt circuitry.

Interrupts With Priority Control

The way around polled interrupts is also the solution to the conflict of multiple interrupts. In the 8080 a special 40-pin chip called the 8259 PIC or priority interrupt controller, handles this job. The 8259 PIC is designed to accept up to eight interrupt inputs, and in response to the inputs it produces one of eight CALL instructions to the desired interrupt program start locations. The 8259 PIC* is designed to operate with the 8228 system controller, and will not work only with the 8080 MPU. The way the PIC handles multiple interrupts is simple. Each input to the chip is assigned a priority level, with 0 the highest and 7 the lowest. This way if a priority interrupt 4 device is requesting service at the same time as a level 2 device, the level 2 device gets serviced first. If a level 1 interrupt occurs during the time the level 2 is executing, it will

---

*In the 6500 and 6800 families, priority interrupt circuits can be constructed in MSI without too much trouble.

cause an interrupt to occur by the PIC and the level 2 program will be temporarily delayed.

The priority approach is an excellent way around which to design a business computer. We can have a printer connected to a low level interrupt so that after a line of text is printed, it signals the computer for the next line. During the time the printer is busy printing the text line, the computer is free to continue with other processing. Often the keyboard, disk, and crt will be attached to the interrupt logic so the printer is made to slow down when these devices need service.

Strobed Status Information

Certain MPUs, such as the 8080, send out a great deal of information about the processor's internal states. Without consuming extra pins on the chip, this information includes the type of instruction being executed, the state of interrupts, and even contains the additional address information. How is this possible?

The answer is a tricky technique called strobed status. What happens is that eight bits of information are gated out on the data bus for a brief instant prior to the execution of an instruction. Since the data bus is not used at this time it doesn't interfere with normal operation. Each of the eight bits represents the state or status of a particular event in the MPU. This is also referred to as "time-multiplexed" status information.

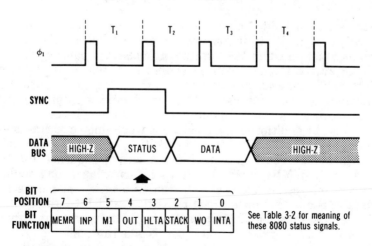

Fig. 3-37. The 8080 status signals appear on data bus during the T_1 and T_2 states of every machine cycle.

Table 3-2. Status Signals Sent Out by the 8080

D_0	INTA*	Interrupt acknowledgment—used to gate a RST instruction onto data bus
D_1	WO	Write output machine cycle (WO = 0: write)
D_2	STACK	Address bus is holding stack pointer
D_3	HLTA	Acknowledgment signal if HALT instruction is executed
D_4	OUT	Indicates address bus contains the 8-bit address of an 8080 output device, and data bus will contain the output data when WR is active (0)
D_5	M1	Indicates the OP CODE fetch cycle, or first byte of an instruction
D_6	INP*	Indicates address bus contains address of input device and input data should be placed on the data bus when DBIN is active.
D_7	MEMR*	Indicates that the data bus will be used for a memory read.

*These 3 signals can control all data flow on 8080 data bus.

In the 8080 the status bits are gated on the data bus during the first two T states of each machine cycle (remember an 8080 machine cycle has 2 to 5 clock pulses called T states). See Fig. 3-37. The actual status signals sent out by the 8080 are listed in Table 3-2. The most interesting are the INP and OUT status bits which occur on data lines D_6 and D_4. These are the famous 8080 I/O port strobe signals which allow using the 256 8080 I/O ports without consuming any address space.

The 8080 processor also outputs memory read and write strobe signals which are normally used to control memory devices, such as the direction of bus transceivers. In a simple low parts count system, the status information can be latched using an 8-bit latch, such as the 8212 shown in Fig. 3-38A. Fig. 3-38B shows how the 8212 latch hooks up to the 8080. For medium to complex systems, the Intel 8228 system bus controller provides five of the major status signals listed in Table 3-2, and in addition buffers each data bus line so it can drive many additional gates.

Fig. 3-39A shows a typical input/output sequence for the low-cost SC/MP processor. Status information, along with 4 bits of address, is strobed onto the data bus, just before the data appear. This is referred to as the valid I/O status time. The status information in this case is a *read cycle flag,* which tells us that the data input cycle is starting; an *instruction fetch flag,* which tells us that the first byte of an instruction is being fetched; a *delay flag,* which tells us that the beginning of a programmed delay cycle is starting (that is, the second byte of the delay instruction is being fetched) ; and a *halt flag*, which tells us that a HALT instruction has been executed. That information requires that 4 bits of the data bus be sent out. Since the other 4 bits of data bus are available, some chips use them as address extension bits. In the SC/MP, the address width of the microprocessor pins is 12 bits, for a maximum address of 4096. The 4 bits on the data bus, available during the address strobe time, contain the "page" information for selecting one of 16 possible 4096-byte pages of memory. For the first 4096 bytes of memory, we can simply use the microprocessor's 12 address pins directly. The remaining 4 bits of information must be latched during any memory read or write. Thus, the processor appears to get 65,536 bytes (16 bits) of address range on 12 address pins!

Start-Up and Halting

Starting a microprocessor is accomplished through the use of the reset pin (usually called $\overline{RES}$ or $\overline{RESET}$). Stopping the processor can be done by an external switch connected to the MPU ready line (RDY) or by executing a software break (interrupt) instruction via the program.

To start a processor from the power completely off condition is called a cold boot or a cold start (assuming that the computer is cold from being off all night). To start up the 6502, for example, the reset pin is pulled low by a 555 (connected as a one-shot) for a brief period (see Fig. 3-40). Upon receiving the low, the processor clears all registers, then executes the program pointed to by the reset vectors stored at FFFE and FFFF. The user is responsible for filling these locations with a vector to the user's monitor or start-up program before the RESET. Naturally this means the vectors must be stored in some form of read-only memory. This could even be 16 diodes (8 per vector-address byte) but you would need an octal Three-State buffer to gate the addresses on the bus.

The actual reset program always initializes important variables and constants in the user's program, sets up the direction of the ports in the PIAs, and then turns over execution to the main user program.

There are two ways to halt or stop a microprocessor. One way uses hardware connected to the ready (RDY) line of the processor. Recall that when RDY on the 6502 (HALT on the 6800) is pulled to logic 0 it puts the processor in a waiting mode until RDY is allowed to go to logic 1 again. The processor will finish out the current instruction first. Another

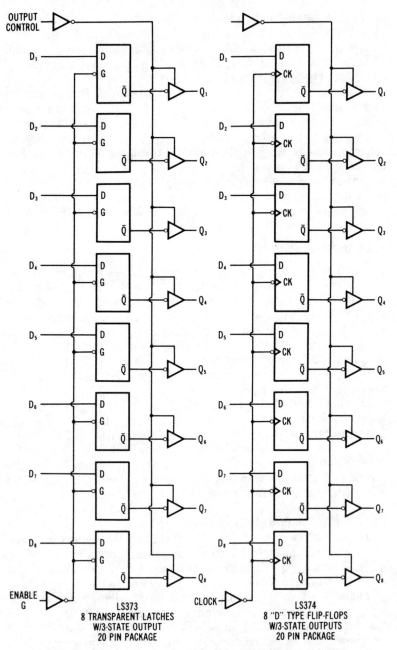

(A) Typical 8-bit input or output latches for implementing I/O ports.

Fig. 3-38. The 8218 octal latch

way to halt the processor is to do it through the program by use of the 6502 break (BRK) instruction. This is called software interrupt, or SWI in the 6800. When the MPU executes a break instruction it acts as if an external IRQ interrupt occurred and vectors through FFFE and FFFF to the users interrupt routine. The program can then go into a programmed loop and signal the user that the BRK instruction was executed.

An interesting way to *stop* a microprocessor is shown in Fig. 3-39B, where a flip-flop and NAND gate are used to generate a manual or programmed halt. A programmed halt is one initiated in the software program, as opposed to a manual halt initiated by a mechanical switch. The Q output of the flip-flop drives the CONT input of the processor, which, when high, allows the next instruction to be fetched and the computer to run. When low, it halts the processor prior to the next instruction fetch cycle. Two things control this flip-flop: a start switch that the user controls for manual start and stop, and a NAND

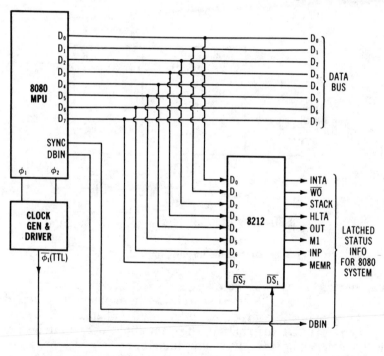

(B) Latched status for 8080 bus occurs when SYNC and 0 are true.

captures system status.

gate monitoring bit D_7 of the data bus. The NAND gate is NANDed with the strobe signal NADS, which occurs when valid status is available on data bus. The NAND gate then drives the clear input of the flip-flop latch. As long as D_7 is not high (halt

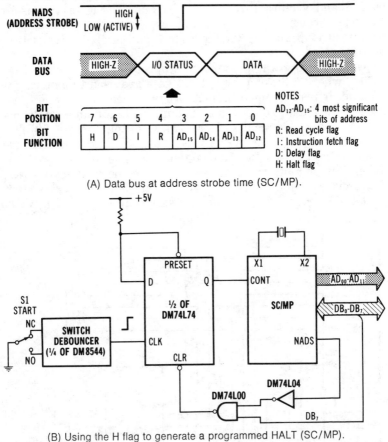

(A) Data bus at address strobe time (SC/MP).

(B) Using the H flag to generate a programmed HALT (SC/MP).

Courtesy National Semiconductor Corp.

Fig. 3-39. Strobed status and programmed HALT.

flag not set), the NAND gate keeps the clear input high and the processor runs. (The start switch can be momentarily closed to stop or start the processor manually.) When the H flag is set by the HALT instruction, the clear input of the latch goes low, which sets the Q output low and stops the processor. Since the HALT instruction is all zeros (00000000), an accidental jump to an empty area of memory will read in all zeros and cause a safe programmed halt.

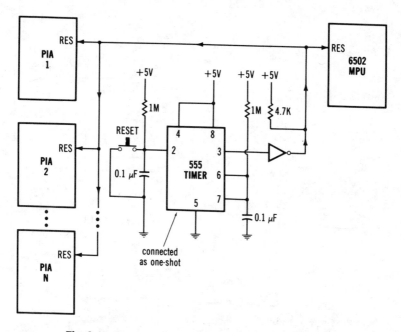

Fig. 3-40. Starting the processor by pulsing RESET low.

Single Instruction Stepping

Often it becomes necessary to step the microprocessor through a program one instruction at a time, particularly during a program debugging session. Sometimes the designer will want to step through the several cycles of a single instruction one cycle at a time. Single stepping can be implemented either mostly in hardware as shown in Fig. 3-41, or mostly in software as shown in Fig. 3-42.

Referring to the hardware logic in Fig. 3-41, we can see that the major control line is the three-input NAND gate to the processor's ready line. The RUN/HALT switch forces RDY to stay at logic 1 when in the RUN mode, while in the HALT mode it puts a logic 0 on RDY, thereby locking the processor from running. The second and third inputs to the NAND gate control single-cycling and single-instruction stepping. The timing diagram in Fig. 3-41B shows that single instruction stepping is accomplished by using the processors SYNC output to gate the RDY line so the MPU executes until SYNC ends. Single cycling of the MPU is done through similar logic. The processor can't be stopped during a memory write cycle. LEDS are used to show which cycle is executing.

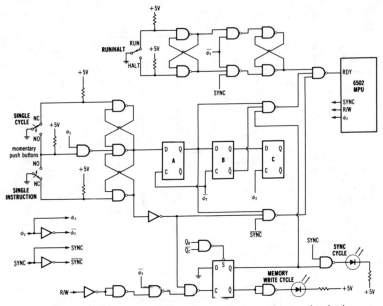

(A) RUN/HALT and single-instruction or single-cycle stepping logic.

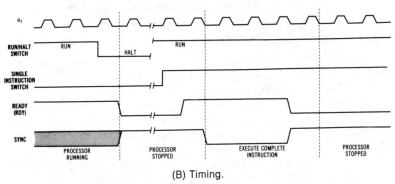

(B) Timing.

Fig. 3-41. Hardware approach to single stepping.

The software approach to single instruction stepping is illustrated in Fig. 3-42. Here the NMI input on the 6502 is utilized to force the processor to an interrupt program that executes one instruction, disassembles it into its mnemonics, displays it and all internal registers on an output device, and then returns control to the system monitor. The user can specify the starting address of the instruction from which to begin single stepping. The program keeps a history of the last address disassembled so the next instruction can be located.

140

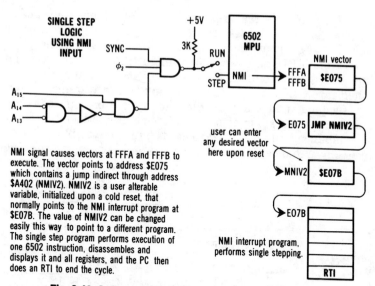

SINGLE STEP
LOGIC
USING NMI
INPUT

NMI signal causes vectors at FFFA and FFFB to execute. The vector points to address $E075 which contains a jump indirect through address $A402 (NMIV2). NMIV2 is a user alterable variable, initialized upon a cold reset, that normally points to the NMI interrupt program at $E07B. The value of NMIV2 can be changed easily this way to point to a different program. The single step program performs execution of one 6502 instruction, disassembles and displays it and all registers, and the PC then does an RTI to end the cycle.

user can enter
any desired vector
here upon reset

NMI interrupt program,
performs single stepping.

Fig. 3-42. Software approach to single-step logic AIM 65 single-board computer.

MPU COMPARISON

In the preceding chapters we have alluded to the slight differences in microprocessors and tried to be general in our discussion. Now we are going to explore the differences between one chip and another. At this writing there are over 100 different microprocessor chips on the market and over 200 different versions of these chips packaged in a computer system. Although it's quite probable the microprocessor field will become even more diverse, there seems to be a reduction process occurring, in that the differences between processors are dwindling. In fact, since the introduction of the first 4-bit machine, a standard of 8 bits has become the popular size for a data word, and 16-bit addresses are typical. Simplified input/output instructions that treat an I/O device as a memory location are a trend. Internal "on-chip" clocks to simplify timing requirements, and Three-State output structures that allow easy peripheral interfacing are on the increase.

MPUs of the 1980s

The most exciting trend today in microprocessor technology is the new superpowerful 16-bit chip—processors that offer ten times the throughput of the older 8-bit predecessors of the 1970s. These 16-bit MPUs pack an incredible amount of advanced mainframe features, including 64-bit multiply and divide, the ability to access megabytes of memory, and instructions that support advanced software disciplines. Further, these new 16-bit MPUs are especially suited to multiprocessing and time sharing systems, due to the way memory may be partitioned into 64K byte segments for multiuser systems.

A second trend today is the enhanced 8-bit micros—more sophisticated versions of older but popular 8-bit MPUs. These new enhanced processors are software compatible with the chip they enhance (the 6809 for example enhances the 6800

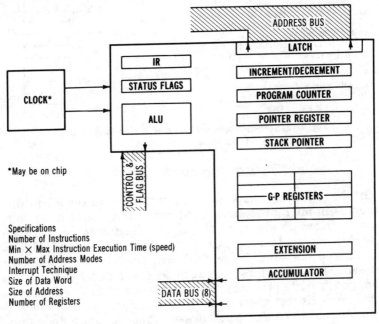

Fig. 3-43. MPU reference diagram.

and can run all its programs), and in addition offer tremendous improvements in addressing, usually by increasing the number of registers on the chip.

The enhanced MPUs have more flexible interrupt structures, and strangely enough smaller instruction sets. The catch here is that each instruction does a lot more than the ones before it.

There are six important areas to examine when evaluating a microprocessor: the instruction set, the number of addressing modes, the speed of execution, the interrupt technique, the number and size of internal registers, and, finally, the size of the address and data word. Fig. 3-43 illustrates a "universal"

MPU block diagram which we will use for our comparisons. It contains all the important registers of a typical microprocessor, the clock circuit, and the system buses.

Instruction Set

Although we will cover this topic in finer detail in the programming section, for now it is important to realize that there are some dramatic instructional differences among today's microprocessor devices. Most of the squeezes the manufacturers make are to simplify the logic inside the chip, reduce the number of pins, and to keep the cost of the mask to an absolute minimum.

The later generations of microprocessors have evolved quite complete instruction sets with rather sophisticated mathematical and logical instruction modes. Most have ALUs that add and subtract, that allow double-precision arithmetic, binary-coded decimal (bcd) arithmetic, as well as signed and unsigned binary and two's complement (see Appendix A). The logical functions of the ALU are also high-powered, including all types of ANDs, ORs, exclusive ORs, rotates, shifts, and complements. Clearly, the absolute number of instructions in the set tells us something about the power of the processor. The low-cost type of processors may have anywhere from 30 to 40 instructions, while the more sophisticated types have upwards of 75 to 200 instructions.

The latest generation of 16-bit and enhanced 8-bit microprocessors has vastly improved instruction sets. Based on research studies of vast amounts of user software, manufacturers have discovered and refined major weak points in microprocessor instruction sets. The new MPUs offer a rich variety of register exchange and transfer instructions, the ability to handle bit, nibble, byte, word, long word, bcd, ASCII, and block (string) data. Instructions for multiply and divide that give 32-bit results, special stack instructions that can save any number of registers at once, and relative mode addressing modes that allow reentrant and recursive programming disciplines are also included in these latest generation supermicroprocessors.

Note that when examining a processor's instruction set, do not let the absolute number of different mnemonics fool you; addressing instructions will have many variations and they may be indexed from several sources. The 6809 for example has only 59 mnemonics compared to the 6800's 72, but it has 268 op codes (legal instruction operation codes), and 1462 distinctly different instruction combinations.

Addressing Modes

Since the microprocessor spends much of its time addressing memory or peripherals, it makes sense to have a large number of addressing instructions. The low-cost microprocessors are limited in this respect and will usually allow a maximum of four types of addressing: *PC* (*Program Counter*) *relative*, where the address is obtained from the current address in the program counter and the displacement located in the operand field; *indexed*, where the address is obtained from some internal pointer register and the displacement is added to it; *immediate* addressing, where the second byte of the instruction is used as the data; and, finally, *auto-indexed*, which provides the same capabilities as indexed, except that the pointer register is incremented or decremented by some value after it is used. Although this sounds like more than enough addressing modes, it turns out that even more sophisticated modes are available in the higher-level processors, and that we can do more with them.

The more expensive 8-bit microprocessors, such as the 6800 and 6502 have additional addressing modes that allow involve index registers and special use of the first 256 bytes of memory (called page zero). New modes include two-byte *zero page* (or *direct*) instructions that act on a location in page zero, three-byte *absolute* (or extended) instructions, which use the trailing two bytes of the instruction to access a location anywhere in the range 0 to 65535 bytes, *accumulator* instructions, where a one-byte instruction specifies one of several internal accumulators. The 6502 has two particularly powerful addressing modes called *indexed indirect* and *indirect indexed*. These modes allow operations on any location in memory, are only two bytes long, and use page zero memory and an index register to form the effective address.

Finally, the addressing range on the new 16-bit microprocessors has increased dramatically. Where the older 8-bit MPUs could only access 64K bytes, the 16-bit Intel 8086, for example, has a 20-bit physical address, and can therefore locate 2 to the 20th bytes which is 1 megabyte (1 megabyte = 1,048,576 bytes). However the 8086 is designed to break the megabyte of memory into four 64K byte "segments" and then provides four 16-bit segment registers which contain a base address that are added to the normal 16-bit effective address. The 8086 is intended to have a 64K segment for code, one for data, one for the stack, and one called extra which would be an additional data segment. This means a program that does not directly

144

change or load these segment registers is said to be dynamically relocatable, and can be moved anywhere inside the megabyte range. Also the I/O instructions OUT and IN can apply to 65,535 ports!

The point is that you probably will never exhaust all the addressing capabilities of the new 16-bit processors, while the modes on the older 8-bit MPUs may be leave a little to be desired for some applications.

The enhanced 8-bit MPUs offer several new kinds of indirect addressing (a powerful minicomputer technique) including (in the 6809) *relative indirect, extended indirect,* and *absolute indirect*. This makes for relocatable programs.

Execution Time

The ultimate speed of any processor depends on so many variables that deciding which is the fastest is quite a complex job. The reason for this is that execution speed is job dependent; one processor may complete a certain program faster than another, but a different program might turn the tables. One easy way to get an idea how fast the computer runs is to pick a standard instruction, one that will be used in your application quite often, and see how long it takes to execute according to the particular manufacturer's specification sheet. (The latter may also be referred to as the Instruction Set Summary Card.) The trick to this method is discovering how many cycles the instruction requires.

The number of cycles is given in the summary card listed under the character N or $\curvearrowright$. This number is then multiplied by the machine cycle time to obtain the speed of the instruction. (Machine cycle time is not the same as clock cycle time. Many clock cycles make a machine cycle.) In the MC6800, the clock time *is* equal to the machine cycle time (1 μs for a 1-MHz clock). An "indexed load" requires 5 MPU machine cycles. Therefore, this instruction takes five times 1 microsecond, or 5 microseconds, to execute.

The SC/MP processor uses a slightly different formula to come up with the cycle time. In this case, the oscillator is internal and a capacitor sets the frequency. The machine cycle, however, is two times this number. Thus, for a 1-microsecond clock time the cycle time is 2 microseconds. An indexed load on SC/MP requires 18 microcycles, and therefore the instruction requires 18 times 2 microseconds, or 36 microseconds. Thus, we can begin to see the difference in execution time required by these two devices to move a byte of data into the accumulator.

Since this is something we may do often, we should ask ourselves if the SC/MP, which is more than five times slower than the 6800, is a worthless machine. Of course, the answer is: Absolutely not. We often find that our application can be handled in a slightly different way so that the time requirements are not so formidable. Or, we may find that a multiprocessor approach will be more effective. Regardless, one should reserve judgment until *all* the various details of the Instruction Set Summary Card have been examined.

It's true that one way to get a general feeling for the execution speed of an MPU is to look at its *range* of instruction execution times, i.e., the fastest and slowest instructions for a fixed clock range. But like judging a horse for a race, you won't really know anything until you write a standard benchmark program for the particular MPU you're interested in. And even a benchmark doesn't tell all. Some MPU processing rates drop drastically for certain kinds of program applications. Sometimes the application literature will point to the kinds of processing the MPU is best suited for. In Chapter 6 we present a useful benchmark that moves a block of data in RAM.

Also, remember that PMOS MPUs are slower than NMOS. Most microprocessors today are either NMOS or CMOS.

Interrupt Technique

The manner in which each manufacturer chooses to implement the interrupt features of a processor has a direct bearing on the ability of the device to handle complex I/O operations. For example, the first processors lacked even a simple interrupt technique, making it very difficult to have an I/O device signal to the CPU that it had completed its task.

The popular 8-bit processors that followed opened the interrupt possibilities by giving the user two kinds: maskable and nonmaskable. The enhanced 8-bit processors add a third "fast" interrupt pin which lets the user decide what, if any, additional registers should be stacked, and thus speeds things up.

To allow multiple prioritized interrupts most popular 8-bit microprocessor manufacturers have a 40-pin priority interrupt controller chip available that allows fairly simple expansion for 8 or more interrupting devices. The Intel 8080 uses the 8259 PIC, while the Motorola 6800 family offers the 6828 PIC.

Keep in mind that if both an IRQ and NMI kind of interrupting pin are provided you will be in position to create fairly sophisticated I/O interface programs.

Size of Address and Data Word

This is perhaps the largest variable among microprocessors, with each company making different sizes for different requirements. The early processors were all 4-bit data-word machines, and were adequate for handling bcd arithmetic and simple calculatorlike jobs. The size of the data word has a direct bearing on the "resolution" of the processor, and 4 bits provide for one part in 16. Arithmetic in a 4-bit machine is done on a digit by digit basis, usually on binary-coded-decimal digits (see Appendix A). With an 8-bit data word, we get better resolution (one part in 256) and the arithmetic process is simplified. The 16-bit machine gets one part in 65,536 but, of course, you must remember that it requires more pins to implement.

The size of the address word gives us a good indicator of the addressing range of the MPU. A 4-bit machine usually has to send out an address in 4-bit chunks, which makes programming rather tedious. Three chunks gives 12 bits, or 4096 words. With the 8-bit machine, addressing is usually accomplished in two 8-bit chunks (first the lsb then the msb), to allow addressing up to 64K bytes. The 16-bit machine offers the best addressing range of all, needing only one word to cover the entire 64K of memory. Although the trend is to use 8-bit data words and 16-bit address words, it is probable that a 16-bit standard for both will eventually occur.

The 8-bit processors, then, usually provide 16 pins for the address, 8 pins for the data bus, and the remaining pins for power, clock, and control. How, then, could manufacturers provide a 16-bit data word without increasing the number of pins beyond 40? The answer is to have the data and address bus share 16 common pins in a time-multiplexed mode. The user then adds a set of 16 latches to hold the address and drive the address bus, and a set of 16 transceivers to form the data I/O bus. A status signal from the processor is used to tell when the high byte or low byte of data is on the 16-line data bus. The data bus for 8-bit oriented memories can then be split into two banks, one for the upper byte and one for the lower.

Moving the data pins onto the address pins has given us eight new pins to define. Four to seven of these are usually made to be additional address pins, the so-called "segment" or "paragraph" address. With four additional address pins (beyond 16) we can get to 1 megabyte of RAM; with seven extra pins—48 megabytes!

This is probably more RAM than anyone would ever use, except in the most demanding application.

Now that we have a better idea of what each of the five microprocessor parameters means, let's take a closer look at individual processors. We will consider the chips in their chronological sequence, covering the five important parameters, as well as some of the peculiarities of the chip design.

4004

The 4004 was the early bird in the field. Introduced in 1973, it is the 4-cylinder model-A processor, in a 16-pin DIP, that started the ball rolling. Originally designed for a Japanese calculator, the 4004 almost emulates a general-purpose computer in the sense that it can be programmed as a different type of calculator. Its main drawback is the difficulty in actually programming it. A 4004 has a 4-bit data word and uses a 4-bit bidirectional bus to send out not only data, but chunks of address. The memory chips are designed to latch the data from the MPU, and thus the MPU will not work with standard memory. Yet with all these drawbacks, designers at that time could see that the chip family offered cost-effective and interchangeable calculator designs.

Inside the 4004 is a 12-bit program counter and an 8-bit instruction register. The 4004 has a total of 45 instructions and a 10.8-microsecond cycle time. Loading from memory into the accumulator requires first sending out three 4-bit chunks of address, which takes a two-word instruction. Thus, 21.6 microseconds are consumed in setting up the address. The returned data are stored in an internal register. Next, the accumulator is actually loaded with the contents of this register, which takes a one-word instruction, or 10.8 microseconds. Thus, the total time is 21.6 + 10.8, or 32.4 microseconds, which is quite slow.

The interrupt on the 4004 is called TEST and isn't really an interrupt. The TEST is really a sense bit and can be tested periodically with a JUMP instruction. Thus, interrupts on the 4004 are ruled out, unless some complex hardware is added outside the chip. Calculators, however, don't really require interrupts to function, so any calculatorlike job can be implemented.

4040

Although the 4040 (Fig. 3-44) didn't come next, historically speaking, it is a revealing chip to examine in the light of the 4004, its little brother. The 4040 is functionally equivalent to the 4004 and upward-compatible. Fourteen new instructions are added for a total of 60 instructions. These additional instructions enhance the 4004's usefulness and show what a general-purpose MPU should approach. First the ALU was improved, and logical and compare instructions were added to it. Seven levels of subroutine nesting were added to the 4004 basic addressing instructions. Eight more pins were added, making the unit a 24-pin LSI chip. Perhaps most important, an interrupt enable input pin and interrupt acknowledge input and

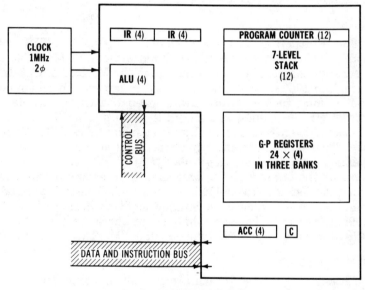

Fig. 3-44. 4040 4-bit MPU.

output instructions were added, along with the internal hardware structure needed to process the interrupt. A HALT instruction was finally added to the instruction set so that the MPU could easily be stopped by the software. Also, the carry bit was brought out to an external pin. However, the bus and address capabilities remained the same, still requiring much multiplexing and indirect programming. These drawbacks notwithstanding, the 4040 has been used in everything from incremental tape recorders to turkey-weighing machines. Its primary advantages are low cost, a moderate-size package, and a well-developed chip set for input/output control. Its main disadvantages are inability to work with standard memory and its small-size data word.

Today except for really high volume applications most 4-bit processors are a dying breed. When the 8-bit devices became available, manufacturers created an artificial price differential to keep the 8-bit machine expensive, and thereby keep a market for 4-bit devices. But the highly competitive nature of the industry quickly eroded the 8-bit MPUs price to under $5.00 in quantity lots, and thus led to the final death blow of the 4-bit device. Yet even after an MPU design dies as a competitive implementation, the chip still must be produced to support the thousands of products and devices built around it.

TMS1000

One 4-bit MPU that hasn't faded away is the TMS1000 family from Texas Instruments. What makes the TMS1000 so special is that a single chip contains RAM, ROM, and I/O logic. The 1000 is intended to be used in low-cost, high-volume applications, such as in microwave ovens, smart tuners, hand-held electronic games, etc. Only 2K nibbles of ROM and 128 nibbles of RAM are provided. No expansion is possible either. The TMS1000 allows no interrupts and is implemented in PMOS rather than more popular NMOS. The instruction set is primitive, but strong on some kinds of control type applications. A TMS1000 would not be a good choice for a micro-computerlike application. Still, with all these drawbacks 5,000,000 TMS1000s were shipped in the second quarter of 1979! Compare this with 700,000 8080s.

8008

Although the 4004 IC chip got the ball rolling, the 8008 caught the attention of an even larger group of enthusiasts, particularly because it was the first 8-bit machine on the market (hence the 8 in 8008). The 8008 manages to get all the important registers, data, I/O, and status pins in a single 18-pin DIP package. The 8008 also has a combined data and address bus. A considerable amount of multiplexing is required to separate the data and address information outside the chip. The chip can address up to 16K bytes of memory, and does so by sending out two bytes of address information which must be latched by the user (contrary to the more recent chips). The secret of the 8008's small package is that the design requires external hardware decoding of its internal machine cycle, and the latching of the various portions of these cycles. There are three state lines (S_4, S_2, and S_3) which are decoded into five time periods. Each 8008 instruction requires some amount of these; an I/O cycle requires the full five steps. The fastest 8008 has a 12.5-microsecond machine cycle time. An indexed load instruction requires first setting up a register with an upper and lower byte that points at the memory location. Since the upper byte is a maximum of 6 bits, the range of addressing is 14 bits wide, which gives an address range of 16K bytes. The remaining bits of the address are latched to provide status information. The actual indexed load from RAM takes 37.5 microseconds. This is close to the same time as the 4004, which takes 32.4 microseconds.

A minimum 8008 system requires about 10 additional MSI ICs. This in itself is not justification to avoid the 8008, as its small 18-pin package size means extremely low cost. In addition, the 8008 has a high-level systems language compiler called *PL/M*. In fact, it was the first processor to offer this capability. This type of programming allows the user to develop an 8008 task on a time-shared terminal (at a nominal monthly cost). The same terminal "outputs" 8008 machine code for running the microprocessor. The user then takes the machine code (usually on paper tape)) and enters it into the 8008 system. Obviously, this speeds up the application development cycle for the 8008, which is probably why it became the microprocessor standard.

Software people were quick to recognize the language potential of the 8008, and it wasn't long before programming manuals from consulting houses became available. These manuals enlightened many engineers about the value of programming, as did the proliferation of companies teaching courses on how to utilize the 4- and 8-bit machines.

About this time, *Radio-Electronics* magazine carried an article about the first hobbyist computer based on the 8008, called the Mark 8. It was a simple and cost-effective design with excellent documentation. The Mark 8 was later modified, and today is remembered as the first commercially available microcomputer.

Like the 4040, the 8008 has the barest of interrupt systems, and suffers from this shortcoming in the more complex applications. The answer to this problem was right around the corner as 8008 users discovered the upgraded 8080.

8080

The 8080 (Fig. 3-45) was the first really high-powered MPU to hit the market. It has a clock period of 500 ns and a typical machine cycle time of about 2 microseconds, which is about five times faster than the 8008. In addition, the 8080 has a 16-bit program counter that allows addressing up to 64K bytes of memory. It can do decimal, binary, and double-precision arithmetic, and has 78 basic instructions.

The price of all this sophistication is the addition of 22 more pins to the old 8008, making the unit a 40-pin LSI ceramic IC. The extra pins are used for addressing (16), data in and out (8), interrupt, reset, and three power supplies (4).

A load the accumulator direct instruction (LDA addr) requires three bytes of instruction. The three bytes set up all the internal counters needed to point to the proper memory location; no latching is needed. The instruction takes 13 clock periods to execute, or 6.5 μs with a 2-MHz clock. This is quite fast by 8008 standards.

In addition, the 8080 has a rich mix of ALU instructions, including rotates, shifts, compares, exclusive ORs, and more. It can do decimal subtraction or addition, which allows simple and easy bcd interfacing. A DAA (decimal adjust the accumulator) instruction is provided to separate the 8-bit number in the accumulator into two 4-bit bcd digits.

The 8080 contains six 8-bit general-purpose working registers and an accumulator. The six general-purpose registers

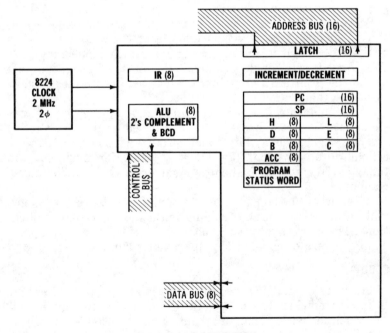

Fig. 3-45. 8080 8-bit MPU.

may be addressed individually or in pairs, providing both single- and double-precision operators. Arithmetic and logical instructions can set or reset four flags.

The 8080 uses an external stack feature in which any portion of memory may be used as a last-in/first-out stack to store or retrieve contents of the accumulator, flags, program counter, and all six of the general-purpose registers. A 16-bit stack pointer controls the addressing of this external stack. This gives the 8080 the ability to handle multiple-level priority interrupts by rapidly saving and restoring processor status. Also, it provides almost unlimited subroutine nesting. Ultimate control of the data and address bus is provided by a HOLD input pin on the 8080. This pin forces the processor to suspend operation, and drives the buses into a high-impedance state. This permits ORing the bus with other controllers for direct memory access (DMA) operations, or multiprocessor operation.

There are a total of 256 directly addressable I/O ports in the 8080, which are controlled by a special I/O instruction in the set, and don't consume address space.

The 8080 was the second microprocessor to hit the hobbyist market and, due to its more sophisticated structure, it was more successful. Today there are probably more 8080 computer systems in use than any other single device, and the 8080 has almost established a record for distribution of microcomputers.

One real attraction of the 8080 is the availability of a high-level programming language (PL/M) and an excellent group of assemblers and editors. Moreover, the first version of the BASIC programming language for a microprocessor appeared especially made for the 8080.

But what really created the major foothold for the 8080 markets was Intel's wise insight to sell a complete microcomputer development system based around the 8080. Intel went all the way with the 8080 microcomputer development system, giving it dual 8-inch floppy disks, an intelligent terminal, etc. Then, they hired a brilliant systems software consultant to design the world's first microcomputer operating system—called ISIS II. At the same time a clever and colorful fellow named Ed Roberts, who owned a floundering calculator company called Mits, had the nerve to try to market a computer around the Intel chip, in "kit" form. When the kit was introduced in *Popular Electronics* magazine in December 1974, Mits was knocked off its foundations with orders, and the $400 Altair was born. Later the designer of ISIS created a new operating system called CP/M and made it work with the Altair and a pair of cheap 8-inch floppies. This was the true beginning of the home computer industry. The Altair went on to flourish, then died when Mits was bought out by Pertec. However, other companies picked up the 8080 chip and CP/M, and to this day it is still considered to hold 50% of the microcomputer operating system market.

Although no one thought much about it at the time, the Altair utilized a poorly organized 100-pin bus, designed in a hurry by Roberts' engineers. Called the S-100 bus, for lack of a better name, this sloppy bus standard led to a mushrooming of hundreds of companies with devices that would plug into the bus. The S-100 bus today is in the process of being better defined by the IEEE.

From this point onward, the microcomputer field expands considerably. Nine other processors were introduced during, and immediately following, the rise of the 8080, and each had a particular reason for its existence. Of all of these, one of the most attractive in terms of its simplicity and ease of utilization is the Motorola MC6800.

6800

The 6800 (Fig. 3-46) was the first serious threat to the 8080 market. The 6800 was developed to be an enhancement of the Intel 8008, during the same period Intel was designing the 8080. Perhaps the most distinguishing feature of the 6800, when compared to the 8080, is its simplicity and ease of implementation. Timing on the 6800 is extremely simple; all instructions take two or more machine cycles and all machine cycles are the same length—one clock period. Thus, a 6800 machine cycle and clock cycle are the same length, as compared to the 8080 which has variable-length machine cycles. Furthermore, the 6800 has no separate I/O instructions—memory and I/O are within the same address space. The 6800 doesn't multiplex status signals on the data bus, and has a much simpler set of control signals, eliminating the need for a bus controller like Intel's 8228.

Where the 8080 uses three power supplies, the 6800 has only one, +5 volts. Finally the 6800 instruction set is much easier to understand; it has fewer instruction types and more memory addressing options, while the 8080 has more one-of-a kind instructions and more internal register manipulation instructions.

As you can see in Fig. 3-46, the 6800 has fewer internal registers than the 8080. There are, however, two 8-bit accumulators (A and B) and a 16-bit program counter, stack-pointer, and index register. The index register is used in memory addressing instructions. With fewer registers, the 6800 instruction set is more memory intensive as compared to the 8080.

The secret of the 6800's success was not due solely to its being a more powerful processor, since the 8080 offered more power than designers were ready for. Rather, the 6800's success was due to the fact that the designers of the 6800 didn't stop at the MPU, but went on to develop a complete family of

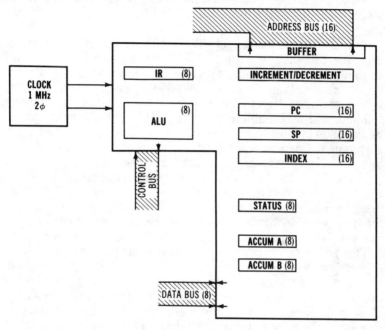

Fig. 3-46. 6800 8-bit MPU.

support ICs. The 6800 family contains, for example, an LSI peripheral interface adapter (PIA) that allows the microprocessor to send and receive 8-bit parallel binary data to two independent I/O devices. The two PIA ports can be programmed at power-up to be either inputs or outputs. The LSI device has all the necessary logic functions needed for parallel interfacing to remote devices, and eliminates a large number of MSI packages. The simplicity of this "family" approach is that almost no extra circuits are required to create a working system.

The complete family contains a MPU, PIA, ACIA (asynchronous interface adapter), modem (low- and high-speed), clock, and various bus interface logic ICs. Today the 8080 has caught up with the 6800 and offers a similar set of support chips.

As a processor, the 6800 has photofinishes in benchmarks with the 8080. As for size, the chip has the same 8-bit data word and 16-bit address range as the 8080. The bus system is completely Tri-State, with inputs for causing the bus to switch into a high-impedance state, or for enabling it at the proper time. An "extended accumulator load" instruction requires 6 μs on the 6800 with a 1-MHz clock, which is a little faster than the 8080 (by .5 μs).

The instruction set of the 6800 looks exceedingly simple, except for the fact that there are seven different types of addressing modes. Learning to use all these can take a while, but a little study reveals some of the 6800's power. The addressing modes include: direct, relative, immediate, indexed, extended, implied, and accumulator. The flexibility of the interface needs of the 6800 is most likely due to its close resemblance to Digital Equipment Corporation's Unibus® concept, where all the various peripheral devices share the bus. Each device on the bus is treated by the CPU as a valid memory address. Therefore, all the memory reference instructions of the 6800 are also used for communicating with peripherals and remote devices. Such a straightforward approach relaxes the interface requirements for both software and hardware designers.

The problem of interrupting the processor while it is in a program, and the subsequent problem of distinguishing between many external interrupting devices, is simplified by the availability of two different interrupt pins on the 6800, the NMI and IREQ. Each of these serves a different function in changing the course of the operation. The nonmaskable interrut, NMI, causes the 6800 to automatically save five different registers in a specific location in memory, and then to vector to another specific location in memory containing the starting address of the interrupt subroutine.

Soon after the introduction of the 6800, a small electronic kit company in New Mexico, called Southwest Technical Products, packaged a neat and simple microcomputer around the 6800. This microcomputer used a simple 50-pin bus called the SS-50. Today large amounts of software exist for the Motorola 6800 microprocessor and the SWTP 6800 microcomputer.

6502

The 6502 was developed at MOS Technology, Inc. by a group of turned-on chip designers who worked on the 6800 at Motorola. Therefore, it is not surprising that the 6502 is an enhancement to the 6800. However the enhancements consist of instruction set changes, bus system alterations, and subjective MPU architectural shifts, so that the differences are subtle, application dependent, and hard to judge fairly. In general, we can say that 6502 follows the Motorola 6800 philosophy of "strength in simplicity," and the 6502 is an incredibly easy MPU to work with; in fact, it's even easier to use than the 6800. However, the fact that the 6502 address bus isn't Three-State and the simpler set of 6502 control signals costs you something. You can't easily float the address bus and data bus during the ϕ_1 clock, so DMA is difficult and interfacing dynamic memories means you must steal machine cycles by inserting wait status, as in the way slow memory is interfaced.

Perhaps the most attractive feature of the 6502 is its inclusion of the complex ϕ_1 and ϕ_2 clock circuitry right on the chip. As shown in Fig. 3-47 the designer only has to add an RC network and inversion gate to get the 6502 clock running.

The 6502 is very fast; a load the accumulator absolute (LDA) takes only 4 microseconds with a 1-MHz clock. This is faster than the 6800 (6 μs) and 8080 (6.5 μs). Some of the fastest BASIC interpreters for home computers have been written in 6502 code.

From an architectural standpoint, if you examine the register sets in Figs. 3-47 (6502) and 3-46 (6800) you can see that the 6502 design team split the 6800's 16-bit index register into two 8-bit registers, and called them the X index and the Y index. (Two index registers it turns out, are much more useful than a single 16-bit index register.) Second, the 6502 team cut the stack pointer to 8-bits, and fixed the stack itself so it always has to reside in the 256 bytes of page one of system* RAM. Third, the 6502 team dropped the second accumulator in the 6800. Then the final touch on the 6502 was to mate the two 8-bit index registers with page zero of memory by instructions that allowed indirect addressing; a powerful mode lacking in the 6800.

The 6502 is a family oriented MPU and provides some interesting support devices we will learn more about later. The 6502 indirect addressing mode adds the second byte of a two-byte instruction to the index register, to obtain an address in base page zero that contains the actual two-byte effective address. This allows sophisticated addressing methods,

---

*Page "zero" is available for special 6502 instructions. Thus, user memory starts at hex 200.

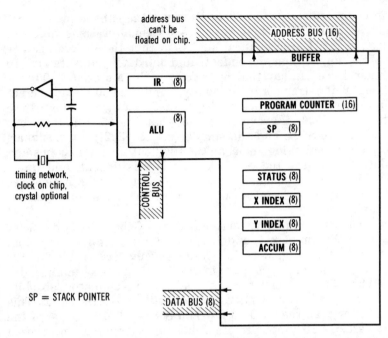

address bus
can't be
floated on chip.

ADDRESS BUS (16)

BUFFER

IR (8)

PROGRAM COUNTER (16)

ALU (8)

SP (8)

timing network,
clock on chip,
crystal optional

CONTROL BUS

STATUS (8)

X INDEX (8)

Y INDEX (8)

ACCUM (8)

SP = STACK POINTER

DATA BUS (8)

Fig. 3-47. 6502 8-bit MPU.

such as placing all important subroutine entry point addresses in page zero.

Eventually, the 6502 microprocessor went on to become the darling of the home computer companies. Commodore Business Machines created their PET 2001 around the 6502, as did Apple with the Apple II color home computer. All in all, the 6502 seems to offer the ultimate refinement in a single-chip microprocessor. But, while all the 8-bit machines were making headlines, another processor with a radically different architecture was introduced. Hosting a 16-bit data word and an especially flexible interrupt structure, the PACE chip from National Semiconductor Corp. kicked off the first of the 16-bit microprocessors.

PACE

The PACE (Fig. 3-48) differs from the previous designs in that all the address and data bits are issued from a single 16-bit–wide port on the chip. Eternal circuit elements, in conjunction with PACE state information, latch and pick up the address or data bits from the same bus. Since the address and data share the same bus, the external structure and pc layout of the system are simplified. Since the processor uses 16-bit data words, resolution of 1 part in 65,536 can be obtained. Only a single memory read is needed to address up to 64K, whereas in the smaller 8-bit machine two bytes of data must be read sequentially.

An indexed load instruction on PACE takes only 4 microseconds, with a 2-MHz clock. This is 20 percent faster than the same instruction on the 6800.

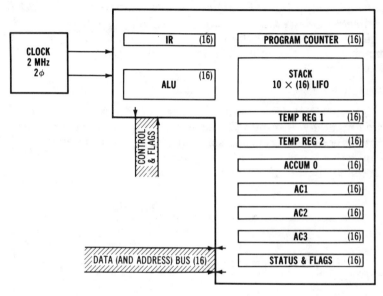

Fig. 3-48. PACE 16-bit MPU.

Internally, the PACE is built like a 16-cylinder Mercedes-Benz, with four 16-bit accumulators, a ten-word "last-in/first-out" (LIFO) stack, two temporary scratchpad registers, and a 16-bit ALU.

Because many microcomputer applications chiefly involve the control of some complex assembly process, or chemical cycling, or mechanical flow control, PACE was designed to be a Processing And Control Element (hence the name PACE). This was accomplished by including rather sophisticated four-level vectored priority interrupt circuitry right on the chip. The hardware can save all the internal registers in the ten-word LIFO stack, along with the vector of the interrupt. No software polling is required, as in many of the 8-bit machines. With this type of interrupt system, the PACE can be used as the master controller of a complex real-time process cycle involving many external devices and sensors.

But the PACE never caught on like the 8080, 6800, and 6502. Why? One reason is that PACE doesn't output TTL compatible signals. Instead it requires special interface chips called BTEs to convert to a TTL bus. Further, since the address and data bus are multiplexed, a special ILE and ALE interface latch is needed. (Of course most MPUs need bus drivers unless the application is low cost, high volume.) The PACE instruction set addressing instructions are rather limited and only a few indirect modes exist. However, until Intel produced the 8086, the PACE remained the only well-known 16-bit MPU on the market, and a popular choice for industrial control applications.

SC/MP

The SC/MP (Fig. 3-49) processor (pronounced "scamp"), also made by National Semiconductor, offered the first really cost-effective microprocessor that could be used in low-cost controller types of operations, particularly ones involving mechanical operations or serial data.

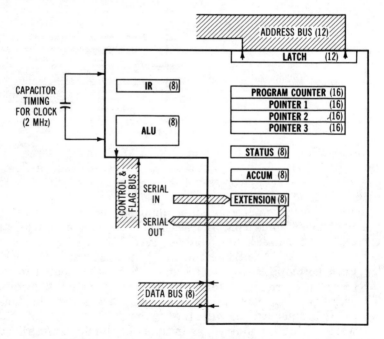

Fig. 3-49. SC/MP 8-bit MPU.

With regard to hardware, the SC/MP is among the simplest of processors to use, hosting three 16-bit pointer (index) registers, a flexible 8-bit ALU, and an "extension" register that can be used either as an internally programmed register or as a serial input or output port. The SC/MP can easily send serial data right off the chip into a receiving device, and vice versa. Moreover, the SC/MP has three external flag pins that can be set or reset under program control.

The IC has two sense inputs, one of which serves as an interrupt pin to allow a single vectored interrupt. Software polling must be used to determine the interrupting device when more than one device is to be serviced. Twelve full bits of address come right off the pins. The remaining 4 bits are available by latching them off the data bus at the proper strobe time. The data word is available on an 8-bit Three-State bidirectional bus, and, just as in the more expensive machines, control of the bus is possible for DMA-type applications.

The SC/MP hardware arrangement has the simple efficiency of the early Volkswagen. The chip needs no clock and uses a single capacitor to set the frequency of the clock. (For more stable applications, a crystal can be used.) The most outstanding feature of the chip, however, is the bus request and bus grant process used in the SC/MP. The SC/MP is designed so that it can work in series with other SC/MPs. This type of mulitiprocessor operation is called *distributed processing*. By simply hooking the chips together in a daisy chain, a priority type of processing is put into action, with each SC/MP working on an individual part of the operation. A bus request pin on the processors allows them to share a common bus.

The SC/MP, being a descendant of the PACE microprocessor, has a very minicomputer structure and thus one would expect the SC/MP to be a popular processor. Yet the SC/MP was held back by its slow PMOS logic, lack of index registers, and the absence of zero page and indirect addressing modes. Still the SC/MP has been found to be a one-of-a-kind microprocessor, perfect for certain low-cost control applications, particularly as a smart peripheral processor for the 16-bit PACE.

2650

The 2650 is produced by Signetics, and although it was a late horse entry in the microprocessor race, the chip has firmly established itself as having the most sophisticated addressing mode on the market, and a group of very informative control signals. The 2650 is designed to use simple TTL interface circuits and does not have a family of support circuits like the 8080, 6800, and 6502.

One drawback of the 2650 is that it only accesses a maximum of 32K bytes of memory because of its 15-pin address bus. This may or may not be a problem depending on the application.

As shown in Fig. 3-50, the 2650 has six 8-bit registers, split into 2 banks of 3 registers each, and an 8-bit accumulator. These registers act like the 6502's index registers, or they can be used as 8-bit accumulators. The stack for the 2650 is on-chip, and holds only eight 15-bit addresses, thus limiting the depth of nested subroutines. But the 2650 makes up for its limited stack with an amazingly rich variety of addressing modes, including four kinds of indirect addressing with auto increment and decrement.

The 2650 interfaces to the external world through I/O ports that don't consume memory space like the 8080 does, but unlike the 8080, the 2650 provides the I/O status pin on the chip and this results in very straightforward I/O decoding.

The 2650 uses an 800-nanosecond clock and a load accumulator absolute instruction takes 4.8 microseconds. The 2650's

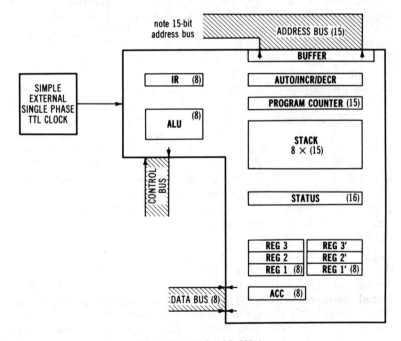

Fig. 3-50. 2650 8-bit MPU.

interrupt is a simple maskable IRQ input and a request acknowledge output. The interrupting device must provide the vector address of the interrupt program.

So far in the microprocessor race, most manufacturers seemed to be stressing computing power for what we can call "high-end" applications. The SC/MP was an exception, as was some of the 6500 and TMS1000 family, but in general MPUs were power hungry, with the single +5 volt supply drawing up to a half ampere. The world was looking for a power-miser MPU. It didn't take long for RCA with its CMOS skills, to introduce one.

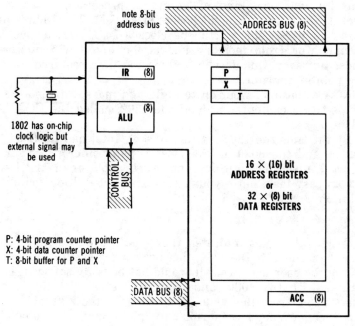

Fig. 3-51. CMOS 1802 8-bit MPU.

1802

The 1802 (made by RCA) uses CMOS technology and is the only MPU suited to battery-powered applications (although a CMOS 8080, the NSC800, has been announced by National Semiconductor). The 1802 is a strange horse of an irregular color—it has a structure that seems to be perfect for one application, and disastrous for another. The 1802 has a very primitive interface to external memory. It relies on an internal scratch pad register bank to point to memory addresses and a pair of 4-bit counters to select from registers in the scratch pad (see Fig. 3-51).

The register bank in the 1802 can contain thirty-two 8-bit data values or sixteen 16-bit addresses or data. Only implied and direct memory addressing modes are supported, with auto increment and decrement.

All the registers in the 1802 must be loaded with an address before the memory address instruction can be used, and this makes the 1802 a poor data-cruncher. There is no decimal mode in the 1802.

The 1802's strong point is in small battery powered devices that involve some kind of minimum processing, such as a pocket timer, or intelligent pocket size DVM. The 1802 is also a fast device. Using a .155 ns clock (6.4 MHz), a load the accumulator from memory instruction takes 3.75 microseconds. However, this doesn't include the time required to load the pointer register.

RCA eventually went on to build and market a remarkable single-board computer around the 1802, called the COSMAC VIP.

By the time the 1802 hit the market, Intel had itself as the leader, and the 8080 as the most popular microprocessor to improve upon. To improve upon such a powerful MPU was not an easy task, but a young company called Zilog found the solution.

Z80

When Zilog first indicated they would produce the Z80 as an enhancement to the 8080, there was much skepticism among microprocessor users that it would not be truly software compatible with the 8080, and would therefore not lure many users away from the 8080. Many thought the Z80 would follow the 6502/6800 scenario, only philosophically enhancing the 8080. Imagine the shock then when the Z80 turned out to be totally software and object-code compatible with the 8080 to the point that a ROM with 8080 code would run on a Z80. Further Zilog did the following magic to the chip: (1) they reduced supply requirements to a single +5 volt, (2) a complete on-chip clock, (3) a fast clock period on the Z80A of 250 nanoseconds (4 MHz), the 8080A is 500 microseconds), (4) automatic on-chip dynamic RAM refresh logic, (5) an additional NMI interrupt pin, (6) a much simplified read/write control philosophy, (7) bus control and bus request logic for simplified DMA.

Zilog could have stopped here and had an excellent product, but they went much further. Examine Fig. 3-52 and you can see the way Zilog upgraded the Z80 architecture while maintaining 8080 compatibility. Z80 has a double set of 8080 programmable registers so in addition to the normal 8080 status register (PWS), A, B, C, D, E, H, and L registers, stack pointer, and program counter, the Z80 has a prime status register (PWS') and A', B', C', D', E', H', and L' registers. This

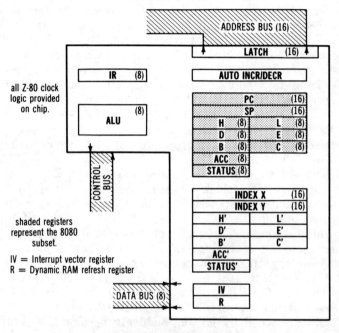

Fig. 3-52. Z80 8-bit MPU.

is a powerful architectural addition to any microprocessor, as it makes the handling of single level interrupts extremely easy —instead of saving registers on the stack you simply switch to a new register set! The 8080 had no indexed addressing. The Z80 however has two 16-bit index registers. Continuing with their obvious philosophy of making life for the designer easier, Zilog added a special 8-bit interrupt vector register, which can hold the high order address byte for a CALL instruction put on the bus by the interrupting device. A table of up to 64 16-bit starting addresses of interrupt programs can be set up in this table. The more primitive 8080 single byte RST vector interrupt mode is also available. Another register Zilog added, the refresh counter, is never used by the programmer, but supersimplifies interfacing the Z80 to dynamic RAM. By providing a zero to 128 address count on the address bus at regular intervals when the memory isn't being accessed, the dynamic RAM interface circuits on Z80 systems can be extremely minimal.

What about the instruction set? Zilog did another clever trick here. In the 8080 almost every one of the OP-CODES possible in a single 8-bit byte were used up. So Zilog took the few remaining codes and used them to specify a second byte of object code, resulting in the Z80 having 16-bit OP CODES, and an entirely new set of instructions. One such incredible new instruction is called the BLOCK MOVE instruction. This single instruction allows moving any contiguous group of bytes from anywhere in RAM to any other place in RAM, or between RAM memory and an input or output port. It also allows single instruction scanning of a block of RAM for a defined value.

The Z80 is a very fast processor, in fact not counting bipolar and bit-slice MPUs, it is the fastest 8-bit MPU you can buy. As an example, you can purchase a Z80A version that uses a 4-MHz clock (250 nanosecond period). A "load the accumulator instruction" (13 clock periods) takes 6.5 microseconds on the 8080A. The Z80 does this in half that— 3.25 microseconds. Moreover, some new Z80 instructions are faster than the equivalent set of instructions needed in the 8080. For example, to load any register pair (RP) with a 16-bit value located at address ADDR takes 20 clock states with the Z80 *LD RP, ADDR* instruction. The 8080 would require 3 instructions and 26 total (clock states).

So Zilog, owned by Exxon, suddenly became the company with the best processor on the market. Obviously the midnight oil began to burn furiously at Intel and Motorola (Motorola's 6800 just couldn't keep up with the Z80).

About this point in the micro's history, designers of the chips began to review the kinds of things the programmers of the chips did with them. Studies revealed a lot, and one of the first companies to put all this user data to use was Motorola, with the 6809.

6809

After the Z80 hit the market, users had time to realize the value of upgrading MPU hardware while maintaining software compatibility. Not to be caught sleeping (or even resting momentarily) Motorola was busy in Austin, Texas creating their own enhancement to the 6800. (Why have another company capitalize on your design?)

But Motorola did more than enhance the 6800—rather, it restructured and simplified the entire 6800 instruction set. This was done to optimize several disciplines of software and programming which Motorola saw as the coming wave. The main goal of the 6809 was to minimize software costs. In what ways can this be done? One way is to write code in a block structured high-level language (like PASCAL or PL/M). Another way is to distribute software code in ROMs. But the problem with most second generation MPUs (like the 6800) is that a ROM can't be sold that will work on most users actual designs.

Motorola felt that to lower costs programs should be written in "position-independent code," that is, programs that can execute anywhere in memory, and contain no absolute addresses (all addresses are relative to the program counter). Also, indirect operations via the stack were called for. This position-independent code means the ROM program could go where the user had room for it.

The 6809 supports these software disciplines and thereby allows software subroutines to be mass-produced and distributed in read-only-memory, just like another IC device. (We should begin to see ROM-bottled algorithms and subroutines in the early 80's. This is a revolution that Motorola will be responsible for starting.)

Physically, as shown in Fig. 3-53, the 6809 is bus compatible with the 6800, using an 8-bit data bus and a 16-bit address bus typical of second generation 8-bit microprocessors. It is not pin compatible with the 6800. The register set of the 6809 however has been mildly expanded to contain a second 16-bit index register, a second 16-bit "user" stack pointer, a new 8-bit condition code register (CCR) and a new 8-bit direct page register (DPR).* The DPR register allows the so-called direct page to be moved anywhere in memory (not just at page zero). The additional user stack is designed to hold local variables and parameters, while the system stack holds return addresses of subroutines vitally necessary for position independent programming. The direct page would normally hold global variables. It would seem that with so few additional registers, the 6809 wouldn't be all that more powerful than the 6800.

---

*In addition, the original two 8-bit accumulators of the 6800 (ACCA and ACCB) can be catenated into a single 16-bit accumulator in the 6809.

The truth is that the power of the 6809 is its instruction set, particularly its addressing modes. The 6809 supports 20 different addressing modes, including a powerful program relative addressing, indexed addressing with 0-, 5-, 8-, or 16-bit offsets, auto increment and auto decrement by 1 or 2, and an extended indirect mode. There is an 8-bit by 8-bit multiply instruction, the ability to perform 16-bit operations on the joined A and B registers, and a multiple push and pull registers instruction. The actual number of instructions in the 6809 has shrunk. Where the 6800 had 72 different mnemonics to memorize, the 6809 has only 59. Yet there are over 1400 valid combinations of 6809 instructions. For example, the 6809 instruction TFR R1;R2 to transfer registers, has 42 valid combinations, but isn't this easier to remember than the 6800's TBA, TAB, TAX . . . etc? On the down side, the 6809 instruction set lacks bit manipulation and block-move instructions.

The 6809 is a speedy processor. The popular version uses a 2-MHz clock. A load the accumulator extended instruction requires 5 cycles, or 2.5 microseconds to execute, which is much faster than the Z80A at 4 MHz (3.25 microseconds) and runs circles around the older 6800 (6 microseconds).

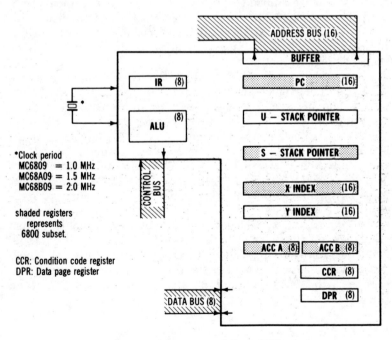

Fig. 3-53. 6809 enhanced 8-bit MPU.

The interrupt structure on the 6809 has been enhanced with a new input called FIRQ, for fast interrupts request. This just forces the PC and CCR to be stacked, allowing user code to stack only those additional registers that are really needed. A SYNC instruction for halting the program when a fast interrupt input occurs allows very fast input-output processing.

The 6809 was designed with a clear philosophy in mind— "down on absolute addressing." But it wouldn't be fair to assume Motorola came to this decision in a vacuum. In fact over 25,000 lines of 6800 source code, gathered from users, were examined. Out of this analysis came the fact that 38% of all MPU instructions were loads and stores. Thus the 6809 designers concentrated on improving this class of instruction, while staying away from great amounts of one-of-a-kind operations.

Note that the 6800 is only "source" code compatible with the 6809. (6800 programs must be compiled to run on the 6809.) With the 6809 on the market it was becoming evident that microprocessor users wanted even more and more power. For many users 8-bits was not enough data; 16-bits would be much better, but no good 16-bit machine existed. Users were running out of address space. Time sharing systems needed megabytes of RAM—second generation devices couldn't easily exceed 64K. So who would be most likely to come out with a 16-bit MPU that would also be an enhancement of a popular MPU? Intel, of course.

8086

With its dominant position in the microprocessor industry, the time was ripe for Intel to make a major move on the market. Recall that Intel started the real microprocessor revolution with the 8080, but since that time the 6800, 6502, 2650, 1802, Z80, and 6809 had appeared, and each took away a chunk of Intel's market. So typical of a leader, Intel made a quantum leap and brought out the 8086; a new 16-bit microprocessor, completely software (source code) compatible with the 8080 and offering up to ten times the throughput of the 8080A.

True, this was not the first 16-bit microprocessor (the PACE from National had been around for some time) but it was the first 16-bit enhancement of the most popular 8-bit processor in the world, and with several years of proven 8080 software it could run 10 time faster.

But Intel, realizing that "16-bit does not a giant make," took the 8086 design one giant step further. Increasing the addressing range of the 8086 to 1 megabyte (16 × 64K bytes) and coupling this with some clever register architecture and bus request circuitry, resulted in the ability to have up to 16 8086s sharing the same large memory—perfect for multiprocessing applications. Or, we can have one 8086 serve 16 individual 64K byte memories, each belonging to a single user —perfect for time-sharing applications.

The 8086 can operate in a minimum or maximum mode depending on a special strap pin. When the strap pin is grounded the 8086 is in the maximum mode, and pins 24 through 31 connect to the 8288 bus controller that then generates MULTIBUS (TM) compatible control signals. When strapped to V_{cc} the 8086 develops its own bus control signals on pins 24-31. In any case, the 8086 requires an external 8284 clock generator chip.

The 8086 provides a powerful interrupt mode, with a thousand bytes set aside for up to 256 4-byte pointers to interrupt locations. Like the 8080 and Z80, the interrupting device puts an 8-bit number on the data bus which is used to vector to the desired pointer.

The 8086 handles I/O operations without using up memory space and can address up to 64K I/O registers, using the DX register as a pointer.

A LOCK output pin provides status for multiprocessor "test and lock set" operations. A special TEST input pin is provided so when a WAIT instruction executes the MPU stops and waits for TEST to become active. TEST is used so the processor can synchronize its program with an external signal, for example in an I/O operation.

Like Motorola's 6809 philosophy, the 8086 contains mechanisms for position independent code, reentrancy, and stack processing. In addition the 8086 offers 8-bit and 16-bit signed arithmetic, including multiply and divide, improved bit manipulation, and a new concept called interruptable byte string operations that allows a string to be scanned and terminated on an interrupt to the processor.

Fig. 3-54 shows how Intel structured the 8086 so it would extend 8080 features symmetrically, across the board. As you can see, the complete 8080 register set has been duplicated. However, now each 8-bit register pair makes a 16-bit data register (AX, RX, CX, and DX). The processor status word has been increased to 16 bits. In addition to the normal 16-bit stack pointer, the 8086 has a 16-bit base pointer, and two 16-bit index registers. These provide offsets that locate the beginning address of 64K byte sections in the total 1 megabyte address space. This approach can allow up to 16 MPUs to share the memory without any addresses overlapping. There is a code, data, stack, and extra segment register; this supports relocatable disciplines.

Physically, the 8086 uses a time-multiplexed 16-bit bus to supply both address and data. Four additional segment pins provide the remaining 4-bits of the 20-bit address. (Of course, not all of this memory must be used.) The signals from the multiplexed address/data bus are separated physically by using latches for the address bus, and transceivers for the data bus.

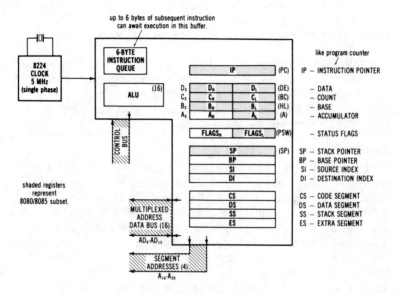

Fig. 3-54. 8086 16-bit MPU.

As to be expected, the 8086 is very fast. A 5-MHz clock is used, giving a 200 nanosecond clock period. One typical instruction (load accumulator absolute), accomplished with a MOV instruction, takes 2.8 microseconds. (An 8-MHz version of the 8086 may be offered, in which case this MOV would occur in 1.75 microseconds.) This is almost as quick as the 6809, and at 8 MHz, it's the fastest MPU we've seen. Intel accomplished this kind of speed by inventing a new fast n-channel silicon process called HMOS. HMOS allowed Intel to squeeze 29,000 transistors onto a 225 mil die.

Of course, the 8086 is quite expensive, by ten dollar 8080 prices, but even an 8080 cost $300 when it first appeared. As production experience grows the price will drop significantly.

Another Intel 8086 feat was to enhance the 8080 architecture, so as to increase the bus throughput and bandwidth. The strategy involved adding an instruction "queuing" mechanism that prefetches up to 6 bytes of the next instruction and stores it until the MPU is ready for it. This greatly reduces dead-time on the address bus.

Finally, anticipating how users might react to the problem of redesign of the pc board due to the 8086's 16-bit wide data bus, Intel created a device called the 8088, an 8-bit data bus version of the 8086 that is completely software compatible but sends out 16-bit data in two 8-bit chunks over an 8-line bus. This clever device allows the user to start using the 16-bit power of the 8086 without the necessity of redesigning the pc board layout.

With such an incredible 16-bit processor on the market, another move in the game of one-upmanship was imminent. What would Zilog do? What about Motorola? It didn't take long for Zilog to launch a broadside blast at the 8086, a blast that would heat up the market even further.

Z8000

If the 8086 could be considered a giant 747 among the popular microprocessors, then the Zilog Z8000 would be an interstellar space station (Fig. 3-55). Like the 8086, the Z8000 is a 16-bit machine, and like the 8086 the Z8000 supports a vast array of advanced programming mechanisms not found in 8-bit microprocessors. But the people at Zilog took the Z8000 several big steps further than the 8086. The Z8000 deviates from the normal by coming in two versions, the 8001 and the 8002. The difference in versions is in the maximum memory that can be accessed. The Z8001 contains a 16-bit address/data bus and a 7-bit "segmented" address bus so it can access directly up to 8 megabytes of address space. (The 8086 can only access 1 megabyte.) Further, there can be up to six such 8 megabyte address spaces in the Z8000 for a maximum of 48 megabytes. The Z8002 is a nonsegmented version of the Z8001, and can address up to six 64K byte address spaces, using its 16-bit address/data bus (a maximum of 384K bytes if all six "spaces" are used). As the result of instructions, status signals are output from the Z8000 to signal what type of address space is being accessed. There are three types of address space: data, program, and stack. Further, each type of space can be "system" space or "normal" space, depending on the instruction mode. Obviously the Z8000 was designed to be in direct competition with larger sophisticated mini and mainframe computers that can service multiple users, giving each user its own 64K of RAM, such as in the PDP-11/35 and IBM 360/370.

Zilog veered from the 40-pin chip standard, coming out with a 48-pin IC and, in doing so, they were able to increase the segmenting for more memory space. But in order to use the advanced memory features of the Z8001 a special memory management unit IC, the MMU, is required. Also in a 48-pin package, the MMU produces the 23-bit physical address bus, handles segmenting size, and provides memory protection and relocation features. The 8086 as yet has no such similar management unit.

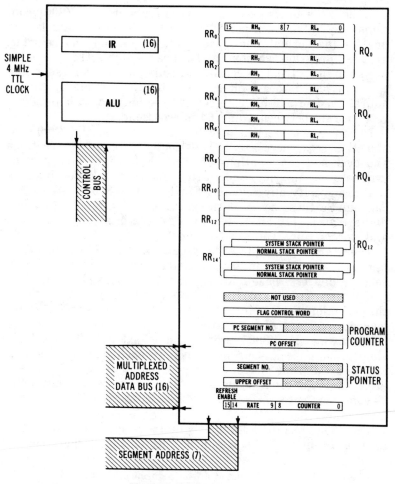

Fig. 3-55. Z8000 16-bit MPU.

Registerwise the Z8000 is unequaled. There are sixteen 16-bit registers, which can be used for "word" operations (a word is 16-bits). These same registers can also be used as thirty-two 8-bit "byte" registers, or as four 32-bit "double-word" or "long word" registers and some instructions specify one of two 64-bit "quadruple word" registers. (A 64-bit number is extremely huge—over 18,500 trillion.)

In the Z8000 any register can serve as an accumulator, an index register, or a memory pointer. The Z8000 has a "register-to-memory" architecture, meaning it is basically a register-oriented processor, with some memory-to-memory operations supported.

In addition to its general purpose registers, the Z8001 contains two 23-bit stack pointers, one for the system stack, and one for the normal stack;* a 16-bit status and flag register, a 23-bit program counter, and a neat 16-bit refresh counter for simplified dynamic RAM refreshing. (The refresh register is divided into a 9-bit row counter that counts up to 256 addresses, and a 6-bit rate control section that can program refresh rate between 1 and 64 microseconds.)

If you're not overwhelmed by now, consider the Z8000 instruction set. There are 110 distinctly different instructions and over 414 combinations of them. Following their goal of symmetry, regularity, and clarity, almost any Z8000 instruction can specify any register. Further, the Z8000 instructions can handle these seven data types: bits, bytes (8-bits), bcd digits, words (16-bits), long words (32-bits), byte strings, and word strings (up to 64K bytes).

There are eight addressing modes in the Z8000, including register, immediate, indirect register, direct address, indexed, relative address, base address, and base indexed. Almost all instructions contain all the address bits necessary to perform the operation, thus no internal extension registers must be pre-loaded to perform the operation.

Speedwise the Z8000 uses a simple external TTL 4-MHz single phase clock. Our microscopic benchmark instruction, load a word from memory into a register, using a 23-bit address range, takes 12 cycles, or 3 microseconds on the Z8001. The nonsegmented Z8002 takes 2.25 microseconds for the same instruction.

The Z8000 has both a multiply and a divide instruction that handles 16-bit or 32-bit signed values, and performs a 16-bit

---

*These stack pointers consist of a 7-bit segment part and a 16-bit offset; 9 bits are unused.

word multiply in under 17.5 microseconds (the PDP-11/45 microcomputer takes 5.56 microseconds to perform the same operation).

To conserve memory and improve throughput, the Z8000 designers used the results of statistical program studies to make the most often used instructions short one-word instructions: jump relative, load byte register immediate, etc., are all one word long (16-bits).

Like the 8086, the Z8000 treats I/O separate from memory, providing special I/O and block I/O instructions that select up to 64K I/O ports. Status signals on the Z8000 distinguish memory addresses from I/O addresses on the address/data bus.

For multiprocessing systems, where several Z8000s will be sharing a common bus, special Multi-Micro mode pins and instructions are provided. To guarantee that the Z8000 components will work together successfully, Zilog has specified its own Z-bus, a "shared" processor bus arrangement.

Interrupts on the Z8000 consist of the normal nonmaskable, a nonvectored maskable, and a vectored maskable. Four types of software "traps" are provided. (Traps are interruptlike sequences followed when, for example, an unrecognized instruction is encountered.) The Z8000 supports privileged instruction, system call, and segment traps.

With the Z8000 the new trend towards high-powered mainframe competitive microprocessors was obvious. Since the Z80 instruction set is a subset of the Z8000 set, special Zilog translator programs allow the Z80 user to take advantage of new Z8000 hardware, without rewriting any software.

One would think things would end here, or at least slow down for awhile. But, hot on the heels of Zilog and Intel, the Motorola design group in Austin, Texas was about to unleash the final volley in the microprocessor race for number one.

68000

If there was ever any doubt that everything in Texas is bigger than anywhere else, the new Motorola MC68000 16-bit microprocessor has finally proved it true. The hot sun and dry weather of Texas apparently inspired the Motorola engineers to go right to the cutting edge of semiconductor technology, and inside the 68000 are no less than 68,000 transistors, almost twice as many as the Z8000 or 8086. Such density goes beyond anything in LSI. By using a process called HMOS (high-density short-channel MOS) a transistor in the 68000 consumes 44% less area than an equivalent NMOS transistor. Such smallness has created a need for new development and etching techniques, and the 68000 is the first of the new VLSI products, Very Large Scale Integration.

By using VLSI, Motorola's engineers and system programmers were able to create a microprocessor with a 32-bit register-to-memory architecture, similar in many ways to the Z8000, but different enough to be unique. The 68000, as shown in Fig. 3-56 contains eight 32-bit data registers and nine 32-bit address/stack registers! That's an incredible package, when you consider that in mid 1978 the most registers you could find in an 8-bit processor were ten 16-bit registers in the Z80.

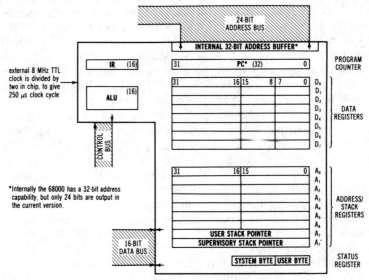

Fig. 3-56. 68000 16-bit MPU.

The 68000 is big on everything. The chip itself has 64 pins, which except for the less popular 9900 from TI, is a record. It may be a problem for the designer who is already hassled by the largeness of 40-pin chips, but when you examine what the extra 24 pins get you, it is worth the added layout complexities. For example, the 24-pin linear address bus of the 68000 is completely separate from its 16-pin data bus. Demultiplexing of the buses is not necessary, and timing and external hardware needs are relaxed.

With its 24-pin address bus, the 68000 can directly access up to 16 megabytes of RAM or ROM. A memory management device from Motorola works with the 68000 to provide advanced memory protection, segmentation, and relocation mechanisms for multiuser type applications, but it is not required to access the full 16 megabytes. There are two kinds of address spaces in the 68000, data space and program space, so that really up to 32 megabytes are available.

The 68000 register set is enormous, and, quite possibly, there are enough registers to manage any program written up until the year 2000. Unlike the Z8000, Motorola does not allow any register to serve as an accumulator or an index register, but rather there are eight registers specifically for data and nine specifically for addresses. There are two 32-bit stack pointers, one for user programs and one for so called supervisory programs. A status bit switches between these stack pointers. A privilege mechanism in the 68000 allows easy management of operating systems with several users.

The 68000 has more addressing modes than the Z8000 and 8086 (14 in the 68000, 7 in the Z8000), but less instructions (56 in the 68000, 110 in the Z8000). This seems to be a continuation of the tradeoffs established by earlier 8-bit microprocessors, namely you can't have lots of general purpose registers and lots of addressing modes at the same time.

The 68000 addressing modes are: register deferred, base plus displacement, indexed absolute, immediate, stack/queue postincrement, and predecrement.

The 56 instructions in the 68000 include operations on bits, bcd digits, bytes, words (16-bits) and long (32-bit) words, but string instructions do not *yet* exist. Apparently, future versions of the 68000 (6800X) will include string processing mechanisms, and probably instructions for handling floating-point data will be included as well.

Multiply and divide instructions are included, and work on regular 16-bit words, signed or unsigned. (A multiply on the 68000 takes about 10 microseconds, which is almost twice as fast as the Z8000.)

The 68000 is as quick as a Texas falcon, executing a MOV memory to register instruction* (reg = 16 bits, memory range = 24 bits) in under 1.5 microseconds. That's fast, offering a throughput of up to 2 million 16-bit word transfers per second.

The 68000 takes another major jack-rabbit leap over the microprocessor pack by including an on-chip 7-bit priority interrupt structure which uses three input pins, and a user initialized table to provide 192 levels of vectored interrupts. Each interrupt can specify a program anywhere in the 24-bit memory space. It is easy to envision a 68000 serving up to 192 terminals, with each terminal controlled by another 68000.

---

*register-deferred addressing.

Like the Z8000 and 8086, the 68000 contains mechanisms for multiprocessing; the bus master/slave relationship is featured and special test and set instructions aid in this area. The 68000 supports stack and queue processing, and provides the ability to control the growth direction of the LIFO stack or FIFO queue.

Obviously, the Motorola people feel the 68000 will be the forerunner of the new trend towards 16-bit microprocessing, with large low cost memory capacity. Whether the 16-bit micro race slows down the sales of 8-bit machines remains to be seen, but one thing is certain—the 16-bit microprocessors are here to stay.

All the processors covered so far have been single-chip designs. Another class of microcomputers is the board-level systems, such as the LSI-11. The LSI-11 is a four-piece chip set on a single pc board. Its processing power and software support make it a device worth knowing about.

LSI-11

The LSI-11 microprocessor is an LSI chip set that emulates exactly the entire instruction set of Digital Equipment Corp.'s PDP-11 computer products. These devices have been in use since 1970, and have acquired an extensive software library, as well as a significant amount of applications experience.

The microprocessor is built around four n-channel MOS chips, which include a control and data element, and two micro-coded (microprogrammed) ROMs. These ROMs are programmed to emulate the PDP-11 instruction set, and have a special routine for debugging on-line programs, operator interface, and bootstrap loading ability.

The LSI-11 is built on a single 8.5-inch by 10-inch circuit board. A second ROM allows hardware multiply and divide operation. Unlike most microprocessors that require some sort of control panel, the LSI-11 is designed to use a regular tty or crt/ASCII keyboard to communicate with the processor. The ROM chip contains all the necessary program code for these operations, along with code for controlling the CPU, examining internal registers, etc.

The address and data word length is 16 bits. The LSI-11 can directly access up to 64K bytes of 16-bit memory and can handle either words (16 bits) or bytes (8 bits) with equal ease. Stack processing in external memory is provided, along with a vectored interrupt input. A daisy-chained priority bus system is used, along with a bus grant output to allow multiprocessor operation. The LSI-11 system is designed to use a master/slave type of bus sharing. Each device using the bus can be a bus receiver or a bus transmitter, and only one device can send on the bus at any given time. This allows a very simple bus interface in the LSI-11, along with simple DMA capability.

As for software, the LSI-11 is the queen of the microprocessors. It contains a special power-fail-restart circuit that saves all important registers whenever the system senses dc power dropping. When power is reestablished, the computer responds with the time that the dropout occurred and the status of the machine at this time. The LSI-11 software library covers almost every possible type of language, including FORTRAN, BASIC, PASCAL, and COBOL. Editors and assemblers are available, as are a large array of user application programs.

THE FUTURE OF MICROPROCESSORS

After reading the comparison of MPUs it should be obvious that the name of the game is increasing performance. Will microprocessor performance continue to improve at its present rate? The answer is a probable yes. And what will the microprocessor look like in the year 2000? It will most likely be a geometric extension of today's devices, that is, given a doubling of transistor density every two years, we will eventually see a 128-bit data word and a 256-bit address bus. Random access memory will eventually be so cheap (given bubble technology) that billion-byte RAMS will not be uncommon. As improvements continue, we will likely see I/O processing right on the CPUs pins—with up to 128 serial ports, 256 parallel I/O ports, and 64 internal A/D converters. We will also see more on-chip number crunching, including instructions for doing transcendental arithmetic, matrix algebra, and even built-in fast fourier analysis functions.

For sure, the future microprocessors will be low power consuming, and considering the emphasis on energy conservation, the future MPUs may be solar powered.

chapter 4

MEMORIES

In its most basic form, computer memory can be represented as a single flip-flop storage unit. A flip-flop is a *two-state* device that can be made to store a single *b*inary dig*it*, or *bit*. Since a bit can be either a 1 or a 0, the flip-flop will store either a 1 or a 0.

The flip-flop remains in either the 1 or 0 state as long as power is applied. At any time, the flip-flop storage unit may be read to determine what state it is in (Fig. 4-1). Also, at any time the state of the flip-flop may be set to a 1 or a 0 by applying the proper logic signal and pulsing the clock input. We call this operation a memory *write*. Determining the flip-flop's state is called a memory *read*.

A word of binary information, such as an 8-bit byte, may be stored in a group of 8 flip-flops, as shown in Fig. 4-2A. If the inputs and outputs of the flip-flops are properly interconnected, the 8 binary digits can be made to enter and exit from the group in sequential or serial fashion (one bit at a time), or move in parallel—all 8 bits at once.

When dealing with registers inside the CPU or memory, programmers usually draw them as shown in Fig. 4-2B. This

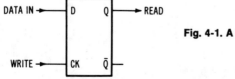

Fig. 4-1. A flip-flop is a 1-bit memory.

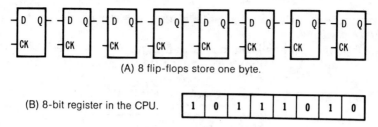

(A) 8 flip-flops store one byte.

(B) 8-bit register in the CPU.

1	0	1	1	1	0	1	0

Fig. 4-2. An 8-bit memory.

simplified model of the storage cells makes it easy to illustrate register and memory locations.

ADDRESSING

By simply increasing the number of these storage flip-flops, we can increase the number of stored bits. But a fundamental problem presents itself: How do we locate a particular storage bit among a group of registers or memory locations?

The solution is to use a form of addressing. We can apply a unique group of binary digits to a group of pins, and a unique storage location becomes available. Fig. 4-3 shows how a typical semiconductor memory device is arranged so that the storage flip-flops, or "cells" as they are sometimes called, can

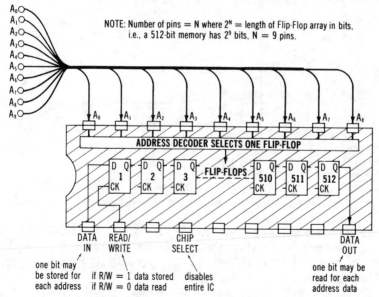

Fig. 4-3. A memory IC is an array of flip-flops.

181

be independently selected with a unique binary code called an *address word*.

Once the cell has been located, an input port on the IC is enabled, and a 1 or a 0 may be written into the cell. Inside the IC

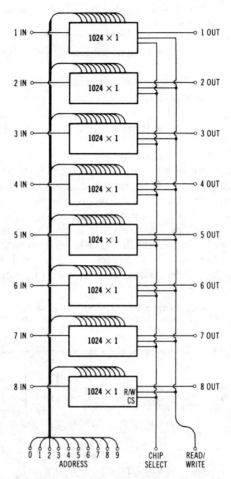

Fig. 4-4. A 1024 word memory (word = 8 bits).

the cells are actually arranged in an x by y matrix, with half the address pins locating the x coordinate of the cells, and the other half of the pins locating the y coordinate. This is explained in detail in Appendix B, but for now it is sufficient to regard the cells as simply a long chain of flip-flops and the address as somehow moving a selector to the correct cell.

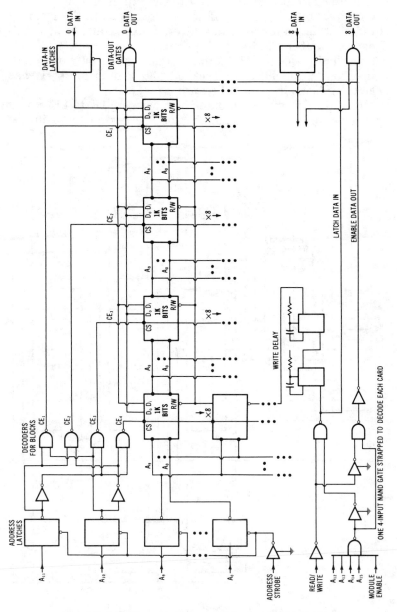

Fig. 4-5. A 4096-word memory which uses 32 1K-bit ICs.

183

To read the state of a cell, the desired address is applied and the read line is enabled. Now the data in the selected cell appear at the output port. Note that the length in bits of the memory is equal to the number of storage flip-flops in the memory chip, and that the number of address pins is equal to n, where 2^n is the number of storage flip-flops. For example, a 256-bit memory chip is usually organized so that it has only one input and output port. Thus, it is called 256×1 memory. It has exactly eight address pins because $2^8 = 256$.

Moderate size microcomputer memories of 1K to 8K words are made up of several smaller ICs. The reason for using so

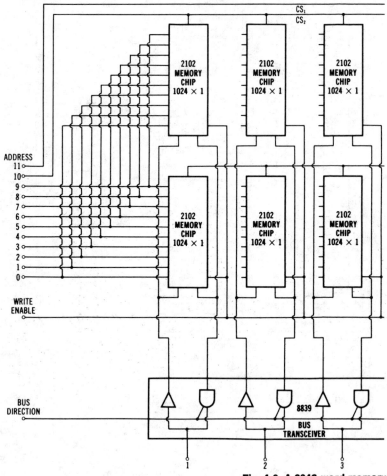

Fig. 4-6. A 2048-word memory

many ICs is because of the number of interconnections necessary. Although at present the maximum chip density has reached 64K bits, for hobbyists or experimenters on a small budget, 1K-bit memories are the easiest to find and use. These are arranged as 1024 × 1, and come in 16-pin packages, making them convenient to use.

How do you arrange these $2^n \times 1$ memory chips into a suitable array on a printed-circuit board for use in a microcomputer system? For example, suppose you have a source of low-cost 1024 × 1 RAM memory chips, and you want to find out how many you need to make 4K words of memory for your 8-bit computer. Eight of the 1024 × 1 ICs arranged as in Fig.

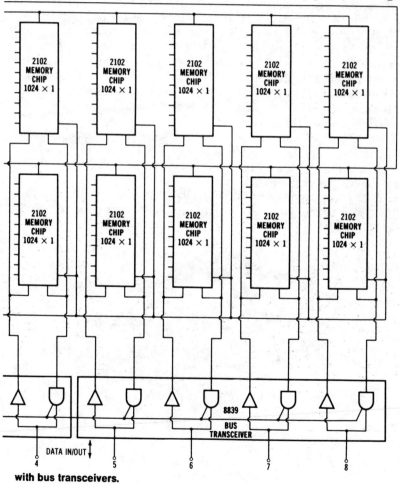

with bus transceivers.

4-4 produce 1024 words, or 1K words, of memory. For every input word, each IC stores one bit of the word ($\frac{1}{8}$ of the word). The address pins of the ICs are connected in parallel, and the 8-bit binary data word is applied to the eight data-in pins. The output word is read off the eight data-out pins. Since eight ICs give 1K words of storage, it takes four of these circuits, or 32 ICs, to make a 4K-word memory. This is shown in Fig. 4-5.

The reader might have noticed that a 4K memory has 2^{12} words of storage and, therefore, requires a 12-bit address. However, our 1024×1 chips have only 10 address pins. The solution to this problem is to use the chip select (CS) pin of the ICs to enable a single block of 1024 words at a time. In effect, we decode the eleventh and twelfth bits of the address into one of four, which in turn selects the desired 1024-word block. Note that we show 16 bits of address in this circuit; bits 12, 13, 14, and 15 are used to select one particular 4K memory card, out of a total of 16 cards. These high-order address bits are decoded by a five-input NAND gate which is hard-wired to strap the card in at the proper address. These cards make up 4K-word pages in the total 64K word memory. There are 16 possible pages, since there are 4 more bits decoded in the address. Fig. 4-6 shows a complete 2048-word microcomputer memory, complete with transceivers for interfacing to a bidirectional data bus. Fig. 4-7 illustrates a commercial semiconductor memory board.

Fig. 4-8 illustrates an 8K byte RAM board suitable for the 8080 microprocessor running in an S-100 bus system. Note

Courtesy Electronic Arrays, Inc.

Fig. 4-7. Photo of memory board.

the use of Three-State bus drivers on the memories output data bus.

MEMORY PAGE AND LINE ORGANIZATION

Most 8-bit microprocessors have instruction sets that treat memory as if it were organized into pages. A page is considered to be 256 bytes long. Each byte is considered to be a line in the page. In a 64K byte address space there are 256 such 256-byte pages. These are usually labeled consecutively, starting with page 0 and continuing to page 255. If hexadecimal notation is used, the 256-byte pages are labeled 00 to FF. If octal is used, this would be 000 to 377. Fig. 4-9 illustrates how memory pages can be visualized in hex notation. Usually the lower 8-bits of the 16-bit address (LSB) selects the line within a page, while the upper 8-bits (MSB) selects one particular page.

SPEED

The 1024-bit 2102 memory chips we have discussed are fabricated by using the "n-channel MOS" manufacturing process. Economy versions of the 2102 have cycle times of under 1 microsecond, and premium versions are under 200 nanoseconds. (*Cycle time* of a memory chip is how long it takes from the time a valid address is applied to the chip, to the time valid data appear at the output of the chip.) Since the microcomputer usually performs most of its instructions by addressing memory, it is often memory read and write (and cycle) times that set the speed limit on certain programs. Some microcomputers will insert a wait command between a memory write or read instruction to slow the processor down to the speed of the memory ICs used.

The fastest memory circuits are ECL, or emitter-coupled logic. This type of logic cell works on current instead of voltage, and a 1 is so many microamperes and a 0 is so many less microamperes. Obviously, it is not a good choice for low-cost easy-to-use computer memory, as logic levels can be checked only with a sophisticated current probe, or by opening the connection physically and inserting a microammeter. Another problem with ECL is that it is so fast that triple-layer pc boards are a must. The middle layer of the board is a ground plane which helps to reduce the rf radiation caused when the ECL gates switch from one state to another. ECL also requires rather hefty power supplies.

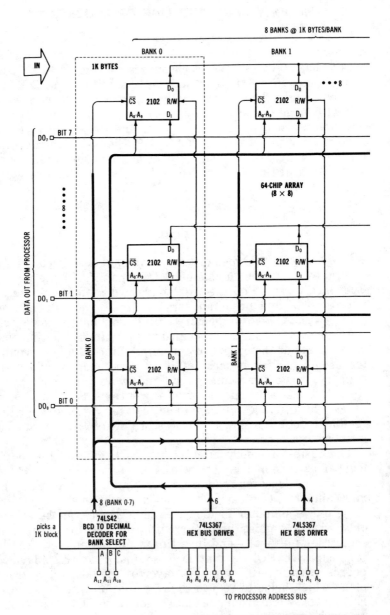

Fig. 4-8. An 8K static RAM (using

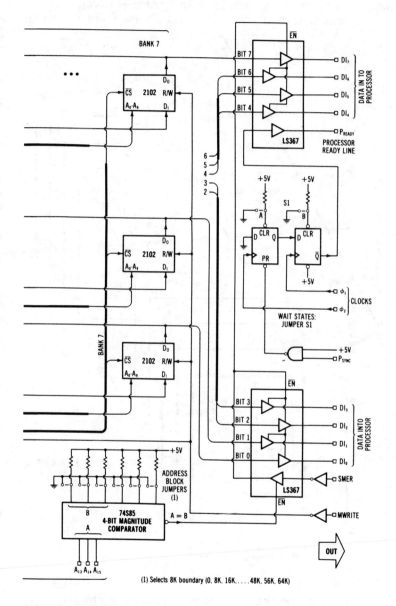

BANK 7

D_0
$\overline{CS}$ 2102 R/W
A_0-A_9 D_1

BANK 7

D_0
$\overline{CS}$ 2102 R/W
A_0-A_9 D_1

D_0
$\overline{CS}$ 2102 R/W
A_0-A_9 D_1

$\overline{EN}$

BIT 7
BIT 6
BIT 5
BIT 4

DI_7
DI_6
DI_5
DI_4

DATA IN TO PROCESSOR

P_{READY}

LS367 PROCESSOR READY LINE

6
5
4
3
2

+5V   +5V

S1

A   B

D CLR Q   D CLR $\overline{Q}$
PR

+5V

ϕ_1
ϕ_2 CLOCKS

WAIT STATES: JUMPER S1

+5V
P_{SYNC}

$\overline{EN}$

BIT 3
BIT 2
BIT 1
BIT 0

DI_3
DI_2
DI_1
DI_0

DATA INTO PROCESSOR

SMER

LS367

$\overline{EN}$

MWRITE

+5V

ADDRESS BLOCK JUMPERS (1)

B
74S85
4-BIT MAGNITUDE COMPARATOR
A

A = B

A_{13} A_{14} A_{15}

OUT

(1) Selects 8K boundary (0, 8K, 16K,....48K, 56K, 64K)

2102s) for the S-100 bus.

Another popular fast memory chip is low-power Schottky-clamped TTL logic (74 *LSXX* series). A Schottky diode is a special type of diode that has a metal in contact with the semiconductor device. This results in no charge storage at the junction, which normally prevents transistors from switching

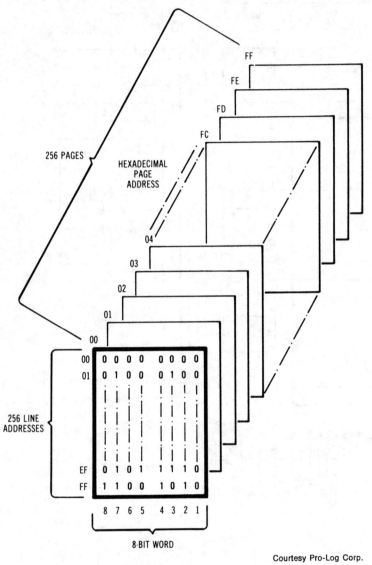

Fig. 4-9. Memory "Page" and "Line" organization in a typical 64K byte memory.

above a theoretical maximum frequency. Schottky diodes are usually gold-dipped and are required on every TTL input. They are, therefore, an expensive form of memory. They are very useful whenever the need for high-speed TTL-compatible memory is needed.

VOLATILITY

The perfect memory uses no power and stores data forever. Typical n-channel and p-channel MOS and TTL ICs dissipate around 250 to 500 milliwatts per chip. A 4096-word memory can easily draw 2 amperes at 5 volts. Obviously, this is far from ideal. If the power lines were to drop out for a few seconds, all the bits would change and the computer memory would end up with pure garbage in it. One approach to this problem is to take advantage of the chip select inputs on the ICs and force the chips into a low-power inoperative state when they are not involved in a memory read or write. Although the amount of power saved can be significant, the amount of additional circuitry may not warrant such a solution. Moreover, the processor must somehow go into a "power down" routine, which would then require some special programming.

A more viable solution to this problem of losing stored information (volatility) is to use memory ICs made of CMOS. This logic family uses two MOS transistors instead of one, as in regular MOS, and draws almost zero power when not being read or written into. The CMOS transistor cells, however, are bigger than the regular MOS types and are thus more expensive. They are perfect whenever low power consumption is required, such as for battery-operated microcomputers in remote locations.

SYSTEM MEMORY—BIG RAMS

As microprocessors increased in computing power and shrunk in cost, more and more general purpose microcomputer products were built around them. These general purpose microcomputer products consisted of such things as development systems, business computers, and even home computers. In these powerful systems high-level languages, such as BASIC, FORTRAN, and PASCAL, were used. Large operating system programs were required. The result of all this software was the need for copious amounts of read-write random access memories, in the range of 16K bytes to 64K bytes. As the

16-bit processors loomed ahead, it became obvious that even larger memories, up to 1 megabyte, would be desirable.

But consider the formidable problems facing the designer of a 64K byte memory using the popular 1K-bit 2102 memory chip, as were used as examples in previous small memories. First to get the full 64K bytes will require 512 of the 1K chips (64 × 8). There will be a total of 512 × 16, or 8,192 pins to solder and 8,192 potential bad solder joints. In the powered-down "standby" mode, each chip consumes about 100 mW. Thus the 512 chips would require 51.2 watts, while idling. Surely there must be a better way.

The obvious solution is a higher density 4,096-bit memory chip, one that consumes less power per bit than the 1K-bit chip. A 4K-bit chip would cut the number of ICs in our 64K byte memory to only 128. Stand-by power would drop too. But manufacturing low cost 4K parts using the well known static memory technology of the 1K part is a problem.

First of all the static memory cell uses three transistors. This results in a large die size (for a high density) which means poor yields and hence higher cost. Of course as the learning curve improved cost would come down, but manufacturers were looking to the eventual 16K-bit chip and wondering how this density problem would be licked. Clearly a smaller cell size was needed.

Dynamic RAM

The answer to the density problem came in the form of a new storage technology called the dynamic RAM cell. The dynamic RAM memory cell is an ingenious way to shrink the size of a storage device. It consists of a single transistor and capacitor. (See Appendix B.) A logic 0 is no charge on the capacitor. The capacitor holds a charge to represent a logic 1. The single MOS transistor of the dynamic RAM cell buffers the capacitor. But the charge on the capacitor, representing a logic 1, will leak off quickly. So external circuitry must be used to periodically refresh *every cell* in a dynamic RAM chip. The cell must be refreshed about every 2 milliseconds. Refreshing can be done by continuously interleaving refresh read cycles with normal processing of the MPU, or can be done on a burst mode, reading every cell in a burst every 2 milliseconds.* Even with the additional refresh circuits, the dynamic RAM approach is cheaper than static—die size is

---

*Reading a cell in a dynamic RAM automatically restores any charge on the capacitor.

smaller, cost is lower, and yield higher. Standby power drain in the dynamic is lower than the static RAM.

How exactly does refreshing work? Fig. 4-10 shows a block diagram of the parts required in an ideal refreshed memory using dynamic chips. A multiplexer switches the RAM chip address lines between two sources, the regular computer address bus and the special "refresh" bus. The refresh bus is

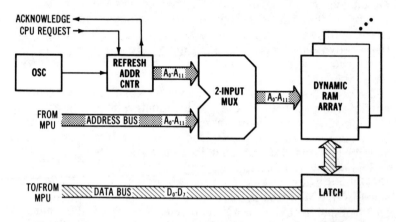

Fig. 4-10. Refreshed dynamic RAM requires an address multiplexer and address counter.

simply the output of a counter driven by a high-speed oscillator. The counter cycles through every memory address, performing a "read" of each cell, thereby refreshing it, and moving to the next. When, during regular processing, the CPU wishes to read or write a memory location, it requests access to the RAM from the refresh logic. The refresh logic acknowledges the request, and temporarily stops refreshing cells while the CPU accesses the memory. The CPU use of the memory is given lower priority than the refreshing and so the system throughout slows down slightly, but this is less than 5%.

The Multiplexed 4K Dynamic RAM

Our dynamic RAMS still have a problem, namely what pinout should be used? The industry favored a 16-pin chip, but consider the minimum number of pins required for the 4K part: 12 address pins, 4 power (+5, −5, +12 volts, and ground), 1 chip select, 1 write enable, 1 data in, and 1 data out. That comes to 20 pins. Even if the −5- and +12-volt supplies were eliminated, we would still need 18 pins. The solution to reducing pins was the old time-multiplexing concept again. Manufacturers divided the 12 address pins of the 4K part to receive two addresses: the *row address* and the *column address*. Two 6-bit address chunks are sent to the chip one at a time, first the lower 6-bits of the address is sent, then the upper 6-bits is sent. Latches inside the chip store the full address. Two new pins, $\overline{RAS}$ and $\overline{CAS}$, are used to strobe the 6-bit addresses in the chip. Fig. 4-11 shows how the 2104 4K-bit dynamic RAM receives the two address chunks.

With refreshing circuitry already required and now additional address multiplexing, designers were slow to go for the 4K dynamic part. Most designers felt the extra demands of continual refreshing made testing and debug of their systems difficult.

Memory density was doubling every year. RAMs were bread and butter products to the semiconductor houses (some say microprocessors were invented to sell more memory chips). At the current rate of density increases, the 16K part was due shortly and the 64K-bit part loomed ahead. (See Fig. 4-12.)

The semiconductor houses were smart and realized that if they could use the same 16-pin package as the 4K RAM, that the 16K RAM would receive a terrific welcome. Further, if it could plug into existing 4K memories and work, designers of

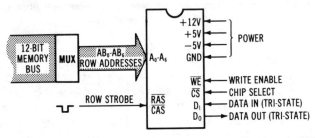

(A) Row addresses (ABO-AB6) are strobed into the chip first, via $\overline{RAS}$.

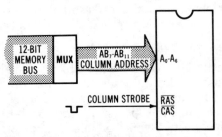

(B) Column addresses (AB7-AB11) are strobed into the chip second, via $\overline{CAS}$.

Fig. 4-11. How a 12-bit address is latched in the 4K dynamic RAMs using 6 pins and $\overline{RAS}/\overline{CAS}$ strobes.

4K memories could very easily upgrade to 16K and then later to 64K. Fig. 4-13 shows how the 4K, 16K, and 64K RAM chips compare and how the 16K chip can easily plug into a 4K bit socket. The 16K chip is simply a 4K chip with the chip select input representing a new address pin (A6). The $\overline{CAS}$ pin serves as the chip select now.

The 64K part went further and removed the old +12 and −5 volt supply pins, moved V_{cc} to pin 8, and added the extra address pin where V_{cc} was. This means 64K RAMs will not easily go into 16K sockets, but rather are made to work alone. The new 64K-bit chips also provide an automatic refresh operation via pin 1, and thus reduce the complexity of external refresh circuitry.

Note that there are three ways to approach the chip's refresh circuits: read cycle refresh, $\overline{RAS}$ only refresh, and $\overline{CAS}$ before $\overline{RAS}$ refresh. Table 4-1 sums up the three methods. By far $\overline{RAS}$ only is the simplest to implement.

Now it was obvious that dynamic RAM offered a better tradeoff for large RAM arrays over the static RAM. What helped pull the resisting designer all the way over to using dynamic RAM was the condensation of the major dynamic RAM multiplexing circuits into a single refresh support part. In Fig. 4-14, the refresh parts of a dynamic RAM memory (inside the dashed line) were integrated by Intel into a refresh controller chip called the i3242. This device contains 7 three-

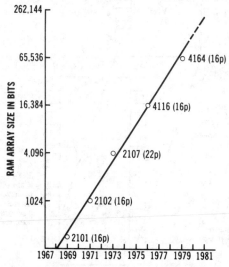

Fig. 4-12. Memory-chip bit density has doubled every year since 1969. By 1983 a typical RAM will store over one million bits.

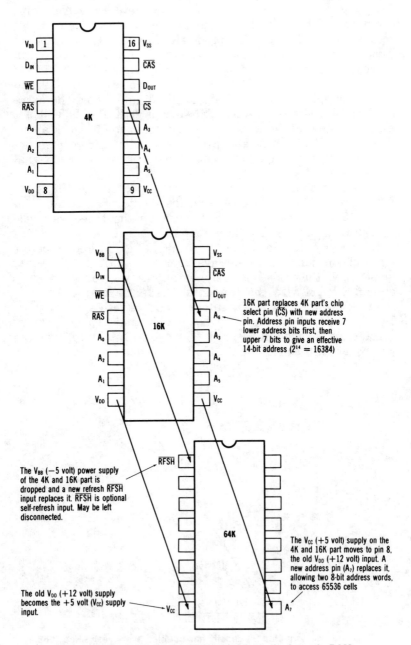

Fig. 4-13. Evolution of the 4K/16K/64K 16-pin dynamic RAM.

The following labels appear in the figure:

4K chip:
Left		Right	
V_{BB}	1	16	V_{SS}
D_{IN}			$\overline{CAS}$
$\overline{WE}$			D_{OUT}
$\overline{RAS}$			$\overline{CS}$
A_6			A_3
A_2			A_4
A_1			A_5
V_{DD}	8	9	V_{CC}

16K chip:
Left	Right
V_{BB}	V_{SS}
D_{IN}	$\overline{CAS}$
$\overline{WE}$	D_{OUT}
$\overline{RAS}$	A_6
A_6	A_3
A_2	A_4
A_1	A_5
V_{DD}	V_{CC}

16K part replaces 4K part's chip select pin ($\overline{CS}$) with new address pin. Address pin inputs receive 7 lower address bits first, then upper 7 bits to give an effective 14-bit address ($2^{14} = 16384$)

64K chip:
$\overline{RFSH}$

V_{CC}

A_7

The V_{BB} (-5 volt) power supply of the 4K and 16K part is dropped and a new refresh $\overline{RFSH}$ input replaces it. $\overline{RFSH}$ is optional self-refresh input. May be left disconnected.

The V_{CC} ($+5$ volt) supply on the 4K and 16K part moves to pin 8, the old V_{DD} ($+12$ volt) input. A new address pin (A_7) replaces it, allowing two 8-bit address words, to access 65536 cells

The old V_{DD} ($+12$ volt) supply becomes the $+5$ volt (V_{CC}) supply input.

196

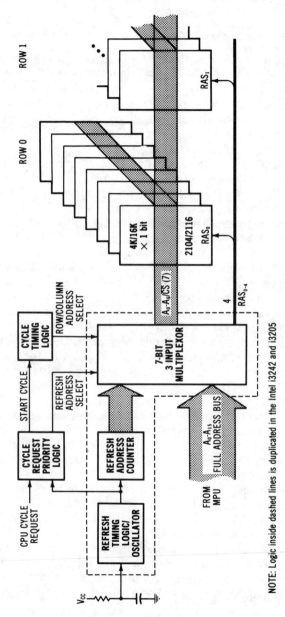

Fig. 4-14. Dynamic address and refresh logic.

197

Table 4-1. Three Methods for Refreshing Dynamic RAMs

1. *read cycle refresh*—We perform 128 read cycles on A_0-A_7 every 2 milliseconds—OR-tied rows not possible.
2. *RAS only refresh*—With RAS clock active we address 128 rows every 2 milliseconds—allows OR-tied rows. Z80 dynamic refresh counter could work here.
3. CAS before RAS—Allows 64 cycles of refresh every 2 milliseconds and loads the bus bandwidth less than the other two methods.

way multiplexers and a refresh counter. Seven bits allow the i3242 to work with either the 4K or the 16K dynamic RAM part. Each row is 4K bytes if 4K devices are used, or 16K bytes per row if 16K devices are used. Four rows are assumed here. Jumpers are used to reconfigure the refresh circuitry for the memory chip being used, as shown in Fig. 4-15.

Fig. 4-16 shows a block diagram of our original goal of a 64K byte memory, only now we are using 16K-bit dynamic RAMs, which means we have only 32 chips and 512 solder connections.* Standby power is a mere 960 milliwatts (27mW per chip). Fig. 4-17 shows a complete schematic of the 64K byte dynamic memory. Note that the board also allows jumpering the base address of the 64K bytes to start anywhere in a 1 megabyte address space.

Because the peak amplitudes of the V_{dd} current transients are about 60 mA, rise and fall times are 5-10 nanoseconds, and pulse widths are 20 nanoseconds, significant noise components in the 10-MHz range are produced. This calls for extremely effective power distribution and decoupling of dynamic RAMs.

Fig. 4-19 illustrates a section of a typical double-sided PC layout for the 2116 16K-bit dynamic RAM. Using both horizontal and vertical grids results in low inductance and low noise levels. Decoupling capacitors are used liberally as shown. Complete details for dynamic RAM design can be found in the Intel *Memory Design Handbook* and the National *Memory Applications Handbook*.

Fig. 4-19 is a photo of a 32K to 128K byte dynamic RAM memory board which uses either 2104 4K dynamic RAMs (for 32K bytes) or 2117 16K dynamic RAMs for 128K bytes. The board is made by Intel and interfaces to their MULTIBUS.

See Appendix C for a nonexhaustive list of random access memories, arranged by numerical part number and revealing RAM organization, number of pins, access time, cycle time, power dissipation, and supplies required.

---

*This memory design works with the 8080 microprocessor.

Cost of RAM

On the low-cost hobby surplus market a static 1024 × 1-bit 2102 RAM goes for about one dollar. This is about 1/1000 cent per bit or about 1 millicent per bit. A larger and more practical MM5257 4096 × 1-bit static RAM is about six dollars, or about 1.5 millicent per bit. However, a 2116 16,348 × 1-bit *dynamic* RAM cost $11.00; which translates to 0.67 millicent per bit! This means a typical bit of dynamic RAM costs one-third to one-half less than a typical bit of static RAM. Of course, this does not include the extra cost of the dynamic RAM refresh circuits, but for a carefully designed 64K byte or greater memory, this extra cost will be less than 0.1 millicent per bit.

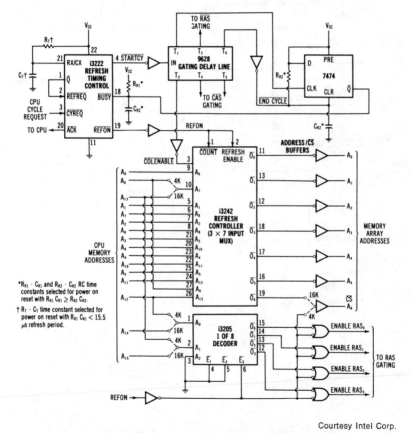

Courtesy Intel Corp.

Fig. 4-15. 4K/16K memory system control using i3242 refresh controller and i3222 refresh timing control chip.

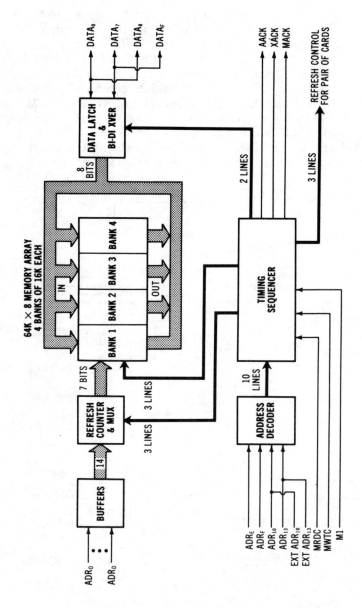

Courtesy National Semiconductor Corp.

Fig. 4-16. Block diagram of an 8080 compatible memory using four banks of 16K bit, 16-pin dynamic RAMs.

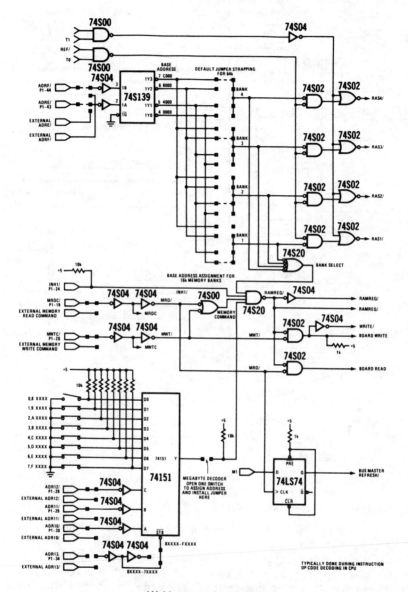

(A) Memory select logic.

Fig. 4-17. Complete schematic diagram of the 64K byte dynamic RAM memory.

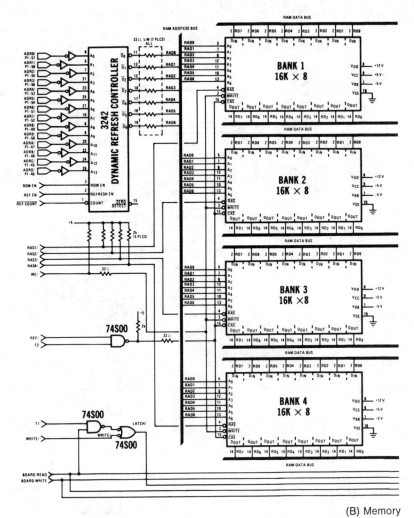

(B) Memory

Fig. 4-17 cont'd. Complete schematic diagram

Quasi-Static Byte-Wide RAM

Although the dynamic RAM is certainly here to stay, especially with the 64K bit 4164, there is another technology looming in the future that promises to greatly simplify the problem of dynamic refresh addressing, and board layout. These are the new quasi-static "byte-wide" memory chips. The byte-wide RAMs are organized as 2K, 4K, or 8K by 8 bits, which results in a maximum of 64K bits in the 8K device. By

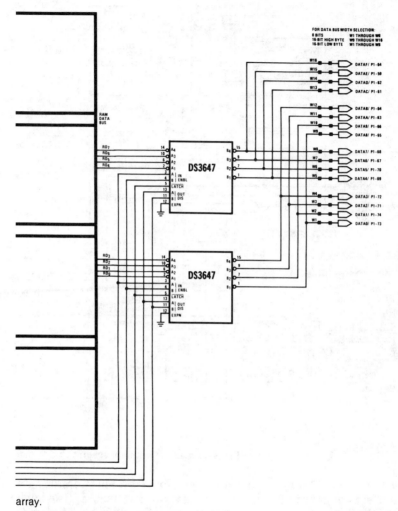

array.

of the 64K byte dynamic RAM memory.

using some simple multiplexing of the data and address pins, we can get the byte-word chip in a 16-pin package. A typical quasi-static chip coming is the Zilog Z6164, which is a 8192 × 8-bit device.

PROMS AND ROMS

As we have seen, read/write memory has a volatility problem when designed around conventional semiconductor mem-

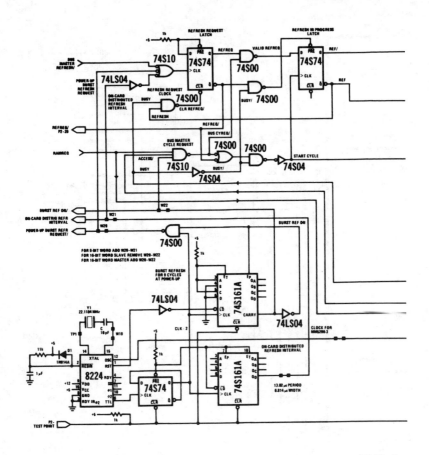

(C) Timing

Fig. 4-17 cont'd. Complete schematic diagram

ory circuits. A more ideal memory would be able to store its contents indefinitely and never lose data. It would also have nearly the same high access speed as semiconductors. The read-only memory, or ROM, serves exactly this purpose.

By setting up the desired bit pattern during the manufacturing process, the data in a ROM memory may be permanently stored. In other words, the ROM memory is identical with a read/write memory except all the bits are fixed to a logic 1 or a logic 0. Thus, if the bit pattern in the ROM is fixed, there will be no data input pins, and the device will only be able to supply data, i.e., read only. As we will see, however, it is possible to write into a ROM if we loosen up on the definitions of writing (Hint: What if the ROM could be "written" once by

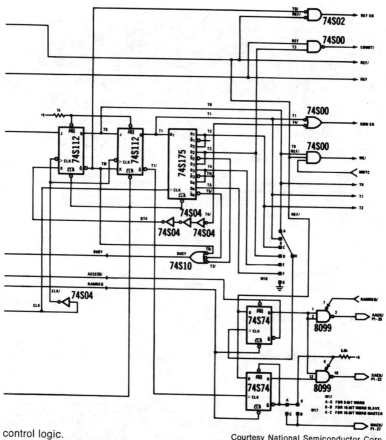

control logic.

Courtesy National Semiconductor Corp.

of the 64K byte dynamic RAM memory.

your computer?). Keep in mind that only the small RAMs have separate data-in and data-out pins. Larger memory chips combine these pins as described under bus systems, and use a read/write control pin to determine the function of the pins. This allows the remaining pins to be used as address pins. A read/write pin won't be found on the ROM, but there will be a chip enable pin that takes the ROM from an inoperative low-power state to the working, read-only state.

The usual way to use a ROM is to design and debug a program in standard read/write memory until it is working correctly. A listing of the bit pattern for the program is then sent to the ROM manufacturer. The manufacturer makes up a special mask and produces the ROM memory chip (actually

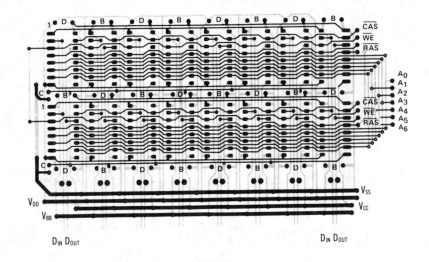

DECOUPLING CAPACITORS

$D = 0.33 \ \mu F \ V_{DD} \ TO \ V_{SS}$
$B = 0.10 \ \mu F \ V_{BB} \ TO \ V_{SS}$
$C = 0.01 \ \mu F \ V_{CC} \ TO \ V_{SS}$

Courtesy Intel Corp.

Fig. 4-18. Recommended two-sided board layout for 2116 16-pin 16K-bit dynamic RAM.

Courtesy Intel Corp.

Fig. 4-19. A 32K to 128K dynamic RAM memory board.

many chips). The user receives the ROM, and places one in the computer where the RAM memory that held the original program was. If no mistakes were made, the program will perform exactly as it did when it resided in RAM. Note, however, that there is no way to correct a mistake in the ROM without starting all over, and that may take months.

A way around the long developmental cycle is to use what is known as programmable read-only memory, or PROM. Although the name may seem like a contradiction in terms, PROMs do exactly what their name says; they are read-only memories that may be programmed or altered. Here, "programmed" means that they are easier to alter than the "mask" ROM.

For example, the most basic form of PROM is made up of diodes. As shown in Fig. 4-20A, a diode can be made to act as either a logic 1 or logic 0. If the diode is placed at the cross junction of an address bus to which several diodes are connected in common, the group will work as a complete word of stored data, as shown in Fig. 4-20B. The diode PROM is programmable in that the diodes may be removed with a soldering iron without damaging the memory.

There are several drawbacks to diode PROM (DPROM). One is its large size when compared with IC memories. Another is its high cost per bit. However, for very short utility programs not exceeding, say, 32 bits (four 8-bit words), diode PROM may work fine. A third drawback to diode PROMs is that the address rows and columns must be decoded with transistors or ICs to select the proper diode in the matrix.

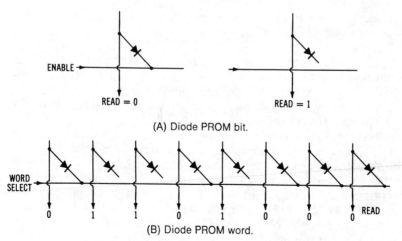

(A) Diode PROM bit.

(B) Diode PROM word.

Fig. 4-20. Functioning of diode PROM.

More useful are the PROMs available with the same packaging as regular RAMs. These PROMs are programmed "electrically" by using a commercial programmer device or a homemade version. There are two types of PROMs now in popular use: fusible-link and erasable programmable.

Fusible-Link PROM

This tye of PROM is like a regular memory IC, but instead of containing flip-flop storage cells, it contains tiny Nichrome fuses at each cell location. The fuse is connected in the PROM cell so that while it is intact, it will cause the cell output to be a logic 0. When it is electrically blown by the programming device, the cell output becomes a permanent logic 1.

Fig. 4-21A shows a popular 64-word fusible-link PROM that can be programmed quite simply. Each input to the PROM is a TTL load, while each output is an open-collector transistor. Fig. 4-21B shows that each bit of the data word is connected to one of 64 word-select columns, depending on which word is addressed. A fuse exists between the data pin and the emitter of a transistor. If the transistor is enabled by addressing the desired word *and* the fuse is intact, the bit will be read as a logic 0. But, if the fuse is blown out, the bit will be raised high and the pin will be at logic 1.

When you buy a new PROM, it may come preprogrammed with all 0's or all 1's. To program this PROM which comes preprogrammed as all 0's, a negative pulse is applied to each output terminal where the initial logic 0 is to be changed to a logic 1 (Fig. 4-21C). The circuit shown in Fig. 4-21D is used, along with a 100-milliampere pulse generator, to burn out the fuse. Two grounds on this chip are brought out on separate pins to isolate the 100-mA current pulse from the TTL input buffers.

The programming procedure is to apply the address of the word with switches A_0–A_5, pulse each individual output terminal wherever a logic 1 is desired, verify that the bit is properly programmed, and continue to the next word, selecting it again with the address switches.

Larger PROMs, for example those of 256 words, are also important in microcomputer applications. A popular fusible-link PROM is the Signetics 8226. Organized as 256×4, two of these memories in parallel make up a low-cost ROM memory system for a microcomputer. Since the PROM is much larger now (1024 cells to be programmed), a more sophisticated programmer is required as compared to the one used with the 64×8 programmer.

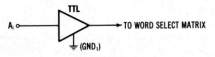

(A) Input circuit (X6).

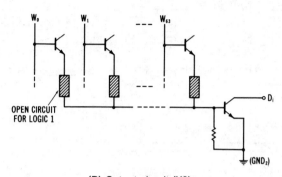

(B) Output circuit (X8).

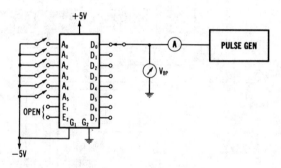

(C) Programming connections.

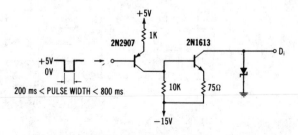

(D) Programming circuit.

Fig. 4-21. Fusible-link PROM (Harris 64 × 8 "HPROM").

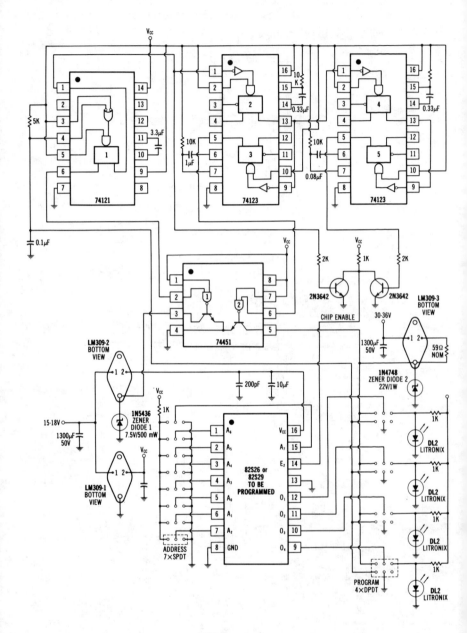

(A) Programmer.

Fig. 4-22. Fusible-link

Fig. 4-22A shows a schematic of such a programmer. It uses toggle switches to select the desired address and momentary push buttons to program the desired bits. As in the previous fusible-link PROM, the output pin of the IC is pulsed with current to blow the fuse. In this circuit, a complete generator is shown. Also, in this type of PROM the programming voltages must be applied in a special sequence, as the timing diagram of Fig. 4-22B shows.

The procedure for using the programmer is to insert the PROM and set up the address of the location to be programmed, using the toggle switches. When any of the output push buttons on the data-out pins are pushed, a sequence of timing pulses triggers the various LM309 current and voltage regulators. After a 1-ms delay, an 85-mA, 22-volt constant-current pulse is enabled for blowing the Nichrome fuse in the chip. When the switch is released, the LED will indicate a logic 1, if it is on. If it is off, it means the bit fuse is still intact and the procedure must be repeated. After the bit is verified, the next bit is programmed, and finally a new word is addressed and the procedure repeated.

The fusible-link PROMs have the same drawback when it comes to correcting mistakes as do the masked PROMs. If the engineer makes a mistake, the entire PROM must be replaced. This simply means PROM programs should be kept short enough so that making a mistake doesn't mean losing many hours of work. Thus, the small 64 × 8 PROMs are preferred to the larger PROMs when used with a simple ROM programmer, since nothing major is lost if a mistake is made. Moreover, if the programmer is controlled by a microcomputer, then the actual programming cycle can be vastly speeded up.

One serious problem that occurred in earlier metal-fusible link PROMs was "regrowth," a chemical-mechanical process

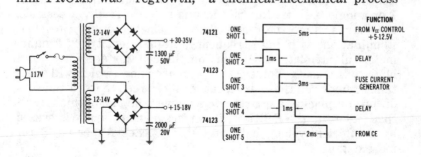

Courtesy Signetics Corp.

(B) Power supply and waveforms.

PROM programmer.

211

where a blown fuse tends to grow back and thus change its logic state. This problem was largely solved by employing silicon links in the PROM instead of metal links. Following a 20-to-30-mA pulse, the silicon link reaches 1400°C, then blows open and in the heating process, coats itself with a layer of silicon dioxide. This effectively insulates the link and prevents regrowth.

Performance—Note that in general, all fusible link PROMs are bipolar TTL and therefore draw more current than MOS-type devices. Typical current drains for TTL PROMs are in the range of 100 to 200 milliamps, which translates to 1/2 to 1 watt per device.

However, access times for TTL are about an order of magnitude better (faster) than an equivalent MOS PROM, and are in the range of 30 to 100 nanoseconds. (MOS PROMs = 300 to 100 nanoseconds.) Bipolar PROMs are configured in 16 pin 256 × 4 packages, on up to 24 pin 2K × 8 packages.

Erasable PROMs

The erasable PROM, sometimes called EPROM, UVROM, or EAPROM, can store data indefinitely like the fusible-link PROM but can also be erased at any time and reprogrammed.

A UVPROM storage cell is made of a single p-channel MOS transistor, with the gate lead floating and insulated from the rest of the circuit. A voltage in excess of 30 volts will cause electrons to avalanche through the insulator and build up a negative charge on the gate. The negative charge causes a conductive inversion layer in the channel connecting the drain and source. Since the surrounding insulating material has a high resistance, the charge on the gate will not decay for many years (see graph in Appendix B). The charged gate thus forms an "on" transistor, and therefore can be programmed as a logic 1 or a logic 0. Since the gate lead is not electrically accessible, the charge cannot be removed by an electric pulse. However, illumination with high-frequency, high intensity, 254 nanometer, ultraviolet (UV) light on the cell surface for ¼ to 1 hour, will cause a photoelectric current to flow, which will eventually remove all the charge, returning the cell to its initial condition. By placing a quartz window over the monolithic circuit that makes up the EPROM, the entire memory array is erased by a sufficiently long bath of UV light. See Appendix B for more details.

The programming requirements for the early versions of the UVPROM were quite demanding as far as timing and power dissipation during programming were concerned. The first, and probably the most popular, UVPROM is the 1702A. This device requires applying the programming pulses to three separate pins and complementing the address and data signals just before these pulses are applied. All the voltages to the UVPROM must be of exact amplitude and duration, and may not be applied for too long, or the chip will burn out. Since the 1702A and similar-type UVPROMs are organized as 256 or 512 8-bit words, hand programming can be agonizing, especially when the program gets above a couple hundred bits. Fig. 4-23 shows an EPROM programmer with ultraviolet compartment.

A more reliable and time-saving way to program these EPROMs is to use the microcomputer to do the job. For example, a program can be developed in RAM where it is easily modified and debugged. Once the program is working properly, the microcomputer can use another program to copy, or move, the contents of the RAM into the EPROM, pulsing the EPROM pins with high voltage and programming the EPROM as it does so. As each programming cycle is finished, the microcomputer checks to see if the bits have programmed properly.

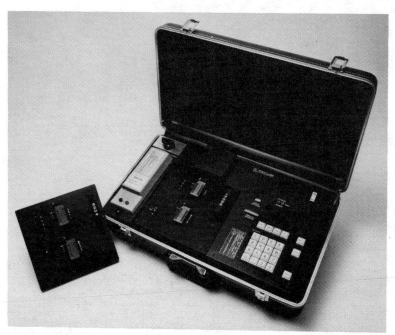

Courtesy Pro-Log Corp.

Fig. 4-23. Commercial EPROM programmer.

Supersimple 2708 UVPROM Programmer

One of the most popular UVPROMs today is the 2708 part. The 2708 is organized as 1K × 8 bits, which makes it good for small microprocessor programs, or for larger programs if a high-end moderate volume application is involved. The 2708 has Tri-State outputs, and dissipates about 400 to 800 mW. Access time is 450 nanoseconds, so in some cases the MPU will need to be halted until the memory can present its data.

Fig. 4-24 is a schematic of a supersimple 2708 programmer that connects to a typical microprocessor PIA port device, and requires only three 74193 counters, a 7406 open-collector inverter, and a pair of transistors.

The I/O port is connected to the input of a 10-bit upcounter so that the program can toggle it and count up the 2708 addresses. The eleventh bit output at the end of the 10-bit counter also goes to the PIA; this is an output that the program can check for the last address of the 2708. Another input on the 2708, the CS/WE, allows the 2708 to be programmed or to be just read. The actual programming pulse is delivered

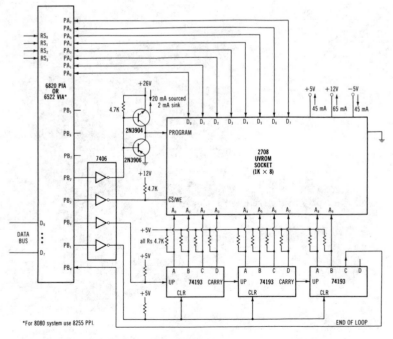

Fig. 4-24. Typical 2708 UVPROM minimum-parts-count programmer.

to the 2708 by a pair of transistors in a push-pull arrangement. A 26-volt, 20-mA pulse is required. Its duration should be about 1 millisecond. The data must be programmed repeatedly. The formula $N \times tpw > 100$ ms determines the number of repeated loops necessary for a fixed pulse width. For a 1 ms tpw, 100 loops are required and since there are 1024 bytes, the 2708 takes about $1024 \times 100 \times 1$ ms or about 103 seconds to program.

The program needed to control the 2708 programmer must consist of an initialization routine that sets up the PIA I/O ports, data pointer, and cycle count; the presentation of the data word and the programming pulse, incrementing the counters and data pointer; testing for the last data entry; testing for a complete programming loop (1024 addresses complete) ; and testing for the end of programming.

The exact program for this interface is left as an exercise for the reader. We will learn about the PIA later.

Notice that one subtle problem arises in using a program to manipulate and move another program. In this case the *copy* program must be written before it can do any copying! Since the most logical place to keep a copy program so that it won't be lost during a power outage would be in a ROM, this would mean we would have to hand program the copy program into the EPROM the first time around. If a mistake is made, we must start all over. The solution to this seemingly circular problem is to hand assemble the copy program the first time around in RAM. Then, after it is debugged and working correctly, have it copy itself into the EPROM! Now the copy pro-

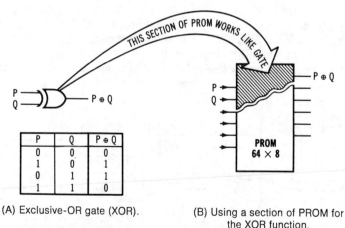

(A) Exclusive-OR gate (XOR).

(B) Using a section of PROM for the XOR function.

Fig. 4-25. Equivalency of gates and PROMs.

gram is safely stored away in a ROM, and can be called by a program as a subroutine at any time, to copy another program into EPROM. We can call the copy a "utility" program, and it can be kept in an EPROM called the "utility" ROM.

Other Uses for EPROMs

Permanent storage of microcomputer programs is not the only use of PROMs. We can further classify PROM as a dedicated component. A dedicated PROM can be programmed to be almost any kind of circuit. This is a consequence of the mathematical similarity between gates and bits. It is possible to take any type of digital gate and write its truth table on paper. So, since a PROM is nothing more than a giant truth table, we can make it work as any gate we wish, as long as we don't run out of bits in the PROM.

In Fig. 4-25A, an exclusive-OR gate and its truth table are shown. The XOR function can be stored in a PROM by simply using two of the input pins and one output pin, as shown in Fig. 4-25B. In this case we are programming the gate function in a low-cost, 64 × 8, fusible-link PROM. Since there are still four input pins left, two more XOR gates can be stored. Notice, however, there are five leftover output pins. These are actually wasted unless we make the inputs also represent other gate functions.

When using PROMs as code converters or large gate circuits, we must constantly look for ways to reduce the required number of input and output pins. This will help us keep the size of the PROM to a minimum.

As the size of the PROM increases, we can do more and more with it. For example, Fig. 4-26A shows a digital comparator circuit made from a 256 × 4 PROM. It compares two 4-bit digital words on the eight input pins and produces the output signal corresponding to the relationship between the two words.

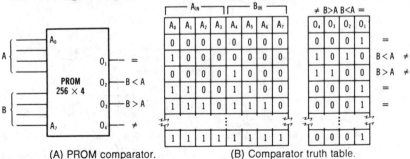

(A) PROM comparator.   (B) Comparator truth table.

Fig. 4-26. PROM as a digital comparator.

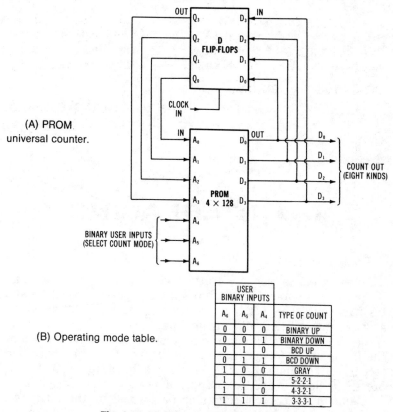

(A) PROM universal counter.

(B) Operating mode table.

USER BINARY INPUTS			
A_6	A_5	A_4	TYPE OF COUNT
0	0	0	BINARY UP
0	0	1	BINARY DOWN
0	1	0	BCD UP
0	1	1	BCD DOWN
1	0	0	GRAY
1	0	1	5-2-2-1
1	1	0	4-3-2-1
1	1	1	3-3-3-1

Fig. 4-27. PROM as a universal counter.

If the words are equal, we get an output from O_1, A = B, and so on. The truth table for the PROM is shown in Fig. 4-26B.

It's not unusual to see a PROM used as a programmable universal counter like the one in Fig. 4-27A. This is a 128 × 4 PROM, used in the feedback loop of a 4-bit synchronous counter. Four of the PROM's input pins are used to select the type of count, such as binary or bcd, and the direction of the count, either up or down. The operating mode table for this circuit is shown in Fig. 4-27B.

PROM selection guide (MOS only) is presented in Appendix D. PROMs are listed by configuration, vendor, part number, access time, output type, power dissipation, and the devices pin-out is presented.

chapter 5

I/O INTERFACING

In the broadest sense, an interface allows us to put 1's and 0's in the computer. It also allows the computer to send 1's and 0's back out. The I/O device, whether it is a crt terminal, seven-segment LED display, or paper-tape punch, converts these 1's and 0's to humanly recognizable form. It is the job of the interface to format the 1's and 0's for the I/O device and to control the housekeeping requirements of the I/O device. Most I/O devices are exceedingly dumb and therefore need a fair amount of control functions performed by the interface. The information, in the form of 1's and 0's, can come from the computer either serially (one bit at a time) or in parallel (all bits at once). In the case of the serial mode, operation is usually slow but inexpensive. In the parallel mode, operation is fast and complex (but not necessarily expensive for short distances).

Compared with the CPU, the interface area is much more diversified and requires an understanding of the many ways a computer can be "talked" to. In a sense, no computer is very useful (except for educational purposes) unless it has some minimum form of I/O.

ELEMENTS OF THE I/O INTERFACE

Fig. 5-1 shows the basic elements found in almost any I/O interface. First there must be some way for the computer to "talk" to or address the I/O interface. This is usually done by assigning a specific memory address to the I/O interface.

Decode logic is then used connected to the address bus so as to produce an enable pulse when the assigned address of the interface appears on bus. This resulting enable pulse is then used to trigger the I/O interface to do something. It may, as shown in the figure, cause an exchange of data on the data bus between the interface and the MPU. But, as the dashed line indicates in the figure, the interface often may not use the data bus at all. For example, in the case of a solid-state relay, or a speaker audible indicator, etc.

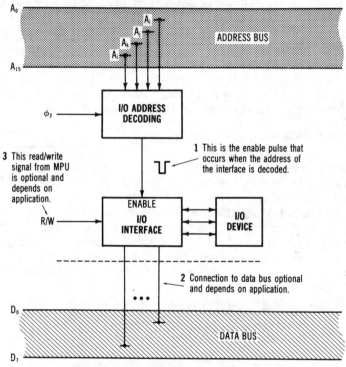

Fig. 5-1. The components of an I/O interface.

Often the clock of the MPU will be involved as an input to the interface to provide a gating function so that address decoders respond only when the address is stable. The read/write line, (or memory read or memory write if 8080) may also be involved in the interface to indicate direction when a data exchange must occur. Sometimes the reset line on the MPU will be extended to the interface so that any registers or flip-flops in it would be cleared or zeroed by the normal reset pulse.

219

Address Decoding

The most fundamental questions the designer must ask when planning an interface are: (1) where in the memory space should the interface go, and (2) how can I minimize hardware and optimize software in the interface? The answer to the first question partly determines the answer to the second. The exact location of the interface in the memory address space depends on how much actual RAM is to be used in the final product, and how many separate I/O devices will be needed. Usually less than 10 I/O devices will be used in a typical application; however, we will usually find that to economize on the hardware decoding a much larger number of addresses will be set aside for I/O interfaces (but not all used). This will become more apparent when we consider the three ways to decode I/O locations in memory. But first let us clear up a confusion that exists about I/O "ports."

Memory-Mapped I/O vs I/O Mapped I/O

The type of I/O interface we have discussed so far is called "memory-mapped" because it treats the interface exactly like it was a valid memory location (Fig. 5-2). All the power of the processor's memory access instructions is available to operate on the interface. But on the down-side, each I/O device consumes what would have been RAM addresses. Another form of I/O, popularized by the 8080, is called I/O-mapped input/output, or sometimes, wrongly called Port I/O. I/O-mapped I/O, as shown in Fig. 5-3, does not use up RAM memory space because it uses a special I/O "port" read or I/O write enable signal put out by the MPU. Two new instructions,

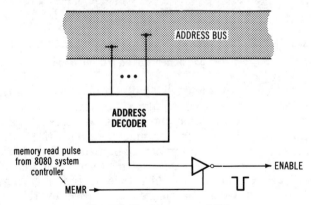

Fig. 5-2. Memory-mapped I/O.

IN n and OUT n are used to input data from input port n or to output data to output port n. The port number n, can be 0 to 255, and is output on the lower 8 bits of the address bus. Decode logic can be used to enable the desired port, as shown in Fig. 5-3. The drawback here is that the OUT or IN instructions only exchange the byte between the MPU and interface; manipulation takes more instructions. In memory-mapped I/O we can do much more and take advantage of advanced addressing modes.

Linear-Address Decoding

The simplest form of address decoding for an interface is linear address decoding. As shown in Fig. 5-4, linear decoding is almost "hardwareless" in that we dedicate a single high-order address bit to address and trigger the I/O device. In our example bit A_{15} of the address bus is used to trigger a 555 connected as a one-shot (or monostable multivibrator). This results in an extended pulse sent to the speaker (in the millisecond range) and causes a "click" sound when triggered. By using address line A_{15}, memory address space is simply split in half; 32K is dedicated to the I/O devices and 32K to system RAM. All addresses greater than or equal to hex 8000 will trigger the speaker. Addresses less than hex 8000 (0000-7FFF) access system memory.

The ϕ_2 clock pulse is used to enable the address pulse inverter shown in the figure. The gate keeps the 555 from being triggered by noise on A_{15} when the bus is floating.

As you can see, linear decoding is quite wasteful of address space. However, it allows approaching zero hardware decod-

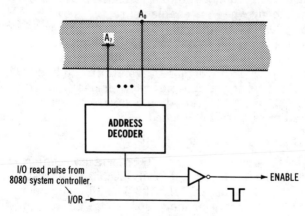

I/O read pulse from 8080 system controller.

I/OR →

ENABLE

Fig. 5-3. I/O-mapped I/O.

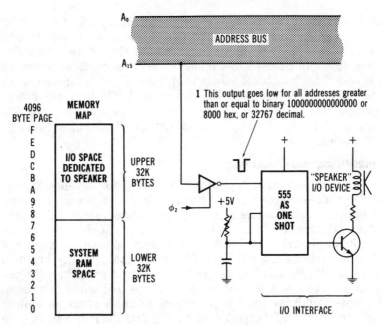

Fig. 5-4. Linear-address decoding.

ing, which in some cases may be a better trade-off. It is often used to enable large ROMs via their chip select inputs.

Fully Decoded Address Decoding

Fully decoded address decoding simply means we decode one unique address, instead of huge chunks of address space. As shown in Fig. 5-5, a 16-input AND gate and a single inverter are used to produce an enable pulse for location FFF7 hex *only*. As you can see, this approach results in a rather complex and awkward wiring arrangement (16 inputs).

Further, every unique I/O location requires a 16-input AND gate and up to 16 inverters to isolate its address. This type of decoding is unusual and not very efficient, but it does illustrate how an AND gate array and inverters are used, when a unique address must be decoded.

Partial Address Decoding

The most popular form of I/O interface decoding is a compromise between linear and fully-decoded address decoding. Fig. 5-6 shows the use of 74LS138 3 to 8 line decoders (binary to octal) to break up memory space into convenient 4K byte "pages" (don't confuse with 256 byte pages). The first decoder attaches to address bits A_{13}, A_{14}, and A_{15}. This results in each of the eight outputs going low for each of the eight upper hex digits of the address word. Thus the upper 32K of memory is decoded and set aside for peripheral devices. However, we can use any of the 4K page outputs to enable several ROMs if desired. The second 74LS138 is tied to the 8XXX hex page

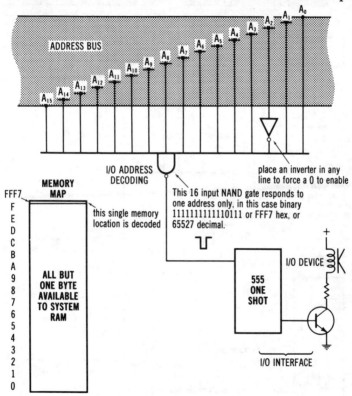

Fig. 5-5. Fully decoded address decoding.

output of the first decoder, and to the lower three address bits A_0, A_1, and A_2. This results in eight new decoded I/O addresses on the beginning of page 8XXX, namely 8XX0, through 8XX7. (The XX refers to the part of the hex address that we don't care about—thus the address 8000 has the same effect as 8220.) Our example shows using address 8XX1 to toggle a flip-flop connected to a speaker and address 8XX0 to clear or reset it.

Partial address decoding is the most efficient form of decoding and results in extremely straightforward designs. Fig.

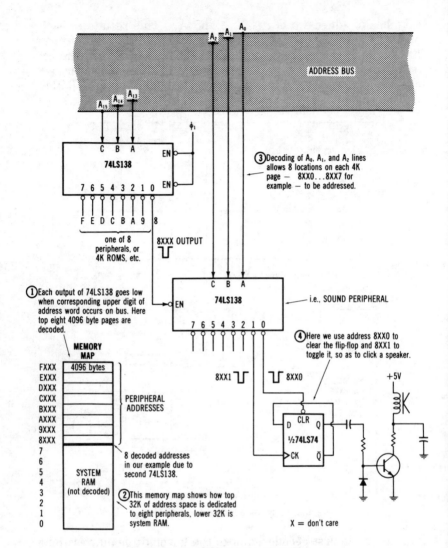

Fig. 5-6. Partial address decoding.

5-7 shows how a typical home computer product utilizes partial address decoding to manipulate several I/O devices, including strobe pulses for analog to digital 555s, keyboard data enables, changing text and graphics modes, and so on.

Fig. 5-8 shows how to represent the address decoding functions symbolically so schematics can be kept simple. The box represents a collection of 74LS138s or similar decoders.

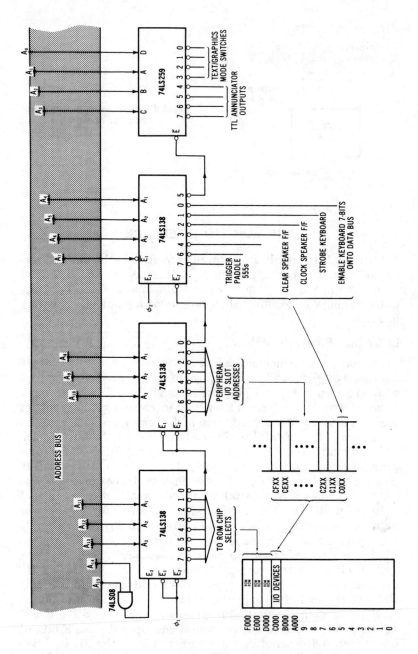

Fig. 5-7. How a popular home computer product decodes memory for RAM, ROM, and I/O ports.

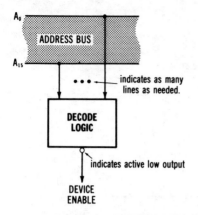

indicates as many lines as needed.

indicates active low output

DEVICE
ENABLE

Fig. 5-8. Symbolic representation of address decoding.

MINIMUM I/O INTERFACE

Perhaps the most basic form of interface is the one the machine-language programmer uses. In this case, the programmer at minimum will be able to enter data directly into the computer memory or examine the contents of a particular memory location.

LEDs and Binary Switches

To specify the memory address we will need a set of 16 address switches, and to set up the data we need a second set of 8 (16 also if it's a 16-bit MPU) switches. The most basic form of front panel control will then consist of a group of toggle switches: 16 for address and eight more for an 8-bit data bus, giving a total of 24 switches. The data bus portion of a schematic for such a panel is shown in Fig. 5-9. The programmer communicates with the panel in 1's and 0's. This can be simplified by grouping the switches by threes or fours and converting mentally to octal or hexadecimal.

In order to keep the toggle switches from shorting out the data bus, we use a 74LS244 octal buffer with Tri-State outputs (one inverter per switch). The enable signal that turns on the buffers comes from the address decoders ANDed with the system clock. In the example, when location 8000 hex is addressed, it enables the Tri-State buffers and transfers the logic state of the switches onto the data bus. So if an instruction such as "load the accumulator with contents of location 8000" (LDA 8000) is executed, we would end up with the 8 bits of the switch byte stored in the accumulator of the MPU. Likewise, the eight LEDs are memory mapped at address 8001H, and therefore a "store accumulator at location 8001" (STA

8001) will place the 8 bits in the accumulator in the 74LS364 octal latch, and in turn the LEDs will display the 8-bit binary number.

Obviously, *some* software is involved in using this binary front panel, but it is quite minimal. Provision for holding 16 more bits for address indicators involves hanging additional latches and LEDs on the data bus, giving each a unique mapped address, and expanding the program to pass address information to the new latches. A new set of 8 switches could work as a 16-bit address input register.

Since the front panel is now a valid memory location, we can write simple programs that do things inside the CPU, and then we can write the results into the front panel display for our analysis. For example, suppose the computer is stopped and we want to know the value of the accumulator. In such a case a short program would reside in a ROM, consisting primarily of a STORE instruction, which puts the contents of the accumulator into the specified panel address.

But as any experienced programmer can tell you, the binary switches are about as useful as sails on a battleship. It takes

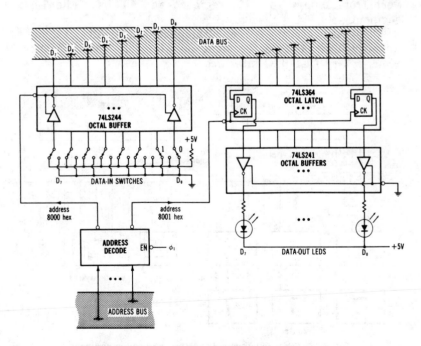

Fig. 5-9. Simple front-panel interface using toggle switches and LEDs.

much more patience and time to set up the proper data and address information, and we must mentally convert machine code into 24 switch settings. Small "bootstrap" programs can be entered through this type of I/O interface, but if constant program reloading is necessary, this will quickly become burdensome. A better solution, and one not requiring much more circuitry, uses thumbwheel switches and LED seven-segment displays.

Octal Thumbwheels and Seven-Segment Displays

This type of interface is much more convenient to use. The data are put onto the bus by using three low-cost octal thumbwheel switches. These have four output lines per digit (coded in binary or bcd). If we choose either coding, and use the three least significant lines on the bus (2^0, 2^1, 2^7), we effectively form an octal digit (3 bits). Since the switches are connected inside to form the proper binary code, all we need to do is connect them to the bus through an octal buffer (Fig. 5-10). The seven-segment LED display requires a latch to hold the incoming data, and three binary to seven-segment decoders to convert from binary to seven-segment and to drive the LED segments.

The logic necessary to define the panel electrically as a valid memory location uses the same decoding shown in the previous binary LED I/O interface.

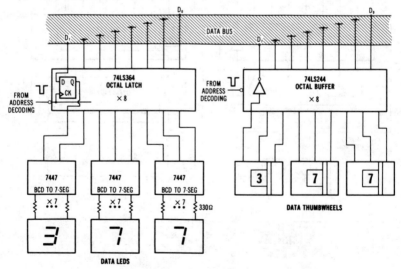

Fig. 5-10. Octal thumbwheel switches and seven-segment display interface.

Some seven-segment LEDs are available with all the 7447 decoders and 7475 latches built in. Of course, their cost is much higher than without these. However, they make wiring up the panel much simpler. But even thumbwheels become tiresome after a while, especially if they are hard to turn. The obvious next step up in convenience is the old familiar calculatorlike keyboard.

Hex Keyboard, Maximum Hardware Circuit

The next level up from the octal thumbwheel display, and the one most often used by the manufacturers of low-cost microcomputer kits, is the hex keyboard and seven-segment display. The design of keyboard technique can be approached in one of two ways. One way involves an operating program that scans the keyboard matrix and determines which key is being pressed. The program then lights the appropriate LED digit. The second technique uses all hardware to generate and light up the digit. The second method is the most obvious; therefore we will cover it first.

Fig. 5-11 shows the details of a simple hex keyboard and 2 digit hex data display, capable of working with almost any microprocessor. The hex keyboard has 16 keys, which would be expensive if regular push-button toggles are used. Instead the keyboard in the figure is a matrix keyboard consisting of four rows (Y_1-Y_4) and four columns (X_1-X_4). The switches short out one particular row and column intersection when pressed. The MM74C922 is a keyboard "encoder" chip that automatically scans the rows and columns looking for a keypress and when one is found, it converts the key to a 4-bit output, which can be Tri-Stated onto the data bus.

In our example, we use a Tri-State gate on bit D_7 of the data bus to allow the program to check the encoder's "data ready" output. When the program finds that data is available in the encoder, it issues a "read" to the memory-mapped address of the encoder, which pulses its output enable pin, and the data for one digit (4 bits) is transferred to the MPU. The output enable pulse also clears the data available flip-flop, so a test for new data (new keypress) can be done repeatedly in a programmed loop.

In this interface, the hexadecimal display is more compact and perhaps more useful than the octal displays, as only two digits are needed for an 8-bit number. However, there is a problem in the decoding of the binary-to-hex for the segment displays. Most 7-segment decoders display the numbers 0 to 9 only, and either blank the display for a >9 binary value,

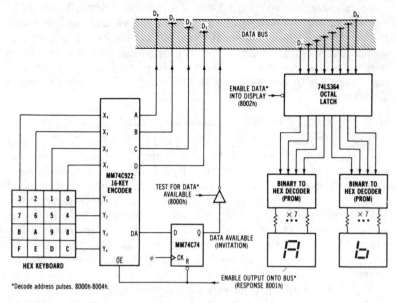

(A) Hex keyboard.

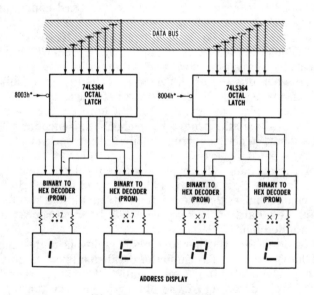

(B) Address part of hex display.

Fig. 5-11. Hex keyboard and seven-segment hex display.

or present a partial segment display for the remaining six values. So the solution (in hardware) is to use a custom PROM for the binary to 7-segment hex decoder.

Like the previous octal display we can add four extra digits to represent an address up to FFFF by hanging two more octal latches on the data bus and giving them their own memory-mapped addresses. See Fig. 5-11B.

The I/O program (sometimes called the I/O driver) must keep track of digits input from the keyboard, and store them in proper order in the display latches.

Hex Keyboard, Software Approach

The software approach to a hex keyboard uses what is called a *scanning and table look-up* technique.. The hardware shown in Fig. 5-12 contains a 5-by-8 matrix-type keyboard. In a scanning type of keyboard, an instruction sequence in the program applies the address of the keyboard to the five "rows" in the key matrix. The eight "columns" of the key matrix are pulled high by resistors, and form the inputs to two 8834 transceivers. The transceivers apply the information from the eight keyboard columns to the data bus. If no key is pressed, selecting and reading the keyboard will put all 0's into the accumulator. But if a key is pressed, a 1 will appear in the accumulator. Since the difference between a key press and no key press is a 1 in the accumulator, we can use a program that simply loops, checking to see when the accumulator becomes nonzero. When it does become nonzero, the program enters the next phase and determines which key was pressed. It does this by applying a row of the address and reading the corresponding data word. The row count is kept in a register, and when the data word finally becomes a number greater than zero, the number of the row containing the pressed key is contained in the register. The register value, along with the data word, is used to form the address in a table of the desired digital value for that key.

In order to minimize the decoders necessary for driving the LEDs, we can use the software to store the corresponding code for each of the 16 possible hex digits. After determining which key was pressed, we need to display its value in the LEDs. The CPU simply looks up the desired digit code stored in a table in memory and then applies this information to the seven segments, via the data bus. Since only one digit can be applied at any given time over the eight data lines, multiple digits are multiplexed by having the CPU scan the display while it also scans the keyboard. The software routine uses a pointer to

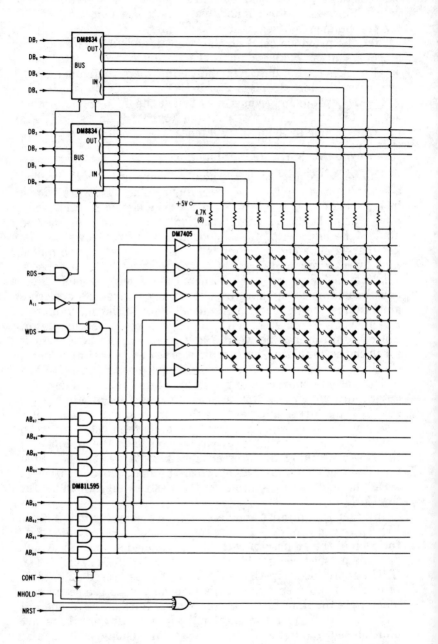

Fig. 5-12. Hex keyboard,

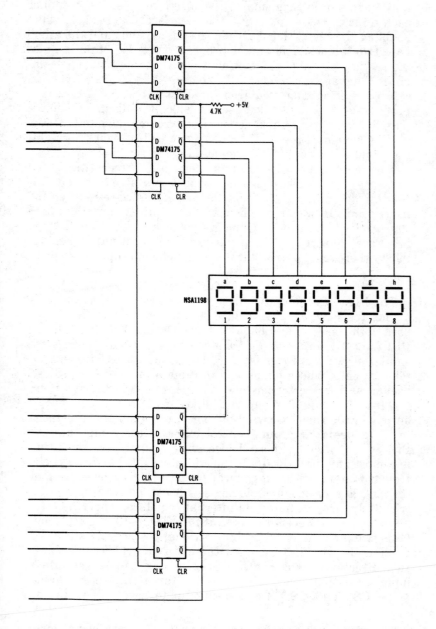

software approach.

233

store the number of digits in the display. Since the individual digits are stored in memory, the program selectively applies each digit to the display, via the data latches (74175), while enabling the respective digit via the address bus and the alternate two latches. The actual program that does this is quite interesting but takes some effort to decipher in a strange computer language.

The multiplexing requirement illustrates an interesting problem with software keyboards. Since the display is multiplexed, the program must constantly execute a loop to keep the display visible. If the CPU breaks down or isn't working right, the panel operation will be rendered useless.

The last approach to building the I/O interface (maximum software) was the best, mainly because multiplexing and putting the decoding functions in the driver software reduced the parts count. However, our design still requires more than nine ICs. And what happens when we require a second and third interface? Most likely the parts count will continue to run up. Surely there must be a better way to handle microprocessor I/O.

The PIA

The PIA was the system designer's answer to a dream. PIA stands for *Peripheral Interface Adapter,* which is the device used with the 6500 and 6800 systems. On the 8080 it's called a PPI for *Programmable Peripheral Interface.* Both devices are similar so we will focus on the PIA device.* The PIA is a 40-pin LSI chip, whose purpose is to replace most of the MSI IC packages, discrete transistors, and passive components of an I/O interface and allow up to 16 lines of bidirectional input or output in the form of two 8-bit ports, to be simply interfaced to the address, data, and control buses of the computer. The PIA is a general purpose device and is capable of operating in almost any mode desired: polled, interrupt, handshack, etc. How can one chip be so general purpose? The answer is that the PIA is a programmable device—it can be configured electrically by programming its internal registers, when the computer is first powered-up. As shown in Fig. 5-13, the PIA contains two independent 8-bit bidirectional peripheral data buses (A and B) for interfacing to the external real world. These 16 bidirectional pins can be "programmed" to act as either input or output lines. The PIA has three chip-select inputs (CS_0, CS_1, and CS_2) for locating up to seven PIAs in the

---

*The justification for bias toward the 6800, 6502 family was given earlier.

memory space of the MPU. There are two register-select inputs, RS_0 and RS_1, which connect to the lower address bus lines (A_0 and A_1) and allow the MPU to select among the

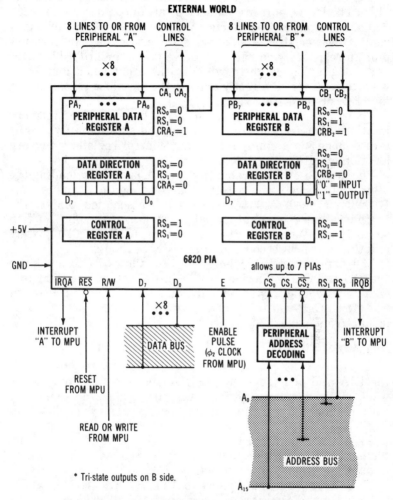

Fig. 5-13. The 6820 PIA occupies four memory locations, but has six internal registers.

internal registers of the PIAs. On the CPU side, the PIA has 8 bidirectional data pins for connecting to the system data bus. In addition to the A and B ports, the PIA provides four control lines ($CA_{1,2}$ and $CB_{1,2}$) that allow the I/O device to communicate through the PIA to the MPU and vice-versa.

These control lines are capable of causing an interrupt to the MPU, and the MPU can then interrogate the PIA to determine which port requires attention.

The driving capabilities of the A and B ports are not exactly alike. The B-side port presents Tri-State outputs so a line specified as an input can be shorted and can deliver 3 mA of a current. However, the A-side drivers contain passive resistive pull-up resistors, and can only drive two standard TTL loads, and can't be loaded down while in the input condition. Thus, we often see port B directly driving the base of a transistor, or an LED, or solid-state relay.

There are six registers in the PIA, but only four memory locations. The technique to accessing the additional two registers is done via a single bit in the "control register" memory location on either the A or B side.

The method of "programming" a PIA is done by loading the 8-bit "data direction registers" (there is one for A and one for B) with 1 or 0. A 1 transforms the associated pin on the peripheral port to an output, while a 0 makes the pin function as an input. When the PIA is reset it puts 0 in all registers and thus all ports become high-impedance inputs.

The data direction register (DDR) allows us to configure the PIA at the beginning of the initialization program and change its configuration on a dynamic basis, under control of the MPU. Can you think of a way such a port could be used in our front panel I/O device?

Hex Keyboard Six-Digit Display PIA Approach

If we are willing to accept the challenge of designing with the PIA and of letting the MPU software to take over more work at the display interface, we can produce an extremely efficient, low parts count, highly flexible display as shown in Fig. 5-14.

By having the program peform digit multiplexing and by having the PIA turn an individual digit segment, we eliminate a ton of additional decoding hardware.

This design uses one PIA; two TTL ICs (a 74LS145 and a 74LS244); and seven transistors, six for digit drivers and one for a speaker output. The approach used here is to have the MPU program continually "poll" the PIA, looking (testing) for a depression of one of the keys. Also the program must continually refresh the digits in the display one at a time and at a rate fast enough so that the eye sees a steady display.

The software for such a display is interesting, but beyond the scope of this book. In a nutshell, however, a table of digits

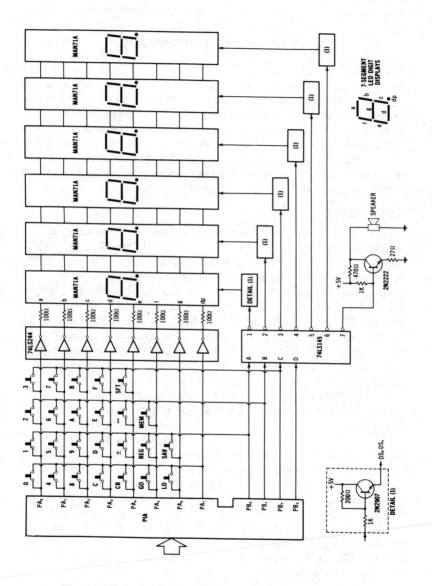

Fig. 5-14. Example of a simple hex keypad, six-digit hex display and speaker interface using PIA.

is kept in system RAM, along with a look-up table of segment codes for each digit and a "map" of the last state of the keyboard so it can easily be tested for a changed condition. Because the MPU must continually scan and test the interface, this approach does tend to slow down the system somewhat.

ALPHANUMERIC INTERFACE

From the simple hex keyboard with hex numbers, the next level up in computer communication is the familiar English alphabet with its numbers and punctuation marks. These can be encoded into binary for entry into the computer. Our first problem is to decide which particular binary codes to associate with the letters and other characters. Luckily, computer scientists realized that this should be standardized so that the storage medium would be universal and one computer could read the tapes and memory of another.

ASCII Standard

The ASCII standard in use today meets the universal requirement with a 7-bit code, shown in Fig. 5-15. The eighth bit of an ASCII character is free for the designer to play with, but often it is used as a parity bit, or to signify reverse video in a crt display. Since there are 7-bits in the ASCII code, a total of 128 possible characters can be represented. However, the ASCII code designates the first 32 character positions as *nonprinting control characters*. For example, the carriage return character (CR) is a control character and has an ASCII value of 13 (0D hex), if parity is 0. You can see from Fig. 5-15 that quite a bit of important information is stored in the ASCII control character set. The remaining 96 characters consist of upper and lower case alphabetic characters, numerals, and punctuation symbols.

To use the table in Fig. 5-15 to convert a alphanumeric or control character to its respective ASCII value, first find the character then locate the hex value for its column and write this down as the MSB.* Next find the value for the symbols row position (the LSB) and write this down to the right of the first character. The result is two digit hex value for the symbol. For example, a lower case "j" is ASCII 6A hex, if $p = 0$, but if $p = 1$, then it's EA hex. Convert to decimal if necessary. The ASCII code for a bell or beep (BEL) is 7, and line feed (LF) is a 10.

---

*Assume a parity of 1 or 0.

HEX		MSD	p = 1	8	9	A	B	C	D	E	F
			p = 0	0	1	2	3	4	5	6	7
			b8	p	p	p	p	p	p	p	p
	BITS		b7	0	0	0	0	1	1	1	1
			b6	0	0	1	1	0	0	1	1
LSD	b4	b3	b2 b5 / b1	0	1	0	1	0	1	0	1
0	0	0	0 0	NUL	DLE	SP	0	@	P	`	p
1	0	0	0 1	SOH	DC1	!	1	A	Q	a	q
2	0	0	1 0	STX	DC2	"	2	B	R	b	r
3	0	0	1 1	ETX	DC3	#	3	C	S	c	s
4	0	1	0 0	EOT	DC4	$	4	D	T	d	t
5	0	1	0 1	ENQ	NAK	%	5	E	U	e	u
6	0	1	1 0	ACK	SYN	&	6	F	V	f	v
7	0	1	1 1	BEL	ETB	'	7	G	W	g	w
8	1	0	0 0	BS	CAN	(	8	H	X	h	x
9	1	0	0 1	HT	EM	)	9	I	Y	i	y
A	1	0	1 0	LF	SUB	*	:	J	Z	j	z
B	1	0	1 1	VT	ESC	+	;	K	[	k	{
C	1	1	0 0	FF	FS	,	<	L	\	l	|
D	1	1	0 1	CR	GS	-	=	M	]	m	}
E	1	1	1 0	SO	RS	.	>	N	^	n	~
F	1	1	1 1	SI	US	/	?	O	___	o	DEL

CONTROL CHARACTERS

NUL Null	**FF** Form Feed	**CAN** Cancel
SOH Start of Heading	**CR** Carriage Return	**EM** End of Medium
STX Start of Text	**SO** Shift Out	**SUB** Substitute
ETX End of Text	**SI** Shift In	**ESC** Escape
EOT End of Transmission	**DLE** Data Link Escape	**FS** File Separator
ENQ Enquiry	**DC1** Device Control 1	**GS** Group Separator
ACK Acknowledge	**DC2** Device Control 2	**RS** Record Separator
BEL Bell (audible or attention signal)	**DC3** Device Control 3	**US** Unit Separator
BS Backspace	**DC4** Device Control 4 (Stop)	**DEL** Delete
HT Horizontal Tabulation (punched card skip)	**NAK** Negative Acknowledge	
LF Line Feed	**SYN** Synchronous Idle	
VT Vertical Tabulation	**ETB** End of Transmission Block	

Fig. 5-15. ASCII standard computer code. See text to use.

The next level up in our front panel would obviously be one that used the ASCII character set. This way we could type in entire word commands to the computer as we would on a typewriter.

We also would need to be able to output characters for display inexpensively. It turns out the ASCII display can be a formidable undertaking, depending on how much like a typewriter it must work. Let's start with the ASCII keyboard.

ASCII Keyboard

There are several ways to approach the design of an ASCII keyboard. The most efficient approach is the row/column scan method, as used in the previous hex keyboard. Since there are 128 ASCII codes, we could easily eat up switches using them all.

The idea is to use the control and escape keys like the shift key so that each character can double as a control or escape code. Thus the BEL control code is *control G*, line feed is *control J*, and so on, where *control* means press the control key while pressing the letter key.

The maximum hardware approach to an ASCII keyboard is to use a ASCII encoder chip, such as the Signetics 2376, as shown in Fig. 5-16. This encoder automatically scans 88 key cross-points and converts a pressed key to its equivalent ASCII 7-bit code, with parity output also provided. A hardware jumper or microswitch allows upper-case only or upper- and lower-case. The nice thing about this approach is the processor doesn't have to scan or otherwise be involved in decoding the keyboard, and is thus free to do other things. The strobe output from the encoder circuit can be used to tell the MPU that a keypress has occurred, by either interrupting the MPU or by being sampled at a moderate rate. The only problem here is cost of the 2376 (moderate) and the parts count (high).

A better approach is to use the design shown in Fig. 5-17, which uses a more advanced version of the PIA, called the RIOT, to scan the ASCII key matrix under computer software control. The RIOT contains 128 bytes of RAM, two I/O ports, and a built-in programmable timer. A 6820 or 6520 PIA could also be used. The software for this design uses the "walking ZERO" approach we described earlier, but an interrupt mode is used instead of polling to free up the processor.

ASCII Display

It's in the ASCII display that the design choices become many. First we must decide on what type of output, hard or

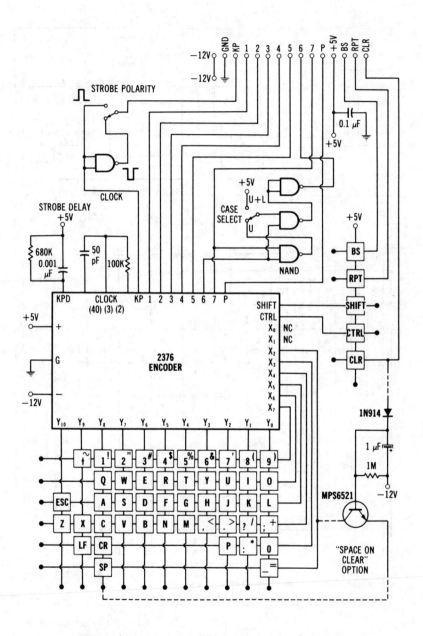

Fig. 5-16. ASCII keyboard, maximum hardware approach.

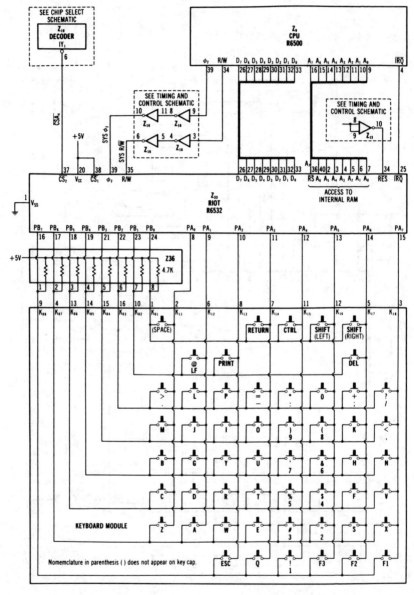

Courtesy Rockwell, Inc.

Fig. 5-17. ASCII keyboard interface using a 6532 RIOT (RAM, I/O, timer chip).

242

soft, is needed. A hard copy output device is a printer, and here an enormous range of possibilities exists. A soft-copy output device can be as simple as a row of twenty solid-state, 16-segment LED character displays, or it can be as complex as a full blown crt screen that displays 24 lines of 80 characters. The direction to take here is mainly a function of portability and cost . . . the crt display is expensive, fragile, heavy, and extremely practical; the solid state row display is cheap, rugged, lightweight, and moderately useful, especially for low cost single board computers that are used for developing assembly programs.

ASCII 20 Character Solid-State Display

The display shown in Fig. 5-18A uses special 16-segment LED displays that produce the limited 64-character ASCII character set shown in Fig. 5-18B. The displays are LD-1415As made by Dial Light and come 4 digits in a 20-pin package. There are five such packages used in the design, resulting in a 20-character row display.

The design is incredibly simple (only one PIA) because each four character section of the 20-character display contains its own memory, decoder, and driver circuit. This greatly simplifies the load on the MPU software, as there is no longer the need to refresh each character, or to multiplex the various digits or to look up the segments in decode table in RAM.

Note that each 4 character display is controlled by seven data lines (D_0-D_6), two address lines (A_0 and A_1), two control lines (W and CW) and a chip select (CE).

The seven data lines connect to the B port of the PIA, while the 5 chip-selects (CE_1-CE_5) and address and write enable lines connect to the A port.

To use the display, the desired data code is placed on D_0-D_6, according to the table in Fig. 5-18B. Next the desired four character group is selected by enabling a chip select line (CE_1-CE_5), and then one of the four characters is selected via address lines A_0 and A_1. The write line is driven low to store and display the data. The display will remain the same until replaced with new data. A cursor character (all segments ON) can be displayed without erasing the actual character "under" the cursor, so the user can see where the next character will be entered.

Understand that because the display memory is "write-only," the software program may have to store a copy of the characters displayed in an internal RAM buffer, but this is relatively easy.

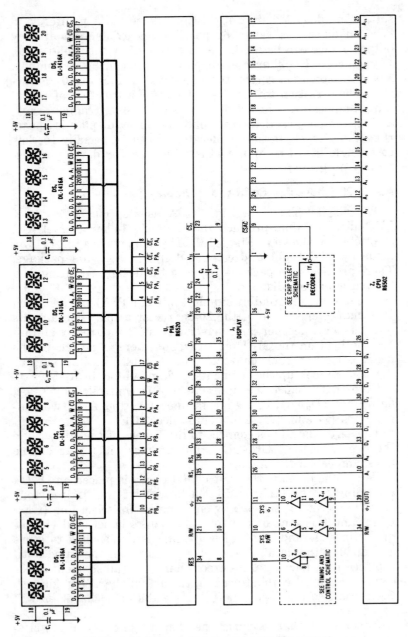

(A) Display interface using row of twenty 16-segment
alphanumeric LED displays.

Fig. 5-18. ASCII solid-state

Memory-Mapped Video Display

Although the single-line 20-character solid-state display is simple, it leaves much to be desired in terms of information density. What we would like in many cases is to display an entire page of text information, or at least several lines. We would also like to have many more than 20 characters on each line, at least 40 and ideally 80 or more.

Such a display exists, doesn't cost a fortune, and you're probably sitting within 100 feet of such a display right now . . . a common television set.

A common television set may be used to display up to 25 lines of 40 characters per line of ASCII text, and if you purchase a $125 special "video-monitor" with a wider (12 MHz) bandwidth than the tv, you can build video circuits to squeeze

CHARACTER SET

			D0	L	H	L	H	L	H	L	H
			D1	L	L	H	H	L	L	H	H
			D2	L	L	L	L	H	H	H	H
D6	D5	D4	D3								
L	H	L	L								
L	H	L	H								
L	H	H	L								
L	H	H	H								
H	L	L	L								
H	L	L	H								
H	L	H	L								
H	L	H	H								

Courtesy Rockwell, Inc.

(B) Figure set for 16-segment alphanumeric LED displays.

display interface and figure set.

over 80 characters per line of ASCII text on a line and still have 24 lines.

We call such a display a video-display because the method sends video televisionlike signals including horizontal and vertical sync pulses, to a raster-scanned television or monitor. In the case of a television, the video signals must be used to modulate an rf signal which is then injected into the tv-antenna terminals.

Fig. 5-19. Output of video display circuit on standard television via rf modulator (16 × 64 characters).

In a video monitor, the rf modulator isn't needed. Fig. 5-19 shows output from a video display circuit designed to drive a television. It displays 16 lines of 64 character lines, and can show upper and lower case. Fig. 5-20A is an example of the output of a high resolution video monitor display, here producing 40 lines of 86 character lines. Fig. 5-20B is a photo of the board that produced this high density display.

The video display is quite a complex circuit and worthy of a book all by itself. A block diagram of a memory-mapped video display circuit is shown in Fig. 5-21. In memory-mapped video I/O the information you can see displayed on the screen is actually stored in ASCII byte format in an area of memory. Circuits in the video display scan this screen memory, convert the bytes in it to video pulses, add the important vertical and

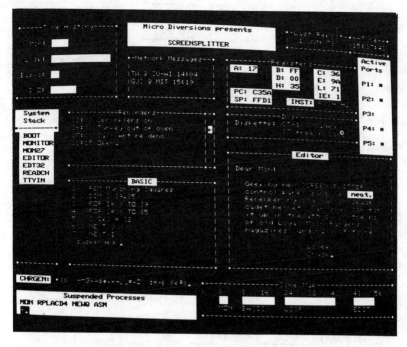

(A) 40 × 86 character video display.

(B) Low cost memory-mapped video board. Plugs directly into an S-100 bus.

Fig. 5-20. High resolution video display and board producing the display.

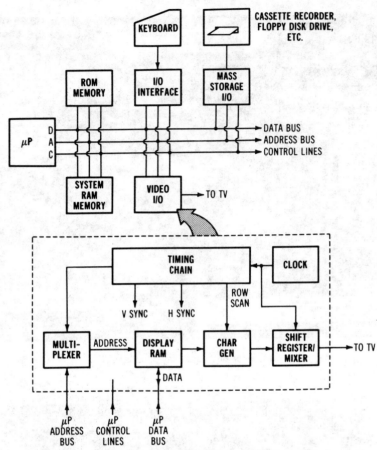

Fig. 5-21. Block diagram of a memory-mapped video display circuit.

horizontal sync pulses, and then pump this composite signal into the rf modulator for television display, or directly into a video monitor. The computer changes the screen information by simply updating the screen memory (see Fig. 5-22).

The characters for the video display can be encoded in a ROM character generator chip as a matrix of dots and the density of the matrix may vary from 5 by 7 to 7 by 9 (see Figs. 5-23A and 5-23B).

SERIAL DATA TRANSMISSION

So far the peripheral I/O devices we have discussed have utilized parallel data transmission, that is, to send eight-bits of data we use eight wires, such as in an 8-line PIA port, or an 8-bit latch on the data bus. But often we would like to send or receive binary data (bits) over a single wire. For example, if you needed to have an ASCII keyboard located several yards from the computer, you would need at least a 12-conductor cable (remember power, ground, parity and

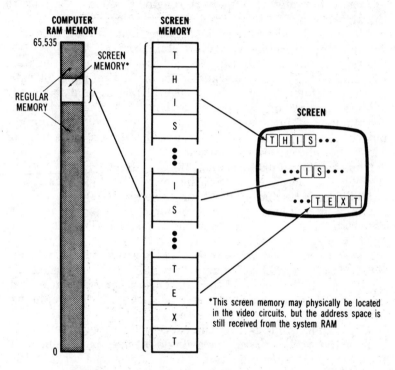

Fig. 5-22. Memory-mapped video. Screen memory is part of regular RAM memory.

strobe signals) to run the distance. Such a cable is quite costly over long distances. A place where parallel data won't work at all is in the storing of binary information on a magnetic recorder tape, where there is only a single read/write head. Eight heads would be needed for the storing of parallel data transmission.

Transferring bits of information over a single wire is called, naturally, serial data transmission. One of the oldest uses of serial data transmission involves the old mechanical "Teletype" or "tty" device, which uses a single wire to serially transmit and receive 8-bit ASCII characters. In fact, today electronic versions of the tty* still retain the same serial transmission format as the tty, but they do it at a much faster speed.

The way an 8-bit quantity, such as an ASCII character, is encoded for serial transmission is shown in Fig. 5-24. As you can see, special "start" and "stop" bits are added to the eight bits of data to allow receiving circuits to identify the ending of an old character, and the beginning of a new one (similar to the strobe function in parallel transmission). As you can see a 1 bit is encoded as a positive voltage and a 0 as a negative voltage. In order to identify one bit from another, the bits are sent at a fixed rate, the receiver synchronizes to the start bit, and samples are made at 16, 32, or 64 times the bit rate. The actual bit rate depends on several factors and is usually specified as so many bits per second or *baud*. The baud rate is the number of bits per second that results from including 7 data bits, 1 parity bit, 1 start bit, and 2 stop bits, for a total of 11 bits per character transmitted.

Thus a 110 baud rate equals $110/11 = 10$ characters/second. At 8 bits per actual character, the real data rate is thus 10×8 $= 80$ bits/sec (including parity in the eighth bit). So you cannot think of 110 baud as a *data rate* of 110 bits per second. The data rate is always lower than the baud rate. The *bit time* is $1/110 = 9.99$ ms.

There are several ways to convert parallel formatted data into serial data, and serial data to parallel data. As usual, the particular method chosen for microprocessor application can use very little hardware and rely heavily on software, or use more hardware and less software.

If you don't mind letting the processor software handle the bulk of the work, you can use a single-bit memory-mapped I/O port for serial communication. This could be one bit of a PIA port, if one spare was available.

ACIA

Another more popular approach to building a serial data transmission circuit is the ACIA. The ACIA is a 40-pin LSI chip that, like the PIA, is programmable and like the PIA contains a wealth of intelligent features. The ACIA stands for *Asynchronous Communication Interface Adapter*, which simply means the data bits can arrive at the receiving end at any time (asynchronously), and do not need to arrive in sync with a system clock (but they must arrive at a constant rate). Al-

---

*Crt terminals with built-in keyboards that link to a remote computer.

most all microprocessor manufacturers produce an ACIA device.

What is special about the ACIA is that it allows the user to program in the number of start and stop bits, the baud rate, the type of parity (even or odd), and so on, at program initialization time.

RS232 and TTY Current Loop

The actual voltage and current levels involved in serial data transmission are also standardized. The tty current loop uses

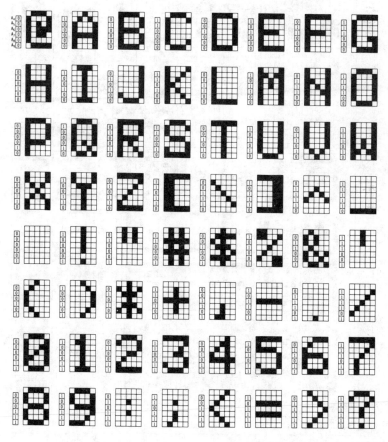

Courtesy National Semiconductor Corp.

(A) ASCII character font.

Fig. 5-23. Video display characters.

20-mA current pulses to represent logic 1, and no current to represent a logic 0. This current loop serial interface is left over from the days of mechanical tty's.

The RS232 is a voltage standard for serial transmission. It is more popular than current loop and its specs are easy to accomplish in hardware, as shown in Fig. 5-25. The recommended maximum cable length is 50 feet, and the maximum data rate is 20,000 bits/second. Note that the RS232 is unbalanced and nonterminated.

A3...A0 →	0000	0011	0010	0011	0100	0101	0110	0111
A6...A4 ↓	D6...D0	D6...D0	D6...D0	D6...D0	D6...D0	D6...D0	D6...D0	D6...D0
000 (R0..R8)	⊠	P	Γ	δ	ε	ζ	η	θ
001 (R0..R8)	P	σ	T	U	Φ	χ	Ψ	ω
010 (R0..R8)		!	"	#	$	%	&	'
011 (R0..R8)	0̸	1	2	3	4	5	6	7
100 (R0..R8)	@	A	B	C	D	E	F	G
101 (R0..R8)	P	Q	R	S	T	U	V	W
110 (R0..R8)	`	a	b	c	d	e	f	g
111 (R0..R8)	P	q	r	s	t	u	v	w

▼ = Shifted Character   The character is shifted three rows to R3 at the top of the font and R11 at

(B) Character font from

Fig. 5-23 cont'd. Video

Cassette Tape Interface

One of the most popular ways to store microcomputer programs and data is on cheap cassette tapes. The job of the interface is to take byte data from memory, convert it to a serial bit stream, and convert the bit stream to a modulated signal that can be stored on the tape. Another job of the cassette interface is to convert the serial modulated bit signals on the tape back to bytes and to place them properly in memory.

1000	1001	1010	1011	1100	1101	1110	1111
D6...D0	D6...D0	D6...D0	D6...D0	D6...D0	D6...D0	D6...D0	D6...D0

the bottom.

6571 character generator ROM.

display characters.

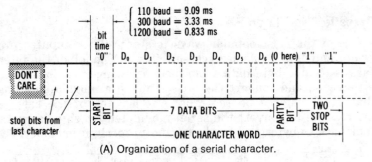

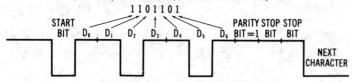

(A) Organization of a serial character.

i) ASCII Z = hex 5A (assuming parity (bit 8) = 1)

ii) hex 5A = binary 1 0 1 1 0 1 1
$$D_6\ D_5\ D_4\ D_3\ D_2\ D_1\ D_0$$

iii) fill in respective bit levels (note reverse order of bits)

1 1 0 1 1 0 1

START
BIT D_0 D_1 D_2 D_3 D_4 D_5 D_6 PARITY STOP STOP
BIT=1 BIT BIT

NEXT
CHARACTER

(B) Example: Encoding ASCII letter Z.

Fig. 5-24. Serial transmission format.

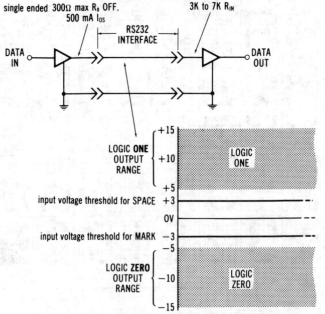

**Fig. 5-25. Electronic Industry Association (EIA) RS-232
serial transmission standard.**

There are hundreds of ways one may encode (format) bit information for storage on tape. The format for one popular pseudo-standard (the 300 Baud KIM standard) is shown in Fig. 5-26. The rate of the KIM-1 audio tape format is 135 bits/second, or 16 bytes/second. By decreasing the number of pulses in a bit period by one-third (one bit = 2.484 ms), we increase data rate to 50 bytes/second. The circuit to implement this format is shown in Fig. 5-27. The circuit uses a few lines of a VIA like a PIA, except that it contains a built-in timer circuit, and a serial data register. The other I/O pins of the VIA are used to control two cassette recorder motors (turn them on and off) and to provide a serial data link to an external terminal, if desired.

Note that in the KIM standard, 8-bit data is converted to 4-bit "nibbles" before it is stored. Also, note that we must

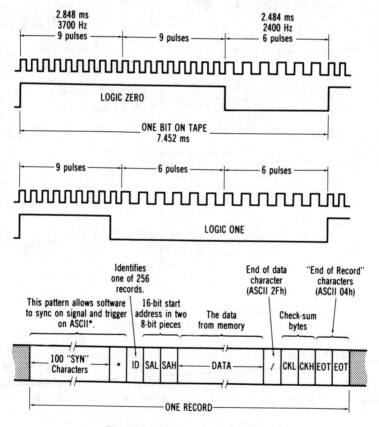

Fig. 5-26. KIM-1 audio tape format.

encode the data's 16-bit memory address* on the tape along with the data. This way when the tape is "read" we can put the data back in its original memory location.

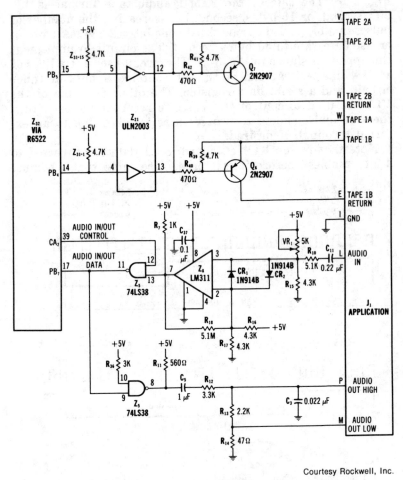

Fig. 5-27. Audio cassette recorder circuit using part of VIA (Versatile Interface Adapter).

As shown in Fig. 5-27, the VIA's control pin CA2 is used as an output to control the audio data direction. When CA2 is high it enables the audio input data from IC to be coupled to the PB-7 pin of the VIA, which is configured as an input. The

---

*Ending address of data doesn't need to be saved.

amplifier Z8 and its associated components provide wave shaping of the possibly noisy tape input signal.

To output data, the CA2 output is made low and this inhibits any noise on the input from mixing with the audio output data. Audio output is routed through PB-7 also, only this time the program sets it as an output. The remaining circuitry is used to control the recorders motors via transistors which open and close the power line of the motor.

chapter 6

PROGRAMMING

The computer's power as a machine lies in the fact that it can be "programmed" to perform various functions at the will of the user. This is the most distinct difference between the computer and any other sophisticated machine that has been created by man. In this chapter, we will learn what is meant by the term "program," and how one goes about writing (or designing) a program. We will work through some examples of commonly required programming techniques, and will discuss in detail the steps involved in writing a program.

EXECUTION OF A PROGRAM

We will begin by defining just what a program is. A *program* is a sequence of steps (or instructions) that must be performed in order for a desired process to be completed. A non-computer example of this is the steps necessary for the refinement of crude oil into gasoline. Mathematical examples are plentiful, such as the formula for determining the area of a circle: $A = \pi r^2$. The sequence of steps necessary for the solution of this formula is as follows:

1. Obtain a value for the radius r.
2. Square the value for the radius (or multiply it times itself).
3. Obtain a value for the constant π.
4. Multiply the squared radius (r^2) by the value for π.
5. Deliver the above product as the area A.

Now there are several ways to go about performing these steps, and as long as the same solution is found, the technique is not important. We intend here to illustrate the procedural nature of this step-by-step approach to problem solving. For each given radius, we must begin with Step 1 and proceed through Step 5 in order to have completed the job. Likewise, a program, stored in the memory of a computer, is a sequence of steps that direct the computer in its processing.

Programs in Memory

As we have learned, the computer is capable of executing only one instruction at a time, and it therefore requires a memory of some sort in which to store the complete set of instructions that make up the program. The amount of memory that is necessary to store the program depends on several factors pertaining to the complexity of the program and the amount of memory necessary to store data used by the program.

Execution of this program consists of taking one instruction at a time from the memory and performing the operation that it specifies. The program counter register (PC) is used by the CPU to step the program through execution, one instruction at a time. The PC usually contains the memory address of the instruction currently being executed. It is automatically incremented by the CPU just before the next instruction is fetched from the memory. The increment is added to the PC arithmetically, and its value reflects the size in words of the particular instruction that has just been executed. This increment varies between different CPUs, but the principle is the same. The normal sequence of executing instructions is to begin at low memory addresses and to proceed by adding positive increments to the PC, in order to step through the program which is arranged in ascending sequence in the memory.

Data in Memory

Various elements of data that are to be used by the program may also be stored in the memory. These may include such things as the value of π, used in the previous example. In order for the program to be able to use this numerical value, the memory location at which it is stored must be known by the program at the time that the value is needed. Another example of data in memory concerns the connection of some I/O device to the computer. Generally speaking, data that have been put in the computer are stored in the memory for future use by the program. In the case of complex I/O devices, where many words of data are being transferred at a fast rate, large blocks of memory may be reserved for storing these large amounts of data. Here again, the program must know exactly where this block is located in the memory and how large it is. The programmer must build these *data addresses* into the program, and he must make certain that all references to the data are consistent with these addresses.

Memory Map

Throughout this chapter, we will develop a program that performs a relatively simple task. That task is to move data stored in one area of memory into another area of memory. This is a very useful operation and is often required as a part of some greater processing goal. Fig. 6-1 shows a simple "map" of how the memory is to be allocated for this program.

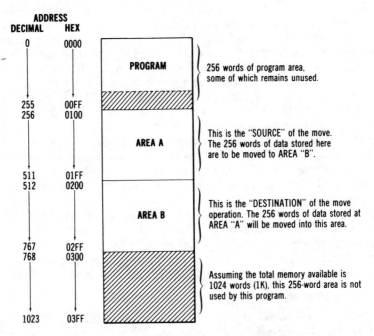

Fig. 6-1. Memory map for MOVE program.

For the purpose of illustration, we will be writing this program to operate on the Motorola MC6800 microprocessor, equipped with 1024 words (1K) of RAM memory. Keeping the development as simple as possible, without too many "bells and whistles," we should be able to get this program into 256 words of the memory. Using hardware, we will arrange it so that when the 6800 is reset, all registers including the program counter are set to zero; thus, the first executable instruction of the program must reside in memory location 1. The PC will be incremented just prior to fetching the instruction so that it points to the first word of the program. Although it is doubtful that we will use 256 words of memory for this program, we will allow some space in memory for expansion if desired.

There are two data areas, each 256 words in length. Our program will move data from area A into area B, one word at a time. Area A begins at memory location 256 (which is actually the 257th word of memory since the addresses start at 0) and extends through location 511. Area B begins at memory location 512 and extends through location 767. Memory locations 768 through 1023 are not used for any purpose by this program.

INSTRUCTION SET

The group of different instructions that a particular CPU is designed to execute is called its *instruction set*. Each manufacturer incorporates a slightly different instruction set into the CPU, according to the intended use of the product. Some are very simple, consisting of only a handful of instructions, while others are quite complex, with the total number of possible instructions ranging to several hundred. There are several different types of instructions, each having its own usefulness. The instructions are given names which are usually abbreviated in the form of some group of characters. Of course, inside the computer, these instructions are stored as binary 1's and 0's. An 8-bit instruction for adding two numbers might be 00101101. This is great for the computer, but it is a bit hard for programmers to remember, so the abbreviation *ADD* might be used in place of the binary code. These abbreviations of the instruction set are known as *mnemonics,* or the *operation codes,* of the instructions.

Just telling the computer to "ADD" is not quite enough. The computer must be told what to ADD, and what this is to be added to. This information is also considered as part of the instruction, and in fact is usually contained in another word (or words) of memory just following the actual operation code part of the instruction. There are exceptions to this as we shall see in the section on addressing modes, but, for the most part, each instruction must have a specified *operand*. This is the "who" that the "what" is to be done to.

Memory Access Instructions

In any instruction set, there are usually several instructions dealing with the operation of putting data into, or getting data out of, the memory. On the other end of this data transfer is usually some CPU register, most likely the accumulator, since this is where most of the "computing" is done. (See Fig. 6-2.) This operation can pertain to only one word of the memory at any given time, and therefore the operand part of the instruction will specify the address of the memory location that is to be affected by the instruction.

Memory access instructions include "LOAD" instructions, which are used to transfer data from the memory to some internal register. In some cases, when there is more than one register that can be loaded in this way, there will be different instructions for each register, with different binary bit patterns to designate the desired register.

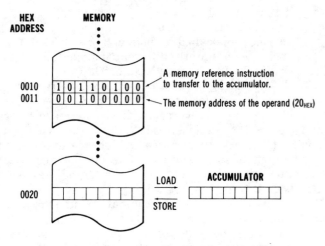

Fig. 6-2. Diagram of memory access instruction.

"STORE" instructions transfer data from some register in the CPU to a specific memory location. Again, where there are different registers that can be affected, the instruction will designate the desired register. The affected memory location can be designated in a number of ways (addressing modes) which will be discussed later in this chapter.

Arithmetic Instructions

The arithmetic instructions allow the program to control the ALU, causing the ALU to perform various types of arithmetic operations upon data stored in the accumulator register and in the memory. These operations are usually restricted to addition (Fig. 6-3) and subtraction in various forms, and only in the more advanced microcomputers will there be instructions for multiplication and division. As we shall see, these operations must be "programmed" by using the available set of instructions. Subtraction is often referred to as a "complement and add" instruction, since binary subtraction is accomplished by complementing the number and then adding, as shown in Appendix A.

In the usual situation involving arithmetic instructions, two numbers are operated on. Some CPUs require that both of these be resident in an internal register before the operation can be performed. The result of the arithmetic will end up in one of the two registers, thereby destroying the original contents. Other CPUs require that only one of the two numbers be resident in an internal register. The other number may be contained in a memory location specified by the operand of the instruction. The result of the arithmetic will be contained in the register after the operation is complete, and the contents of the memory location will remain unchanged.

The numerical values used in the execution of these arithmetic instruction are represented as signed binary numbers. Generally speaking, the sign (+ or −) is designated by the most significant bit of the data word. A 0 bit indicates a positive number, while a 1 bit indicates a negative number. The next seven bits in the word represent the binary equivalent of the numerical value. We can see that in seven bits we can represent a number no larger than 127. Therefore, in an 8-bit signed binary data word, we can represent numbers from −128 to +127.

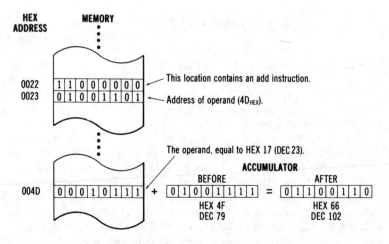

Fig. 6-3. Diagram of ADD instruction.

As positive and negative numbers are added and subtracted, the ALU automatically keeps track of the sign of the result. However, if the result of the arithmetic yields a number larger than +127, a processing error will occur, and the number will probably be mistaken by the computer for a negative number.

Logical and Shift Instructions

The ALU can also be controlled by the program to perform various types of "bit-manipulation" instructions. These are processed very similarly to the arithmetic instructions, in the sense that there must be data in an internal register, usually the accumulator. Shift instructions cause the contents of the accumulator to be shifted left or right in the register, bit by bit. This type of instruction does not access the memory at all but operates only on the contents of the accumulator. There are several good uses for this operation, one of which is that if we shift all the bits of a data word one bit to the left, we have in effect multiplied it by 2. (See Fig. 6-4.) Another use for this

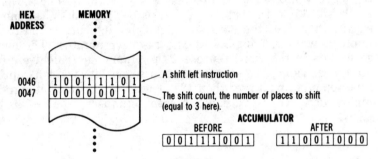

Fig. 6-4. Diagram of SHIFT LEFT instruction.

operation occurs when the program needs to determine which bits in a data word are 1's and which are 0's. If we start shifting the bits to the left, one at a time, every time a 1 bit ends up in the most significant bit of the accumulator, the word will look like a negative number. This condition can be used to tell the program whether the bit was a 1 or a 0.

The logical instructions provided by most microprocessors consist generally of the common logical operations AND, OR, and EOR. These require two operands, usually one in the accumulator and the other residing in some memory location. The standard approach here is that first one word of data is loaded into the accumulator and then the logical instruction is executed using the word from memory. The contents of the accumulator after the operation will contain the logical outcome, and the original contents will have been destroyed. The contents of the memory location are not altered by the logical operation. The truth tables for these instructions are shown in Fig. 6-5. The two data words are logically processed, one bit at a time.

These instructions are also useful in determining which bits of a given data word are 1's and which are 0's. For example, suppose we want to know if bit 4 of a word is set (equal to 1). We can load it into the accumulator and execute a logical AND instruction between it and a mask word that is set aside somewhere in memory and has bit 4 equal to 1 and all the other bits equal to 0's. If the desired bit is a 1, then the result in the accumulator will be the same as the mask word. If it is not a 1, the result in the accumulator will be all 0's.

AND TRUTH TABLE		
P	Q	PQ
1	1	1
1	0	0
0	1	0
0	0	0

OR TRUTH TABLE		
P	Q	P+Q
1	1	1
1	0	1
0	1	1
0	0	0

EOR TRUTH TABLE		
P	Q	P⊕Q
1	1	0
1	0	1
0	1	1
0	0	0

Fig. 6-5. Truth tables for AND, OR, and EOR instructions.

Register Manipulation Instructions

To facilitate the use of the various internal CPU registers by the program, there are instructions that perform operations on these registers. Most common are those instructions regarding the "index" or "pointer" registers. These are used for many purposes by the program. The programmer can assign them to be used for some general-purpose register, perhaps storing the address of some memory location that is accessed frequently. Some microprocessors dedicate one of these registers to contain the address of a special part of the program that is used to process an interrupt.

There are some instructions that allow the program to load a value into the desired register. These may be useful if there is something that needs to be done a fixed number of times by the program (such as read 80 characters from an input device). Here, the desired index register can be loaded with the value 80 and decremented (subtracted by one) each time a character is read. When the value in the index register is equal to zero, all 80 characters have been read.

Some instructions allow the program to store the contents of a given register in a location in memory. These offer the programmer the ability to save the contents of an index register while it is being used for some other temporary purpose, and then later restore it to its original value.

Certain microprocessors allow the program to access other registers besides the index registers, but they are exceptions. The National Semiconductor SC/MP has an "extension register," which is used similarly to the accumulator and is also used for the serial I/O port, as described in the section entitled "Input/Output Control."

There are some instructions that allow the program to exchange, or swap, two registers. This swap can be used to transfer the contents of the program counter to some index register for use at a later time. Since these are usually 16-bit registers in 8-bit processors, they generally must be manipulated in two parts, the most significant bits (MSBs) contained in one word and the least significant bits (LSBs) contained in another word.

Jump or Branch Instructions

Jump or branch instructions are capable of altering the program counter. This means that the program can "decide" which instruction to execute next, and need not always execute the very next instruction in the memory. The instruction may specify that a certain number of words be skipped over in the program and that execution be continued at some other address; or, an absolute memory address may be part of the JUMP instruction, telling the processor to jump to that address and resume execution.

These instructions give the programmer a great deal of flexibility in designing programs. If need be, the program can be made to jump ahead in the sequence of instructions, ignoring parts that do not pertain to a particular situation. The program can even be directed to jump back to some known point to repeat execution of instructions already executed.

In many cases, these jump or branch instructions must be accompanied by some necessary condition in order for the jump to occur. These conditions usually depend on the accumulator, which may be tested for several states, including positive, negative, odd, even, overflow, and carry conditions. The programmer may specify that the jump occur only if the result in the accumulator is a positive number, or perhaps the opposite. In this way, the program may be controlled by the results of various arithmetic operations involving the accumulator. This gives the programmer some real potential computing power, since what computers do best is impartially test for the existence of certain conditions and then invariably perform some desired process, based upon the test.

ADDRESSING MEMORY

Among the CPUs available today, the method used to address memory locations varies considerably in complexity. As we have seen, many of the instructions access the memory in order to store something there or to retrieve something previously stored. At the time that the instruction is being executed, the memory address of the location involved must be available to the CPU. This can be accomplished in many ways, depending on several factors, mainly the modes of addressing that are supported by the particular microprocessor in question. In this section, we will discuss some of the most popular forms of addressing memory.

Program-Counter Relative Addressing

This type of memory addressing allows the CPU to access words in memory that are located within a certain range of the

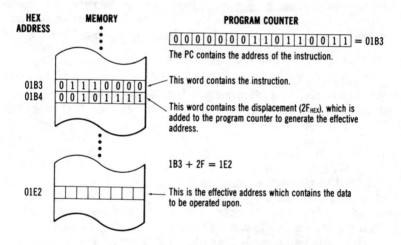

Fig. 6-6. Diagram of PC relative addressing.

current value in the program counter register. Since the PC contains the memory address of the instruction at execution time, the memory location being accessed by the instruction is within a certain range of the instruction itself. This range is generally limited by the word length of the microprocessor. The word directly following the instruction usually contains the displacement value which is added to the value in the PC to derive the effective address. (See Fig. 6-6.) This displacement can be positive, addressing memory locations with addresses larger than the address of the instruction, or it can be negative, addressing memory locations with addresses that are smaller than the instruction address. We can see that an 8-bit machine can accommodate displacement values of −128 to +127. This establishes the range about the PC value, within which the effective address must be.

The effective address is the address of the operand of the instruction. It is the contents of this address that are to be used during the execution of the instruction. This mode of addressing is useful for accessing memory locations that are close to the location of the instruction itself. Instructions using this mode of addressing will usually execute faster than other modes because only one memory access is necessary to load the displacement value into the CPU.

When the displacement is to be negative (that is, when the word to be addressed has an address that is smaller than the current value in the PC), the value of the displacement is stored in two's complement form. This data form is described in Appendix A, and the programmer should be familiar with its use, since many circumstances require a reference to a memory location with an address that is smaller than the address of the instruction currently being executed.

Pointer-Register Relative Addressing

Pointer-register relative addressing is very similar to PC relative addressing just described. The only exception is that a designated pointer register is used instead of the program counter to derive the effective address.

The displacement value is again stored in the word of memory directly following the word containing the instruction (Fig. 6-7). Its value can be either positive or negative, and it is added to the value stored in the designated pointer register at execution time to produce the effective address of the instruction. It is the contents of the memory location at the effective address that become the operand of the instruction.

This addressing mode is very useful in several ways. For one thing, the pointer register is usually a 16-bit register which can contain a value up to 65,535 in unsigned binary. This means that memory locations quite far away from the address of the instruction can be accessed. In fact, since the displacement value is still used in deriving the effective address, any memory location within the range of the displacement from the value in the pointer register can be accessed by the instruction.

Another benefit of this type of memory addressing is that the value in the pointer register can easily be modified by the program during execution. This means that the programmer need not know exact effective address at the time the program

268

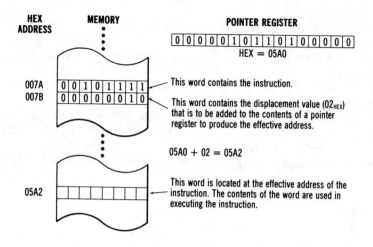

Fig. 6-7. Diagram of pointer-register relative addressing.

is written. However, the programmer must have some logical means for getting this information together at the time the instruction is to be executed, and for setting up the pointer register with the appropriate value.

Direct Addressing

In the direct addressing mode, the effective address is stored as an absolute binary number, usually occupying the two memory locations directly following the instruction itself. (See Fig. 6-8.) No program counter or pointer registers are involved.

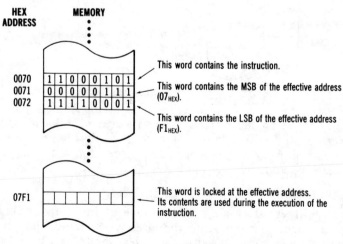

Fig. 6-8. Diagram of direct addressing.

The 8 most significant bits (MSBs) of the 16-bit effective address are stored in the word directly following the instruction, and the 8 least significant bits (LSBs) of the effective address are stored in the next word of memory. In some processors, such as the 8080, the order of these high and low address bytes are reversed.

This mode allows addressing any of 65,535 words of memory as the operand of the instruction. It is used mainly in situations where other modes are not sufficient. Memory locations can be accessed without regard for the limited range of a relative

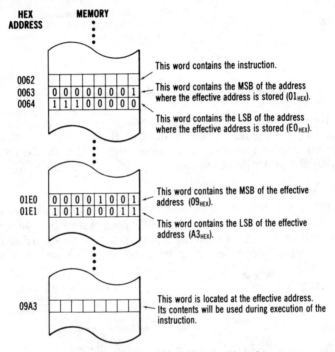

Fig. 6-9. Diagram of indirect addressing.

addressing mode, and also without requiring that a pointer register be set up and waiting. The only drawback to this mode of memory addressing is that it generally takes longer to execute, since two memory accesses are necessary just to acquire the effective address.

Indirect Addressing

The indirect addressing mode is one of the more sophisticated methods of generating the effective address. Not all of the microprocessors currently available offer this type of addressing. Its electronic support requirements are outside of the allowable cost effectiveness of some of the simpler CPUs, and it is mainly found in the more advanced general-purpose CPUs.

The unique feature of indirect addressing is that an intermediate step is involved. The operand of an instruction using this mode is an intermediate memory location that contains the actual effective address of the instruction. This intermediate address can be derived either by the PC or pointer-register relative displacement technique, or it can be defined "directly" as shown in Fig. 6-9. At this intermediate address is stored the effective address, usually occupying two memory locations: one for the MSB and the other for the LSB of the effective address. The CPU then proceeds to use this address and the data stored there during execution of the instruction.

The main advantage of this type of memory addressing is that the exact effective address of the instruction need not be known by the programmer at the time that the program is written. The address of the intermediate location is built into the instruction. Now, during execution of the program, the actual effective address may be determined by the program and placed in the intermediate memory location prior to the execution of the instruction.

The drawback here is, again, the fact that several memory accesses are necessary just to get the effective address into the CPU. These indirect instructions will take longer to execute than other types of memory addressing modes.

Immediate Addressing

Fig. 6-10 illustrates the immediate addressing mode. The operand address is also the effective address. The contents of the displacement word (which directly follows the instruction) are used as the operand for this type of instruction. No further memory accesses are necessary to complete execution of the instruction. Obviously, this type of addressing has many potential uses when a separate memory location for the data is not

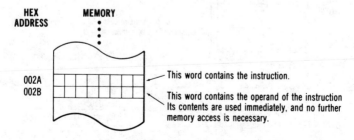

Fig. 6-10. Diagram of immediate addressing.

required. Because it requires no further memory accessing, this type of instruction usually has one of the fastest execution times.

Auto-Indexed Addressing

Auto-indexed addressing is basically the same as pointer-register addressing, but there is usually no displacement value in the word following the instruction. There is, however, one quite helpful variation on the pointer register principle. Whenever an instruction of this type is executed, the contents of the designated pointer register can be altered by some factor. The National Semiconductor SC/MP microprocessor is designed to use the value in the displacement word to alter the designated pointer register. If the value of the displacement is positive, it is added to the value in the pointer register after the memory fetch has been made. If the value of the displacement is negative, it is subtracted from the value in the pointer register before the memory fetch is made.

This feature is very useful when there are large areas of data stored sequentially in the memory that must all be operated upon by the program. (See Fig. 6-11.) A pointer register

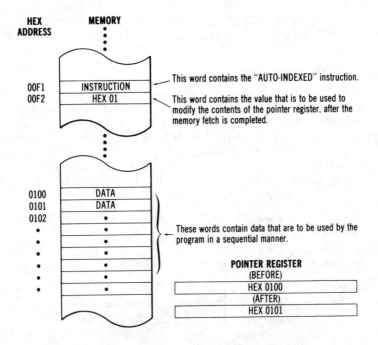

Fig. 6-11. Diagram of auto-indexed addressing.

can be set up to contain the memory address of the first word in the data area (lower memory address). The displacement word of the instruction that is to fetch these data words from the memory is set up to contain a binary 1. Each time this instruction is executed during the course of the program, the value in the pointer register will be incremented by 1 directly after the data are fetched. Thus, the next time the instruction is executed, the pointer register will contain the address of the next data word in the area.

Going one step further, the programmer should be aware that any value can be used as the increment if it is stored in the displacement word of the instruction. If this value were equal to 2 in the previous example, then every other data word in the area would be processed by the program as it was worked through.

INPUT/OUTPUT CONTROL

Input/output control refers to any situation in which the program has to execute instructions as part of a data transfer to or from a device. Most computer systems incorporate some sort of input/output device in order to interface the computer with the "real world." This may be as simple as a hex keyboard and LED display, or as complex as an ASCII keyboard and video display module. In any case, there will most likely be a need to control these devices at the will of the program.

There are two popular forms of I/O control: the *bus* type and the *instruction* type. Bus I/O is used as though the I/O device were just another memory location. In fact, the I/O interface is directly connected to the address and data busses, and is wired to respond to accesses of certain memory addresses. Instruction-type I/O control is accomplished through the use of special I/O instructions in the instruction set. These instructions access the I/O bus, which is not the same as any of the busses to which memory is connected. Input/output operations are conducted independently of the memory.

Both types of I/O control are useful to the programmer. We will look at an example of each, stressing the programming ramifications.

I/O on the Memory Bus

This I/O configuration utilizes the Motorola MC6800 microprocessor and the peripheral interface adapter (PIA). The I/O devices connected to the system include an ASCII keyboard and a video display module. Fig. 6-12 illustrates this input/output configuration.

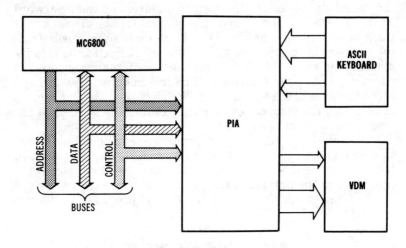

Fig. 6-12. I/O on the memory bus.

The PIA is an I/O interface that will control two devices. It is connected directly to the memory busses, at a special address. To operate the I/O devices, the program accesses this special address, and the PIA buffer becomes available to the program.

The input operation involves the receiving of characters from the ASCII keyboard. When a key is depressed, the PIA interrupts the processor and tells it that there is a character in the keyboard buffer. The program currently being executed must be put aside momentarily, and a JUMP instruction must be executed. The JUMP instruction goes to a series of instructions that will get the word containing the key-press information from the PIA buffer and put it into a CPU register. From there, it can be operated upon immediately, or it can be stored in a memory location until some later time. Once this has been done, the processor again resumes execution at the point in the original program where it was interrupted. This sequence of events occurs every time that a key is pressed, so the program instructions used to process this I/O operation must always be stored in the memory at some known location. These instructions are relatively simple for this example, since the PIA is treated just as if it were a memory location. When the character is ready to be read into the computer, the program simply executes a LOAD instruction, which transfers the contents of the PIA buffer into a CPU register.

The output operation involves transferring ASCII characters from the CPU to the video display module. We will assume that this vdm has its own internal memory in which the several hundred characters displayed on the screen are stored. The characters to be displayed on the screen are transferred, one at a time, to the PIA. This also can be accomplished with a simple STORE instruction, which addresses the special memory locations occupied by the PIA registers.

Special Instructions for I/O

This example of special instruction I/O uses the National Semiconductor SC/MP microprocessor. The I/O device is a Teletype keyboard and printer, in the conventional current loop with the Teletype control interface (Fig. 6-13). The actual entry into the CPU is done through the use of the special extension register inside the SC/MP. The MSB and LSB are connected directly to pins on the chip package. This register is controlled by special instructions in the program.

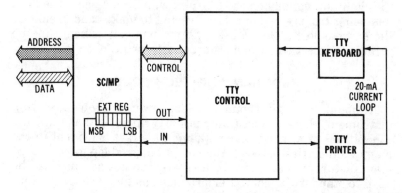

Fig. 6-13. Special I/O bus.

Bearing in mind that Teletype is a serial code, with the bits being transferred one at a time, notice in Fig. 6-13 that the Teletype control unit is connected to the serial I/O pins on the SC/MP. When a serial I/O instruction is executed, the logic level on the IN pin is transferred to the MSB of the extension register and the LSB of the same register is transferred to the OUT pin. All the other bits in the register are shifted one bit to the right.

The Teletype control unit must signal the processor when each of the data bits is present on the input pin. The program in midexecution is interrupted, and a jump is forced to the area of the program that is designed to process the I/O. The special serial I/O instruction is used to capture the bit and to shift it into the extension register in the CPU. After a certain num-

275

ber of bits have been read into the computer in this manner, the bit pattern in the extension register will be a representation of one character of input data.

For output operations, a character of the data to be output is loaded into the extension register. Then, through a time-delayed looping program, the serial I/O instruction is used to shift the bits out to the Teletype controller one at a time, at the correct rate of speed. The programmer would probably write the necessary instructions into a subroutine that could be used over and over to process the I/O. This subroutine could be incorporated in several programs for controlling the Teletype I/O.

A word about the Teletype controller. It is an interface that is in series with the 20-milliampere current loop, common to Teletype operation. The making and breaking of this current loop, which is used to encode each character, is converted to a changing voltage signal and applied to the IN pin. Likewise, the changing voltage on the OUT pin, which represents the data bits being transferred out, is converted to makes and breaks of the current loop. This causes the mechanical elements in the printer to select the proper character to print.

PROGRAMMING TECHNIQUES

Although the digital computer is a powerful problem-solving instrument, there are certain rules or principles that limit the capabilities of any digital computer. This fact is evident in the many similarities between the computer products of different manufacturers. These similarities are due not so much to the wish to standardize computer products, as they are to the limitations of the binary logic system.

For this reason, there are many instances where the programming method used to achieve some desired processing goal is precluded by the hardware features of the particular CPU. Such a simple operation as the addition of two numbers requires that the two numbers to be added first be identified (usually by memory addresses specifying the memory locations in which the numbers are stored). Next, one of the numbers must be loaded into a CPU register available to the ALU. The other number must also be made available to the ALU. This can be done with certain microprocessors by specifying its memory location address as the operand of the ADD instruction. Other processors require that both numbers be loaded into two separate CPU registers before the ADD can take place. Once the arithmetic has been accomplished, the result is usually present in some CPU register, and it may either be used in another arithmetic instruction directly following or be stored in a specified memory location for future use.

Other, more complex operations also will be found to follow certain procedural rules demanded by the binary processing approach. We will examine three of the most common programming techniques in terms of their procedural requirements, and not in consideration of any given manufacturer's product. The emphasis will be upon the step-by-step approach to achieve the processing goal, rather than on actual instructions for any particular CPU.

Iteration

Many times in the course of executing a program it becomes necessary to repeat a particular operation several times. This repeating process is known as *iteration*. It is a very common programming technique and can be implemented in a number of ways. The basic goal of iteration is to cause something to occur for a given number of times, or until some other condition is met. This technique can be used for counting events or for generating sequences of memory address for accessing large tables of information.

There are four general steps to the iteration process:

1. Initialize the counter. This initial condition is usually a word in memory or in a general-purpose register in the CPU. Either the counter can be initialized to zero and added to until some desired value is reached, or it can be initialized to the value and subtracted from until zero is reached.
2. Increment (or decrement) the counter each time that the process to be iterated is executed.
3. Test the counter each time the iterative process is completed, to see if it has reached the desired number.
4. Go back to the beginning of the iterative process if the desired number has not been reached.

Processing of this type is often called *looping*, since the same sequence of instructions is executed several times under the management of the counter. The program "loops" back to the beginning until the desired value is reached by the counter (Fig. 6-14).

The iteration process is useful when many elements of data are to be subjected to the same processing. These data may be read from some input device, one element at a time, or they may all be stored in the memory in sequential locations. Here, an internal CPU general-purpose register would probably be used for the counter. This could be initialized to the address

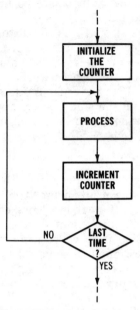

Fig. 6-14. Flowchart of the iteration process.

of the lowest memory location that contained the data, and incremented by one until the last memory location containing data had been processed.

Multiplication

Although some of the more powerful microcomputers have a "built-in" hardware multiplication circuit in their ALU, most multiplication is still performed by software. The program is actually a sequence of steps designed to perform the multiplication according to a binary algorithm. (The term *algorithm* is really synonymous with "procedure" and implies that the desired operation must be done in small steps leading toward the end product.)

The first step is to choose a multiplication algorithm that can be suitably programmed to provide all the requirements of the application. One most important consideration is that the "product" of the two numbers multiplied together will have as many digits as the sum of the digits of the two numbers. (Zeros may occur on the left-hand side.) Also, the magnitude of the product of the two numbers may easily exceed the range of an 8-bit data word, and it may be necessary to write a more complex program, using two words to store each of the numbers. Furthermore, we must consider the requirements that are necessary for keeping track of the sign (+ or −) of the product.

Clearly, we can see that this "simple" task of multiplying two numbers, using software, can get quite complex. We will therefore discuss the concept within a limited set of rules.

1. The multiplicand and the multiplier will always be positive numbers.
2. The numeric value of the multiplicand and the multiplier shall not exceed 15_{DEC} (1111_{BIN}), and therefore may be stored in only 4 bits.

Now, the multiplication algorithm that we will use is stated below.

(1) Test the least significant bit (LSB) of the multiplier for 1 or 0.
    (a) If it is 1, add the multiplicand to the result (initialized to zero). Then go to (2).
    (b) If it is 0, go to (2).
(2) Shift the multiplicand to the left, one bit.
(3) Shift the multiplier to the right, one bit, and go back to (1).

A simplified flowchart of this procedure is shown in Fig. 6-15.

Let's go through an example of the use of the algorithm, using the problem $9 \times 11 = 99$.

R = 00000000   First we must initialize the result to zero.

MC = 00001011   The multiplicand, 11_{DEC}.

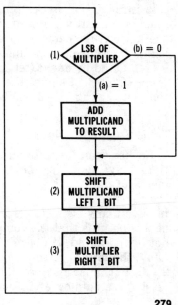

Fig. 6-15. Simple flowchart of binary multiplication algorithm.

MP = 00001001   The multiplier, 9_{DEC}.
R   = 00001011   LSB = 1; add multiplicand to result, 11_{DEC}.
MC = 00010110   Shift multiplicand left one bit, 22_{DEC}.
MP = 00000100   Shift multiplier right one bit, 4_{DEC}.
                LSB = 0.
MC = 00101100   Shift multiplicand left one bit, 44_{DEC}.
MP = 00000010   Shift multiplier right one bit, 2_{DEC}.
                LSB = 0.
MC = 01011000   Shift multiplicand left one bit, 88_{DEC}.
MP = 00000001   Shift multiplier right one bit, 1_{DEC}.
R   = 01100011   LSB = 1; add multiplicand to result, 99_{DEC}.

There are a few more steps that must be added to the algorithm if it is to be programmed for execution by a computer. First of all, the multiplicand and the multiplier must be located at some specific address in memory. There must also be a designated memory location in which the result (product of the multiplication) is to be stored. The reader may also have observed that the very first thing that has to be done is to initialize the result to zero. Then, each time that the LSB of the multiplier is 1, the multiplicand is added to the result, until the last bit of the multiplier has been tested. This introduces an interesting question: How will the computer know when the last multiplier bit has been tested? The program must supply this information by keeping track of which bit of the multiplier is currently being examined. To accomplish this, we may use a word in memory to store the number of the bit (NB) being examined. This must be initialized to one, and then be incremented by one, after each bit is tested, until it is equal to four, which will signal the program that the multiplication is completed. Fig. 6-16 shows an expanded flowchart of the program.

Table Search Routines

Rather than involving a lot of data, some computer applications may involve a complex process that uses only a few elements of data during execution. Others, especially those relating to some sort of data processing operation, will most likely involve many elements of data. One thing we must remember at this point is that the computer, though having memory, does not have a mind. It doesn't know how to spell nor does it even know the letters of the English alphabet. It can be told to add 2 + 2, but must also be told what "2" is. This almost constant need for a catalog of information is filled by a programming

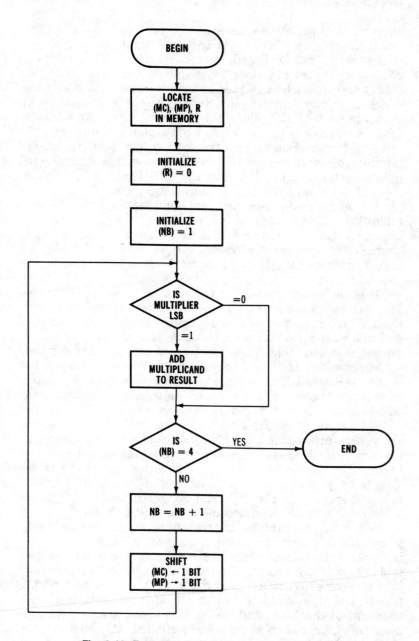

Fig. 6-16. Expanded flowchart of multiplication program.

technique known as *data tables* and the related *table search routines*.

As an example, a data table may be used in a computer system employing an ASCII keyboard as an input device. As a key is depressed, the keyboard interface encodes it into binary code. Once transferred into the memory of the computer, the binary code must be analyzed by some program to determine which character it represents. In doing so, the program may scan a table of all the possible characters, comparing each one to the character that was input, until a match occurs.

To carry the example one step further, consider the following. Suppose that part of the processing required that the input character be converted from the ASCII code to some other form of character encoding, such as Baudot (the old-style five-level Teletype code). For this, we could set up a second data table that would contain all of the Baudot character codes in the same sequence as the ASCII table. Then, when the input character was matched with an entry in the ASCII table, the corresponding entry in the Baudot table would provide the converted code.

These tables are usually in the form of areas of the memory that incorporate any number of sequential memory locations. Then, accessing of these memory locations can be controlled by a register in the CPU which "points" to the particular entry in the table. This register can then be incremented, or decremented, as it is used with instructions in the pointer register relative addressing mode. Of course, if there are going to be several tables used in conjunction with one another, there will have to be several registers to manage them.

Tables of this type are known as *sequential access* tables because they are usable only by starting at the beginning (or low-order end of the table) and proceeding through the entries in an ascending sequence to the high-order end of the table. This technique is quite adequate as long as the size of the table is kept fairly small. The computing time required to fully scan a large table would soon become a detriment to the operation of the overall program. In this regard, there are "faster" table search routines that don't have to start at the beginning of the table but can start at some likely point in the middle of the table. This likely point must be determined by the program based on some predefined rules regarding the information that is to be stored in the table. The details of these routines exceed the scope of this book, and the reader should, at this point, be aware of their existence and their usefulness. At this time, we shall remain with the sequential search technique as used for the ASCII to Baudot conversion.

As shown in Fig. 6-17, there are two tables in memory. One contains the characters of the alphabet in ASCII code, while the other contains the same alphabet in Baudot code. Once the input character has been read and is ready to be converted, the routine begins with the initializing of address pointers A and B. Pointer A is set to the memory address that contains the first entry of the ASCII table. According to the memory map shown in the illustration, this would be a hexadecimal value of 0120. Also, the B pointer is set equal to the memory address that contains the first entry of the Baudot table. This would be the hexadecimal value of 0190. The next step, then, is to compare the input character with the first entry in the ASCII table, to determine if they do match. If the two characters do not match, then the program must determine if the end of the table has been reached. This can be accomplished by comparing the A pointer register value to the address that represents the last entry in the table. This, according to the memory map, is

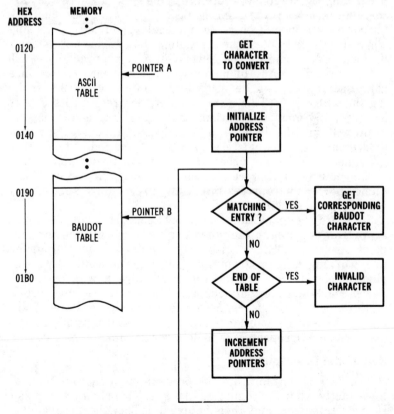

Fig. 6-17. Flowchart and memory map for table searching.

the hexadecimal value 0140. If the A pointer register does not contain this value, then the end of the table has not yet been reached, and both the A and B pointer registers are incremented by one. This will make them "point" at the next entry in the tables. The program then goes back to compare the input character with the next table entry, and so on, until either a match is found or the end of the table is reached. If the end of the table is reached and no match has been found, then the input character must then be an invalid ASCII character and some provision must be made for the program to handle this situation.

Notice that here we have not only an example of table searching, but also another example of the iteration process.

WRITING A PROGRAM

Regardless of the particular computer being used, or the programming language, there are some general ideas that are common to most programming tasks. In some cases, the programming task may become noticeably difficult, especially when the upper limit of the computer's features is approached. For example, some of the lower-power microprocessors will only allow addressing of memory locations that are within a rather small range of the location of the instruction that is doing the addressing. This means that if the program itself is to be large, any memory locations that contain data for the program will most likely have to be addressed through the use of a hardware pointer register (a premium commodity to the programmer). This same program task, when programmed on a higher-power microprocessor, can be done with ease. These higher-power microprocessors allow direct addressing of any word in a memory up to 64K.

So, there are many differences between the approaches that a programmer might use when dealing with a high-, or low-power processor. However, if we were to observe a programmer working at a programming job, we would not always be able to tell whether the job was for a high-power, or a low-power machine. There are certain things that need to be done, and in a definite sequence, no matter what the machine. These are what we will explore in this section as we program a Motorola MC6800 microprocessor to do a very simple task.

Sequential Description

The very first thing that the programmer must do is to define exactly what the computer's task is. This should begin as a simple statement, and then be expanded as the programmer develops the approach. For our example program, we will define its purpose:

> To MOVE the contents of one area of memory into another area of memory.

Of course, these areas of memory have been designated for the storage of some sort of data. The object of our program is to create an exact duplicate of the first area and place it in the other area of memory. At this point we should recall the discussion regarding the memory map. Fig. 6-18 is a duplicate of the memory map that pertains to this programming job.

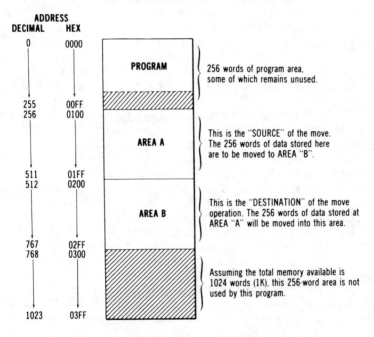

Fig. 6-18. Memory map for MOVE program.

Recall that this MOVE program is going to be written for execution on a Motorola MC6800 microprocessor equipped with 1K of read/write memory. As we see in the memory map, the first 256 words of the 1K memory are reserved for the program itself. The second 256 words of the memory are allocated for the A area. This is the "origin" of the MOVE operation. It consists of the data that are to be moved into the B area, or "destination." The B area is located in the third block of 256 words in the 1K memory. The fourth block of 256 words is not used by this program.

Now we know where everything is located in the memory, and we have a general idea of what the program is to do. At this point, we can become more specific. We begin with a list of the basic operations that must occur in order to realize the defined purpose of the program. This list would start as follows:

1. LOAD a word from area A into the accumulator.
2. STORE the word in area B.
3. END after doing these steps 256 times.

Here we have the three most basic elements of this program. We can see from this list that we are going to be using "memory access" instructions to LOAD and STORE these words. These instructions require that the operand (the object of the action of the instruction) be defined as a memory address at the time the instruction is to be executed. Therefore, we will need to keep track of memory addresses for both the A and B areas.

The easiest way to fulfill this requirement is to make use of the MC6800's extended addressing mode. In this mode, the operand address is specified in the two words immediately following the word in the program that contains the instruction. So, the two words directly following the LOAD instruction will specify the address of the A area word to be loaded into the accumulator. Likewise, the two words directly following the STORE instruction will specify the address of the word in area B that is to receive the contents of the accumulator. Since these words following the instructions can be treated as just another memory location, they too can be modified during the execution of the program, so that the address that they specify can be changed. Each time that a word is transferred from area A into area B, the program must also modify these addresses by adding one, thereby "pointing" them to the next word in both areas.

Another consideration at this time is how to determine when the full 256 words have been moved and when it is time for the program to end. This brings back our old friend, "iteration." We will need to initialize a counter of some sort, increment it each time a word is moved, and test it to see if the total 256 words have been moved. For this, we can also use just another word of memory. It will be initialized to zero before the program begins and then incremented by one each time that a word of data is moved from area A into area B. Since the MC6800 is an 8-bit device, the largest unsigned binary number that can be stored in one word is 255. If this value is incremented, as it will be after the last data word has been moved, all the bits of the word will be cleared to zero, and the zero condition bit in the status register will be set to one. So, to test the counter to determine when the last data word has been moved, we need only test for all zeros, which will indicate that the counter has just been incremented from 255 to 256. When this occurs, the move operation will be complete, and the program can be ended with a HALT instruction.

Now, we can expand the sequential description further as in the following:

1. CLEAR the counter to zero.
2. LOAD (extended) a word from area A into the accumulator.
3. STORE (extended) the word in area B.
4. INCREMENT the counter by one.
5. TEST the counter. If zero, GO TO (8).
6. INCREMENT area A address and area B address.
7. GO TO (2).
8. HALT.

There is one last thing to consider. The extended-mode LOAD and STORE instructions that transfer the data from the A area to the B area find the operand memory address contained in the two words immediately following the instruction in the program. The first of these words contains the most significant bits (MSBs) of the memory address, and the second word contains the least significant bits (LSBs) of the address. The two words, linked together, form a 16-bit unsigned binary number, which is the absolute address of the operand. In order to increment these addresses, a one is added to the second word of the pair (LSB). Now, at some point, this second word may possibly contain all 1 bits (255_{DEC}). If we add a one to this word, it will result in an arithmetic carry, clearing all the bits in the word to zero and setting the zero condition bit in the status register. At this point, we must now increment the first word of the address pair that contains the most significant bits (MSBs). It is obvious that incrementing the addresses will require several instructions. At this time the sequential description appears as follows:

1. CLEAR the counter to zero.
2. LOAD (extended) a word from area A into the accumulator.
3. STORE (extended) the word in area B.
4. INCREMENT the counter by one.
5. TEST the counter. If zero, GO TO (13).
6. INCREMENT the LSB of the area A address.

7. TEST the LSB portion. If not zero, GO TO (9).
8. INCREMENT the MSB portion of the area A address.
9. INCREMENT the LSB of the area B address.
10. TEST the LSB portion. If not zero, GO TO (2).
11. INCREMENT the MSB portion of the area B address.
12. GO TO (2).
13. HALT.

Note here that this program has been designed for the sake of illustration of the programming steps. The beginning A and B area addresses will be "built into" the LOAD and STORE instructions as we hand-assemble the program later in this section. After the program has finished execution, the processor will simply stop. This is not the usual method of programming a computer, since most computers are not dedicated solely to such simple tasks as moving data from one place in the memory to another.

Flowcharting

Flowcharting is the most often neglected element of the programming task. By the time the programmer has come this far in the development of the program, he does not really need a flowchart to know what his program is doing. The designer of a program is so intimately involved with the program that he knows all the "ins and outs" and the "whys and wherefores" of every instruction. What most programmers fail to think about is that perhaps someday in the future, some other programmer will have to sit down and try to figure out how the program works.

This, then, is the primary reason for flowcharting: to document the logical operation of the program in a way that can be understood by any programmer. This can save great amounts of time and trouble if for some reason the program is inherited by a programmer unfamiliar with it.

Some would argue that this is not the time to draw a flowchart of the program, since subsequent testing of the program might reveal a logic error which would necessitate the modification of the program. They might say that it would be better to wait until the program had been thoroughly checked out and tested before the flowchart was drawn. This sounds great, except for the inevitable situation in which the programmer is halfway finished with a program, and suddenly disappears in search of more money, a bigger computer, more important assignments, and so on.

So, at least a rough flowchart should be drawn at this time. It doesn't have to be a work of art, but it should be neat and

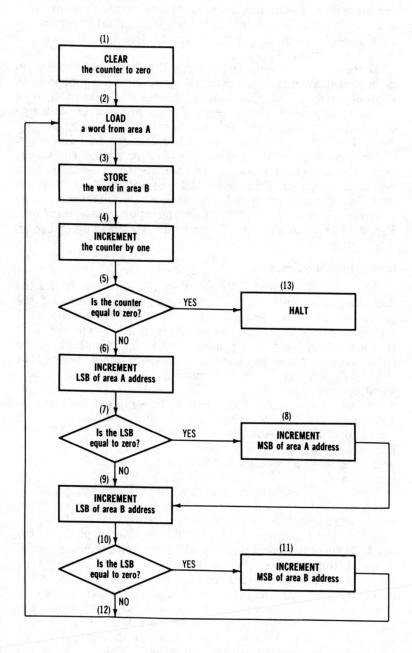

Fig 6-19. Flowchart of the MOVE program.

readable and of course disclose any parts of the program that may not be readily noticed. Later, after the final program has been accepted, a final flowchart can be drawn to replace this working drawing.

There are really only two shapes that are predominant in flowchart drawings. The rectangle represents some process to be done by the CPU. The diamond represents a decision to be made, usually based on the result of some process. The outcome of the decision may result in the rerouting of the program, indicated by the arrows connecting the rectangles and diamonds. Some sort of description should be written inside (or alongside) the flowchart elements to indicate the operation they represent. Also, since the sequential description of the program will already have numbered steps, these same numbers can be transcribed onto the flowchart in the appropriate positions. Fig. 6-19 is a flowchart of the program which is described in this section.

Instruction Sequence

By using the sequential description of the program and the flowchart drawing to help visualize the overall nature of the program, we can determine the actual CPU instructions. Of course, we have had these instructions in mind ever since we first started to design the program. The fact that the MC6800 CPU accommodates an extended addressing mode means that the two data areas can be addressed through the use of a two-word operand that follows the instructions. The MC6800 instruction set also offers increment and decrement instructions (INC and DEC), making the task of maintaining a counter a simple one. Finally, the basic arithmetic logic of the MC6800 led to the "testing for zero" concept used in incrementing the area addresses, as well as in determining when 256 words had been moved.

Next we will use the information provided by the manufacturer. This information describes each of the instructions from a hardware standpoint. Fig. 6-20 is a reproduction of the Instruction Set Summary card provided by Motorola Corp. for the MC6800 chip. Using this, we will construct the basic framework of the program. We will begin by writing down the mnemonics (abbreviations) for each of the instructions, in the order that they are to executed. Realizing that each instruction must have some sort of operand, we will also write in a name designating the object of the operation. Also, for each instruction, we will write a short description (similar to the sequential description) of the operation which is performed in the computer.

As an example, we will now work through Table 6-1, one step at a time, while using the sequential description as a guide and the Instruction Set Summary card. Observe the following: First, at Step (1) we must clear the counter to zero. This counter is to be a word in memory, located near the program. Its actual address can be determined later, so for now we will use the CLR instruction with a symbolic operand called COUNTER. This instruction will set all the bits in the operand to 0.

In Step (2), we must load a word from the A area into the accumulator. We decided to use the extended addressing mode, which will specify the address of the operand in the two words

Table 6-1. Instruction Sequence for the MOVE Program

Step	Label	Mnemonic	Operand	Description
1		CLR	COUNTER	Clear the counter to zero
2	MOVE	LDAA	AREAA	Load accumulator A with a word from data area A
3		STAA	AREAB	Store accumulator A in a word in data area B
4		INC	COUNTER	Increment the counter by one
5		BEQ	HALT	Branch to HALT if counter became zero
6		INC	LSBA	Increment the LSB of the address for data area A by one
7		BNE	INCB	Branch if not equal to zero to increment area B address
8		INC	MSBA	Increment the MSB of the A area address
9	INCB	INC	LSBB	Increment the LSB of the address for data area B by one
10		BNE	MOVE	Branch if not equal to zero to MOVE another word
11		INC	MSBB	Otherwise, increment MSB of B area address
12		BRA	MOVE	Then branch always to MOVE another word
13	HALT	WAI		This is the HALT for the program

immediately following the instruction word. Again, the actual address will be worked out later. Since the MC6800 has two accumulators, we will elect to use the A accumulator only. Looking at the Instruction Set Summary card, we find that the instruction we wish to use is called LDAA. For now, we will

ACCUMULATOR AND MEMORY OPERATIONS	MNEMONIC	IMMED			DIRECT			INDEX			EXTND			INHER			BOOLEAN/ARITHMETIC OPERATION (All register labels refer to contents)	COND. CODE REG.					
		OP	~	#	OP	~	#	OP	~	#	OP	~	#	OP	~	#		5 H	4 I	3 N	2 Z	1 V	0 C
Add	ADDA	8B	2	2	9B	3	2	AB	5	2	BB	4	3				$A+M \to A$	↕	●	↕	↕	↕	↕
	ADDB	CB	2	2	DB	3	2	EB	5	2	FB	4	3				$B+M \to B$	↕	●	↕	↕	↕	↕
Add Acmltrs	ABA													1B	2	1	$A+B \to A$	↕	●	↕	↕	↕	↕
Add with Carry	ADCA	89	2	2	99	3	2	A9	5	2	B9	4	3				$A+M+C \to A$	↕	●	↕	↕	↕	↕
	ADCB	C9	2	2	D9	3	2	E9	5	2	F9	4	3				$B+M+C \to B$	↕	●	↕	↕	↕	↕
And	ANDA	84	2	2	94	3	2	A4	5	2	B4	4	3				$A \cdot M \to A$	●	●	↕	↕	R	●
	ANDB	C4	2	2	D4	3	2	E4	5	2	F4	4	3				$B \cdot M \to B$	●	●	↕	↕	R	●
Bit Test	BITA	85	2	2	95	3	2	A5	5	2	B5	4	3				$A \cdot M$	●	●	↕	↕	R	●
	BITB	C5	2	2	D5	3	2	E5	5	2	F5	4	3				$B \cdot M$	●	●	↕	↕	R	●
Clear	CLR							6F	7	2	7F	6	3				$00 \to M$	●	●	R	S	R	R
	CLRA													4F	2	1	$00 \to A$	●	●	R	S	R	R
	CLRB													5F	2	1	$00 \to B$	●	●	R	S	R	R
Compare	CMPA	81	2	2	91	3	2	A1	5	2	B1	4	3				$A-M$	●	●	↕	↕	↕	↕
	CMPB	C1	2	2	D1	3	2	E1	5	2	F1	4	3				$B-M$	●	●	↕	↕	↕	↕
Compare Acmltrs	CBA													11	2	1	$A-B$	●	●	↕	↕	↕	↕
Complement, 1's	COM							63	7	2	73	6	3				$\bar{M} \to M$	●	●	↕	↕	R	S
	COMA													43	2	1	$\bar{A} \to A$	●	●	↕	↕	R	S
	COMB													53	2	1	$\bar{B} \to B$	●	●	↕	↕	R	S
Complement, 2's (Negate)	NEG							60	7	2	70	6	3				$00-M \to M$	●	●	↕	↕	①	②
	NEGA													40	2	1	$00-A \to A$	●	●	↕	↕	①	②
	NEGB													50	2	1	$00-B \to B$	●	●	↕	↕	①	②
Decimal Adjust, A	DAA													19	2	1	Converts Binary Add of BCD Characters into BCD Format	●	●	↕	↕	↕	③
Decrement	DEC							6A	7	2	7A	6	3				$M-1 \to M$	●	●	↕	↕	④	●
	DECA													4A	2	1	$A-1 \to A$	●	●	↕	↕	④	●
	DECB													5A	2	1	$B-1 \to B$	●	●	↕	↕	④	●
Exclusive OR	EORA	88	2	2	98	3	2	A8	5	2	B8	4	3				$A \oplus M \to A$	●	●	↕	↕	R	●
	EORB	C8	2	2	D8	3	2	E8	5	2	F8	4	3				$B \oplus M \to B$	●	●	↕	↕	R	●
Increment	INC							6C	7	2	7C	6	3				$M+1 \to M$	●	●	↕	↕	⑤	●
	INCA													4C	2	1	$A+1 \to A$	●	●	↕	↕	⑤	●
	INCB													5C	2	1	$B+1 \to B$	●	●	↕	↕	⑤	●
Load Acmltr	LDAA	86	2	2	96	3	2	A6	5	2	B6	4	3				$M \to A$	●	●	↕	↕	R	●
	LDAB	C6	2	2	D6	3	2	E6	5	2	F6	4	3				$M \to B$	●	●	↕	↕	R	●
Or, Inclusive	ORAA	8A	2	2	9A	3	2	AA	5	2	BA	4	3				$A+M \to A$	●	●	↕	↕	R	●
	ORAB	CA	2	2	DA	3	2	EA	5	2	FA	4	3				$B+M \to B$	●	●	↕	↕	R	●
Push Data	PSHA													36	4	1	$A \to M_{SP}, SP-1 \to SP$	●	●	●	●	●	●
	PSHB													37	4	1	$B \to M_{SP}, SP-1 \to SP$	●	●	●	●	●	●
Pull Data	PULA													32	4	1	$SP+1 \to SP, M_{SP} \to A$	●	●	●	●	●	●
	PULB													33	4	1	$SP+1 \to SP, M_{SP} \to B$	●	●	●	●	●	●
Rotate Left	ROL							69	7	2	79	6	3				M	●	●	↕	↕	⑥	↕
	ROLA													49	2	1	A 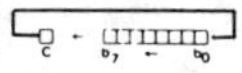	●	●	↕	↕	⑥	↕
	ROLB													59	2	1	B	●	●	↕	↕	⑥	↕
Rotate Right	ROR							66	7	2	76	6	3				M	●	●	↕	↕	⑥	↕
	RORA													46	2	1	A 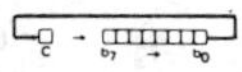	●	●	↕	↕	⑥	↕
	RORB													56	2	1	B	●	●	↕	↕	⑥	↕
Shift Left, Arithmetic	ASL							68	7	2	78	6	3				M	●	●	↕	↕	⑥	↕
	ASLA													48	2	1	A 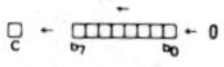	●	●	↕	↕	⑥	↕
	ASLB													58	2	1	B	●	●	↕	↕	⑥	↕
Shift Right, Arithmetic	ASR							67	7	2	77	6	3				M	●	●	↕	↕	⑥	↕
	ASRA													47	2	1	A 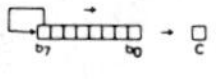	●	●	↕	↕	⑥	↕
	ASRB													57	2	1	B	●	●	↕	↕	⑥	↕
Shift Right, Logic	LSR							64	7	2	74	6	3				M	●	●	R	↕	⑥	↕
	LSRA													44	2	1	A 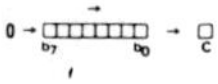	●	●	R	↕	⑥	↕
	LSRB													54	2	1	B	●	●	R	↕	⑥	↕
Store Acmltr.	STAA				97	4	2	A7	6	2	B7	5	3				$A \to M$	●	●	↕	↕	R	●
	STAB				D7	4	2	E7	6	2	F7	5	3				$B \to M$	●	●	↕	↕	R	●
Subtract	SUBA	80	2	2	90	3	2	A0	5	2	B0	4	3				$A-M \to A$	●	●	↕	↕	↕	↕
	SUBB	C0	2	2	D0	3	2	E0	5	2	F0	4	3				$B-M \to B$	●	●	↕	↕	↕	↕
Subract Acmltrs	SBA													10	2	1	$A-B \to A$	●	●	↕	↕	↕	↕
Subtr. with Carry	SBCA	82	2	2	92	3	2	A2	5	2	B2	4	3				$A-M-C \to A$	●	●	↕	↕	↕	↕
	SBCB	C2	2	2	D2	3	2	E2	5	2	F2	4	3				$B-M-C \to B$	●	●	↕	↕	↕	↕
Transfer Acmltrs	TAB													16	2	1	$A \to B$	●	●	↕	↕	R	●
	TBA													17	2	1	$B \to A$	●	●	↕	↕	R	●
Test, Zero or Minus	TST							6D	7	2	7D	6	3				$M-00$	●	●	↕	↕	R	R
	TSTA													4D	2	1	$A-00$	●	●	↕	↕	R	R
	TSTB													5D	2	1	$B-00$	●	●	↕	↕	R	R

Fig. 6-20. MC6800 Instruction

simply refer to the operand symbolically as AREAA, the A area. Notice here the "label" that has been attached in Table 6-1 to this instruction: MOVE. This point in the program is where the MOVE operation begins. It is "branched" to, as we see on the flowchart, for each word to be moved, until all 256

INDEX REGISTER AND STACK		IMMED			DIRECT			INDEX			EXTND			INHER				5	4	3	2	1	0
POINTER OPERATIONS	MNEMONIC	OP	~	#	OP	~	#	OP	~	#	OP	~	#	OP	~	#	BOOLEAN/ARITHMETIC OPERATION	H	I	N	Z	V	C
Compare Index Reg	CPX	8C	3	3	9C	4	2	AC	6	2	BC	5	3				$(X_H/X_L) - (M/M + 1)$	•	•	⑦	↕	⑧	•
Decrement Index Reg	DEX													09	4	1	$X - 1 \rightarrow X$	•	•	•	↕	•	•
Decrement Stack Pntr	DES													34	4	1	$SP - 1 \rightarrow SP$	•	•	•	•	•	•
Increment Index Reg	INX													08	4	1	$X + 1 \rightarrow X$	•	•	•	↕	•	•
Increment Stack Pntr	INS													31	4	1	$SP + 1 \rightarrow SP$	•	•	•	•	•	•
Load Index Reg	LDX	CE	3	3	DE	4	2	EE	6	2	FE	5	3				$M \rightarrow X_H, (M + 1) \rightarrow X_L$	•	•	⑨	↕	R	•
Load Stack Pntr	LDS	8E	3	3	9E	4	2	AE	6	2	BE	5	3				$M \rightarrow SP_H, (M + 1) \rightarrow SP_L$	•	•	⑨	↕	R	•
Store Index Reg	STX				DF	5	2	EF	7	2	FF	6	3				$X_H \rightarrow M, X_L \rightarrow (M + 1)$	•	•	⑨	↕	R	•
Store Stack Pntr	STS				9F	5	2	AF	7	2	BF	6	3				$SP_H \rightarrow M, SP_L \rightarrow (M + 1)$	•	•	⑨	↕	R	•
Indx Reg → Stack Pntr	TXS													35	4	1	$X - 1 \rightarrow SP$	•	•	•	•	•	•
Stack Pntr → Indx Reg	TSX													30	4	1	$SP + 1 \rightarrow X$	•	•	•	•	•	•

JUMP AND BRANCH		RELATIVE			INDEX			EXTND			INHER				5	4	3	2	1	0
OPERATIONS	MNEMONIC	OP	~	=	OP	~	=	OP	~	=	OP	~	=	BRANCH TEST	H	I	N	Z	V	C
Branch Always	BRA	20	4	2										None	•	•	•	•	•	•
Branch If Carry Clear	BCC	24	4	2										$C = 0$	•	•	•	•	•	•
Branch If Carry Set	BCS	25	4	2										$C = 1$	•	•	•	•	•	•
Branch If = Zero	BEQ	27	4	2										$Z = 1$	•	•	•	•	•	•
Branch If ≥ Zero	BGE	2C	4	2										$N \oplus V = 0$	•	•	•	•	•	•
Branch If > Zero	BGT	2E	4	2										$Z + (N \oplus V) = 0$	•	•	•	•	•	•
Branch If Higher	BHI	22	4	2										$C + Z = 0$	•	•	•	•	•	•
Branch If ≤ Zero	BLE	2F	4	2										$Z + (N \oplus V) = 1$	•	•	•	•	•	•
Branch If Lower Or Same	BLS	23	4	2										$C + Z = 1$	•	•	•	•	•	•
Branch If < Zero	BLT	2D	4	2										$N \oplus V = 1$	•	•	•	•	•	•
Branch If Minus	BMI	2B	4	2										$N = 1$	•	•	•	•	•	•
Branch If Not Equal Zero	BNE	26	4	2										$Z = 0$	•	•	•	•	•	•
Branch If Overflow Clear	BVC	28	4	2										$V = 0$	•	•	•	•	•	•
Branch If Overflow Set	BVS	29	4	2										$V = 1$	•	•	•	•	•	•
Branch If Plus	BPL	2A	4	2										$N = 0$	•	•	•	•	•	•
Branch To Subroutine	BSR	8D	8	2											•	•	•	•	•	•
Jump	JMP				6E	4	2	7E	3	3				See Special Operations	•	•	•	•	•	•
Jump To Subroutine	JSR				AD	8	2	BD	9	3					•	•	•	•	•	•
No Operation	NOP										01	2	1	Advances Prog Cntr Only	•	•	•	•	•	•
Return From Interrupt	RTI										3B	10	1		⑩					
Return From Subroutine	RTS										39	5	1	See special Operations	•	•	•	•	•	•
Software Interrupt	SWI										3F	12	1		•	S	•	•	•	•
Wait for Interrupt	WAI										3E	9	1		•	⑪	•	•	•	•

CONDITIONS CODE REGISTER		INHER				5	4	3	2	1	0
OPERATIONS	MNEMONIC	OP	~	=	BOOLEAN OPERATION	H	I	N	Z	V	C
Clear Carry	CLC	0C	2	1	$0 \rightarrow C$	•	•	•	•	•	R
Clear Interrupt Mask	CLI	0E	2	1	$0 \rightarrow I$	•	R	•	•	•	•
Clear Overflow	CLV	0A	2	1	$0 \rightarrow V$	•	•	•	•	R	•
Set Carry	SEC	0D	2	1	$1 \rightarrow C$	•	•	•	•	•	S
Set Interrupt Mask	SEI	0F	2	1	$1 \rightarrow I$	•	S	•	•	•	•
Set Overflow	SEV	0B	2	1	$1 \rightarrow V$	•	•	•	•	S	•
Acmltr A → CCR	TAP	06	2	1	$A \rightarrow CCR$	⑫					
CCR → Acmltr A	TPA	07	2	1	$CCR \rightarrow A$	•	•	•	•	•	•

CONDITION CODE REGISTER NOTES:
(Bit set if test is true and cleared otherwise)

① (Bit V) Test: Result = 10000000?
② (Bit C) Test: Result = 00000000?
③ (Bit C) Test: Decimal value of most significant BCD Character greater than nine?
(Not cleared if previously set)
④ (Bit V) Test: Operand = 10000000 prior to execution?
⑤ (Bit V) Test: Operand = 01111111 prior to execution?
⑥ (Bit V) Test: Set equal to result of N ⊕ C after shift has occurred
⑦ (Bit N) Test: Sign bit of most significant (MS) byte of result = 1?
⑧ (Bit V) Test: 2's complement overflow from subtraction of LS bytes?
⑨ (Bit N) Test: Result less than zero? (Bit 15 = 1)
⑩ (All) Load Condition Code Register from Stack. (See Special Operations)
⑪ (Bit I) Set when interrupt occurs. If previously set, a Non-Maskable Interrupt is required to exit the wait state.
⑫ (ALL) Set according to the contents of Accumulator A.

LEGEND:
OP   Operation Code (Hexadecimal);
~   Number of MPU Cycles;
#   Number of Program Bytes;
+   Arithmetic Plus;
−   Arithmetic Minus;
•   Boolean AND;
M_SP Contents of memory location pointed to be Stack Pointer;
+   Boolean Inclusive OR;
⊕   Boolean Exclusive OR;
M̄   Complement of M;
→   Transfer Into;
0   Bit = Zero;

00   Byte = Zero;
H   Half carry from bit 3;
I   Interrupt mask
N   Negative (sign bit)
Z   Zero (byte)
V   Overflow, 2's complement
C   Carry from bit 7
R   Reset Always
S   Set Always
I   Test and set if true, cleared otherwise
•   Not Affected
CCR   Condition Code Register
LS   Least Significant
MS   Most Significant

Set Summary card.

have been moved. Therefore, we must have some way of referencing this particular instruction. Hence, the symbolic label, MOVE.

In Step (3), once the word from area A has been loaded into the accumulator, it must be stored in the B area. To do this, we will use another extended addressing mode instruction, STAA. Also, the symbolic operand AREAB is assigned at this time. The actual memory location address will be figured later.

Now that the program has just moved one word from area A into area B, Step (4) says we must increment the counter by one. The MC6800 instruction set conveniently includes an instruction just for this purpose. It is called INC, and it will add one to the specified operand. The operand in this case of course is COUNTER, which was set to zero at Step (1). Now, if the 256th word has just been moved, the COUNTER prior to being incremented will equal 11111111 (255 in unsigned binary). Adding one to this binary number will cause all the bits to be set to zero, and the zero condition bit in the status register will also be set. This offers a simple way of testing to see if all 256 words have been moved. If the COUNTER value is ever equal to zero after it is incremented, we know that it has been incremented for the 256th time, and the job is finished. We will use a *conditional branch* instruction called BEQ (branch if equal to zero) to cause the program to branch to the address specified in the operand. In this case, we will assign the symbolic operand HALT. This will be an instruction, somewhere in the program, that will cause the CPU to stop.

If the COUNTER is not equal to zero, then there are more words to be moved, and at Step (6) we begin to increment the data area addresses. This operation can also make use of the INC instruction, except that in this case the operand will be the LSB of the A area address. Since this is actually the second word following the LDAA instruction at Step (2), we will assign the symbolic name LSBA to the operand at this time. Here again, we will make use of the same fact that if arithmetic overflow has occurred, the contents of the LSB of the A area address will be equal to zero after it is incremented. If this is true, then we will also have to increment the MSB of the area A address.

In Step (7), we will use another conditional branch instruction to cause the program to ignore the MSB incrementing operation if the LSB is not equal to zero. The instruction is called BNE (branch if not equal to zero). So, if the LSB of the A area address is not zero after it is incremented, the program will branch to the address specified by the operand of the BNE instruction. Since this will be some other part of the program, we will assign the symbolic name INCB as the operand for now and work out the exact memory address later.

However, if the result of incrementing the LSB of the A area address yields a value of zero, the program will not branch at Step (7) but will proceed to execute the instruction at Step (8). This instruction is the INC operation to be performed on the MSB of the A area address. Again, since we are still dealing in symbolic terms, we will assign the operand called MSBA.

Step (9) is the first part of the incrementing of the B area address. Here again, we begin by first using the INC instruction to increment the LSB of the B area address. The symbolic operand LSBB is assigned to this instruction. The same principle applies here: if arithmetic carry occurs as a result of incrementing the LSB of the B area address, a value of zero will be contained in the address word; otherwise, the result will be nonzero.

In Step (10), we observe the same type of testing of the LSB of the B area address. The BNE instruction (branch if not equal to zero) causes the program to branch back to the MOVE label if no arithmetic carry has occurred.

If the contents of the LSB of the B area address are zero after it is incremented, then the program will proceed to execute the instruction at Step (11). The MSB of the B area address is incremented by using the same INC instruction. Again, we have assigned the symbolic name MSBB as the operand.

In Step (12), we must branch back to the beginning of the MOVE operation. The addresses have been incremented, and it is now time to move another word. Since this is a branch that must always be made, we will use the instruction called BRA (branch always) to cause the program to go back to the address specified in the operand. This, of course, is the symbolic label MOVE.

Step (13) is the instruction that is to be executed when the entire 256 words have been moved from area A into area B. Here we have used the instruction called WAI (wait), which will cause the CPU to stop executing instructions. This marks the end of the program and bears the symbolic label HALT.

Hand Assembly

Now that the instruction sequence has been established, we may proceed to determine the actual memory addresses of the instructions, as well as the binary bit patterns that represent the instructions themselves. Rather than use binary notation, however, we will use the hexadecimal abbreviation of binary. Referring to the manufacturer's Instruction Set Summary card once again, we see that here, too, the hexadecimal notation is used to designate the equivalent binary bit pattern for the instruction. There are several approaches to the hand-assembly task, any one of which is probably just as valid as the next. The object, of course, is to produce a functional program in the least amount of time, with the least amount of frustration for the programmer.

For the purpose of this illustration, we will add two more columns to the instruction sequence, shown in Table 6-2. These two columns will be added between the Step and Label columns, and will be called "Address" and "Word," respectively. The Address column will contain the memory addresses, in sequential order, beginning with the first word of the program. The word column will contain the hexadecimal representation of the contents of the memory locations. In reality, these two columns should be planned for when the instruction sequence is determined. However, for simplicity's sake, they were not introduced into our illustration until now.

Remembering that a word of memory is to be used for the COUNTER, and also that the first instruction to be executed is the one that is contained in memory location 0001, we will assign the counter to be contained in memory the location 0000. The actual contents of the COUNTER are of no consequence, since it is cleared to zero as the program begins.

Memory location 0001 contains the first instruction of the program. This is the CLR instruction that is to clear the COUNTER to zero. From the Instruction Set Summary card, we see that this instruction may be used in either the indexed or the extended addressing modes. For the sake of simplicity, we shall elect to use the extended mode, which specifies the operand by means of the two words immediately following the instruction. Therefore, memory location 0002 will contain the MSB of the operand address, while location 0003 will contain the LSB of the address. The operand in this case is the COUNTER located at address 0000. So, we can now fill in the Word column for the following addresses:

0001 = 7F   Operation code for CLR instruction.
0002 = 00   MSB of the address for COUNTER.
0003 = 00   LSB of the address for COUNTER.

The next instruction is located at memory location 0004. This is the LDAA instruction, which is to load a word from the A area into the accumulator. Here again, we will use the extended addressing mode to provide a 16-bit absolute memory address for the operand, to be located in the two words that immediately follow the instruction. First of all, we can fill in the operation code for the instruction, as found on the Instruction Set

Summary card. Memory location 0004 will therefore contain B6, the code for the extended mode LDAA instruction. The operand for this instruction will be a word in the A area. When this instruction is executed for the first time, it should cause the first word in the area to be loaded into the accumulator. From the memory map (Fig. 6-18), we can see that the first word of area A is located at memory address 0100 hexadecimal. Thus, we may now fill in the Word column for addresses 0004 through 0006 as follows:

0004 = B6   Operation code for LDAA instruction.
0005 = 01   MSB of address of first A area word.
0006 = 00   LSB of address of first A area word.

Step (3) is coded as follows. Now that the program has loaded a word from A area into the accumulator, the next step is to store it in the B area at the corresponding location. For this, we will use the STAA instruction, also in the extended addressing mode. The memory location 0007 will contain the operation code for the instruction, and the next two memory locations will contain the address of the operand. The operand in this case is to be the B area word in which the contents of the accumulator are to be stored. Referring again to the memory map, we see that the B area begins at memory location 0200, hexadecimal. From this and the Instruction Set Summary card, we can fill in the Word column for the following memory locations:

0007 = B7   Operation code for STAA instruction.
0008 = 02   MSB of address of first B area word.
0009 = 00   LSB of address of first B area word.

Since we are using the hexadecimal notation throughout this example, we observe that the next memory location is designated as 000A, the hexadecimal equivalent of ten. It is in this location that we shall find the next instruction in the program: from Step (4). Here, we are to increment the COUNTER, since we have just completed the moving of one word from the A area into the B area. For this, we shall use the INC instruction, also in the extended addressing mode. The operand in this case is the COUNTER, which is really located at memory address 0000. Now we can fill in the Word column for memory locations 000A through 000C as follows:

000A = 7C   Operation code for INC instruction.
000B = 00   MSB of the address of COUNTER.
000C = 00   LSB of the address of COUNTER.

Table 6-2. Hand-Assembled Instruction Sequence for MOVE

Step	Address	Word	Label	Mnemonic	Operand	Description
1	0000	7F	COUNTER	CLR	COUNTER	This word is used for COUNTER (The remaining descriptions are the same as in Table 4-1)
	0001	00				
	0002	00				
2	0004	B6	MOVE	LDAA	AREAA	
	0005	01				
	0006	00				
3	0007	B7		STAA	AREAB	
	0008	02				
	0009	00				
4	000A	7C		INC	COUNTER	
	000B	00				
	000C	00				
5	000D	27		BEQ	HALT	
	000E	12				
6	000F	7C		INC	LSBA	
	0010	00				
	0011	06				

Line	Address	Hex	Label	Mnemonic	Operand
7	0012 0013	26 03		BNE	INCB
8	0014 0015 0016	7C 00 05		INC	MSBA
9	0017 0018 0019	7C 00 09	INCB	INC	LSBB
10	001A 001B	26 E8		BNE	MOVE
11	001C 001D 001E	7C 00 08		INC	MSBB
12	001F 0020	20 E3		BRA	MOVE
13	0021	3E	HALT	WAI	

The next step to be programmed is Step (5). Here, we must test the COUNTER to determine if arithmetic carry has occurred as a result of the foregoing INC instruction. This will be evidenced by the contents of COUNTER becoming zero as a result of the INC instruction, and the "zero" status flag in the CPU will be set. This allows us to use the BEQ (branch if equal to zero) instruction to accomplish the test. This instruction can be used only in the relative addressing mode, as observed from the Instruction Set Summary card. The displacement value that is to be arithmetically added to the PC register to produce the operand address is found in the word immediately following the instruction. The operand for this instruction consists of the address of the memory location to which the branch is to be made. This particular branch is to be made to the end of the program, designated as HALT. This is a WAI instruction that is located at memory address 0021.

Recall that the operation of "relative addressing mode" involves arithmetically adding a displacement value to the current value of the PC register, in order to obtain the actual address of the operand. It is important to note here that while any given instruction is being executed by the MC6800, the PC register actually contains the address of the *next* instruction in the program. Therefore, when calculating the displacement value the programmer must be aware of this fact. The PC register, at the time the branch is executed, contains the address of the BEQ instruction plus 2 since it is pointing to the next instruction in the program, the INC located at address 000F. (The BEQ remembers, is a two byte instruction.) To make the PC register contain the address of the WAI instruction located at 0021, we must add the displacement value, 12, hexadecimal. From this information we can fill in the Word column for memory addresses 000D and 000E as follows:

000D = 27   Operation code for BEQ instruction.
000E = 12   Displacement value to cause branch.

At this point, we must remember that if the "zero" status flag is not set at the time the BEQ instruction is executed, the program will not branch but instead will execute the next instruction, which is located at memory address 000F. Here we must increment the LSB of the A area address. This is, of course, the 16-bit address stored in the two words of memory immediately following the LDAA instruction. The first word contains the MSB of the address, while the second word contains the LSB of the address. Therefore, it is the word located at memory address 0006 that we must increment.

We will use the INC instruction in the extended addressing mode to accomplish the incrementing of the LSB of the A area address. This, like all extended mode instructions, will require three words of memory as follows:

000F = 7C   Operation code for INC instruction.
0010 = 00   MSB of location of LSB of A area address.
0011 = 06   LSB of location of LSB of A area address.

After incrementing the LSB of the A area address, the program must check to see if an arithmetic carry has occurred as a result of the increment operation. Again, if this has happened, the LSB of the address will have become zero, and the "zero" status flag inside the CPU will have been set. These conditions allow us to use the BNE instruction (branch if not equal to zero) to cause the program to branch around the instructions that will increment the MSB of the address (which need be done only if the carry has occurred). The instruction to which we will want to branch is at Step (9) and carries the label INCB. Here again, we will use the relative addressing mode to derive the actual memory address to which the branch is to be made. The current contents of the PC register are arithmetically added with the contents of the displacement word that immediately follows the instruction. Since the PC register contains the address of INC instruction 0014, and label INCB is located at memory address 0017, we must add the displacement 03 to the PC register to cause the branch. Therefore:

0012 = 26   Operation code for BNE instruction.
0013 = 03   Displacement value to cause branch.

However, if at this point the arithmetic carry has occurred as a result of incrementing the LSB of the A area address, we must also increment the MSB of the address. This is contained at memory location 0005. When the "zero" status flag in the CPU is set, the previous branch instruction will not be executed. Rather, the next instruction in the program will be executed. This will be another INC instruction, also in the extended addressing mode, which will increment the MSB of the A area address and require three words of memory.

0014 = 7C   Operation code for INC instruction.
0015 = 00   MSB of location of MSB of A area address.
0016 = 05   LSB of location of MSB of A area address.

At Step (9), then, we must begin to do the same thing to the B area address. This is, of course, the 16-bit address stored in the two words immediately following the STAA instruction at address 0007. Again, we will use the INC instruction in the extended addressing mode to accomplish the incrementing of the

B area address. This will require three words of memory as follows:

0017 = 7C   Operation code for INC instruction.
0018 = 00   MSB of location of LSB of B area address.
0019 = 09   LSB of location of LSB of B area address.

After the LSB of the B area address has been incremented, the program must check to see if there has been an arithmetic carry as a result of the execution of the INC instruction. This is done in the same manner as it was for the A area address; the BNE (branch if not equal to zero) instruction is used to cause a branch around the instructions for incrementing the MSB of the B area address. Here again, the BNE instruction is executed in the relative addressing mode. The PC register at this time will contain the address of the INC instruction, 001C. The location to which the branch is to be made is back at the beginning of the MOVE process. Since this is a branch "backwards," the displacement contained in the word immediately following the branch instruction must contain a negative value, in two's complement form. (See Appendix A for a development of this format.) Since the location to which the branch is to be made is memory address 0004, a displacement of negative 18 must be arithmetically added to the PC register. In two's complement notation, this is E8, hexadecimal. Therefore:

001A = 26   Operation code for BNE instruction.
001B = E8   Displacement value to cause branch.

Step (11) is the incrementing of the MSB of the B area address in the event that arithmetic carry occurred as a result of incrementing the LSB of the address. This is also accomplished through the use of the INC instruction and is executed only when the previous branch instruction was not executed. This is another extended addressing mode instruction, requiring three words of memory. The first contains the operation code, while the second and third contain the location of the B area address, which is actually the word immediately following the STAA instruction at memory address 0007. So, we fill in:

001C = 7C   Operation code for INC instruction.
001D = 00   MSB of location of MSB of B area address.
001E = 08   LSB of location of MSB of B area address.

Assuming that the MSB of the B area address required incrementing, the next instruction to be executed will be that contained at memory location 001F. Since the next thing we must do is to branch back to MOVE the next word from area A into area B, we will use the BRA (branch always) instruction.

This instruction will be executed in the relative addressing mode. Again, since the PC register contains the value 001F, and the MOVE label is located at address 0004, a negative displacement must be arithmetically added to cause the branch. That displacement value is negative 1B, which is E5 in two's complement notation. So, the next two words can be filled in:

001F = 20   Operation code for BRA instruction.
0020 = E5   Displacement value to cause branch.

Finally, at memory address 0021, we have the WAI instruction, which is branched to after all 256 words have been moved from area A into area B. This instruction requires only one word of memory and will cause the CPU to stop executing instructions. From the Instruction Set Summary card, we can fill in the Word column:

0021 = 3E   Operation code for WAI instruction.

Now we have finished hand-assembling the MOVE program. It has taken 0021 words hexadecimal, or 33 words decimal, to contain the complete program. We have traced the development of the program from the original, defined objective, through the initial sequential description, and on to the actual arrangement of the instructions. The two-digit hexadecimal numbers in the Word column are the actual "machine code" that must be stored in the memory at the specified addresses in order for the program to function.

Hand assembly of a program is obviously a very detailed process, even when only a small, simple program is concerned. If our aim is to program a computer to do some really complex task, hand assembly will probably not be practical. An "operating system" of some sort would have to be used, so that the programmer would not have to figure out the binary codes himself. One thing can be said in favor of the hand-assembly technique—it demands that the programmer fully understand the operation of the computer at the fundamental level. The programmer must know (or know where to find out) what the effects of processing each instruction will be, and must be able to use this knowledge to create a program that fulfills the processing objective. The beginner in microcomputer experimentation will undoubtedly write his first program using this approach. Methodically, the programmer will enter each instruction into its proper memory location via the front panel switches and lights. Once the program is loaded into memory, the programmer will pause for a moment, finger poised over the *start* switch, wondering if anything has been forgotten. If nothing has, the programmer will be rewarded with the satisfaction of a successful run.

chapter **7**

OPERATING SYSTEMS

If you've just waded through the last chapter, trying to put together a simple little program, and are about at your wits end . . . relax. There are only a handful of programmers who really enjoy this kind of programming. In reality, if a computer system is to be of any value to the "noncomputer" user, it must be a lot easier to use. Hexadecimal is wonderful, and calculating negative offsets for return branches is challenging to the "really into-it" computer buff. But what if we want to be able to just "push the right buttons" and have the computer work for us?

To realize the foregoing dream will require some very sophisticated programs, the kind that you won't want to hand-assemble. Since a computer can be programmed to do any kind of task in a prescribed sequence, why not program it to help us write programs? It could carry on a simple dialogue with us, in order for us to issue commands to it. These programs would then create new programs, according to descriptions of the proposed function. Now that sounds more like it!

WHAT IS AN OPERATING SYSTEM?

An operating system is a group of programs that all run on a particular type of computer. These programs make the computer act just like we want it to. There are programs that can help write new programs. There are other programs that manage the computer resources (mass storage). In general, there can be any number of different programs within an operating system, all of them contributing to make the computer easier to use.

But, what kind of hardware would be required to support a complex operating system? Since "computing power" is directly proportional to the amount and complexity of the hardware, it would seem that the more sophisticated the computer was to be, the more hardware would be required. This is basically correct. It is also the reason why the evolution of the microcomputer has been so dramatic. As the hardware has improved over the years, the cost has continued to decrease. The combination of these two factors has made highly complex computer systems possible at a reasonable cost. This is in contrast to the first microcomputers on the market, which *had* to be programmed by means of the hand-assemble technique.

Since microcomputers have been around for a while, there have been great strides made in improving their design. Improved computers (which usually don't break down frequently) have found their way into serious application areas. The microcomputer is finally being accepted as a viable alternative to the traditional "main-frame" computers. For one thing, any computer design that has been in practice for a few years will have developed a "track record." The more of these computers that are put into service (and stay in service) the more enhancements will be made, often by the users themselves. This is how an operating system is born. So, when we use the term "operating system" we are really referring to a combination of hardware and software that when working together comprise a framework within which YOUR OWN applications may be realized.

Disk Operating System (DOS)

By far the most flexible operating system in use today is known as a "disk operating system" or DOS. The key element of this type of system is the use of a disk (usually floppy) as the mass-storage media. This provides a means of storing large amounts of programs and data in a relatively easy to handle form. Since a higher degree of complexity in the operating system usually requires larger amounts of mass storage, the disk is utilized well in this area.

Fig. 7-1 is an illustration of a typical hardware configuration for a disk operating system. Of course, we must begin with some kind of microcomputer. Any kind will do, as long as it is capable of interfacing to a disk drive of some sort. The computer should also contain sufficient RAM memory to accommodate the types of operations that are going to be required. This can vary anywhere from a minimum of about 16K bytes on up to a megabyte or more.

Since we have a disk operating system, we will have a disk drive connected to the computer. There are many different types of disk drives available today. Some are known as "hard disks" since they utilize a rigid disk platter. By far the most popular type in use today is the so called "floppy disk." Even within this type, there are several subtypes. There are "mini-floppys," a little smaller than the "standard floppy." There are also double-sided floppys, known as "flippys," and

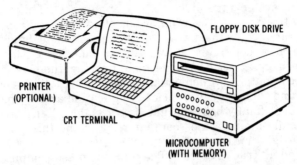

Fig. 7-1. Typical hardware for a disk operating system.

even "dual density" floppys. Although all of these different types of floppys will work, there is one factor which should be considered . . . compatibility. It will be most advantageous to be able to take a floppy disk from one computer, and use it on another computer. This may be done in order to make a "back-up" copy of a floppy, or to exchange different programs with other users. With this in mind, microcomputer users have found that the so called "IBM compatible" format standard floppy diskette provides the most common media. There are many manufacturers who are making a dual floppy disk drive unit, which contains two spindles, and two separate read/write heads. This means that there are actually two disks that can be in the system at the same time.

In order to communicate with the computer, we will have to have some sort of I/O device. Most common here is a device known as a crt terminal. It has a regular typewriter keyboard as an input device, and a crt screen as an output device. Both housed in one compact unit, these I/O devices provide a means to issue instructions to the computer, and receive information back. Here again, there are several different types of terminals available. Some have fixed character sets and can only deal with the numerals and characters of the alphabet. Others will also accommodate special user-programmed characters, and even graphic capabilities. The major difference between different types of terminals is the number of characters that can be displayed on the screen. Some have 24 lines of 80 characters each. Others have 32 lines of 64 characters, 25 lines of 40, and so on. You should decide which is best for your needs, by experimenting with all of them at your local computer store.

An optional part of the hardware system is a printer. Depending upon the nature of your application, a printer may or may not be necessary. If you are going to be developing new programs of significant size, then you should have a printer in order to keep a "hard copy" of the programs. Also, if your application requires that any kind of reports must be generated, a printer will be a must. In some cases, you may be able to do without a printer, especially if you know someone else who has one on a system that is compatible with yours. There are several different types of printers available, again differing primarily in the number of characters that can be printed on one line. There are some which use adding machine tape for paper, and only print 40 characters on a line. Others use regular "fan-fold" computer paper, and can print over 100 characters on a line.

Cassette Tape Operating System

As its name implies, this cassette type of operating system utilizes an ordinary cassette tape to store programs and data. The tape can be read into the computer, as easily as playing a music tape. Things can be stored on the tape just as music can be recorded. Of course, the sounds that are recorded on the cassette will not sound very musical, because they are really binary information that has been tone-encoded. Although cassette tape systems are not as fast as disk systems, they are usually less expensive.

Fig. 7-2 shows a typical hardware configuration for a cassette tape operating system. Notice that the computer itself also contains the keyboard. There are several computers of this type available on the market today. Here again, this keyboard is usually quite like a typewriter, and is used as the primary input device of the system. Being built right into the computer housing, this type of arrangement allows for easy transportation of the heart of your computer. This computer will also require some RAM. Here, the complexity of the application will dictate the amount of RAM that is required. These systems can operate with a minimum of about 4K bytes, on up to about 64K bytes in some of the larger ones. It is also necessary that the computer itself contains a cassette tape interface.

The mass storage device for this system is, of course, the ordinary cassette tape recorder. Its auxiliary input, and earphone output are connected to the interface of the computer so that data can be stored on the tape and also read from the tape. You may have to play with the volume settings on the tape recorder until you find out what works best for your system. Regular tape cassettes can be used with this system, although it is recommended that the "long-playing" tapes not be used since they are usually made from much thinner tape and will have a tendency to stretch at the ends. Besides, most

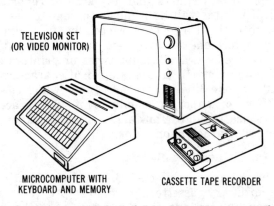

TELEVISION SET
(OR VIDEO MONITOR)

MICROCOMPUTER WITH
KEYBOARD AND MEMORY

CASSETTE TAPE RECORDER

Fig. 7-2. Typical hardware configuration for cassette tape operating system.

of the programs and data that you will store on a tape will only require a few seconds of tape to store. You will find that most of your tapes will be totally blank after a few minutes of programs. A very useful variation that is available is the continuous loop tape. These are found in various time durations from 30 seconds to several minutes. This means that you don't have to worry about rewinding your tapes. Just let them keep going forward until the program comes around again.

A very common output device for this type of system is an ordinary television set. Sometimes, a video monitor can be used instead of a tv. The basic idea is that the computer must have a video generator built into it. The effect is that the generator will output a composite video signal, sometimes with color information. This can then be fed directly into a video monitor, or through a device known as a modulator, to the terminals on the back of an ordinary television set. What it amounts to is an inexpensive crt terminal.

Although it is not shown in the illustration, a printer could be connected to this system. It seems however, that the applications which are implemented on this type of system rarely require hard copy output. When they do, the printer device can usually be one of the simpler ones that won't cost an arm and a leg.

One important thing to consider about a cassette tape operating system is that before any tape can be used to either read or write some data, the cassette itself must be manually set up in the recorder. The user must then manually press the RECORD and PLAY buttons on the recorder and then, while the tape is running, command the system to perform the I/O function. Granted, there are cassette tape systems that have automated these functions to some degree, generally requiring the modification of the recorder itself. If your application requires many different programs and/or data files to be stored on tape, you will find that you are doing a lot af manual tape handling.

ANATOMY OF AN OPERATING SYSTEM

Having described an operating system as being a collection of programs, we can see that this is quite a broad description. This collection of programs could be related to only one given application area, such as accounting, or, it could be a general purpose collection that would lend itself to many different application areas. Obviously, entire books could be written about such systems, so we have decided to try to generalize in our discussion of the operating system. We will present some of the major components of a typical operating system.

Start-Up Programs

First things first. Before we can do anything with the operating system, we must start the computer, and initialize everything so that the operating system can begin. Since the operating system is going to be doing many different types of operations with the computer, it will be keeping track of the status of various things such as interrupt driven I/O devices. To initialize the system we must run a special program.

All computers have some prescribed way of causing program execution to begin at a specified memory location, simply by pressing a button, or setting a switch on the front panel. Whatever the internal method may be, the end result is that no matter what is happening at the time, the computer can be made to branch to some predetermined place in memory, and begin running whatever program is stored there. The program that must be stored there is our "start-up" program.

Often referred to as "bootstrap" or "cold-start" programs, start-up programs do not necessarily have to be very large. The common procedure is that the start-up program is stored in ROM which is given the designated address. When the button is pressed, the program executes. What happens now differs between the disk operating system and the cassette tape system.

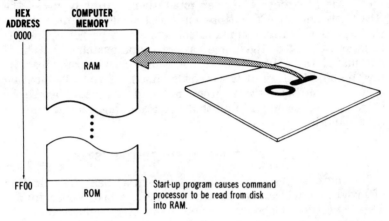

Fig. 7-3. Starting up a disk operating system using a "bootstrap."

The main objective of the start-up program is to initialize the system, and then to transfer execution to another part of the operating system known as the "command processor." This program is usually stored on disk in a disk system, and in ROM on a cassete system. As illustrated in Fig. 7-3, the bootstrap program reads the command processor from the disk into the RAM and then executes it.

Fig. 7-4 shows how a typical cassette operating system is started up. Usually, the command processor is stored in another part of the ROM. Therefore, all that the start-up program has to do is to initialize the system, and then pass control to the command processor, already in ROM.

Command Processor

The command processor is really the heart of any operating system. Sometimes referred to as "monitors" or "supervisors," these programs are intended to provide the dialogue between the operator and the system. It is through the command processor that every user-initiated operation is begun, and it is

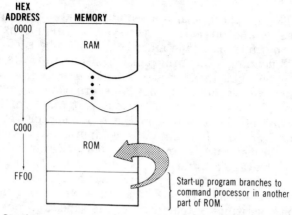

HEX
ADDRESS

0000

C000

FF00

MEMORY

RAM

ROM

Start-up program branches to
command processor in another
part of ROM.

Fig. 7-4. Starting up a cassette tape system with ROM command processor.

the command processor that is returned to after everything is completed.

There is usually some character which is displayed in the first position of a line on the screen whenever the command processor is waiting for a user directive. This character, known as a "prompt" may sometimes be replaced by an entire word like "READY." When the prompt is being displayed on the screen, the command processor is ready to input a command through the keyboard. The command processor is programmed to recognize certain words or characters which are entered, and to consider anything that it does not recognize as an error.

Perhaps the simplest form of a command is to enter the name of a program that is to be executed. This command would pertain only to a disk operating system. Upon entering the program name, the command processor would call in another part of the operating system to check to see if the program requested was stored on the disk currently on the system. If the program was found, control would be passed to another part of the operating system which would read the program from the disk into RAM, and begin executing it. If the system could not locate the program specified, an error message of some sort would be displayed on the screen so that the operator would know that the program could not be located on the disk. At this point, the command processor would be ready to accept another command.

The cassette tape system does not ordinarily support such commands. There are some rather sophisticated tape systems that allow the operator to enter a program name via the keyboard. The system will then attempt to locate the program on the cassette tape currently on the system. This means that all of the programs on a tape must be preceded by some kind of a "label" defining what program it is. Most tape systems are a lot simpler than this.

Usually, you would store only one program on a tape, or keep track of the location of various programs on the same tape by noting the reading on the tape counter. To read a program from the tape into the computer, you would first place the proper cassette in the recorder and rewind it. Then, resetting the tape counter, you would advance the tape to the correct point where the program is located. Then, you would enter the command "LOAD" via the keyboard. This would start the operating system reading the tape, and putting the program into RAM in order to be executed.

The command processor is sort of like the hub at the center of the wheel. All the other parts of the operating system can be reached through the command processor, and once it is in control, all normally completed functions return to it for further commands. As we discuss other parts of the operating systems, we will take into consideration how they interface to the command processor.

High-Level Programming Language

High-level programming language is the part of an operating system that anyone who plans to do his/her own programming will get very familiar with. In order to make the computer perform the way we want it to perform, there must be a means to communicate our desires to it. Most of the computers available today have had some form of programming language developed for them. There could easily be as many different computer programming languages as there are computers. This would mean that most programmers would only know one or two computer languages, and be able to program only one or two different types of computers. Fortunately, this is not the case.

While it is true that computers will have their differences, programming language is not usually one of them. This is due in part to the development of the so-called "high level" programming languages. Why the name "high level"? Because, in comparison to some of the earlier methods of programming computers (such as the example in Chapter 6), languages of today are levels higher in potential. One of these high level languages is known as BASIC. It is the most popular programming language used on small systems as well as some larger ones. Originally developed at Dartmouth College, this language is easily learned, and can perform very powerful tasks readily.

Here is an example of a simple BASIC program that might help you learn the metric system. The program will request that the user enter his/her name, height in inches, and weight in pounds. Then, it will convert these measures to metric units, and print out the answer.

```
1000 REM ---- METRIC CONVERTER
1010 INPUT "WHAT'S YOUR NAME"; N$
1020 INPUT "WHAT IS YOUR HEIGHT IN INCHES"; H
1030 INPUT "AND YOUR WEIGHT IN POUNDS"; W
1040 REM ---- CONVERT UNITS HERE
1050 LET H1 = 2.54  *  H
1060 LET W1 = W / 2.2
1070 REM ---- NOW PRINT THE ANSWER
1080 PRINT "OK"; N$
1090 PRINT "YOU ARE "; H1; " CENTIMETERS TALL"
1100 PRINT "AND YOU WEIGH "; W1; " KILOGRAMS"
1110 END
```

Now, in order for this program to actually run, there must be some sort of input/output device connected to the computer. Let's suppose that it is a terminal with a keyboard and crt screen. Here is what would happen:

```
RUN
WHAT'S YOUR NAME? MICHAEL
WHAT IS YOUR HEIGHT IN INCHES? 68
AND YOUR WEIGHT IN POUNDS? 150
OK MICHAEL
YOU ARE 172.7 CENTIMETERS TALL
AND YOU WEIGH 68.2 KILOGRAMS
```

All of the text which is underscored would be entered by you. Everything that is not underscored is displayed by the program. When you type RUN, the command processor will know that you want to execute the program which is currently in RAM. Let's assume that our metric program has already been entered into the computer, and is ready to go. When the command processor executes the program, the statements are executed in statement number sequence, the first being 1000.

Statement 1000, the REM statement, is known as a "remark" statement. It does not cause the computer to do anything. It is included in the program as a means to document what the program is all about. So, statement 1000 is really just the title of the program.

The next three INPUT statements are executed in sequence to get the information required from the operator. This information will have to be entered from a keyboard/terminal configuration of some sort, in order for the interactive dialogue between the program and the operator to occur. Each INPUT statement contains within it a question, which is displayed on the screen (or printer) before each piece of information is input. Notice the "N$" following the "WHAT'S YOUR NAME" question in statement 1010. This is called a variable name. It was assigned by the programmer to represent the operator's name when it is entered. Later on in the program, when the name must be displayed, the program will only need to refer to "N$" in order to obtain the name. The same is true for the operator's height "H" and weight "W". These pieces of information are entered by the operator, and assigned to variables in order that they may be used again later in the program.

Statement 1040 is another REMark indicating that the metric conversion is processed in the next statements. The LET statement in BASIC is also referred to as an assignment statement. Constructed like a mathematic equation, the LET statement will take the value obtained by evaluating the right side of the equation, and assign it to the variable found on the left side of the equal sign. Since there are 2.54 centimeters per inch, the height "H" is multiplied by 2.54 and assigned to the variable "H1". At about 2.2 pounds per kilogram, the weight must be divided by 2.2 in order to obtain "W1". If you were to perform these calculations yourself, using a calculator, it would probably take you about 10 to 15 seconds. The program will do them so fast that the answer will be displayed as soon as you have entered your weight by way of the keyboard.

Now for the output. The PRINT statement is used to accomplish this. Notice that both messages (enclosed in quotes) and variables may be output by the PRINT statement. Each PRINT statement causes a new line to begin. After all of the information has been output, the program will END, and control will be passed back to the command processor. This need not necessarily be the case. What if we had a group of people to whom we wanted to demonstrate our computer? We could type RUN each time that a new person wanted to convert his/her height and weight, or, we could modify the program slightly, so that it would keep repeating until we entered the word END instead of a name. Here is how we could change the program.

```
1000 REM ---- METRIC CONVERTER II
1010 INPUT "WHAT'S YOUR NAME"; N$
1015 IF N$ = 'END' THEN GOTO 1110
1020 INPUT "WHAT IS YOUR HEIGHT IN INCHES"; H
1030   .
1040   .
1050   .
1060
1070
1080
1090
1100
1105 GOTO 1010
1110 END
```

We have not included statements 1030 through 1100 since they will remain unchanged in our new version of the program. The most significant change is the addition of statement 1015. This is known as an IF statement, and can be used to test a variable for a certain value. Here, we have used it to test the value of N$, which is the name that was just entered. If the value happens to be the word "END," then the program will GOTO statement 1110, which is the END of the program. If N$ is not equal to "END" the program will proceed to the next statement, and operate as usual.

One other statement has been added to the program. At statement 1105, we have added a GOTO statement, which will send the program back to statement 1010 as soon as it has finished PRINTING out all of the converted information. By doing this, we have forced the program to "loop" continuously until someone enters "END" when the program asks "WHAT'S YOUR NAME".

We have shown only a few BASIC statements, and yet it is obvious that it is very easy to write programs using this language. With its simple input/output commands, and the powerful IF statement, sophisticated programs can be written to deal with all kinds of data relevant decisions. Once you learn a high-level language like BASIC, you won't ever want to think about "hand-assembly" again.

There are however, some things that BASIC can't do. One of the most common things it can't do is to interface with strange breeds of I/O devices. These tasks require a different kind of language known as symbolic assembly language.

Symbolic Assembly Language

Symbolic assembly language is quite like machine language in that every machine instruction which comprises the program must be defined by the programmer. Recalling the MOVE program from Chapter 6, you will see that each instruction has a unique mnemonic and operand. Table 6-1 illustrates how these mnemonic symbols are connected together to form the program. For example, the symbol for "load the A accumulator" is LDAA. The symbol for a branch instruction is BRA.

The one big difference between symbolic assembly and hand assembly is that the programmer does not have to figure out all of the actual binary codes that will make a machine-executable program. All that has to be done is to write the assembly program in much the same way that a BASIC program is written, and then use the "assembler" program to put it all together.

The assembler is a part of the operating system which allows the programmer to write complex machine code programs without having to get down to the level of the machine to do it. The assembler will scan the symbolic program which the programmer has entered, and convert it to a machine language program all by itself.

Operating System Utility Programs

A good operating system will always contain some handy utility programs that will save a programmer hours when the structure of the system has to be changed, especially in the disk operating system, where programs and data are being manipulated by the system on disk. There will be need to create new files, copy from one file to another, and modify and delete files that are no longer needed. All of these functions can be provided by a "disk utility program."

The disk utility program is generally accessed directly through the command processor. It will allow the user to do any number of functions like adding or deleting files, and sometimes will include such features as a disk to printer DUMP. This means that if there is something in a file that you want to see quickly, you can have the disk utility program print it out on your printer, or display it on your terminal.

At this time, we should take a look at how a typical disk operating system utilizes the disk storage space (Fig. 7-5). The outer-most cylinders on the disk usually contain the most commonly used part of the operating system, the command processor. In this way, when a disk is mounted in the drive unit, the first thing that the read/write heads will come to will be the command processor.

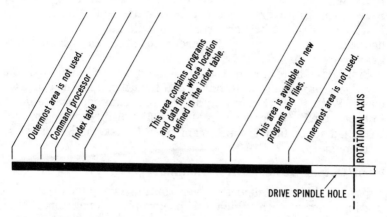

Fig. 7-5. Cross-section view of a typical disk layout.

Next on the disk is an index table that contains the names and locations of all of the other programs or files that are stored on the disk. It is through this index table that the command processor and disk utility program can find the sought-after data.

The bulk of the disk is used to store the programs and data files for the particular system. It is this area that is maintained by the disk utility program. Also, there is an area that is available for the addition of new programs or files to the disk. When the disk utility program adds a new file to the disc, it puts it into the available area, which is then decreased in size.

When a file or program is to be removed from the disk, the disk utility program can be called upon to DELETE the program or file. This can be done in different ways depending upon the type of system. Some disk utility programs will actually erase the file from the disk entirely, and repack everything down to fill the unused space. Others may only erase the name of the file from the index table, which will render it inaccessible.

In some cases, the disk utility program may be invoked directly by another part of the operating system. An example of this is given by the way that BASIC programs are written with a disk operating system.

The BASIC statements are created by the programmer and are typed into the keyboard. As each statement is typed in, it is stored in memory. When all of the statements of the program have been entered, the programmer may decide to

RUN it right away, or to SAVE it on the disk. By typing SAVE (program name), the programmer will automatically invoke the disk utility program that will take care of all the necessary "housekeeping" in order to effect saving the program on the disk.

Similarly, a program that is stored on the disk can be LOADed into memory so that it can be either modified or executed. With BASIC running, all the programmer has to do is to type LOAD (program name). The disk utility program will be called in to find the program on the disk, and to read it into memory.

Input/Output Device Driver Routines

An input/output device driver routine is a part of the operating system with which the programmer/operator should not have to deal too often. It is usually very important when a new computer is being hooked up for the first time, or whenever the hardware or software configuration is changed.

For each I/O device connected to the system, there must be an I/O driver routine. This is a program that controls the operation of the device. It handles the transmission of data to or from the device, as well as some of the mechanical functions peculiar to certain devices. For example, let's take the case of an ASCII keyboard.

In BASIC, all you have to do to read the keyboard is to write a statement:

    1010 INPUT "WHAT IS YOUR NAME"; N$

But think about what is required at the hardware level in order for all of this to happen. First of all, the characters within quotes have to be transmitted to the output device (no small task in itself), and then, characters entered from the keyboard must be stored in a variable called "N$". When the program is performing an INPUT statement, it is really the keyboard driver routine that has control of the computer. When a key is pressed, the hardware signals the keyboard driver routine that there is a character in the hardware buffer. The driver routine must load the character from the buffer into one of the CPU registers, and then do a number of tests upon it. First of all, the routine must check to see if the character just entered was the result of pressing the RETURN key, in which case it will assume that the INPUT is complete. Besides the RETURN key, there are usually several other keys which have special functions. These may include BACKSPACE, RUB OUT, ESCAPE, etc.

Sidetrip: One very useful application of these special function keys allows the operator to "re-boot" the system in the event that something has malfunctioned. A commonly encountered method of achieving this is through the keyboard driver routine. Many systems use the convention of entering a "control C" (CNTL and "C" keys pressed at the same time) to cause a re-boot of the command processor, and re-initialization of the system.

If the driver routine finds that the character which was entered is not one of the special function characters, it will add it to those characters which were previously entered until the RETURN key is pressed. Then, the routine will pass the entire string of characters that were entered to the variable N$ of the BASIC program.

As you might have guessed, the device driver routines used to handle reading and writing a floppy disk are even more complex. But here again, from a BASIC program, all the programmer has to do is to write a statement like

```
1000 READ #1 N$; H; W
```

to cause the program to read data from the disk file which has been labeled #1, and store that data in the variables N$, H, and W. There is no need to think about the sector address on the disk at which the data is located or how to tell if the data has been read correctly. The I/O device routine for the floppy disk will take care of all of that.

The same is true when the programmer wants to LOAD or SAVE a program on the disk. Although the disk utility program may be handling the management part of doing the job, the disk driver routine is really doing the work.

Due to the size and complexity of some disk I/O routines, the latest trend has been to store these routines in ROM which is located right on the I/O interface board. That way, RAM memory is not required just to keep the driver available, and can be used for user application programs instead.

OPERATING MODES

Writing a program in BASIC involves dealing with certain abstract concepts regarding the particular application, and representing these concepts within the framework of the BASIC programming language. However, when the program is actually being run, these concepts must be broken down into CPU instructions that perform the task one step at a time. There are currently two common methods of making this conversion. They are:

INTERPRETING
and
COMPILATION

Interpretive Mode

Using the interpretive mode, the BASIC program statements are "interpreted" at the time that they are to be executed. This is done by a part of the operating system known as the BASIC Interpreter. The numbered program statements are stored in RAM during execution in the sequence that they are to be executed. They are also stored in the same form as they were entered. All of the characters that were typed as the source statement are stored in RAM.

As each statement comes up for execution, the BASIC interpreter must scan it to determine what kind of statement it is. REMark statements for example are ignored by the interpreter. The interpreter will determine which other parts of BASIC will be required to carry out the operations that have been programmed by the statement. INPUT and PRINT statements will of course have to be done by the I/O routines of BASIC. LET statements are handled by another part, and IF statements by still another part. The interpreter's main job is to coordinate the operation of all of the other parts of BASIC according to the sequence of statements created by the programmer.

Compiled Mode

An operating system which uses the compiled mode will execute the very same programs that an interpreter will except that it will be done in a different manner. In a compiled system, the BASIC statements are not in the RAM during execution. Also, a program that has just been typed in cannot be directly executed. It must first be compiled into actual CPU instructions by a special program known as the compiler.

In many ways, the operation of the interpreter and the compiler are alike. They each must scan the BASIC statements and determine what sequence of steps must be performed. The difference is that the interpreter does it right away, and the compiler just creates a machine executable "object program" that can then be run or stored. When the compiler has finished compiling the program, it will usually call in the disk utility program to effect saving the object program on the disk. Then, the program can be RUN directly from the command processor, since it is already converted into CPU instructions, and is all ready to be executed.

Pros and Cons

We might think that the differences between the interpretive and compiled modes are transparent to the programmer. They are not. There are several factors that must be taken into consideration in deciding which is best for your particular application.

First of all, there will be a distinct difference in the amount of RAM memory required by the same program in an interpreted vs compiled environment. Since the interpretive mode requires that all of the BASIC statements be stored in RAM during execution, there will definitely not be optimum utilization of memory. REMark statements will take up some of the memory, and there will be a natural tendency on the part of the programmer to either leave them out completely, or at least to make them rather sparse. This means that programs will be harder to understand for someone other than the author.

In a compiled environment, the only thing that needs to be resident in RAM during execution is the object program itself. Remember that this is composed of actual CPU instructions, and therefore will require less memory than the same program in an interpretive environment. This equates to the ability of a compiled environment to execute more complex programs in a smaller sized RAM.

Another factor that cannot be overlooked is execution speed. A program that is being interpreted at execution time will require longer to run than a program that has been compiled into object code. The increased execution time is due to the number of CPU cycles that are used by the interpreter itself in its job of deciding what to do.

Of course, the job of compiling a BASIC source program into machine executable code will require some time, but it only has to be done once. Then, each time that the program is executed, the same object code that was generated by the compiler is used.

Perhaps of greatest importance to the programmer is the ease of developing a new program and getting it to work. Here is where the interpretive mode seems to outshine the compiler. Since all of the BASIC source statements are resident in RAM during execution, they can be quickly changed in the event that things don't seem to be working correctly. For example, let's suppose that you have just entered the following program which is to compute the speed of a dragster, given the distance and elapsed time. Here's the program.

```
1000 REM ---- DRAGSTER
1010 INPUT "ENTER THE DISTANCE IN FEET"; D
1020 INPUT "ENTER THE TIME IN SECONDS"; T
1030 REM ---- CONVERT TO MILES, HOURS
1040 LET D1 = D / 5280
1050 LET T1 = T / 60
1060 REM ---- COMPUTE SPEED
1070 LET S = D1 / T1
1080 PRINT "SPEED WAS "; S; " MILES PER HOUR"
1090 END
```

It's really pretty straightforward. First, the distance and time must be entered by the operator. Then they are converted from feet to miles, and seconds to hours respectively. The speed is computed as the distance divided by the time, and then it is printed out. Let's simulate a RUN.

```
RUN
ENTER THE DISTANCE IN FEET? 1320
ENTER THE TIME IN SECONDS? 12.4
SPEED WAS 1.2096774 MILES PER HOUR
```

What! That can't be right. Going the quarter mile in a little over 12 seconds means we should be doing better than a mile a minute. What's going on here?

Now, we can take advantage of one of the best features of the interpreter known as the immediate mode. Since all the program is still in RAM, let's take a look at what is going on. We can examine the contents of the variables in the program by simply using the PRINT statements without a statement number.

```
PRINT D    1320
PRINT T    12.4
```

Well, everything looks OK here, let's go on.

```
PRINT D1   .25
PRINT T1   .20666667
```

Hmmm. Well, 1320 feet is ¼ mile all right, but there's something fishy about the conversion from seconds into hours; .20666667 hours is about ⅕ of an hour, or 12 minutes. Pretty slow dragster . . . does the quarter mile in 12 minutes flat. Must be something wrong with our conversion from seconds to hours. Look at statement 1050. Sixty seconds in an hour right? Wrong! How embarrassing, only off by a factor of 60. Anyway, let's fix the program right now, and try it again. This can be done by simply reentering statement 1050.

```
1050 LET T1 = T / 3600
```

All the rest of the program will remain unchanged. Now, let's try it again.

```
RUN
ENTER THE DISTANCE IN FEET? 1320
ENTER THE TIME IN SECONDS? 12.4
SPEED WAS 72.580645 MILES PER HOUR
```

Now that's more like it.

Pretty simple mistake really. Simple to fix too, thanks to the immediate mode of the interpreter. If this program had been developed using a compiler, we would have had to stare at the source statements until the answer jumped out and hit us between the eyes. Then, we would have to edit the source program file on the disk and then compile it again before it would work correctly.

The previous example, although almost trivial in nature should give you some kind of clue as to the relative ease with which much more complicated programs can be "de-bugged" using the interpretive mode instead of the compiled mode. You should bear in mind though that this advantage is only realized when a new program is being developed, or when an older program has to be modified, thereby creating the possibility of introducing new bugs into an already proven program. Once a program has been "shaken down" and is running properly, the compiled version will be the most efficient way to go. It will require less memory, and run faster than the interpreted program.

ADVANCED OPERATING SYSTEMS

Have you ever seen one of those time-lapse movies of a flower opening, or the formation of cumulonimbus clouds? If you could see the evolution of computer technology, it would bear a striking resemblance. The field is mushrooming as new devices are perfected and as our understanding of how to use them grows. Fantastic things are being done with computers today. Giant speeding mainframe systems are at work day and night at the nation's banks and insurance companies. Silently, the rack-mounted minis guard the premises of hundreds of warehouses. There are computer systems that have only one function—to manage the job flow of other computers.

Have you traveled by air recently? All of the airlines have computer terminals everywhere. Somewhere lurks a mammoth computer system grinding out the reservations and confirmations and cancellations . . . and never complaining once. Well

. . . hardly ever. Behind the scenes, there is big brother, the air traffic controller. Gazing into the array of dots and blips that represent people traveling through the sky in silver ships. Just about as "real-time" as real-time gets. Can you imagine the complexity of the operating system that connects the computer with the radar in so precise a way that we entrust it with our lives?

All of this is attributable to the emergence of tremendously sophisticated operating systems. These are systems that would have been impractical a few years ago if for no other reason than the amount of memory that they require. A few years ago, we dreamed of having a computer with 64K bytes of RAM. Now, it is not uncommon to find that amount of memory or more being totally dedicated to the operating system.

These kinds of operating systems include such features as "time-sharing," and "automatic scheduling." That's how all of those terminals at the airline seem to be working at the same time. They are all connected to the same computer, which in turn is connected to the many megabytes of disk storage that is necessary to store the reservation data. The operating system is constantly polling all the terminals to see if there is any data that must be either sent or received. If there is data, the operating system will initiate the transmission, and then go on to service the next terminal. Think about this the next time you are waiting in line at the airport, and the reservation clerk tells you, "The computer is down." Why . . . the poor little thing probably needs a rest.

We see a lot of this kind of thing these days. One computer doing all kinds of different jobs for many different people, apparently at the same time. Of course, it's not really happening "simultaneously." After all, there is only one CPU in this computer, and it can only execute one instruction at a time. So it does a few instructions of your job and then puts you in suspended animation for a period while it does a few instructions of mine, and then his, and then hers, and then someone else's, and then the new guy, and then finally back to you again. Can you imagine the operating system that has to keep all of us straight? These are examples of one computer doing many jobs.

What about the case of several computers all working on the same job? We've seen a little of this kind of thing with the NASA space projects, and the like, but these are really several different computers, each working on a different job that all happens to be very closely related in the overall project. Each of these computers is still executing CPU instructions, *one at a time*. That is because our technology approaches problem solving as a sequence of events, each of which should lead us closer to the solution. Most of the time, this sequence builds upon itself, and each step is somewhat dependent upon the previous one. Even our consciousness operates this way. While you may think that you can do two things at the same time, or think about two things at the same time, or listen to the stereo while you do your homework (ha ha), you can't. Your conscious mind is a "serial processor" and that is why computers are also. That is the only way that we know how to build them.

Fantasies abound just thinking about some computer scientist eventually developing a true "parallel processor." Think about it. A computer that was really composed of many CPUs, each capable of operating independent from the others, but with the ability to communicate with the others at the speed of light. In much the same way as Einstein revolutionized modern physics, one of you reading this book may someday have an astounding impact upon the computer phenomena.

APPENDICES

NUMBERING SYSTEMS

"What's one and one and one and one and one and one and one and one and one and one?"
"I don't know," said Alice. "I lost count."
"She can't do addition," said the Red Queen.
(Lewis Carroll, *Through the Looking Glass*)

No one knows when the first number was recorded, but most likely it dates back to Biblical times. Among the oldest system of numbers was that of the Chinese, which was first based on a system of laying sticks in patterns and later was based on symbols drawn with pen and ink (Fig. A-1).

Calculating in these number systems was exceedingly difficult. This was because each time the basic numerals were exceeded, a new numeral had to be invented. In Roman numerals, when you needed to count above 100, you used a C, and above 1000 an M. The real problem came when these numbers had to be multiplied. The actual process of counting took place on counting boards, such as the Chinese abacus, where answers were converted back to the notation system.

Our current decimal system is much more streamlined than those of the ancient civilizations. We only have to learn the 10 basic symbols and the positional notation system in order to count to any number. For example, what is the meaning of the number 256? In positional notation, the value of each digit is determined by its position. The four in 4000 has a different value than the 4 in 400. Thus, in 256 we have three digits, and each must be "interpreted" in light of where it is in order and relation to the other digits. We learn that the rightmost digit is interpreted as the number of "ones," the next to the left as the number of "tens," and the next digit as "hundreds." The general formula for representing numbers in the decimal system using positional notation is:

$$a_1 10^{n-1} + a_2 10^{n-2} + \ldots + a_n$$

which is expressed as $a_1a_2a_3 \ldots a_n$, where n is the number of digits to the left of the decimal point. Therefore,

$$256 = (2 \times 10^2) + (5 \times 10^1) + (6 \times 10^0)$$
$$= 2 \text{ hundreds} + 5 \text{ tens} + 6 \text{ ones}$$

In the decimal system we use 10 as the basic multiplier. We call 10 the *base* or *radix*. Most of recorded history shows mankind counting in the decimal system (base 10). However, it is not difficult to imagine a race of one-armed people who used the quinary system (base 5). We see examples of the duodecimal system in clocks, rulers, the dozen, and so on.

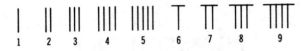

(A) Chinese "stick" number system.

(B) Chinese "pen-and-ink" number system.

Fig. A-1. First number systems.

THE BINARY SYSTEM

Although the seventeenth-century German mathematician Leibnitz was given most of the credit for invention of the binary number system with a base of 2, it was probably the ancient Chinese who realized the simple and natural way of representing numbers as powers of 2.

Early computers used relays and switches as their basic elements. The operation of a switch or a relay is itself binary in nature. A switch can either be on (1) or off (0). Modern computers use transistors like those found in televisions and radios. These components can be arranged to be in one or two "states": on or off. As a matter of fact, the more distinctly different the two states, the more reliable the computer's operation.

The idea is to make the devices work in such a manner that even slight changes in their characteristics will not affect the operation. The best way of doing this is to use a *bistable device*, which has two states.

If a bistable device is in stable state X, an energy pulse will drive it to state Y; and if the bistable component is in stable state Y, an energy pulse will drive it to state X. It is easy for a bistable component to represent the number 0 or 1:

stable state X = 1

stable state Y = 0

Counting

The same type of positional notation used in the decimal system is used in the binary. Since there are only two possible states for a numeral, either we count the position value or we don't count it. The general rule is: The binary number $a_1 a_2 a_3 \ldots a_n$ is expressed in decimal as:

$$a_1 2^{n-1} + a_2 2^{n-2} + \ldots + a_n$$

Therefore, the binary number 11010 is converted to decimal as follows:

$$N = a_1 2^{5-1} + a_2 2^{4-1} + a_3 2^{3-1} + a_4 2^{2-1} + a_5 2^{1-1}$$
$$= a_1 16 + a_2 8 + a_3 4 + a_4 2 + a_5 1$$

Substituting the values for a_1, a_2, a_3, a_4, and a_5:

$$11010 = (1 \times 16) + (1 \times 8) + (0 \times 4) + (1 \times 2) + (0 \times 1)$$
$$= 16 + 8 + 0 + 2 + 0$$
$$= 26 \text{ (decimal system)}$$

Table A-1 lists the first 20 binary numbers.

Table A-1. The First 20 Binary Numbers

Decimal	Binary	Decimal	Binary
1	1	11	1011
2	10	12	1100
3	11	13	1101
4	100	14	1110
5	101	15	1111
6	110	16	10000
7	111	17	10001
8	1000	18	10010
9	1001	19	10011
10	1010	20	10100

A simpler way to convert binary numbers to decimal is to use a weighting table (Fig. A-2). This is simply a reduction of the expansion formula just presented. Write down the value of the positions in the binary number over the binary digits, arrange them as an addition, and add them.

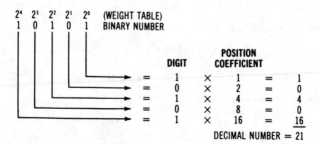

Fig. A-2. Binary-to-decimal conversion using the weighting method.

Frequently we will want to convert in the opposite direction, from decimal to binary. For this method we repeatedly divide the decimal number by 2, and the remainder after each division is used to indicate the coefficients of the binary number to be formed. Fig. A-3 shows the conversion of 47_{10} to binary. Note that decimal 47 is written 47_{10} and that binary numbers are given the subscript 2 if there is danger of confusing the number systems.

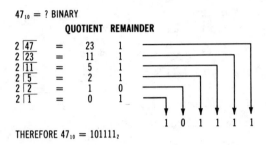

THEREFORE $47_{10} = 101111_2$

Fig. A-3. Decimal-to-binary conversion using the division method.

Fractional numbers are treated in the same manner as in the decimal system. In the decimal system:

$$0.128 = (1 \times 10^{-1}) + (2 \times 10^{-2}) + (8 \times 10^{-3})$$

In the binary system:

$$0.101 = (1 \times 2^{-1}) + (0 \times 2^{-2}) + (1 \times 2^{-3})$$

Binary Addition and Subtraction

Addition in binary is as easy as addition in decimal, and follows the same rules. In adding decimal $1 + 8$, we get a sum of 9. This is the highest-value digit. Adding 1 to 9 requires that we change the digit back to 0 *and carry 1*. Similarly, adding binary $0 + 1$, we reach the highest-value binary digit, 1. Adding 1 to 1 requires that we change the 1 back to a 0 and carry 1, i.e., $1 + 1 = 10$. Thus, for example, add binary 101 to 111:

$$\begin{array}{r} 101_2 = 5_{10} \\ +\ 111_2 = 7_{10} \\ \hline 1100_2 = 12_{10} \end{array}$$

The four rules of binary addition are:

$$0 + 0 = 0$$
$$0 + 1 = 1$$
$$1 + 0 = 1$$
$$1 + 1 = 0, \text{ carry } 1$$

Here are some examples:

$$\begin{array}{rr} 101 & 5 \\ +\ 110 & 6 \\ \hline 1011 & 11 \end{array} \qquad \begin{array}{rr} 11.01 & 3\tfrac{1}{4} \\ 101.11 & 5\tfrac{3}{4} \\ \hline 1001.00 & 9 \end{array}$$

332

Subtraction is just inverted addition. It is necessary to establish a convention for subtracting a large digit from a small digit. This condition occurs in binary math when we subtract a 1 from a 0. The remainder is 1, and we borrow 1 from the column to the left. Just as in decimal subtraction, if the digit on the left is a 1, we make it a zero, and if it's a zero, we make it a 1. The rules for binary subtraction are:

$$0 - 0 = 0$$
$$1 - 0 = 1$$
$$1 - 1 = 0$$
$$0 - 1 = 1, \text{ borrow } 1$$

Here are two examples:

10000	16	110.01	6¼
− 11	− 3	−100.1	−4½
1101	13	1.11	1¾

Binary Multiplication and Division

There are only four basic multiplications to remember in the binary system, instead of the usual 100 we memorize in the decimal system. The binary multiplication table is:

$$0 \times 0 = 0$$
$$1 \times 0 = 0$$
$$0 \times 1 = 0$$
$$1 \times 1 = 1$$

The following examples illustrate how easy binary multiplication is compared with decimal. The rule to remember is: "copy the multiplicand if the multiplier is a 1, and copy all 0's if the multiplier is a 0. Then add down, as in decimal multiplication."

Binary	Decimal	Binary	Decimal
1100	12	1.01	1.25
×1010	×10	×10.1	×2.5
0000	120	101	625
1100		1010	250
0000		11.001	3.125
1100			
1111000			

Binary division is also very simple. Division by zero is forbidden (meaningless), just as in decimal division. The binary division table is:

$$\frac{0}{1} = 0$$

$$\frac{1}{1} = 1$$

Examples of binary division are:

Binary	Decimal
101	5
101)11001	5)25
101	
101	
101	

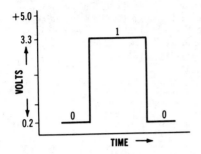

(A) Binary digit representation (TTL).

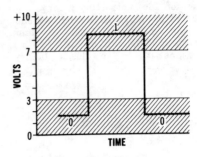

(B) Binary digit representation (CMOS).

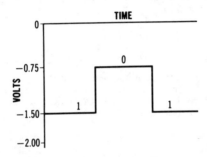

(C) Binary digit representation—negative logic (ECL).

Fig. A-4. Representing binary numbers.

Because of the difficult binary additions and subtractions that result when the numbers are large, octal or hexadecimal notation is often used.

Representing Binary Numbers

Information in digital computers of today is processed by the switching and storing of electrical signals. Computers operating in the binary number system need represent only one of two values (1 and 0) at a time. A single wire can be utilized for this purpose. A method for representing a binary digit on a signal line is shown in Fig. A-4A. In this method a small positive voltage is used to represent a 0, and a larger positive dc voltage is used to represent a 1.

Much importance is placed on the actual voltage values used to represent the binary digit. Usually, the circuitry used to transmit and receive these signals determines the range of voltages. The most ideal circuit is one in which the two logic levels are far apart (Fig. A-4B).

Note that the "1" signal is positive with respect to the "0" signal. This convention could also have been reversed, i.e., the negativemost signal

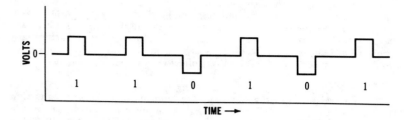

(A) RZ method of representing binary digits.

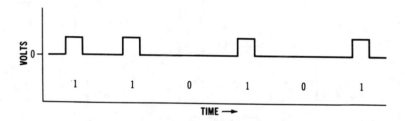

(B) NRZ method of representing binary digits.

Fig. A-5. Pulse representation of binary numbers.

called a "1" and the more positive signal a "0." (See Fig. A-4C.) Usually, one convention is chosen by the designer and then used throughout the computer.

Pulse Representation of Binary Numbers

Binary digits are often transmitted and received as a burst of pulses. Fig. A-5A shows a system in which a positive pulse represents a 1 and a negative pulse a 0. The signal line remains at some in-between value when no pulse is being sent. This technique is used frequently in magnetic recording, and is called *return-to-zero* (RZ) encoding.

A more popular technique is shown in Fig. A-6B. A 1 is represented by a pulse, and a 0 as no pulse. The receive circuitry must keep in synchronization with the incoming signal in order to know when a binary digit is occurring. This technique is called *non-return-to-zero* (NRZ) encoding.

Serial and Parallel Transmission

So far, methods of representing and transmitting a single binary digit have been illustrated. We will find that it is often necessary to transmit complete binary numbers, which is accomplished by transmitting each binary digit over its own wire. Thus, an n-digit binary number would require n wires or signal lines. This is called *parallel transmission*. Fig. A-6A illustrates an 8-bit binary number (10010101) being transmitted over eight parallel lines. In such a system each line is assigned a different

335

weight, based on the positional notation of the binary number system. The leftmost binary digit is assigned the weight of 2^{n-1}, where n is the number of binary digits (8 in this case).

The other method of transmitting binary data is called *serial transmission*. In this method the signals representing the binary digits are transmitted one at a time in sequence, usually starting with the rightmost digit (Fig. A-6B). This method requires some synchronization in order to distinguish several 0's or 1's that follow each other in a sequence.

Negative Numbers

The normal way to express a negative number is to place a minus sign in front of the number. When a negative number is subtracted from a positive number, we *change the sign and add*. For example, $256 - (-128) = 256 + 128 = 384$.

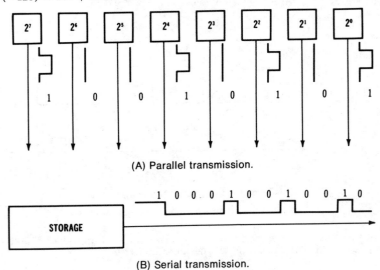

(A) Parallel transmission.

(B) Serial transmission.

Fig. A-6. Parallel and serial transmission.

Digital computers use binary storage devices to store and represent binary digits. Seven such devices can represent the binary numbers from 0000000 to 1111111 (0 to 127_{10}). However, if we wish to increase the range to include the negative numbers from 0000000 to -1111111, we need another binary digit, or bit. This bit is called the *sign bit* and is placed in front of the most significant digit of the binary number.

The convention for the sign bit is: If the sign bit is 0, the number is positive; and if the sign bit is a 1, the number is negative. The remaining digits form the absolute value of the number. This numerical storage mode is called *signed binary*. Fig. A-7A shows signed binary numbers from $+127$ to -127, and the signed binary number line is shown in Fig. A-7B.

Signed binary, although frequently used, has a few minor flaws that make it less flexible than other codes for negative numbers. Any arithmetic operation requires checking the sign bit and then either adding or subtracting the numerical values, based on the signs.

INTEGER	SIGNED BINARY CODE							
	s	b_7	b_6	b_5	b_4	b_3	b_2	b_1
+127	0	1	1	1	1	1	1	1
+126	0	1	1	1	1	1	1	0
⋮				⋮				
+3	0	0	0	0	0	0	1	1
+2	0	0	0	0	0	0	1	0
+1	0	0	0	0	0	0	0	1
0	0	0	0	0	0	0	0	0
−1	1	0	0	0	0	0	0	1
−2	1	0	0	0	0	0	1	0
−3	1	0	0	0	0	0	1	1
⋮				⋮				
−126	1	1	1	1	1	1	1	0
−127	1	1	1	1	1	1	1	1

(A) Seven-bit–magnitude table.

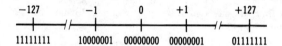

(B) Signed binary number line (seven-bit magnitude).

Fig. A-7. Signed binary code.

The Use of Complements

The use of complemented binary numbers makes it possible to add or subtract binary numbers using only circuitry for addition. To see how negative numbers are used in the computer, consider a mechanical register, such as a car mileage indicator, being rotated backwards. A five-digit register approaching and passing through zero would read as follows:

```
00005
00004
00003
00002
00001
00000
99999
99998
99997
etc.
```

It should be clear that the number 99998 corresponds to −2. Furthermore, if we add

$$
\begin{array}{r}
00005 \\
+\ \underline{99998} \\
1\quad 00003
\end{array}
$$

and ignore the carry to the left, we have effectively formed the operation of subtraction: $5 - 2 = 3$.

The number 99998 is called the *ten's complement* of 2. The ten's complement of any decimal number may be formed by subtracting each digit of the number from 9, and then adding 1 to the least significant digit of the number formed. For example:

<table>
<tr><td>normal
subtraction</td><td colspan="2">ten's complement
subtraction</td></tr>
<tr><td>89
− 23
66</td><td>89
− 23</td><td>89
+ 77
1 66</td></tr>
</table>

⌐► 1 66
└─DROP CARRY

Two's Complement

The two's complement is the binary equivalent of the ten's complement in the decimal system. It is defined as that number which, when added to the original number, will result in a sum of zero, ignoring the carry. The following example points this out:

$$
\begin{array}{ll}
1101 & \text{number} \\
0011 & \text{two's complement} \\
\hline
1\ 0000 & \text{sum}
\end{array}
$$

⌐►
└─IGNORE CARRY

The easiest method of finding the two's complement of a binary number is to first find the one's complement, which is formed by setting each bit to the opposite value:

$$
\begin{array}{ll}
11011101 & \text{number} \\
00100010 & \text{one's complement}
\end{array}
$$

The two's complement of the number is then obtained by adding 1 to the least significant digit of the one's complement:

$$
\begin{array}{ll}
11011101 & \text{number} \\
00100010 & \text{one's complement} \\
\underline{+1} & \text{add one} \\
00100011 & \text{two's complement}
\end{array}
$$

The complete signed two's complement code is obtained for negative numbers by using a 1 for the sign bit, and two's complement for the magnitude of the number. Fig. A-8A shows the signed two's complement code, and its number line is shown in Fig. A-8B.

In contrast to the signed binary code, in the signed two's complement code, numbers can be added without regard to their signs and the result will always be correct. The following examples should make this clear:

$$
\begin{array}{lll}
\begin{array}{rr}
0000101 & 5 \\
+1111110 & +\ (-2) \\
\hline
1\ 0000011 & 3
\end{array}
&
\begin{array}{rr}
1111011 & -5 \\
+0000010 & +\ (+2) \\
\hline
11111101 & (-3)
\end{array}
&
\begin{array}{rr}
1111011 & -5 \\
+1111110 & +\ (-2) \\
\hline
1\ 1111001 & (-7)
\end{array}
\end{array}
$$

└─IGNORE   └─IGNORE

INTEGER	SIGNED 2's COMPLEMENT CODE							
	s	b_7	b_6	b_5	b_4	b_3	b_2	b_1
+127	0	1	1	1	1	1	1	1
+126	0	1	1	1	1	1	1	0
⋮				⋮				
+3	0	0	0	0	0	0	1	1
+2	0	0	0	0	0	0	1	0
+1	0	0	0	0	0	0	0	1
0	0	0	0	0	0	0	0	0
−1	1	1	1	1	1	1	1	1
−2	1	1	1	1	1	1	1	0
−3	1	1	1	1	1	1	0	1
⋮				⋮				
−126	1	0	0	0	0	0	1	0
−127	1	0	0	0	0	0	0	1
−128	1	0	0	0	0	0	0	0

(A) Seven-bit–magnitude table.

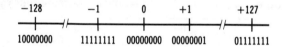

(B) Two's complement number line.

Fig. A-8. Signed two's complement code.

Notice that it is impossible to add +64 to +64 in a 7-bit code and +128 to +128 in an 8-bit code. Also note that in comparing the two systems, signed binary and two's complement, the largest negative two's complement number that can be represented in 8 bits is −128, while in signed binary it's −127. Changing a negative integer from signed binary to two's complement requires simply complementing all bits except the sign bit, and adding 1.

Binary-Coded Number Representation

Since computers operate in the binary number system, while people use the decimal system, it was only natural that some intermediate system be developed. Computers, and some calculators and "intelligent" instruments, use a *binary-coded decimal* system. In such systems, a group of binary bits is used to represent each of the 10 decimal digits.

The binary-coded decimal (bcd) system is called a "weighted binary code" with the weights 8, 4, 2, and 1, as shown in Table A-2. Notice that 4 binary bits are required for each decimal digit, and that each digit is assigned a weight: the leftmost bit has a weight of 8; the rightmost bit a weight of 1.

There's a slight problem with using 4 bits to represent 10 decimal values. Since $2^4 = 16$, the 4 bits could actually represent 16 values. However, the next choice down, 3 bits, allows only 2^3, or 8, possible digits, which is insufficient. To represent the decimal number 127 in bcd, 12 binary bits are required instead of seven if we use pure binary:

$$\begin{array}{ccc} 1 & 2 & 7 \\ 0001 & 0010 & 0111 \end{array}$$

The bcd system has another property that makes it less flexible for binary computation in the computer. The difficulty lies in forming complements of its numbers. As was pointed out, it is common practice to perform subtraction by complementing the subtrahend and adding 1. When the bcd 8-4-2-1 system is used, the complement formed by inverting all the bits may produce an illegal bcd digit. For example, complementing the bcd number 0010 (2_{10}) gives 1101 (13_{10}), which is not a bcd code.

To solve this problem, several other codes have been developed. For example, the *excess-three code* is formed by adding 3 to the decimal number and then forming the bcd code. For example:

$$\begin{array}{rl} 4 & \text{number} \\ +3 & \text{add for excess-three} \\ \hline 7 & \end{array}$$

$$7 = 0111 \quad \text{convert 7 to bcd}$$

Table A-2 also shows the excess-three codes for the 10 decimal digits. Now the complement of the excess-three code doesn't form any illegal bcd digits, i.e., 10_{10} or above.

Table A-2. Binary-Coded Number Representation

Decimal Digit	Binary-Coded Decimal	Excess-3 Coded Binary	2-4-2-1 Coded Binary			
			Weight of Bit			
			2	4	2	1
0	0000	0011	0	0	0	0
1	0001	0100	0	0	0	1
2	0010	0101	0	0	1	0
3	0011	0110	0	0	1	1
4	0100	0111	0	1	0	0
5	0101	1000	1	0	1	1
6	0110	1001	1	1	0	0
7	0111	1010	1	1	0	1
8	1000	1011	1	1	1	0
9	1001	1100	1	1	1	1

The excess-three code is not a weighted code, since the sum of the bits does not equal the number being represented. On the other hand, the bcd 8-4-2-1 code is weighted but forms illegal complements.

A weighted code that does form legal complements is the *2-4-2-1 code* in Table A-2.

OCTAL NUMBER SYSTEM

It is probably quite evident by now that the binary number system, although nice for computers, is a little cumbersome for human usage. For example, communicating binary 11011010 over a telephone would be "one-one-zero-one-one-zero-one-zero," which is quite a mouthful. Also, it is easy to make errors when adding and subtracting large binary numbers. The octal (base 8) number system alleviates most of these problems and is frequently used in the microcomputer literature.

The octal system uses the digits 0 through 7 in forming numbers. Table A-3 shows octal numbers and their decimal equivalents.

Table A-3. First 13 Octal Digits

Decimal	Octal	Binary	Decimal	Octal	Binary
0	0	0	7	7	111
1	1	1	8	10	1000
2	2	10	9	11	1001
3	3	11	10	12	1010
4	4	100	11	13	1011
5	5	101	12	14	1100
6	6	110	13	15	1101

Octal numbers are converted to decimal numbers by using the same expansion formula as that used in binary-to-decimal conversion, except that 8 is used for the base instead of 2.

$$(octal)\ 167 = (1 \times 8^2) + (6 \times 8^1) + (7 \times 8^0)$$
$$= (1 \times 64) + (6 \times 8) + (7 \times 1)$$
$$= 64 + 48 + 7$$
$$= 119\ (decimal)$$

A *weighting table* (Fig. A-9) is a quick way to convert octal values to decimal.

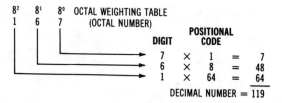

Fig. A-9. Octal-to-decimal conversion.

The primary use of octal is as a convenient way of recording values stored in binary registers. This is accomplished by using a grouping method to convert the binary value to its octal equivalent. The binary number is grouped by threes, starting with the bit corresponding to $2^0 = 1$ and grouping to the left of it. Then each binary group is converted to its octal equivalent. For example, convert 11110101 to octal:

```
   011   110   101   binary number
     3     6     5   octal equivalent
 implied 0
```

The largest 8-bit octal number is 377_8, and the largest 7-bit octal number is 177_8. Negative octal numbers in 8-bit signed two's complement cover 377_8 (-1_{10}) to 200_8 (-128_{10}).

Conversion from decimal to octal is performed by repeated division by 8 and using the remainder as a digit in the octal number being formed. Fig. A-10 illustrates this method.

$$1376_{10} = ? \text{ OCTAL}$$

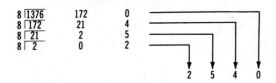

QUOTIENT REMAINDER

$$
\begin{array}{llll}
8\,\overline{|1376} & 172 & 0 \\
8\,\overline{|\ 172} & 21 & 4 \\
8\,\overline{|\ 21} & 2 & 5 \\
8\,\overline{|\ 2} & 0 & 2 \\
\end{array}
$$

2   5   4   0

THEREFORE $136_{10} = 2540_8$

Fig. A-10. Decimal-to-octal conversion.

Addition in Octal

Octal addition is easy if we remember the following rules (which we will find also apply to hexadecimal):

1. If the sum of any column is equal to or greater than the base of the system being used, the base must be subtracted from the sum to obtain the final result of the column.
2. If the sum of any column is equal to or greater than the base, there will be a carry, equal to the number of times the base was subtracted.
3. If the result of any column is less than the base, the base is not subtracted and no carry will be generated.

Examples:

octal	decimal		octal		decimal
5 = 5			35 =		29
+3 = 3			+63 =		+51
8			1 10 8		
−8			−8 −8		
10 = 8			1 2 0 =		80

Octal Subtraction

Octal subtraction can be performed directly or in the complemented mode by using addition. In direct subtraction, whenever a borrow is needed, an 8 is borrowed and added to the number. For example:

$$2022_8 - 1234_8 = ?$$

$$
\begin{array}{r}
2022_8 \\
1234_8 \\
\hline
566_8 \\
\end{array}
$$

Octal subtraction may also be performed by finding the eight's complement and adding. The eight's complement is found by adding 1 to the seven's complement. The seven's complement of the number may be found by subtracting each digit from 7. For example:

$$377_8 - 261_8 = ?$$

a)
$$
\begin{array}{r}
777 \\
-261 \\
\hline
516 \\
+1 \\
\hline
517
\end{array}
$$
    (second number)

    7's complement

    8's complement

b)
$$
\begin{array}{r}
377 \\
+517 \\
\end{array}
$$
    (first number)

    8's complement of 261

$$
\begin{array}{rrr}
9 & 9 & 14 \\
-8 & -8 & -8 \\
\hline
1 & 1 & 6 = 116_8
\end{array}
$$

Octal Multiplication

Octal multiplication is performed by using an octal multiplication table (see Table A-4) in the same manner as a decimal table would be used. All additions are done by using the rules for octal addition. For example:

$$17_8 \times 6_8 = ?$$

octal

$$
\begin{array}{r}
17 \\
\times 6 \\
\end{array} =
$$

$$
\begin{array}{rrr}
1 & 11 & 2 \\
-0 & -8 & -0 \\
\hline
1 & 3 & 2 = 132_8
\end{array}
$$

decimal

$$
\begin{array}{r}
15 \\
\times 6 \\
\hline
90
\end{array}
$$

$$177_8 \times 27_8 = ?$$

octal

$$
\begin{array}{r}
177 \\
\times 27 \\
\hline
1371 \\
376 \\
\end{array} =
$$

$$
\begin{array}{rrrr}
5 & 11 & 13 & 1 \\
-0 & -8 & -8 & -0 \\
\hline
5 & 3 & 5 & 1 = 5351_8
\end{array}
$$

decimal

$$
\begin{array}{r}
127 \\
\times 23 \\
\hline
381 \\
254 \\
\hline
2921
\end{array}
$$

Numbers are multiplied by looking up the result in the table. The result of any product larger than 7 (the radix or base) is carried and then octally added to the next product. The results are then summed up by using octal addition.

Table A-4. Octal Multiplication Table

×	0	1	2	3	4	5	6	7
0	0	0	0	0	0	0	0	0
1	0	1	2	3	4	5	6	7
2	0	2	4	6	10	12	14	16
3	0	3	6	11	14	17	22	25
4	0	4	10	14	20	24	30	34
5	0	5	12	17	24	31	36	43
6	0	6	14	22	30	36	44	52
7	0	7	16	25	34	43	52	61

Octal Division

Octal division uses the same principles as decimal division. All multiplication and subtraction involved, however, must be done in octal. Refer to the octal multiplication table. Some examples:

$$144_8 \div 2_8 = ?$$

$$\frac{144_8}{2_8} = \frac{100_{10}}{2_{10}} = 50_{10} = 62_8$$

$62_8 \div 2_8 = ?$

$$\begin{array}{r} 31 = 31_8 = 25_{10} \\ 2\overline{)62} \\ 6 \\ \hline 02 \\ 2 \\ \hline 0 \end{array}$$

$1714_8 \div 22_8 = ?$

$$\begin{array}{r} 66 = 66_8 = 54_{10} \\ 22\overline{)1714} \\ 154 \\ \hline 154 \\ 154 \end{array}$$

THE HEXADECIMAL SYSTEM

Hexadecimal is another important and often-used computer number system. "Hex" uses the radix 16 and therefore has 16 digits. The first 10 digits are represented by the decimal digits 0 through 9, and the remaining six are indicated by the letters A, B, C, D, E, and F. There is nothing special about these letters, and any other letters could have been used. Table A-5 shows the first 16 hexadecimal digits.

Table A-5. First 16 Hexadecimal Digits

Binary	Hexadecimal	Decimal
0000	0	0
0001	1	1
0010	2	2
0011	3	3
0100	4	4
0101	5	5
0110	6	6
0111	7	7
1000	8	8
1001	9	9
1010	A	10
1011	B	11
1100	C	12
1101	D	13
1110	E	14
1111	F	15

Binary numbers are easily converted to hex by grouping the bits in groups of four, starting on the right, converting the results to decimal, and then converting to hex. For example:

$$\begin{array}{llll} 1000 & 1010 & 1101 & \text{binary} \\ 8 & 10 & 13 & \text{decimal} \\ 8 & A & D & \text{hex} = 8AD_{16} \end{array}$$

As you can probably tell, hex is preferred over octal whenever the binary number to be represented is 16 bits or more. This is because the hex code is more compact than the octal equivalent.

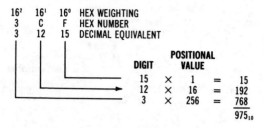

Fig. A-11. Hexadecimal-to-decimal conversion.

Conversion from hexadecimal to decimal is straightforward but time-consuming. The expansion formula, or a weighting table with an intermediary hex-to-decimal conversion, is used as shown in Fig. A-11.

Conversion from decimal to hex is performed by repeatedly dividing by 16, and converting the remainder to a hex digit. The quotient becomes the next number to divide. This is shown in Fig. A-12.

$975 = ?_{16}$

	QUOTIENT	REMAINDER IN DECIMAL	REMAINDER IN HEX
975/16	60	15	F
60/16	3	12	C
3/16	0	3	3

3 C F

Fig. A-12. Decimal-to-hexadecimal conversion.

Hexadecimal Addition

Addition in hex is similar to the addition procedure for octal, except the hex digits are first converted to decimal. For example:

$$3CF + 2AD = ?$$

$$
\begin{array}{r}
+\ 2AD = +2 \quad 10 \quad 13 \\
3CF = 3 \quad 12 \quad 15 \\
\hline
6 \quad 23 \quad 28 \\
-0 -16 -16 \\
\hline
6 \quad\ \ 7 \quad 12 = 67C
\end{array}
$$

Subtraction in Hexadecimal

Subtraction in hex may be accomplished by either the direct or the complement method. In the direct method, the hex digits are converted to decimal. If a borrow is required, 16 is added to the desired number and the digit borrowed from is decreased by 1. In the complement method, the sixteen's complement of the subtrahend is determined and the two numbers are added. The sixteen's complement is found by adding 1 to the fifteen's complement. The fifteen's complement is found by subtracting each of the hex digits from F. For example:

$$2BD - 1CE = ?$$

FFF =	15	15	15	
−1CE	− 1	12	14	second number
	14	3	1	15's complement
			+ 1	
	14	3	2	16's complement
2BD =	+ 2	11	13	first number
1	16	14	15	
	−16	−0	−0	
ignore carry	0	14	15	= EF (answer)

Hexadecimal Multiplication

Direct hex multiplication is rather tedious and time-consuming. This is because there are 256 entries in a hex multiplication table. The best method is to convert to decimal by using the expansion polynomial and then convert back from decimal to hex after computation.

MEMORIES

This appendix classifies memories as read/write and read-only types. Several examples of each type are given.

READ/WRITE MEMORIES

Read/write memories are memories in which the stored information is available at any time and can be changed during normal operation of the system. Bipolar memories, static and dynamic MOS memories, as well as CMOS and SOS cells, are of this type.

Bipolar Memory

The simple bipolar-transistor cell is made of bipolar npn transistors in a cross-coupled configuration, as shown in Fig. B-1. Two emitters are diffused into the memory-cell transistors to permit connection of the cell to read and write circuits.

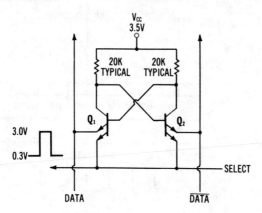

Fig. B-1. Bipolar (TTL) storage cell.

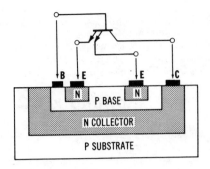

Fig. B-2. Dual-emitter npn transistor schematic symbol and physical cross section.

Fig. B-2 shows the basic bipolar cell building block: a two-emitter npn transistor. Either one of the two emitters is capable of conducting base-emitter current. When conducting, either emitter will turn the transistor on. To operate the transistor, a biasing voltage, positive with respect to the voltage to be used on the emitters, is provided by pull-up resistors. A negative-going voltage on either emitter will then turn the device on.

Fig. B-3 shows how two dual-emitter transistors are biased and cross-coupled to form a memory cell in a 16-by-4 bipolar RAM. In the normal nonaccessed state, the DATA and $\overline{\text{DATA}}$ (D and $\overline{\text{D}}$) lines are held at a positive potential so that they are nonconducting. In this state, the cell simply stores a 1 or a 0. If Q_1 is turned on, it shorts out the biasing resistor for Q_2; thus, Q_2 is off and the biasing resistor for Q_1 is not shorted. This is the state for storing 1. For storing 0, Q_2 is on and Q_1 is off.

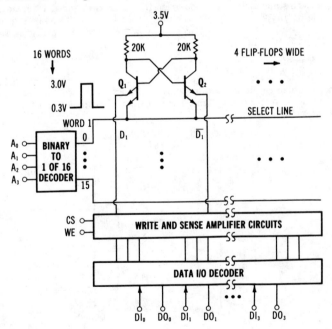

Fig. B-3. Sixty-four–bit bipolar RAM organized 16 by 4.

The SELECT line is normally biased at about 0.3 volt to allow the cell to retain its data. To read data from this cell, the SELECT line is brought high to about 3 volts. A differential amplifier (not shown) connected to the DATA and $\overline{\text{DATA}}$ lines senses the state of the cell. If Q_1 is on, the DATA line will be more positive than the $\overline{\text{DATA}}$ line, indicating 1. If Q_2 is on, the $\overline{\text{DATA}}$ line will be more positive than the DATA line, indicating a 0 is stored in the cell. Many cells can share the same DATA and $\overline{\text{DATA}}$ lines with one common differential amplifier attached. In this configuration, only one cell is selected at a time by placing a positive voltage on its SELECT line. The other cells are not affected by the DATA and $\overline{\text{DATA}}$ lines, as their SELECT lines are at a lower potential (0.3 V).

Writing is similar to reading, in that the cell to be affected is selected by applying a positive voltage to the SELECT line. To write a 0, the cell selected, then the $\overline{\text{DATA}}$ line is brought low to about 2 volts. This turns Q_2 on. Transistor Q_2, being on, shorts the base-bias resistor to Q_1, turning Q_1 off. After writing, the $\overline{\text{DATA}}$ line is returned to its 0.3-V normal state. Writing a 1 is the same, except that the DATA line, rather than the $\overline{\text{DATA}}$ line, is brought low.

Bipolar cells commonly use two types of npn transistor technologies. Regular npn's are used for medium- and low-speed memories. Schottky-clamped npn's are used to make ultrafast-access bipolar memories. In both cases, cell configurations are essentially the same.

Typical standby power for the bipolar cell is about 800 microwatts. Read current is about 150 microamperes; delay is on the order of 20 nanoseconds for the Schottky bipolar memory.

Static MOS Memory

Although bipolar memory cells are high-speed devices, and are well understood, they have quite a few drawbacks when used as dense-memory ICs. The biggest drawback is that bipolar cells use large amount of power to keep the "on" transistor on, and this limits the maximum attainable density. MOS (*M*etal-*O*xide *S*emiconductor) transistors are by far the transistors most often used for memory ICs, and they continue to be improved each year.

While bipolar transistors require two types of current carriers—holes and electrons—MOS devices require only one major current carrier, namely electrons for n channel, and holes for p channel. They are called *unipolar* for this reason.

There are two possible modes of operation of MOS devices: the enhancement mode and the depletion mode. Early MOS technology was depletion mode only, which uses a physical channel diffused in the production process. Later, enhancement mode caught on. These enhancement-mode devices simply induce the electronic equivalent of a channel, further simplifying the MOS device. Enhancement is by far the most commonly used mode of operation for memories.

A primary distinction between MOS and bipolar arises from the fact that bipolar transistors are "bulk" devices. The active region of recombination lies quite a distance from the base surface. MOS devices, on the other hand, utilize a surface effect, which takes place at the insulator interface. These factors add up to make a MOS transistor three-terminal solid-state device that requires almost no input current to operate, quite in contrast to the current-operated bipolar device. MOS input impedance is on the order of 10^{14} ohms.

A final reason for the dominance of MOS in memory is that it inherently uses up less area on the silicon chip, a major cost factor in high-

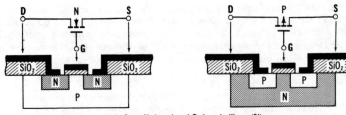

N & P = N doped and P doped silicon (Si)

(A) NMOS inverter schematic symbol and cross section.

(B) PMOS inverter schematic symbol and cross section.

Fig. B-4. MOS transistors.

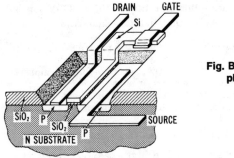

Fig. B-5. PMOS inverter physical layout.

density chips. Furthermore, the MOS transistor can act like a high-value resistor on the chip by tying its drain to the gate. This eliminates the need to diffuse separate resistors on the chip. Values greater than 10^4 ohms result due to the constant-current–source mode of MOS operation.

The fabrication of MOS can be either p channel or n channel. For sheer speed, NMOS is the choice, as the mobility of electrons (the primary current carrier) is three to four times that of the holes in the PMOS. This

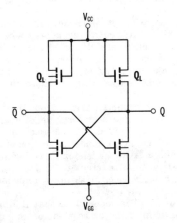

Fig. B-6. Simplest type of MOS storage element.

means three to four times reduction in area for equivalent performance. NMOS is unfortunately harder to make than PMOS. Fig. B-4 illustrates the schematic and cross section for n- and p-channel MOS transistors.

Fig. B-5 shows the actual physical structure of a p-channel MOS inverter. As we can see, the transistor is composed mostly of a silicon dioxide layer, deposited on an n substrate, with a large well occurring where the drain, gate, and source are formed. The channel is made of p-type holes, moving between the drain and source, with the voltage on the gate controlling the movement.

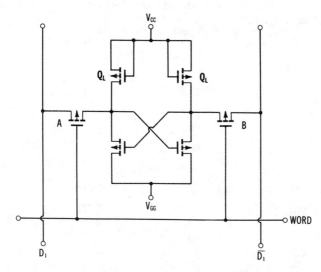

**Fig. B-7. Six-transistor PMOS storage element
with sense transmission gates A and B.**

There are a number of ways to make a MOS memory cell using MOS transistors. Fig. B-6 shows the simplest type of MOS storage element. Here the inverters are cross coupled, as in the bipolar cell, to form a simple flip-flop. Instead of depositing or diffusing separate resistors for drain loads as in the bipolar cell, two additional MOS transistors, Q_L, are diffused as constant-current loads. By connecting the MOS gate to the drain, the device acts like a high-value current source and hence a high-value resistor taking up very little space.

The actual implementation of the MOS storage element is demonstrated in Fig. B-7. This is a PMOS six-transistor cell with six interconnects. The number of interconnects tells us how many connections must be made to each storage element to use it as a memory. Obviously, the smaller that this number of interconnects can be made, the less costly the final IC will be. To read data from the cell (i.e., to determine the state of the flip-flop), the WORD line is raised and the data lines (D_1 and $\overline{D}_1$) are sensed. This means that the state is output to an external circuit. To write data into the cell, the WORD line is raised, turning on A and B gates, and the appropriate data line (D_1 or $\overline{D}_1$) is forced to change state. This will in turn cause the flip-flop to change to the desired state.

NMOS cells, on the other hand, differ in complexity from the PMOS structure. The tradeoff is usually speed for a higher power dissipation.

351

The cell in Fig. B-8 is an eight-transistor static cell, used in the Signetics 2602 static 1024×1 RAM. Transistors Q_1 and Q_2 provide pull-up current for the static flip-flop consisting of Q_3 and Q_4. Transistors Q_5/Q_7 and Q_6/Q_8 are two transmission gates connecting the cell to true and inverted data bus lines shared with other cells. When both X and Y select lines are at logic 1, the transmission gates open (conduct). To write a logic 1, the write circuit (not shown) places logic 1 on the DATA line and logic 0 on the $\overline{\text{DATA}}$ line, and then selects the cell by bringing both the X and Y select lines for that cell to logic 1. This sets the cell to Q4 on and Q3 off. Writing a logic 0 is the same process with DATA and $\overline{\text{DATA}}$ reversed. Reading is done by opening the transmission gates and sensing the DATA and $\overline{\text{DATA}}$ logic levels. The state of the cell appears on these lines.

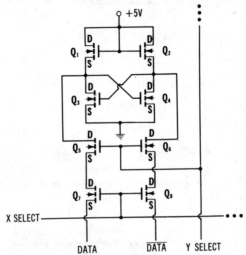

Fig. B-8. Static NMOS storage element (Signetics 2602).

CMOS and SOS Cells

CMOS devices are simply made of PMOS and NMOS inverters connected in series. If we tie the two drains together, an almost ideal complementary-symmetry inverter stage results. Such an ideal inverter is almost impossible to implement with npn/pnp pairs because neither device will turn completely off. Fig. B-9 shows the simplified CMOS stage and its cross section.

The basic CMOS storage element is much like earlier devices, in that two inverters are cross coupled to form the flip-flop. This is shown in Fig. B-10.

Storage cell selection and sensing of states are done by using PMOS transmission gates as shown in Fig. B-11. The p-channel transmission gates require a ground on the word line to select the desired cell.

CMOS memories exhibit all the characteristics of MOS flip-flops with some important extras, including very low power dissipation (milliwatts), low propagation delay, and high noise immunity. Actual storage cells require about six transistors per cell, and the actual cell area is much larger than equivalent PMOS and NMOS types.

352

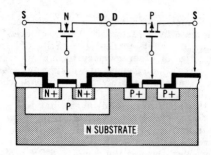

Fig. B-9. CMOS transistor schematic symbol and cross section.

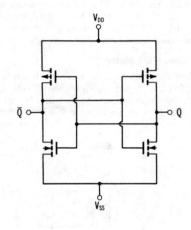

Fig. B-10. CMOS storage element.

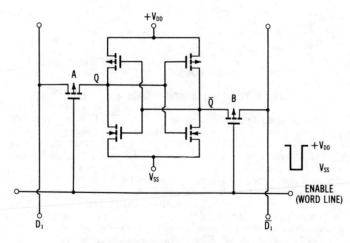

Fig. B-11. Six-transistor CMOS storage cell with
sense transmission gates A and B.

At present, CMOS memories have up to 1024 bits per chip. This figure will doubtlessly increase by a factor of 10, 100, or even 1000 if technology continues to advance at its present rate. Still, CMOS memories will lag behind the densities of other memory technologies due to the extra transistors. CMOS has the side benefit of working quite well in the linear mode, making CMOS attractive to system designers who want to combine linear and digital functions.

One problem with CMOS devices involves what is known as *parasitic conduction*. This is a result of a p substrate being near a p source and drain, and results in a breakdown and conduction. Such conduction paths require the additional step of creating isolation barriers in the manufacturing process. Moreover, there is the common MOS problem of parasitic capacitance resulting from a layer of silicon dioxide separating a metal gate and a conducting substrate. The only way to eliminate the capacitance is to reduce the substrate area, or start with another base for the substrate—such ideas have resulted in SOS technology, or *Silicon On Sapphire*. In SOS, the substrate-to-node capacitance is reduced, and therefore speed is increased as compared with CMOS.

Dynamic MOS Memory

The dynamic cell is a more simple structure than the static cell. Fig. B-12 shows a simple dynamic PMOS storage element. The figure shows that the presence or absence of *charge* on one of the flip-flop gates maintains a logic 1 or a logic 0 on the flip-flop output. How is this accomplished? MOS gates typically have an input impedance of 10^{9} ohms in

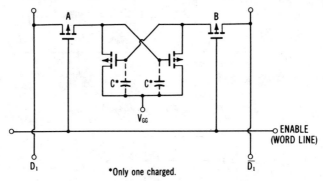

Fig. B-12. Dynamic MOS storage element.

parallel with a distributed capacitance of 2 pF. Because the capacitance is across such a large resistance, it can hold a charge for about 2 milliseconds. (This results from $t = RC$, which means that the charge on the gate for a logic 1 will leak off to 0.7 of its original logic 1 value in approximately 2 ms.) Since a typical processor with a cycle time of a few microseconds can execute many instructions in this period, some smart memory designer realized he could easily stop everything in the processor every 2 ms, quickly charge the memory cell back up (say in 1 μs) and then continue executing instructions. As far as overall processor time is concerned, the recharge delay will hardly be noticed, and the dynamic cell will appear to act like a static cell. Transistors are used on each flip-flop to sense and select one and only one cell. These are labeled A and B in Fig. B-12.

354

Even simpler cells than this can be constructed to operate in the dynamic mode. Fig. B-13 shows two *one*-transistor memory cells that rely on the capacitance (labeled C_s) that is distributed between the source and the substrate. Such small cells allow extremely high bit density on a chip. The following paragraphs describe the result of applying such a structure to make up a 4096-bit memory chip. The chip is produced by Texas Instruments and is called the TMS 4030. It is an amazing device packing over 4000 bits into a tiny 1-by-½-inch IC.

The MOS transistors used in the TMS 4030 are n channel and are used like transmission gates. When a logic 1 is written, the row and data/sense lines are raised to V_{DD} and C_s charges to V_{DD}. When data are being read, the row and data/sense lines are raised and sensed for logic 1 or 0.

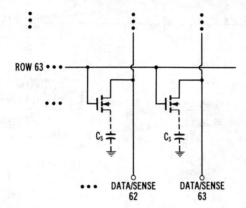

ROW 63 • • •

• • •

DATA/SENSE 62   DATA/SENSE 63

Fig. B-13. Two one-transistor dynamic MOS storage elements.

Fig. B-14 shows the structure of the TMS 4030 4K memory chip. When the chip enable input goes low (logic 0), an internal clock, with edge called ϕ_0, equalizes the voltages on the column inputs on either side of a "sense amplifier." Sixty-four of these differential sense amplifiers run across the center of the chip as illustrated, one for each column. Simultaneously, a voltage halfway between a logic 1 and a logic 0 is developed across a memory capacitor in an unused "dummy" bit row, of which there are two running on either side of the differential sense amplifiers. A pulse voltage generator circuit pumps charge to the dummy cells.

To refresh the memory, first an address is applied and the row decoders select one of 64 rows and the dummy bit row on the opposite side of the differential amplifier. (For a read, the above action occurs and one of the 64 columns is decoded. The charge on the cell at the selected row and the selected column is on one side of the differential amplifier, while the charge on the cell of the dummy row and the selected column is on the other side of the differential amplifier.) Since the dummy bits idle at one-half the supply voltage, the selected bits will be above or below this, i.e., a logic 1 or a logic 0, depending on the charge on C_s previously written. Now clock signal edge ϕ_0 occurs, and the differential sense amplifier latches into the sensed state. The states of the 64 bits in the selected row are now effectively restored. This is quite similar to the read/restore operation of magnetic core memory.

After the ϕ_0 clock edge, the column decoder passes the selected column into the column preamplifier. The selected logic 1 or logic 0 appears on

355

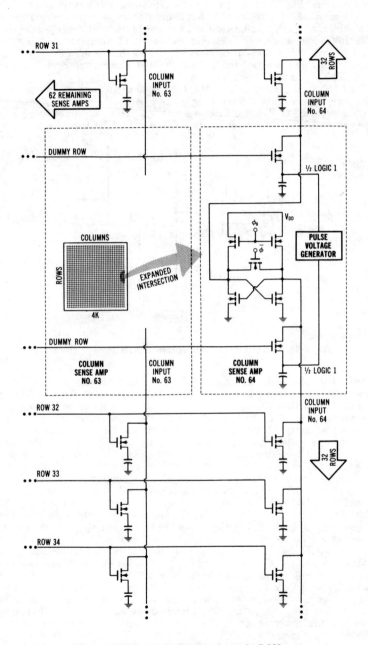

Fig. B-14. TMS 4030 4096-bit dynamic RAM.

the single data output lead. To write into memory, the column decode circuit selects one of the 64 columns to the "data-in" line. During the write, the sense amplifier on the selected column latches like a set/reset flip-flop, and new data are written into the row selected by the row decode address. The other bits on the row are simply refreshed during this write operation.

The complete block diagram of the memory chip is shown in Fig. B-15. This diagram shows how the simple cell structure forces a rather complex amount of peripheral circuitry. Yet, as far as external requirements are concerned, the device functions in a straightforward manner.

As far as updating is concerned, we need to refresh the row bits (i.e., addresses A_0–A_5) for 0.9 μs every 2 ms (a duty cycle of about 2000:1). A simple shift register can do the refreshing, cycling through the six addresses with a 1-MHz clock.

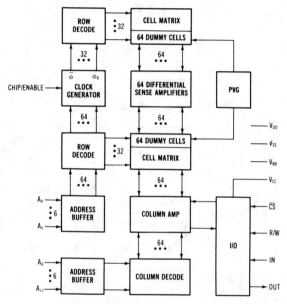

Fig. B-15. TMS 4030 block diagram.

READ-ONLY MEMORIES

The job of the ROM (*R*ead-*O*nly-*M*emory) cell is to permanently store a logic 1 or a logic 0. Such a simple function can be implemented in a number of ways, depending on the type of semiconductor material used.

Diode Matrix ROM

Perhaps the simplest example of a ROM memory is the diode matrix ROM shown in Fig. B-16. With the diodes connected as shown, addressing a bit requires raising the WORD line to logic 1 and grounding the DATA line. If a diode is connected at the selected row and column, the bit will be read as a logic 1 because the diode is forward-biased and provides a low-impedance current path to +5 volts through a cathode resistor. If no diode is connected, the output will be read as a logic 0 by a transistor pulling the row line to ground.

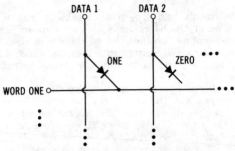

Fig. B-16. Diode connections in a ROM.

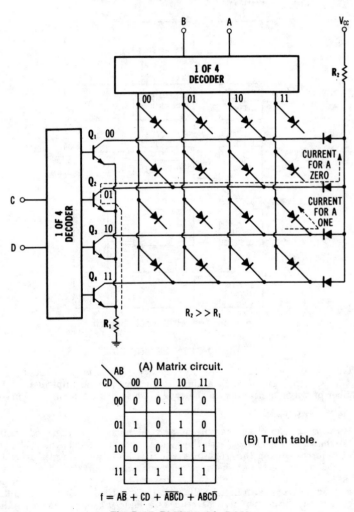

(A) Matrix circuit.

AB CD	00	01	10	11
00	0	0	1	0
01	1	0	1	0
10	0	0	1	1
11	1	1	1	1

(B) Truth table.

$$f = A\bar{B} + CD + \bar{A}BCD + ABC\bar{D}$$

Fig. B-17. Diode matrix ROM.

Fig. B-17 shows how to make a simple 4-by-4 ROM memory using a diode matrix and TTL decoders. If we select a cell by applying a 4-bit address, a diode present at the junction of the selected row and column will provide a low-impedance current path to +5 volts, and a logic 1 will be read. If no diode is present (and R_2 is much greater than R_1), the output will be pulled low by a transistor (current path B) and a logic 0 will be read.

Note that we can easily remove the diodes with a soldering iron. In a way, then, we could say the diode ROM is "programmable." The 1's and 0's that are fixed by the diodes' positions can be reconfigured. Thus, we could call this ROM a PROM, or Programmable *ROM*. But, if the device is programmable (i.e., you *can* change the bit pattern), isn't it a RAM? The answer to this dilemma has to do with how we define "program-

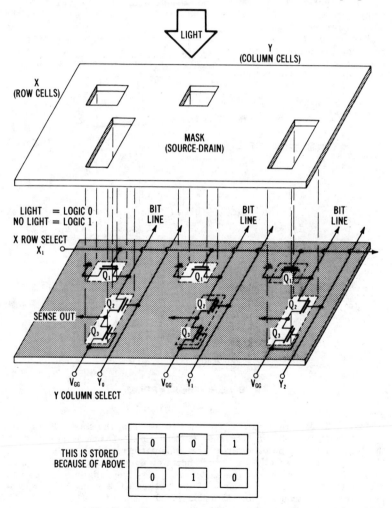

Fig. B-18. Mask programming a static ROM.

mable." In the memory industry, ROM cells are distinguished from PROM devices in that the ROM is an integrated circuit, usually programmed by the manufacturer, while the PROM is programmed by the user. Thus, the diode ROM is technically a PROM if we change the diodes, and only a ROM if we don't change the diodes. In large quantities, ROMs are "mask-programmed."

Mask-Programmed ROM

Consider a logic 1 to be stored at a permanent location in a memory matrix or cell location. A special template or mask is designed and reduced photographically to an extremely small size. The mask is made so that it allows light to expose only those cells that are to be logic 0's. Fig. B-18 shows the schematic symbol and masking operation for a MOS ROM cell. (Remember, this is occurring on a microscopic level.) Transistor Q_1 being accessible through the mask holes allows Q_1 to be included in the manufacturing diffusion process. Now when the memory chip is operating, and the bit or data line is sensed, or is taken to logic 0, a logic 0 will be read due to the inclusion of Q_1. On the other hand, no light through the mask over Q_1 will take Q_1 out of the circuit, and then raising the bit line will cause a logic 1 to be read.

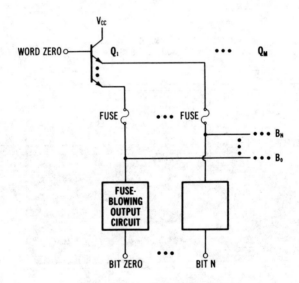

Fig. B-19. Fusible-link PROM.

Masked ROMs are organized in many sizes, from the small 32×8 size up to the large 2048×8. The code pattern for the ROM is supplied by the designer to the manufacturer. This code pattern will be in the form of 1's and 0's on either tabular boxed sheets of paper, 80-column computer cards, or computer paper tape. Often a higher-level language is used to develop the binary code, especially if the masked ROM is used in a microprocessor. Turnaround time is the main drawback of the masked ROM, usually running two to three weeks.

360

PROM Cells

As was pointed out, PROM cells do the same thing as ROM cells, with the exception that the user usually does the programming. There are two basic types of PROM: fusible-link, which can be written in only once and may not be changed later, and ultraviolet erasable (sometimes mistakenly called electrically alterable), which can be written in and erased many times.

Fusible-Link PROM

Fig. B-19 shows the fusible-link cell. Selecting a WORD enables one multiple-emitter word transistor, for example Q_1 in the figure. Each emitter is connected through a 200-angstrom–thick Nichrome fuse to the bit column. With all fuses intact, all bits are logic 0. To program a bit in a word, the word is addressed in the normal manner, and the bits of the

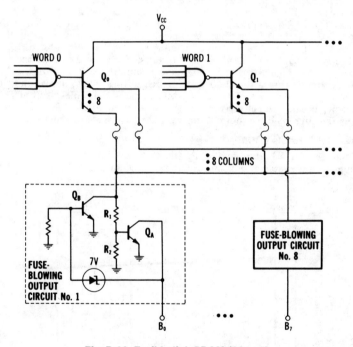

Fig. B-20. Fusible-link PROM (32 × 8).

word to be made a logic 1 are raised to a voltage that trips a comparator on the output pin. The comparator, in turn, directly grounds the selected emitter. Voltage V_{CC} is then raised above the normal +5 volts to +12.5 volts, which is enough to blow the respective fuse. Each bit of the word is programmed in this manner, until the entire word is complete. All circuits with blown fuses will be read as logic 1's during a read cycle.

There are other alternatives to using Nichrome fuses: polycrystalline silicon links (which don't suffer from a "grow back" condition) and back-to-back diodes.

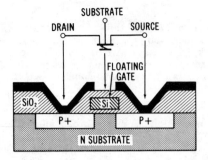

Fig. B-21. UVROM (FAMOS) inverter cell.

Fig. B-20 shows a typical fusible-link PROM memory IC organized as 32 words by 8 bits per word. The 32 words are implemented with 32 npn transistors with 8 emitters per transistor. Each emitter has a fuse in series with it. To program the PROM, a word is first selected via a five-input NAND gate, which turns on one of the transistors through R_1 in series with R_2. To store a logic 1 in the first bit of the eight-bit word, the respective output pin is raised to +8 volts. This breaks down the comparator zener diode, turning on Q_B and grounding one side of the fuse. The V_{cc} line is raised to +12.5 volts, which puts 4.5 volts across the fuse, causing it to blow open. The other 7 bits in the word, unless raised about the zener breakdown, effectively see the series resistance of $R_1 + R_2$, which keeps the current low enough to prevent the fuse from blowing.

Ultraviolet Erasable PROM

The need for a highly flexible PROM that could be used to develop and debug digital systems and microcomputers led to the development of the

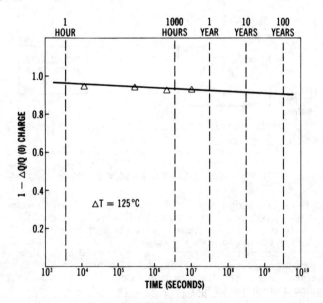

Fig. B-22. UVROM charge decay.

ultraviolet erasable PROM, or UVROM. This device is also called FAMOS for *F*ield *A*lterable *MOS*.

The UVROM cell, as shown in Fig. B-21, is similar in makeup to the standard PMOS cell, with the exception that the silicon gate is floating electrically from the source, drain, and substrate material. It is insulated by a thin layer of silicon dioxide.

A logic 1 is programmed into the cell by applying a high-voltage pulse between the source and drain of the cell. This causes an electron avalanche between these elements, which results in a buildup of negative charge on the floating gate. The charge will decay at an extremely slow rate, as Fig. B-22 shows.

Since the gate is negatively charged, the PMOS channel is enhanced, and a low resistance will exist between the source and drain. An extrapolation of the charge decay shows that this initial charge will drop less than 30% over 100 years.

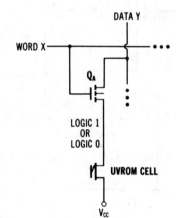

Fig. B-23. UVROM storage element.

Erasing the logic 1 is accomplished by bombarding the device with ultraviolet light. A quartz window on the chip allows the UV to enter. This results in the flow of photocurrent from the floating gate back to the substrate, thereby discharging the gate to its original state of nonconduction.

Fig. B-23 shows the basic UVROM memory cell. Once the *cell* is programmed to a logic 1 or 0, raising the WORD and DATA lines enables the cell state to appear through Q_A, causing either V_{CC} (logic zero) or V_{DD} (logic 1) to be read.

Fig. B-24A shows a single FAMOS cell along with its associated decoding, sensing, and programming circuits. Fig. B-24B shows how the 2048 cells in a UVROM chip are arranged in 8 planes of 8 × 32 cells. Each plane contains 256 FAMOS cells, located at the row/column intersects. The planes are stacked on top of each other, so that there are 8 bits (one on each plane) which share the same row/column intersect. This group of 8 bits can be treated as an 8-bit word being located at a specific (X, Y) coordinate.

To program a word, the address of the word (row/column intersect) is encoded on the address lines A_0–A_7. The bit pattern to be programmed is encoded on the D_0–D_7 data lines by grounding those bits which are to be

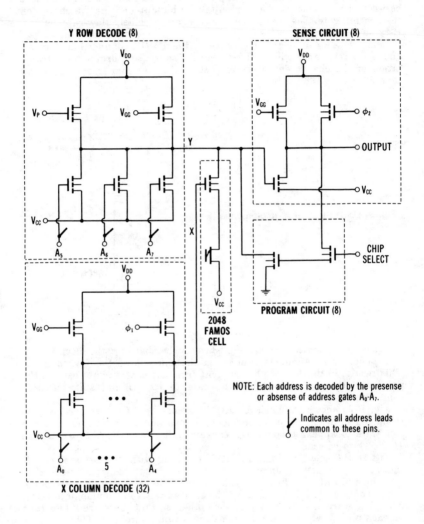

(A) FAMOS cell with associated circuitry.

Fig. B-24. Use of

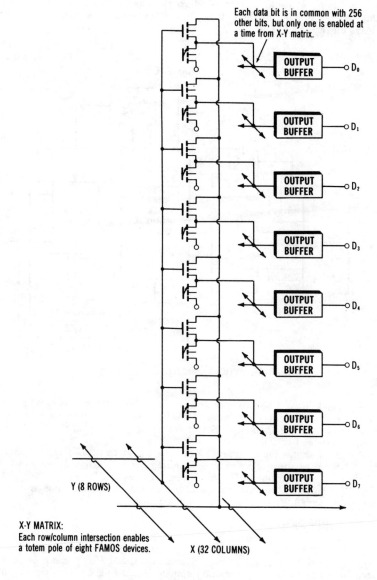

Each data bit is in common with 256 other bits, but only one is enabled at a time from X-Y matrix.

OUTPUT BUFFER ○ D_0

OUTPUT BUFFER ○ D_1

OUTPUT BUFFER ○ D_2

OUTPUT BUFFER ○ D_3

OUTPUT BUFFER ○ D_4

OUTPUT BUFFER ○ D_5

OUTPUT BUFFER ○ D_6

OUTPUT BUFFER ○ D_7

Y (8 ROWS)

X-Y MATRIX:
Each row/column intersection enables a totem pole of eight FAMOS devices.

X (32 COLUMNS)

(B) Matrix of FAMOS cells in 2048-bit memory.

FAMOS cells.

365

programmed as logic 1, while setting the logic 0 lines at −40 volts. A −50-volt, 5-milliampere, 5-millisecond pulse is then applied to the V_{GG} and V_{DD} lines while V_{CC} is held at +12 volts. This will produce enough charge on the floating gate to turn it on, programming a logic 1. Once this has been done, the only way that the logic can be changed to a logic 0 is by using ultraviolet light to allow the charge to leak off. Of course this process is done to the entire chip at the same time, which in effect clears all the bits to logic 0.

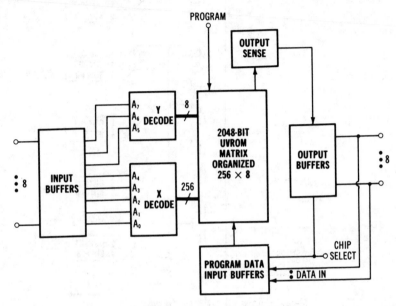

Fig. B-25. UVROM memory IC block diagram.

The clock inputs shown (ϕ_1 and ϕ_2) are two-phase, allowing either static or dynamic operation of the UVROM—static being easier to implement, and dynamic the more efficient. For static operation, the clocks are simply returned to V_{CC}.

Fig. B-25 shows the complete block diagram of the UVROM. Although the UVROM requires complex programming for its storage, its erasability offers a generous tradeoff. Programmers for these ROMs have a hex keyboard for entry of the data words. They also have ultraviolet lamps which can erase the 2048 bits in less than ten minutes.

Dynamic ROM Cells

Although a dynamic ROM might sound like a contradiction in terms, the watchful reader might have anticipated this possibility when we covered UVROMs in the last section. Remember, the UVROM could be operated in either the static or dynamic mode, depending on whether or not two clocks, ϕ_1 and ϕ_2, were available.

In essence, the dynamic ROM uses the same capacitor charge principle that is used in the dynamic RAM covered earlier, except that the bits are

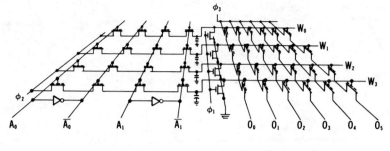

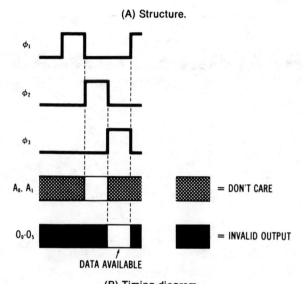

This gate may be present or absent as per program.

(A) Structure.

(B) Timing diagram.

Fig. B-26. Mask-programmed 4 × 6 dynamic ROM.

made either 1 or 0 by the absence or presence of physical gates on the chip. Fig. B-26A shows a mask-programmed dynamic ROM, while Fig. B-26B is a timing diagram for this simple memory. Such a ROM is rarely advertised as being dynamic; however, careful examination of certain manufacturers' data sheets reveals that the clock must stay high to keep the data from leaking off.

RAM SELECTION AID

		·tion	Organization	No. of Pins	Electrical Characteristics Over Temperature				
					Access Time Max.	Cycle Time Max.	Power Dissipation Max.[1] Operating/Standby	Supplies[V]	
		·oded	256x1	16	1500ns	1500ns	685mW/340mW	+5, -9	
		Fully	256x1	16	1000ns	1000ns	685mW/340mW	+5, -9	
		·ecoded	1024x1	18	300ns	580ns	400mW/64mW	+16, +19	
		·ecoded	1024x1	18	150ns	340ns	437mW/76mW	+19, +22	
		·ecoded	1024x1	18	205ns	580ns	400mW/64mW	+16, +19	
		·ecoded	1024x1	18	145ns	340ns	627mW/10mW	+19, +22	
		·ecoded	1024x1	18	145ns	400ns	570mW/10mW	+19, +22	
		·O	256x4	22	350ns	350ns	300mW	+5	
		·O	256x4	22	250ns	250ns	350mW	+5	
		·O	256x4	22	450ns	450ns	300mW	+5	
			1024x1	16	350ns	350ns	275mW	+5	
			1024x1	16	250ns	250ns	325mW	+5	
			1024x1	16	450ns	450ns	275mW	+5	
		High Speed Static	1024x1	16	450ns	450ns	275mW	+5	
2102A-6	1024	High Speed Static	1024x1	16	650ns	650ns	275mW	+5	
2102AL	1024	Low Standby Power Static	1024x1	16	350ns	350ns	165mW/35mW	+5	
2102AL-2	1024	Low Standby Power Static	1024x1	16	250ns	250ns	325mW/42mW	+5	
2102AL-4	1024	Low Standby Power Static	1024x1	16	450ns	450ns	165mW/35mW	+5	
M2102A-4	1024	Static, T_A = -55°C to +125°C	1024x1	16	450ns	450ns	350mW	+5	
2104A-1	4096	16 Pin Dynamic	4096x1	16	150ns	320ns	420mW/18mW	+12, +5, -5	
2104A-2	4096	16 Pin Dynamic	4096x1	16	200ns	320ns	384mW/18mW	+12, +5, -5	
2104A-3	4096	16 Pin Dynamic	4096x1	16	250ns	375ns	360mW/18mW	+12, +5, -5	
2104A-4	4096	16 Pin Dynamic	4096x1	16	300ns	425ns	360mW/18mW	+12, +5, -5	
2107A	4096	22 Pin Dynamic	4096x1	22	300ns	700ns	458mW/2mW	+12, +5, -5	
2107A-1	4096	22 Pin Dynamic	4096x1	22	280ns	550ns	516mW/2mW	+12, +5, -5	
2107A-4	4096	22 Pin Dynamic	4096x1	22	350ns	840ns	450mW/2mW	+12, +5, -5	
2107A-5	4096	22 Pin Dynamic	4096x1	22	420ns	970ns	376mW/2mW	+12, +5, -5	
2107B	4096	22 Pin Dynamic	4096x1	22	200ns	400ns	648mW/4mW	+12, +5, -5	
2107B-4	4096	22 Pin Dynamic	4096x1	22	270ns	470ns	648mW/4mW	+12, +5, -5	
2107B-5	4096	22 Pin Dynamic	4096x1	22	300ns	590ns	648mW/5mW	+12, +5, -5	
2108-2	8192	16 Pin Dynamic	8192x1	16	200ns	350ns	828mW/24mW	+12, +5, -5	
2108-4	8192	16 Pin Dynamic	8192x1	16	300ns	425ns	780mW/24mW	+12, +5, -5	
2111A	1024	Static, Common I/O with Output Deselect	256x4	18	350ns	350ns	300mW	+5	
2111A-2	1024	Static, Common I/O with Output Deselect	256x4	18	250ns	250ns	350mW	+5	
2111A-4	1024	Static, Common I/O with Output Deselect	256x4	18	450ns	450ns	300mW	+5	
2112A	1024	Static, Common I/O without Output Deselect	256x4	16	350ns	350ns	300mW	+5	
2112A-2	1024	Static, Common I/O without Output Deselect	256x4	16	250ns	250ns	350mW	+5	
2112A-4	1024	Static, Common I/O without Output Deselect	256x4	16	450ns	450ns	300mW	+5	

SILICON GATE MOS

Courtesy Intel Corp.

369

	Type	No. of Bits	Description	Organi-zation	No. of Pins	Access Time Max.	Cycle Time Max.	Power Dissipation Max.[1] Operating/Standby	Supplies[V]
						Electrical Characteristics Over Temperature			
SILICON GATE MOS	2114	4096	Static, Common I/O	1024x4	18	450ns	450ns	710mW	+5
	2114-2	4096	Static, Common I/O	1024x4	18	200ns	200ns	710mW	+5
	2114-3	4096	Static, Common I/O	1024x4	18	300ns	300ns	710mW	+5
	2114L	4096	Static, Common I/O	1024x4	18	450ns	450ns	370mW	+5
	2114L-3	4096	Static, Common I/O	1024x4	18	300ns	300ns	370mW	+5
	2115A	1024	Static, Open Collector	1024x1	16	45ns	45ns	660mW	+5
	2115A-2	1024	Static, Open Collector	1024x1	16	70ns	70ns	660mW	+5
	2115AL	1024	Static, Open Collector	1024x1	16	45ns	45ns	395mW	+5
	2115AL-2	1024	Static, Open Collector	1024x1	16	70ns	70ns	395mW	+5
	M2115A	1024	Static, Open Collector	1024x1	16	55ns	55ns	690mW	+5
	M2115AL	1024	Static, Open Collector	1024x1	16	75ns	75ns	415mW	+5
	2115	1024	Static, Open Collector	1024x1	16	95ns	95ns	525mW	+5
	2115-2	1024	Static, Open Collector	1024x1	16	70ns	70ns	660mW	+5
	2115L	1024	Static, Open Collector	1024x1	16	95ns	95ns	345mW	+5
	2125A	1024	Static, Three-State	1024x1	16	45ns	45ns	660mW	+5
	2125A-2	1024	Static, Three-State	1024x1	16	70ns	70ns	660mW	+5
	2125AL	1024	Static, Three-State	1024x1	16	45ns	45ns	395mW	+5
	2125AL-2	1024	Static, Three-State	1024x1	16	70ns	70ns	395mW	+5
	M2125A	1024	Static, Three-State	1024x1	16	55ns	55ns	690mW	+5
	M2125AL	1024	Static, Three-State	1024x1	16	75ns	75ns	415mW	+5
	2125	1024	Static, Three-State	1024x1	16	95ns	95ns	525mW	+5
	2125-2	1024	Static, Three-State	1024x1	16	70ns	70ns	660mW	+5
	2125L	1024	Static, Three-State	1024x1	16	95ns	95ns	345mW	+5
	2116-2	16384	16 Pin Dynamic	16384x1	16	200ns	350ns	828mW/24mW	+12, +5, -5
	2116-3	16384	16 Pin Dynamic	16384x1	16	250ns	375ns	816mW/24mW	+12, +5, -5
	2116-4	16384	16 Pin Dynamic	16384x1	16	300ns	425ns	780mW/24mW	+12, +5, -5
	2147	4096	High Speed Static	4096x1	18	60-90ns	60-90ns	500mW/50mW (Typical)	+5
SCHOTTKY BIPOLAR	3101	64	Fully Decoded	16x4	16	60ns	60ns	525mW	+5
	3101A	64	High Speed Fully Decoded	16x4	16	35ns	35ns	525mW	+5
	3104	16	Content Addressable Memory	4x4	24	30ns	40ns	625mW	+5
SILICON GATE CMOS	5101-8	1024	Static CMOS RAM	256x4	22	800ns	800ns	150mW/2 5mW	+5
	5101L	1024	Static CMOS RAM	256x4	22	650ns	650ns	135mW/20µW	+5
	5101L-1	1024	Static CMOS RAM	256x4	22	450ns	450ns	135mW/20µW	+5
	5101L-3	1024	Static CMOS RAM	256x4	22	650ns	650ns	135mW/1mW	+5
	M5101-4	1024	Static CMOS RAM (-55°C to 125°C)	256x4	22	800ns	800ns	168mW/1mW	+5
	M5101L-4	1024	Static CMOS RAM (-55°C to 125°C)	256x4	22	800ns	800ns	168mW/400µW	+5

Courtesy Intel Corp.

MOS PROM SELECTION AIDS AND PINOUTS

The following table contains information arranged by bit storage capacity and package size. Both 4 and 8 bit PROMs are included; however, 8 bit PROMs predominate. Manufacturers are listed alphabetically within each category. Manufacturer's part numbers do not include package style information, as this would unduly complicate the table. Designer information is obtained from manufacturer's catalogs and data sheets as well as by direct interface with the factories. However, like all such tabulations, it is subject to change. Critical parameters should be verified by the manufacturer.

Parameters which are tabulated include output type (open collector or tri-state), max access time (address to output valid), technology and max operating power. Where military equivalents differ from commercial grade parts, those parameters are shown in parenthesis. The unprogrammed or erased state is also tabulated. Pinout style information is grouped at the end of the tables.

CONFIGURATION	VENDOR	PART NUMBER COMM	PART NUMBER MIL	OUTPUT TYPE	ACCESS TIME (NS)	TECHNOLOGY	ERASED STATE	POWER, MILLIWATTS	PINOUT TYPE	COMMENTS
256x4 16 PIN	HARRIS	HM6610-5 HM6611-5	HM6610-2 HM6611-2	OC TS	275 275	CMOS CMOS	H H	50 50	A16 A16	• Fusible Link: Access time with VCC=10V; 500 μW power consumption when deselected.
512x4 24 PIN	TOSHIBA	3181		—	—	—	—	—	—	
1024x4 24 PIN	INTERSIL	IM6603I IM6603AI IM6653		TS TS TS	280 (TYP) 150 (TYP) —	CMOS CMOS CMOS	H H H	0.6 0.6 0.6	A24 A24 A24	•5V only
256x8 24 PIN	AMD	AM1702A AM1702AL AM1702A-1 AM1702AL-1 AM1702A-2 AM1702AL-2		TS TS TS TS TS TS	1000 1000 550 550 650 650	PMOS PMOS PMOS PMOS PMOS PMOS	L L L L L L	676 — 676 — — 676	B24 B24 B24 B24 B24 B24	•AM1702AD is a one-time programmable version
	INTEL	1702* 1702A 4702A 1702A-2 1702A-6 1702AL 1702AL-2	M1702A	TS TS TS TS TS TS TS	1000 1000 (850) 1700 650 1500 1000 650	PMOS PMOS PMOS PMOS PMOS PMOS PMOS	L L L L L L L	— 885 (960) — 959 885 221 221	B24 B24 B24 B24 B24 B24 B24	•1602A is a one-time programmable version
	MITSUBISHI	M58563S (1702A)		TS	—	—	—	—	—	

Courtesy Pro-Log Corp.

MOS PROM Selection Aid (cont'd.)

CONFIGURATION	VENDOR	PART NUMBER COMM * MIL	OUTPUT TYPE	ACCESS TIME (NS)	TECHNOLOGY	ERASED STATE	POWER, MILLIWATTS	PINOUT TYPE	COMMENTS
256x8 24 PIN	MOSTEK	MK3702-1	TS	550	PMOS	L	—	B24	• MK3602 is a one-time programmable version
		MK3702-2	TS	750	PMOS	L	—	B24	
		MK3702-3	TS	1000	PMOS	L	—	B24	
	NATIONAL SEMI-CONDUCTOR	MM1702AQ	TS	1000	PMOS	L	885	B24	• MM1702AD is one-time programmable version
		MM5203Q MM4203Q	TS	1000	PMOS	H	—	C24	• Can be used as 256x8 or 512x4
	NEC	μPD454D	TS	800	NMOS	L	245 (TYP)	K24	• Electrically Erasable
	SIGNETICS	1702A	TS	1000	PMOS	L	—	B24	
512x8 24 PIN	AMI	S5204A	TS	750	PMOS	L	750	D24	
		S6834	TS	575	PMOS	L	750	E24	
		S6834-1	TS	750	PMOS	L	750	E24	
	ELECTRONIC ARRAYS	EA2704	TS	—	NMOS	H	—	F24	
	FAIRCHILD	F2704	TS	—	NMOS	H	—	F24	
	INTEL	2704*	TS	450	NMOS	H	800	F24	
	INTERSIL	IM66041	TS	280(TYP)	CMOS	H	0.6	G24	
		IM66041A1	TS	150(TYP)	CMOS	H	0.6	G24	
		IM6654	TS	—	CMOS	H	0.6	G24	• 5V only
	NATIONAL	MM5204 MM4204	TS	1000 (TYP)	PMOS	L	680 (850)	D24	
		MM5204-1Q	TS	700	PMOS	L	680	D24	
		MM2704Q*	TS	450	NMOS	H	800	F24	
	SIGNETICS	2704	TS	450	NMOS	H	800	F24	
1Kx8 24 PIN	AMD	AM2708 AM9708	TS	450	NMOS	H	800	H24	
	ELECTRONIC ARRAYS	EA2708	TS	—	NMOS	H	—	H24	
	FAIRCHILD	F2708	TS	—	NMOS	H	—	H24	
	FUJITSU	MB8518E	TS	650	NMOS	H	800	H24	
		MB8518H	TS	450	NMOS	H	800	H24	
	INTEL	2708 M2708	TS	450 (450)	NMOS	H	800 (750)	H24	• 2608 is one-time programmable part
		2708-1	TS	350	NMOS	H	800	H24	
		2708L	TS	450	NMOS	H	425	H24	
		8708	TS	450	NMOS	H	800	H24	• Equivalent to 2708
		2758	TS	450	NMOS	H	525/132	I24	• Single +5 volt supply. Power down mode.
	INTERSIL	7708 (2708)	TS	—	NMOS	H	—	H24	
	MITSUBISHI	M58732S (2708)	TS	450	NMOS	H	800	H24	
		M58732S1 (2708)	TS	650	NMOS	H	800	H24	
	MOSTEK	MK2708	TS	—	NMOS	H	—	H24	
	MOTOROLA	MCM68708	TS	450	NMOS	H	1100	H24	
		MCM2708	TS	450	NMOS	H	1100	H24	
		MCM68A708	TS	300	NMOS	H	1100	H24	
		MCM27A08	TS	300	NMOS	H	1100	H24	
	NATIONAL	MM2708	TS	450	MNOS	H	800	H24	
		MM2708-1	TS	350	MNOS	H	800	H24	
	SIGNETICS	2708	TS	450	MNOS	H	800	H24	
	TI	TMS2508	TS	—	NMOS	—	—	I24	• Single +5 volt supply
		TMS2708	TS	450	NMOS	H	800	H24	
		TMS27L08	TS	450	NMOS	H	475	H24	
	TOSHIBA	TMM322	—	—	NMOS	H	—	H24	

Courtesy Pro-Log Corp.

CONFIGURATION	VENDOR	PART NUMBER COMM	MIL	OUTPUT TYPE	ACCESS TIME (NS)	TECHNOLOGY	ERASED STATE	POWER, MILLIWATTS	PINOUT TYPE	COMMENTS
2Kx8 24 PIN	AMI	S4716**		TS	250	VMOS	H	525/132	I24	*Non-standard programming
	ELECTRONIC ARRAYS	EA2716**		TS	—	—	—	—	I24	
	FAIRCHILD	F2716**		TS	—	—	—	—	I24	
	FUJITSU	MBM2716**		TS	—	—	—	—	I24	
	INTEL	2716	M2716	TS	450	NMOS	H	525/132	I24	*2616 is one-time
		2716-2		TS	390	NMOS	H	525/132	I24	programmable part.
		2716-1		TS	350	NMOS	H	525/132	I24	Power down mode
	MOSTEK	MK2716 (T)		TS	450	NMOS	H	525/132	I24	
	MOTOROLA	TMS2716		TS	450	NMOS	H	1168	J24	*3 power supplies
		TMS27A16		TS	300	NMOS	H	1168	J24	*3 power supplies
		MCM2716		TS	450	NMOS	H	525/132	I24	*Single 5 volt power supply
		MCM27A16		TS	350	NMOS	H	525/132	I24	*Single 5 volt power supply
	NEC	μPD2716**		TS	—	—	—	—	I24	
	SIGNETICS	2716**		TS	—	—	—	—	I24	
	TI	TMS2716		TS	450	NMOS	H	700	J24	
		TMS2516		TS	—	NMOS	H	525/132	I24	
	TOSHIBA	TMM323**			—	—	—	—	I24	
1Kx8 28 PIN	NEC	μPD458D		TS	450	NMOS	L	1110	A28	*Electrically Erasable
1Kx8 40 PIN	INTEL	8741			—	—	L	675	A40	*Single-chip Microprocessor
		8748			—	—	L	675	B40	with EPROM on chip
2Kx8 40 PIN	INTEL	8755*		①	400	NMOS	H	900	C40	*Single-chip I/O
		8755A		①	400	NMOS	H	900	C40	with EPROM
	FAIRCHILD	38E70			—	—	—	—		*Single-chip Microprocessor with EPROM on chip
4Kx8 24 PIN	INTEL	2732		TS	—	NMOS	H	—	M24	
	TI	2532		TS	450	NMOS	H	840/132	L24	

* Obsolete PROM
** Under Development
① Internal address contains latches and two 8-bit ports.

Courtesy Pro-Log Corp.

MOS PROM Pinouts

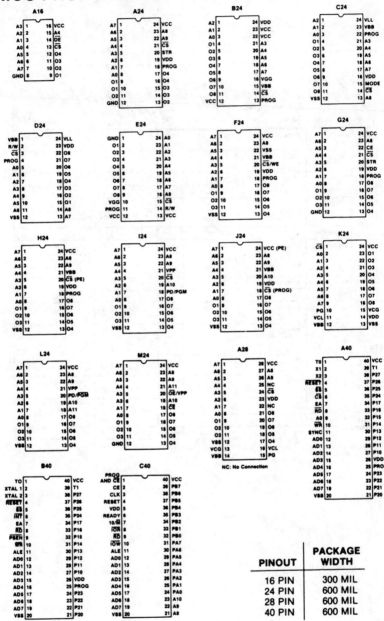

PINOUT	PACKAGE WIDTH
16 PIN	300 MIL
24 PIN	600 MIL
28 PIN	600 MIL
40 PIN	600 MIL

Courtesy Pro-Log Corp.

MICROCOMPUTER
MATH TABLES

The following tables and lists are provided to help you perform typical math calculations that arise in computer usage quickly and easily. Table E-1 is a hexadecimal addition table for finding the sum of two single hex digits (each digit may have a maximum hex value of F). Table E-2 is a hex multiplication table for finding the product of two hex digits; maximum digit value again is F. Table E-3 is an interesting way to convert between hex and decimal for hex values of up to FFFFFF (six digits). Each column (col 1-6) represents one hex digit. To convert a hex value to decimal simply add up the values found in each column for the respective digit in the hex number. Thus F00F hex equals $61,440 + 0 + 0 + 15 = 61,455$ decimal.

Table E-4 is a list of the decimal values of the powers of 2 (up to 2^{24}) and the decimal values of the power of 16 (up to 16^{15}). By using the middle table you can determine the decimal equivalent of powers to 2^{60}. Table E-4 will be useful for address range and segment calculations.

Tables E-5 and E-6 are for finding the hex values for a backward or forward relative branch. These are the hex values that must be inserted in the offsets for relative branches.

To use the tables count off the decimal difference between the location of the branch instruction and the label you are branching to. Then use this number in the forward relative table if the jump is forward, or the backward relative table if the jump is backward, to determine the hexadecimal offset. The hex offset is then made part of the branch instruction. It's the backward branch that causes most problems in relative offset calculations.

Table E-7 defines the way the three important Boolean functions OR, AND, and XOR (exclusive OR) work at the logic bit level, and how these functions may be used to set, clear, or complement bits.

Table E-1. Hexadecimal Addition Table

0	1	2	3	4	5	6	7	8	9	A	B	C	D	E	F
1	02	03	04	05	06	07	08	09	0A	0B	0C	0D	0E	0F	10
2	03	04	05	06	07	08	09	0A	0B	0C	0D	0E	0F	10	11
3	04	05	06	07	08	09	0A	0B	0C	0D	0E	0F	10	11	12
4	05	06	07	08	09	0A	0B	0C	0D	0E	0F	10	11	12	13
5	06	07	08	09	0A	0B	0C	0D	0E	0F	10	11	12	13	14
6	07	08	09	0A	0B	0C	0D	0E	0F	10	11	12	13	14	15
7	08	09	0A	0B	0C	0D	0E	0F	10	11	12	13	14	15	16
8	09	0A	0B	0C	0D	0E	0F	10	11	12	13	14	15	16	17
9	0A	0B	0C	0D	0E	0F	10	11	12	13	14	15	16	17	18
A	0B	0C	0D	0E	0F	10	11	12	13	14	15	16	17	18	19
B	0C	0D	0E	0F	10	11	12	13	14	15	16	17	18	19	1A
C	0D	0E	0F	10	11	12	13	14	15	16	17	18	19	1A	1B
D	0E	0F	10	11	12	13	14	15	16	17	18	19	1A	1B	1C
E	0F	10	11	12	13	14	15	16	17	18	19	1A	1B	1C	1D
F	10	11	12	13	14	15	16	17	18	19	1A	1B	1C	1D	1E

Courtesy Pro-Log Corp.

Table E-2. Hexadecimal Multiplication Table

1	2	3	4	5	6	7	8	9	A	B	C	D	E	F
2	04	06	08	0A	0C	0E	10	12	14	16	18	1A	1C	1E
3	06	09	0C	0F	12	15	18	1B	1E	21	24	27	2A	2D
4	08	0C	10	14	18	1C	20	24	28	2C	30	34	38	3C
5	0A	0F	14	19	1E	23	28	2D	32	37	3C	41	46	4B
6	0C	12	18	1E	24	2A	30	36	3C	42	48	4E	54	5A
7	0E	15	1C	23	2A	31	38	3F	46	4D	54	5B	62	69
8	10	18	20	28	30	38	40	48	50	58	60	68	70	78
9	12	1B	24	2D	36	3F	48	51	5A	63	6C	75	7E	87
A	14	1E	28	32	3C	46	50	5A	64	6E	78	82	8C	96
B	16	21	2C	37	42	4D	58	63	6E	79	84	8F	9A	A5
C	18	24	30	3C	48	54	60	6C	78	84	90	9C	A8	B4
D	1A	27	34	41	4E	5B	67	75	82	8F	9C	A9	B6	C3
E	1C	2A	38	46	54	62	70	7E	8C	9A	A8	B6	C4	D2
F	1E	2B	3C	4B	5A	69	78	87	96	A5	B4	C3	D2	E1

Courtesy Pro-Log Corp.

Table E-3. Hexadecimal and Decimal Conversion

HEXADECIMAL COLUMNS											
6		5		4		3		2		1	
HEX	DEC	HEX	DEC	HEX	DEC	HEX	DEC	HEX	DEC	HEX	DEC
0	0	0	0	0	0	0	0	0	0	0	0
1	1,048,576	1	65,536	1	4,096	1	256	1	16	1	1
2	2,097,152	2	131,072	2	8,192	2	512	2	32	2	2
3	3,145,728	3	196,608	3	12,288	3	768	3	48	3	3
4	4,194,304	4	262,144	4	16,384	4	1,024	4	64	4	4
5	5,242,880	5	327,680	5	20,480	5	1,280	5	80	5	5
6	6,291,456	6	393,216	6	24,576	6	1,536	6	96	6	6
7	7,340,032	7	458,752	7	28,672	7	1,792	7	112	7	7
8	8,388,608	8	524,288	8	32,768	8	2,048	8	128	8	8
9	9,437,184	9	589,824	9	36,864	9	2,304	9	144	9	9
A	10,485,760	A	655,360	A	40,960	A	2,560	A	160	A	10
B	11,534,336	B	720,896	B	45,056	B	2,816	B	176	B	11
C	12,582,912	C	786,432	C	49,152	C	3,072	C	192	C	12
D	13,631,488	D	851,968	D	53,248	D	3,328	D	208	D	13
E	14,680,064	E	917,504	E	57,344	E	3,584	E	224	E	14
F	15,728,640	F	983,040	F	61,440	F	3,840	F	240	F	15
7654		3210		7654		3210		7654		3210	
Byte				Byte				Byte			

Table E-4. Powers of 2 and Powers of 16

2^n	n	$2^0 = 16^0$		16^n	n
256	8	$2^4 = 16^1$			
512	9	$2^8 = 16^2$		16	1
1 024	10	$2^{12} = 16^3$		256	2
2 048	11	$2^{16} = 16^4$		4 096	3
4 096	12	$2^{20} = 16^5$		65 536	4
8 192	13	$2^{24} = 16^6$		1 048 576	5
16 384	14	$2^{28} = 16^7$		16 777 216	6
32 768	15	$2^{32} = 16^8$		268 435 456	7
65 536	16	$2^{36} = 16^9$		4 294 967 296	8
131 072	17	$2^{40} = 16^{10}$		68 719 476 736	9
262 144	18	$2^{44} = 16^{11}$		1 099 511 627 776	10
524 288	19	$2^{48} = 16^{12}$		17 592 186 044 416	11
1 048 576	20	$2^{52} = 16^{13}$		281 474 976 710 656	12
2 097 152	21	$2^{56} = 16^{14}$		4 503 599 627 370 496	13
4 194 304	22	$2^{60} = 16^{15}$		72 057 594 037 927 936	14
8 388 608	23			1 152 921 504 606 846 976	15
16 777 216	24				

Table E-5. Backward Relative Branch Table

MSD\LSD	0	1	2	3	4	5	6	7	8	9	A	B	C	D	E	F
8	128	127	126	125	124	123	122	121	120	119	118	117	116	115	114	113
9	112	111	110	109	108	107	106	105	104	104	102	101	100	99	98	97
A	96	95	94	93	92	91	90	89	88	87	86	85	84	83	82	81
B	80	79	78	77	76	75	74	73	72	71	70	69	68	67	66	65
C	64	63	62	61	60	59	58	57	56	55	54	53	52	51	50	49
D	48	47	46	45	44	43	42	41	40	39	38	37	36	35	34	33
E	32	31	30	29	28	27	26	25	24	23	22	21	20	19	18	17
F	16	15	14	13	12	11	10	9	8	7	6	5	4	3	2	1

Courtesy Pro-Log Corp.

Table E-6. Forward Relative Branch Table

MSD\LSD	0	1	2	3	4	5	6	7	8	9	A	B	C	D	E	F
0	0	1	2	3	4	5	6	7	8	9	10	11	12	13	14	15
1	16	17	18	19	20	21	22	23	24	25	26	27	28	29	30	31
2	32	33	34	35	36	37	38	39	40	41	42	43	44	45	46	47
3	48	49	50	51	52	53	54	55	56	57	58	59	60	61	62	63
4	64	65	66	67	68	69	70	71	72	73	74	75	76	77	78	79
5	80	81	82	83	84	85	86	87	88	89	90	91	92	93	94	95
6	96	97	98	99	100	101	102	103	104	105	106	107	108	109	110	111
7	112	113	114	115	116	117	118	119	120	121	122	123	124	125	126	127

Courtesy Pro-Log Corp.

Table E-7. Boolean Laws of Operation for 0 to 1

OR (+)
$0 + X = X$ meaning: if $X = 1$, $0 + 1 = 1$; if $X = 0$, $0 + 0 = 0$
$1 + X = 1$ meaning: if $X = 1$, $1 + 1 = 1$; if $X = 0$, $1 + 0 = 1$
AND (•)
$0 • X = 0$ meaning: if $X = 1$, $0 • 1 = 0$; if $X = 0$, $0 • 0 = 0$
$1 • X = X$ meaning: if $X = 1$, $1 • 1 = 1$; if $X = 0$, $1 • 0 = 0$
XOR ($\oplus$)
$0 \oplus X = X$ meaning: if $X = 1$, $0 \oplus 1 = 1$; if $X = 0$, $0 \oplus 0 = 0$
$1 \oplus X = X$ meaning: if $X = 1$, $1 \oplus 1 = 0$; if $X = 0$, $1 \oplus 0 = 1$

Example of eight bit operations

Operand	X X X X X X X X	X X X X X X X X	X X X X X X X X
Operator OR	1 1 0 1 0 0 0 1	AND 1 1 0 1 0 0 0 1	XOR 1 1 0 1 0 0 0 1
	1 1 X 1 X X X 1	X X 0 X 0 0 0 X	X X X X X X X X

Summary
OR = Set any bits where the OR operator equals 1
AND = Reset any bits where the AND operator equals 0
XOR = Complement any bits where the XOR operator equals 1

Courtesy Pro-Log Corp.

Bibliography

ABBREVIATIONS

DD	Department of Documents
DPB	Department of Printed Books
DSR	Department of Sound Records
HO	Home Office
IWM	Imperial War Museum
LAB	Ministry of Labour
MEPO	(MEPOL) Metropolitan Police
MRC	Modern Records Centre
MUN	Ministry of Munitions
PRO	Public Record Office

UNPUBLISHED SOURCES

BRUNEL UNIVERSITY LIBRARY

Barker, Lottie. "My Life as I Remember It, 1899–1920," TS, 70 pp.
Lord, Annie. "My Life," MS, 12 pp.
Meadowcroft, Charlotte. "Bygones," MS, 35 pp.

FAWCETT LIBRARY

Women's University Settlement Thirtieth Annual Report, March 1917, Women's
University Settlement Collection.

IMPERIAL WAR MUSEUM

Department of Documents

Adams, Margaret H. "Reminiscences of W.W.I experiences; The Visitor." P348 W/W/1 T.
Airey, Miss Edith. 81/9/1.
Castle, Mrs. Olive. "First World War Reminiscences," Misc. 61, item 948.
Kaye, Mrs. P.371 T.
Taylor, Miss O. M. "Recollections of the Great War, 1914–1918." 83/17/1.
West, Miss G. M. Diary 1916–1918. 77/156/1.

Department of Photographs

Department of Printed Books

Williams, Joan. "A Munition Workers' [sic] Career At Messrs. Gwynne's— Chiswick. 1915–1919."
Women's Work Collection. Particularly Emp., Mun.

Department of Sound Records

Interviews by Southampton Oral History Project.
Oral History Recordings. War Work 1914–1918. Pt. 2, Industry and Agriculture.

Library

A. Darter, "Woolwich Arsenal 1917–18," 323.1, K.48004.

MODERN RECORDS CENTRE, UNIVERSITY OF WARWICK

Institute of Personnel Management Papers.
YWCA Papers.

PUBLIC RECORD OFFICE, KEW

Home Office
Metropolitan Police
Ministry of Labour
Ministry of Munitions

GOVERNMENT PUBLICATIONS

Annual Report of the Chief Inspector of Factories and Workshops for the Year 1916. Vol. 14. Cd. 8570. 1917–18.
Annual Report of the Chief Inspector of Factories and Workshops for the Year 1920. Cmd. 1403. 1921.

History of the Ministry of Munitions. 12 vols. 1918–23. Reprint. Sussex: Harvester Microform Press, 1976.

Industrial Fatigue Board. Report no. 13. *A Statistical Study of Labour Turnover in Munition and Other Factories.* 1921.

Ministry of Munitions. *Official History of the Scottish Filling Factory No. 4 (National), Georgetown, Renfrewshire.* Glasgow, 1919.

Ministry of Reconstruction. *Report of the Women's Employment Committee.* Cd. 9239. 1919.

Parliamentary Debates, Commons.

Parliamentary Papers.

Report of the War Cabinet Committee on Women in Industry. Cmd. 135. 1919.

U.S. Dept. of Labor. "Migration of Women's Labor Through the Employment Exchanges in Great Britain." In *Employment of Women and Juveniles in Great Britain during the War: Reprints of the Memoranda of the British Health of Munition Workers Committee.* Washington: Government Printing Office, 1917.

Working Classes Cost of Living Committee. *Report of the Committee appointed to Enquire into and report upon (i) the actual increase since June, 1914, in the Cost of Living to the working classes and (ii) any counterbalancing factors (apart from increase of wages) which may have arisen under War conditions.* Cd. 8980, 1918, vol. 7.

UNPUBLISHED PAPERS AND THESES

Barnett, L. Margaret. "Upgrading the Diet of Working Women: Canteens and Hostels in Munitions Factories in Britain During World War One." Paper delivered at the annual meeting of the North American Conference on British Studies, October 1990.

Hirst, T. F. "An Investigation of the Incorporation of Women Into the Engineering Trades in South London Between 1914–1918." M.Ed. thesis, University of Reading, 1976.

Hogg, Sallie Heller. "The Employment of Women in Great Britain 1891–1921." D.Phil. thesis, Oxford University, 1967.

Ineson, Antonia. "Science, Technology, Medicine, Welfare and the Labour Process: Women Munition Workers in the First World War." M.Phil. thesis, University of Sussex, 1981.

Kozak, Marion. "Women Munition Workers During the First World War with Special Reference to Engineering." D.Phil. thesis, University of Hull, 1976.

Mohun, Arwen. "Women, Work and Technology: The Steam Laundry Industry in the United States and Britain 1880–1940." Ph.D. thesis, Case Western Reserve University, 1992.

Rubin, Gerry R. "The Enforcement of the Munitions of War Acts, 1915–1917, with particular reference to Proceedings before the Munitions Tribunal in Glasgow, 1915–1921." Ph.D. thesis, University of Warwick, 1984.

Stark, Julie Gordon. "British Food Policy and Diet in the First World War." Ph.D. thesis, London School of Economics and Political Science, 1984.

Thom, Deborah. "Women Munition Workers at Woolwich Arsenal in the 1914–1918 War." M.A. thesis, University of Warwick, 1975.

NEWSPAPERS AND MAGAZINES

Banbury Guardian
Common Cause
Daily Mail
The Engineer
Georgetown Gazette (magazine of the Scottish National Filling Factory at George-
    town), PRO, MUN 5/154/1223/30.
Girls' Friend
Girls' Own Stories
Labour Woman
The Limit (magazine of the White and Poppe factory, Coventry), IWM, DD, 76/
    103/2.
Modern Woman
Newsletter (YWCA)
Our Girls
Our Own Gazette (YWCA)
Pioneer and Labour Journal (Woolwich)
Police Review and Parade Gossip
Punch
Sheffield Weekly Independent
The Suffragette
The Tatler
The Times
The Vote
The War-Worker
Woman At Home
Woman Engineer
Woman Worker
Woman's Dreadnought (later *Workers' Dreadnought*)
Woman's Life

MISCELLANEOUS NEWSPAPER ARTICLES

Fawcett Library. Clippings on women in the First World War.
Trades Union Congress Library. Gertrude Tuckwell Collection. Press clippings.
"Women in Munition Works." Vols. 1, 2. IWM, DPB, Women's Work Collection.
    Press cuttings.

INTERVIEWS

Mrs. Annie Davy, who worked at the Faversham explosives factories during
    W.W.I. Interviewed at her home in Faversham, Kent, 27 July 1989.
Mr. James Wilkie, Sr., and Mr. James Wilkie, Jr., husband and son of Sarah
    Wilkie, who worked as a welder from 1917 to 1920 at Beardmore's shipyard
    at Dalmuir, Clydebank, Scotland. Interview at the home of Mr. Wilkie, Jr.,
    in Santa Barbara, California, on 14 May 1986 two months after Sarah's death.

BOOKS AND PERIODICALS

Abbott, Edith. "The War and Women's Work in England," *Journal of Political Economy* 25, no. 7 (July 1917): 641–78.

Adams, R. J. Q. *Arms and the Wizard: Lloyd George and the Ministry of Munitions 1915–1916.* London: Cassell & Co., 1978.

Adams, R. J. Q. and Philip P. Poirier. *The Conscription Controversy in Great Britain, 1900–18.* Columbus: Ohio State University Press, 1987.

Adamson, R., and H. Palmer-Jones. "The Work of a Department for Employing Expectant Mothers in a Munition Factory," *British Medical Journal* 2 (21 September 1918): 309–10.

Alberti, Johanna. *Beyond Suffrage: Feminists in War and Peace, 1914–28.* New York: St. Martin's Press, 1989.

Alec-Tweedie, Mrs. "The War of Liberation: The Woman's Army," *English Review* (January 1917).

———. *Women and Soldiers.* London: John Lane, 1918.

Allen, Mary S. *Lady In Blue.* London: Stanley Paul & Co., 1936.

———. *The Pioneer Policewoman.* London: Chatto & Windus, 1925.

Allen, Mary S., and Julie Helen Heyneman. *Women at the Crossroads.* London: Unicorn Press, 1934.

"The Amended Munitions Court," *The Englishwoman* 37 (March 1918): 218–24.

Anderson, Adelaide M. "Factory and Workshop Law." Ch. 6 in *Woman in Industry: From Seven Points of View,* ed. Gertrude M. Tuckwell et al. London: Duckworth & Co., 1908, 143–81.

———. *Women in the Factory: An Administrative Adventure 1893 to 1921.* London: John Murray, 1922.

———. *Women Workers and the Health of the Nation.* London: John Bale, Sons & Danielson, 1918.

Andrews, Irene Osgood, and Margarett A. Hobbs. *Economic Effects of the War Upon Women and Children in Great Britain.* New York: Oxford University Press, 1918.

Bailey, Peter. *Leisure and Class in Victorian England: Rational Recreation and the Contest for Control, 1830–1885.* London: Routledge & Kegan Paul, 1978.

Barnett, L. Margaret. *British Food Policy in the First World War.* London: Allen and Unwin, 1985.

Beaufoy, S. L. G. "Well Hall Estate, Eltham: An Example of Good Housing Built in 1915," *Town Planning Review* 21 (October 1950): 259–71.

Beckett, Ian F. W. "Total War." In *War, Peace and Social Change in Twentieth-Century Europe,* ed. Clive Emsley, Arthur Marwick, and Wendy Simpson. Milton Keynes: Open University Press, 1989, 26–44.

Beddoe, Deirdre. *Back to Home and Duty: Women Between the Wars, 1918–1939.* London: Pandora, 1989.

Bedford, Madeline Ida. "Munition Wages." In *Scars Upon My Heart: Women's Poetry & Verse of the First World War,* ed. Catherine Reilly. London: Virago, 1981, 7–8.

Berg, Maxine. "Women's Work, Mechanisation and the Early Phases of Industrialisation in England." In *The Historical Meanings of Work,* ed. Patrick Joyce. Cambridge: Cambridge University Press, 1987, 64–96.

Bird, M. Mostyn. *Woman At Work: A Study of the Different Ways of Earning a Living Open to Women.* London: Chapman & Hall, 1911.

Blanch, Michael. "Imperialism, Nationalism and Organized Youth." In *Working-Class Culture: Studies in History and Theory,* ed. John Clark, Chas. Critcher, and Richard Johnson. London: Hutchinson, 1979.

Bland, Lucy. "In the Name of Protection: The Policing of Women in the First World War." In *Women in Law: Explorations in Law, Family & Sexuality,* ed. Julia Brophy and Carol Smart, 23–49. London: Routledge & Kegan Paul, 1985.

Bondfield, Margaret G. "Women's Trade Unions." In *The Woman's Year Book 1923-1924,* ed. G. Evelyn Gates. London: Women Publishers Ltd., n.d., 332–37.

Booth, Charles. *Notes on Social Influences and Conclusion.* Final vol. of *Life and Labour of the People in London.* London: Macmillan & Co., 1903.

Boston, Sarah. *Women Workers and the Trade Union Movement.* London: Davis Poynter, 1980.

Bowley, A. L. *Prices and Wages in the United Kingdom 1914–1920.* London, 1921.

Bowley, Ruth. "The Pursuits of Leisure: Amusements and Entertainments." In *Life and Leisure,* vol. 9 of *The New Survey of London Life & Labour,* ed. London School of Economics and Political Science. London: P. S. King & Son, 1935, 41–53.

Braybon, Gail. *Women Workers in the First World War: The British Experience.* London: Croom Helm, 1981. Reprint, Routledge, 1990.

Braybon, Gail, and Penny Summerfield. *Out of the Cage: Women's Experiences in Two World Wars.* London: Pandora, 1987.

British Association for the Advancement of Science. *Draft Interim Report of the Conference to Investigate into Outlets for Labour after the War.* Manchester, 1915.

British Women's Emigration Association. *Annual Report 1918.* Keighley: Wadsworth & Co., The Rydal Press, 1919.

Brittain, Vera. *Testament of Youth.* 1933. Reprint. N.p.: Wideview Books, 1980.

———. *Women's Work in Modern England.* London: Noel Douglas, 1928.

Brookes, Barbara. "Women and Reproduction, c. 1860–1939." In *Labour and Love: Women's Experience of Home and Family 1850–1940,* ed. Jane Lewis. Oxford: Basil Blackwell, 1986, 149–71.

Bryder, Linda. "The First World War: Healthy or Hungry?" *History Workshop Journal* 24 (Autumn 1987): 141–57.

Burnett, John. *Useful Toil: Autobiographies of Working People from the 1820s to the 1920s.* Harmondsworth: Penguin, 1984.

Burnett, John, David Vincent, and David Mayall, eds. *The Autobiography of the Working Class: An Annotated, Critical Bibliography, Vol. II 1900-1945.* New York: New York University Press, 1987.

Cable, Boyd. *Doing Their Bit: War Work at Home.* London: Hodder and Stoughton, 1916.

Cadogan, Mary, and Patricia Craig. *Women and Children First: The Fiction of Two World Wars*. London: Victor Gollancz, 1978.

Caine, Hall. "Britain's Daughters at Dangerous Tasks," *Current History* 5 (December 1916): 423–25.

———. *Our Girls: Their Work for the War*. London: Hutchinson & Co., 1916.

Carrington, Charles, ed. *The Complete Barrack-Room Ballads of Rudyard Kipling*. London: Methuen & Co., 1973.

Carrothers, W. A. *Emigration From The British Isles: With Special Reference To The Development Of The Overseas Dominions*. London: P. S. King & Son Ltd., 1929.

Chadwick, Mrs. Ellis. "The Women Munitioners: Their Bit," *The Englishwoman* (September 1916).

Chinn, Carl. *They Worked All Their Lives: Women of the Urban Poor in England, 1880–1939*. Manchester: Manchester University Press, 1988.

Cohen, Lizabeth. *Making a New Deal: Industrial Workers in Chicago, 1919–1939*. Cambridge: Cambridge University Press, 1990.

Cole, G. D. H. *Labour In War Time*. London: G. Bell and Sons, 1915.

———. *A Short History of the British Working Class Movement 1789–1947*. London: George Allen & Unwin, 1948.

———. *Trade Unionism and Munitions*. Oxford: Clarendon Press, 1923.

———. *Workshop Organization*. Oxford: Clarendon Press, 1923.

Collier, D. J. *The Girl In Industry*. London: G. Bell and Sons, 1918.

Collins, Mary Gabrielle. "Women at Munition Making." In *Scars Upon My Heart: Women's Poetry & Verse of the First World War*, ed. Catherine Reilly. London: Virago, 1981, 24.

Cooke, Miriam, and Angela Woollacott, "Introduction." In *Gendering War Talk*, ed. Cooke and Woollacott. Princeton: Princeton University Press, 1993, ix–xiii.

Cooper, Helen, Adrienne Munich, and Susan Squier, eds. *Arms and the Woman: War, Gender and Literary Representation*. Chapel Hill: University of North Carolina Press, 1989.

Corbett, Mary Jean. *Representing Femininity: Middle-Class Subjectivity in Victorian and Edwardian Women's Autobiographies*. New York and Oxford: Oxford University Press, 1992.

Cosens, Monica. *Lloyd George's Munition Girls*. London: Hutchinson & Co., 1916.

Cott, Nancy. *The Grounding of Modern Feminism*. New Haven: Yale University Press, 1987.

Crosthwait, Elizabeth. "'The Girl Behind the Man Behind the Gun': The Women's Army Auxiliary Corps, 1914–18." In *Our Work, Our Lives, Our Words: Women's History & Women's Work*, ed. Leonore Davidoff and Belinda Westover. London: Macmillan Education, 1986, 161–81.

Culleton, Claire A. "Gender-Charged Munitions: The Language of World War I Munitions Reports," *Women's Studies International Forum* 11, no. 2 (1988): 109–16.

Cummins, Iris A. "The Woman Engineer," *The Englishwoman* 46 (April 1920).

Cunningham, Hugh. "The Language of Patriotism." In *History and Politics*, vol. 1

of *Patriotism: The Making and Unmaking of British National Identity,* ed. Raphael Samuel. London: Routledge, 1989, 57–89.

———. "Leisure." In *The Working Class in England 1875–1914,* ed. John Benson. London: Croom Helm, 1985.

———. "Leisure and Culture." In *People and Their Environment,* vol. 2 of *The Cambridge Social History of Britain 1750–1950,* ed. F. M. L. Thompson. Cambridge: Cambridge University Press, 1990, 279–339.

Daggett, Mabel Potter. *Women Wanted: The Story Written in Blood Red Letters on the Horizon of the Great World War.* New York: George H. Doran Co., 1918.

Davies, E. Chivers. "Communal Kitchens," *The Englishwoman* 34, no. 101 (May 1917): 89–100.

Dekker, Rudolf M., and Lotte C. van de Pol. *The Tradition of Female Transvestism in Early Modern Europe.* New York: St. Martin's Press, 1989.

Dellheim, Charles. "The Creation of a Company Culture: Cadburys, 1861–1931," *American Historical Review* 92, no. 1 (February 1987): 13–44.

Dewar, George A. B. *The Great Munition Feat 1914–1918.* London: Constable & Co. Ltd., 1921.

Dewar, Katharine C. *The Girl.* London: G. Bell and Sons, 1921.

Dougan, David. *The Great Gun-Maker: The Story of Lord Armstrong.* Newcastle: Frank Graham, 1970.

Drake, Barbara. "The Tea-Shop Girl," *Women's Industrial News* 17, no. 61 (April 1913): 115–29.

———. *Women in the Engineering Trades.* London: Fabian Society and George Allen & Unwin, 1917.

———. *Women in Trade Unions.* London: Labour Research Department and George Allen & Unwin, 1920. Reprint. London: Virago, 1984.

Durand, Ralph. *A Handbook to the Poetry of Rudyard Kipling.* New York: Doubleday, Page & Co., 1914.

Dwork, Deborah. *War Is Good for Babies and Other Young Children: A History of the Infant and Child Welfare Movement in England 1898–1918.* London and New York: Tavistock Publications, 1987.

Dyhouse, Carol. *Girls Growing Up in Late Victorian and Edwardian England.* London: Routledge & Kegan Paul, 1981.

E. M. "The Training of the Welfare Worker," *The Englishwoman* 31 (September 1916): 240–51.

Eksteins, Modris. *Rites of Spring: The Great War and the Birth of the Modern Age.* Boston: Houghton Mifflin, 1989.

"Empire Migration," *Edinburgh Review* 236 (July 1922): 200–208.

"The Employment of Women in Munition Factories." In *Excerpt Minutes of Proceedings of the Meetings of the Institution of Mechanical Engineers.* London: Institution of Mechanical Engineers, 15 March 1918.

Fairbanks, A. H. M. "Woman's Position in Industry: The Women's Industrial League," *The Englishwoman* 41 (January 1919): 1–3.

Farnol, Jeffery. *Great Britain At War.* Boston: Little, Brown, 1918.

Fawcett, Millicent Garrett. *The Women's Victory—And After: Personal Reminiscences.* London: Sidgwick & Jackson, 1920.

Ferguson, Neal A. "Women's Work: Employment Opportunities and Economic Roles, 1918–1939," *Albion* 7 (Spring 1975): 55–68.

Forman, Charles. *Industrial Town: Self-Portrait of St. Helens in the 1920s.* London: Granada Publishing, 1979.

Foxwell, Agnes K. *Munition Lasses: Six Months as Principal Overlooker in Danger Buildings.* London: Hodder and Stoughton, 1917.

Fraser, Helen. *Women and War Work.* New York: G. Arnold Shaw, 1918.

Fussell, Paul. *The Great War and Modern Memory.* London: Oxford University Press, 1975.

Gagnier, Regenia. *Subjectivities: A History of Self-Representation in Britain, 1832–1920.* New York and Oxford: Oxford University Press, 1991.

Gates, G. Evelyn, ed. *The Woman's Year Book 1923–1924.* 1st ed. London: Women Publishers Ltd., n.d.

Geertz, Clifford. *The Interpretation of Cultures: Selected Essays.* New York: Basic Books, 1973.

Gilbert, Sandra M. "Soldier's Heart: Literary Men, Literary Women, and the Great War," *Signs* 8, no. 3 (Spring 1983): 422–50.

Gittins, Diana. *Fair Sex: Family Size and Structure, 1900–39.* London: Hutchinson, 1982.

Gluck, Sherna Berger. *Rosie the Riveter Revisited: Women, the War and Social Change.* New York: Meridian, 1987.

Glucksmann, Miriam. "In a Class of Their Own? Women Workers in the New Industries in Inter-war Britain," *Feminist Review* 24 (October 1986): 7–37.

———. *Women Assemble: Women Workers and the New Industries in Inter-war Britain.* London and New York: Routledge, 1990.

Gore, Elizabeth. *The Better Fight: The Story of Dame Lilian Barker.* London: Geoffrey Bles, 1965.

Gould, Jenny. "Women's Military Services in First World War Britain." In *Behind the Lines: Gender and the Two World Wars,* ed. Margaret Randolph Higonnet et al. New Haven: Yale University Press, 1987, 114–25.

Graves, Robert, and Alan Hodge. *The Long Week-End: A Social History of Great Britain 1918–1939.* 1940. Reprint. New York: Norton Library, 1963.

H. S. "Early Phases of Food Control," *Edinburgh Review* 227 (January 1918): 108–30.

Hamilton, Peggy. *Three Years or the Duration: The Memoirs of a Munition Worker, 1914–1918.* London: Peter Owen, 1978.

Handbook and Report of the National Council and Union of Women Workers of Great Britain and Ireland, 1917–1918. London, 1918.

Harrison, Brian. "For Church, Queen and Family: The Girls' Friendly Society 1874–1920," *Past and Present* 61 (November 1973): 107–38.

Harroden, Beatrice. *Our Warrior Women.* London: Witherby & Co., 1916.

Hartley, C. G. *Women's Wild Oats: Essays on the Re-fixing of Moral Standards.* London: T. Werner Laurie Ltd., 1919.

Harvey, David. *The Condition of Postmodernity: An Enquiry into the Origins of Cultural Change.* Oxford: Basil Blackwell, 1989.

Higonnet, Margaret Randolph, Jane Jenson, Sonya Michel, and Margaret Collins

Weitz, eds. *Behind the Lines: Gender and the Two World Wars.* New Haven: Yale University Press, 1987.

Hilton, John. "Public Kitchens," *Quarterly Review* 229 (January 1918): 162–175.

Hinton, James S. *The First Shop Stewards' Movement.* London: George Allen & Unwin, 1973.

Hogg, O. F. G. *The Royal Arsenal: Its Background, Origin, and Subsequent History.* 2 vols. London: Oxford University Press, 1963.

Holmes, Alec. "The Munition Worker: A Play in One Scene," *The Englishwoman* 33 (March 1917): 255–70.

Holt, Richard. *Sport and the British: A Modern History.* Oxford: Clarendon Press, 1989.

Holton, Sandra Stanley. *Feminism and Democracy: Women's Suffrage and Reform Politics in Britain 1900–1918.* Cambridge: Cambridge University Press, 1986.

———. "The Suffragist and the 'Average Woman,'" *Women's History Review* 1, no. 1 (1992): 9–24.

Hope, F. W. *Report on the Physical Welfare of Mothers and Children.* Carnegie United Kingdom Trust, 1917.

Hurwitz, Samuel J. *State Intervention in Great Britain: A Study of Economic Control and Social Response 1914–1919.* 1949. Reprint. London: Frank Cass & Co., 1968.

Hutton, J. E. *Welfare and Housing: A Practical Record of War-Time Management.* London: Longmans, Green and Co., 1918.

Hynes, Samuel. *A War Imagined: The First World War and English Culture.* London: The Bodley Head, 1990.

Ineson, Antonia, and Deborah Thom. "T.N.T. Poisoning and the Employment of Women Workers in the First World War." In *The Social History of Occupational Health,* ed. Paul Weindling. London: Croom Helm, 1985, 89–107.

Inman, P. *Labour in the Munitions Industries.* London: HMSO and Longmans, Green and Co., 1957.

Joint Committee on the Employment of Barmaids. *Women As Barmaids.* London: P. S. King & Son, 1905.

Jones, Gareth Stedman. "Class Expression Versus Social Control? A Critique of Recent Trends in the Social History of 'Leisure,'" *History Workshop* 4 (Autumn 1977): 162–70.

———. *Languages of Class: Studies in English Working Class History 1832–1982.* Cambridge: Cambridge University Press, 1983.

Jones, Stephen G. *Sport, Politics and the Working Class: Organised Labour and Sport in Inter-war Britain.* Manchester: Manchester University Press, 1988.

Joyce, Patrick. *Work, Society and Politics: The Culture of the Factory in Later Victorian England.* New Brunswick, N.J.: Rutgers University Press, 1980.

Keegan, John. *The Face of Battle: A Study of Agincourt, Waterloo and the Somme.* London: Penguin, 1978.

Kelly, Eleanor T. *Welfare Work in Industry: By Members of the Institute of Industrial Welfare Workers.* London: Sir Isaac Pitman & Sons, 1925.

Kent, Susan Kingsley. *Sex and Suffrage in Britain, 1860–1914.* Princeton: Princeton University Press, 1987.

Kinnaird, Emily. *Reminiscences [of the YWCA].* London: John Murray, 1925.

Knight, Lynn. "Introduction." In *We That Were Young,* by Irene Rathbone. 1932. Reprint. New York: Feminist Press at CUNY, 1989, ix–xxv.

Knight, Patricia. "Women and Abortion in Victorian and Edwardian England," *History Workshop* 4 (Autumn 1977): 57–68.

Lawrence, A. Susan. "Women On War Work," *Labour Woman* 3 (August 1915): 315.

Lears, T. J. Jackson. "The Concept of Cultural Hegemony: Problems and Possibilities," *American Historical Review* 90, no. 3 (June 1985): 567–93.

Leed, Eric J. *No Man's Land: Combat and Identity in World War I.* Cambridge: Cambridge University Press, 1979.

Levine, Philippa. "'Walking the Streets in a Way No Decent Woman Should': Women Police in World War One," *Journal of Modern History* (forthcoming March 1994).

Lewis, Jane. "The Working-Class Wife and Mother and State Intervention, 1870–1918." In *Labour and Love: Women's Experience of Home and Family 1850–1940,* ed. Jane Lewis. Oxford: Basil Blackwell, 1986, 99–120.

Liddington, Jill. *The Life and Times of a Respectable Rebel: Selina Cooper 1864–1946.* London: Virago, 1984.

———. *The Road to Greenham Common: Feminism and Anti-Militarism in Britain since 1820.* Syracuse, N.Y.: Syracuse University Press, 1991.

Liddington, Jill, and Jill Norris. *One Hand Tied Behind Us: The Rise of the Women's Suffrage Movement.* London: Virago, 1978.

Liverpool Women's War Service Bureau. *Report August 7th, 1914–August 7th, 1915.* Liverpool, 1915.

Livingstone-Learmonth, Agnes, and Barbara Martin Cunningham. "Observations on the Effects of Tri-Nitro-Toluene on Women Workers," *The Lancet* 2 (12 August 1916): 261–64.

Lloyd, E. M. H. *Experiments in State Control at the War Office and the Ministry of Food.* Oxford: Clarendon Press, 1924.

Lock, Joan. *The British Policewoman: Her Story.* London: Robert Hale, 1979.

Loughnan, Naomi. "Munition Work." In *Women War Workers,* ed. Gilbert Stone. New York: Thomas Y. Crowell Co., 1917, 25–45.

Lown, Judy. *Women and Industrialization: Gender at Work in Nineteenth-Century England.* Cambridge: Polity Press, 1990.

Lowndes, M. "Domestic Service: Certain Considerations," *The Englishwoman* 41 (March 1919): 109–12.

MacDonagh, Michael. *In London During The Great War: The Diary of a Journalist.* London: Eyre and Spottiswoode, 1935.

MacDonald, Sarah. *Simple Health Talks With Women War Workers.* London: Methuen & Co., 1917.

Mack, Amy Eleanor. "Oiling the Human Wheels," *Pearson's Magazine* 43, no. 7 (February 1917): 131–42.

Malcolmson, Patricia E. *English Laundresses: A Social History, 1850–1930.* Urbana: University of Illinois Press, 1986.

Manchester, Salford and District Women's War Interests Committee. *Women in the Labour Market (Manchester & District) during the War.* Manchester: William Morris Press, 1917.

Marcus, Jane. "Afterword." In *We That Were Young,* by Irene Rathbone. 1932. Reprint. New York: Feminist Press at CUNY, 1989, 467–98.

———. "The Asylums of Antaeus; Women, War and Madness: Is There a Feminist Fetishism?" In *The Difference Within: Feminism and Critical Theory,* ed. Elizabeth Meese and Alice Parker. Philadelphia: John Benjamins Publishing, 1988.

Marshall, Catherine, C. K. Ogden, and Mary Sargant Florence. *Militarism Versus Feminism: Writings on Women and War.* 1915. Rev. ed., ed. Margaret Kaminer and Jo Vellacott. London: Virago, 1987.

Martin, Hugh. *The Girl He Left Behind Him: The Story of a War-Worker.* Published for the YWCA. London: Witherby & Co., 1916.

Marwick, Arthur. *The Deluge: British Society and The First World War.* London: The Bodley Head, 1965.

———. *Women At War 1914–1918.* London: Fontana, 1977.

Mason, M. H. "Public Morality: Some Constructive Suggestions," *Nineteenth Century* 82 (July 1917): 185–94.

McCalman, Janet. "The Impact of the First World War on Female Employment in England," *Labour History* 21 (November 1971): 36–47.

McCrone, Kathleen E. *Playing the Game: Sport and the Emancipation of English Women, 1870–1914.* Lexington: University Press of Kentucky, 1988.

McFeely, Mary Drake. *Lady Inspectors: The Campaign for a Better Workplace 1893–1921.* New York & Oxford: Basil Blackwell, 1988.

McKenna, Elaine. *Better Than Dancing: The Wandering Years of a Young Australian, Mary Brennan.* Richmond, Victoria: Greenhouse Publications, 1987.

McLaren, Barbara. *Women of the War.* London: Hodder and Stoughton, 1917.

Michel, Sonya. "Danger on the Home Front: Motherhood, Sexuality and Disabled Veterans in American Postwar Films." In *Gendering War Talk,* ed. Miriam Cooke and Angela Woollacott. Princeton: Princeton University Press, 1993, 260–79.

Mitchell, David. *Women on the Warpath: The Story of the Women of the First World War.* London: Jonathan Cape, 1966.

Monk, Una. *New Horizons: A Hundred Years of Women's Migration.* London: HMSO, 1963.

Mosse, George L. *Fallen Soldiers: Reshaping the Memory of the World Wars.* New York: Oxford University Press, 1990.

"Mothers in Factories," *The Englishwoman* 41 (January 1919): 9–11.

Munson, James, ed. *Echoes of the Great War: The Diary of the Reverend Andrew Clark 1914–1919.* Oxford: Oxford University Press, 1985.

National Council of Women of Great Britain and Ireland. *Annual Council Meeting in Harrogate, 8th, 9th, & 10th October 1918.* Occasional paper no. 80. N.p., n.d.

———. *The History of the Official Policewomen.* London, 1922.

Newsome, Stella. *Women's Freedom League 1907–1957.* London: Women's Freedom League, n.d.

Niven, M. M. *Personnel Management, 1913–63: The Growth of Personnel Management and the Development of the Institute.* London: Institute of Personnel Management, 1967.

"On War Service. Some Thoughts on Factory Life," *The Englishwoman* 41 (January 1919): 18–20.

"Origin of the Women's Legion," *War Service Legion and Women's Legion, 1915–1918.* N.p., n.d.

"Overworked Women," *The Englishwoman* 36, no. 106 (October 1917): 1–12.

Owings, Chloe. *Women Police: A Study of the Development and Status of the Women Police Movement.* New York: Frederick H. Hitchcock, 1925.

Pankhurst, E. Sylvia. *The Home Front: A Mirror to Life in England during the First World War.* London: Hutchinson & Co., 1932.

Pedersen, Susan. "Gender, Welfare and Citizenship in Britain during the Great War," *American Historical Review* 95, no. 4 (October 1990): 983–1006.

———. "The Failure of Feminism in the Making of the British Welfare State," *Radical History Review* 43 (1989): 86–110.

Peel, C. S. *How We Lived Then, 1914–1918: A Sketch of Social and Domestic Life in England During the War.* London: John Lane The Bodley Head Ltd., 1929.

Peiss, Kathy. *Cheap Amusements: Working Women and Leisure in Turn-of-the-Century New York.* Philadelphia: Temple University Press, 1986.

Pember Reeves, Maud. *Round About a Pound a Week.* 1913. Reprint. London: Virago, 1979.

Pennybacker, Susan. "'It Was Not What She Said But the Way in Which She Said It': The London County Council and the Music Halls." In *Music Hall: The Business of Pleasure,* ed. Peter Bailey. Milton Keynes: Open University Press, 1986, 118–40.

Pepper, Simon, and Mark Swenarton. "Home Front Garden Suburbs for Munition Workers," *Architectural Review* 163 (April-June 1978): 366–75.

Percival, Arthur. "The Faversham Gunpowder Industry and Its Development," *Faversham Papers,* no. 4. Kent: The Faversham Society, 1967.

Perkin, Harold. *The Rise of Professional Society: England Since 1880.* London and New York: Routledge, 1989.

Peto, D. O. G. "The Training of Women Police and Women Patrols," *The Englishwoman* 32 (October 1916): 22–27.

Phillips, Mary E. "The Effect of the War on Women in Factories and Workshops," *Our Outlook* (YWCA) 9, no. 96 (April 1916): 75.

Pierson, Ruth Roach. "Experience, Difference, Dominance and Voice in the Writing of Canadian Women's History." In *Writing Women's History: International Perspectives,* ed. Karen Offen, Ruth Roach Pierson, and Jane Rendall. Bloomington and Indianapolis: Indiana University Press, 1991, 79–106.

Private (W.A.A.C.) on Active Service. *The Letters of Thomasina Atkins.* New York: George H. Doran Co., 1918.

Proud, E. Dorothea. *Welfare Work: Employers' Experiments for Improving Working Conditions in Factories.* London: G. Bell & Sons, 1916.

Pursell, Carroll. "'Am I A Lady or An Engineer?': The Origins of the Women's Engineering Society in Britain 1918–1927," *Technology and Culture* 34 (January 1993): 78–97.

Purvis, June. *Hard Lessons: The Lives and Education of Working-Class Women in Nineteenth-Century England.* Cambridge: Polity Press, 1989.

Radway, Janice A. *Reading the Romance: Women, Patriarchy and Popular Literature.* Chapel Hill: University of North Carolina Press, 1984.

Rathbone, Eleanor F. "The Remuneration of Women's Services." In *The Making of Women: Oxford Essays in Feminism,* ed. Victor Gollancz. London: George Allen & Unwin, 1917, 100–127.

Roberts, Elizabeth. *A Woman's Place: An Oral History of Working-Class Women 1890–1940.* Oxford: Basil Blackwell, 1984.

Roberts, Robert. *The Classic Slum: Salford Life in the First Quarter of the Century.* Manchester: Manchester University Press, 1971.

Rose, Lionel. *The Massacre of the Innocents: Infanticide in Britain 1800–1939.* London: Routledge & Kegan Paul, 1986.

Rose, Sonya. *Limited Livelihoods: Gender and Class in Nineteenth-Century England.* Berkeley: University of California Press, 1992.

Ross, Ellen. "Labour and Love: Rediscovering London's Working-Class Mothers, 1870–1918." In *Labour and Love: Women's Experience of Home and Family 1850–1940,* ed. Jane Lewis. Oxford: Basil Blackwell, 1986, 73–96.

———. "Survival Networks: Women's Neighbourhood Sharing in London Before World War I," *History Workshop* 15 (Spring 1983): 4–27.

Rowntree, B. Seebohm. *The Human Needs of Labour.* London: Thomas Nelson and Sons, 1918.

Rowntree, B. Seebohm, and Frank D. Stuart. *The Responsibility of Women Workers for Dependants.* Oxford: Clarendon Press, 1921.

Scott, J. D. *Vickers: A History.* London: Weidenfeld and Nicolson, 1962.

Scott, Joan W. "The Evidence of Experience," *Critical Inquiry* 17, no. 4 (Summer 1991): 773–97.

Scott, W. Herbert. *The Story of Barnbow: Embodying a Complete Record of War Work and Service at the No. 1 Filling Factory, Leeds.* Leeds: Jns. D. Hunter & Sons, 1919.

Shadwell, A. "The Welfare of Factory Workers," *Edinburgh Review* 224 (October 1916): 361–81.

Smith, Bonnie. *Changing Lives: Women in European History Since 1700.* Lexington, Mass.: D. C. Heath and Co., 1989.

Smith, Ellen. *Wage-Earning Women and Their Dependants.* London: The Fabian Society, 1915.

Smith, Harold. "The Issue of 'Equal Pay for Equal Work' in Great Britain, 1914–19," *Societas* 8 (Winter 1978): 39–51.

———. "Sex vs. Class: British Feminists and the Labour Movement, 1919–1929," *The Historian* 47, no. 1 (November 1984): 19–37.

———, ed. *British Feminism in the Twentieth Century.* Amherst: University of Massachusetts Press, 1990.

Smith, Helen Zenna. *Not So Quiet . . . Stepdaughters of War.* 1930. Reprint. New York: Feminist Press at CUNY, 1989.

Smith, Robinson. "Efficiency," *Quarterly Review* 229 (January 1918): 110–20.

Society for the Oversea Settlement of British Women. *Report of S.O.S.B.W. Year Ending December 31st, 1920.* N.p., n.d.

Soldon, Norbert C. *Women in British Trade Unions 1874–1976.* Dublin: Gill and Macmillan, 1978.

Standing Joint Committee of Industrial Women's Organisations, Report Presented to the Joint Committee on Labour Problems After the War. *The Position of Women After the War.* London: Cooperative Printing Society Ltd., 1917.

Stanley, Beryl. "Women in Unrest, 1914–1918," *Labour Monthly* 22 (August 1940): 458–64.

Steedman, Carolyn Kay. *Landscape For A Good Woman: A Story of Two Lives.* New Brunswick, N.J.: Rutgers University Press, 1987.

Stevenson, John. *British Society 1914–45.* Harmondsworth: Penguin, 1984.

Strachey, Ray, ed. *Our Freedom and Its Results.* London: Leonard & Virginia Woolf, 1936.

Stubbs, M. H. *Friendship's Way: Being the History of the Girls' Friendly Society, 1875–1925.* London, 1926.

Stubbs, Patricia. *Women & Fiction: Feminism & The Novel 1880–1920.* London: Methuen & Co., 1981.

Summerfield, Penny. "Women, War and Social Change: Women in Britain in World War II." In *Total War and Social Change,* ed. Arthur Marwick. New York: St. Martin's Press, 1988, 95–118.

Summers, Anne. *Angels and Citizens: British Women as Military Nurses 1854–1914.* London: Routledge & Kegan Paul, 1988.

Theweleit, Klaus. *Male Fantasies.* Vol. 1. Minneapolis: University of Minnesota Press, 1987.

Thom, Deborah. "Tommy's Sister: Women at Woolwich in World War I." In *Minorities & Outsiders,* vol. 2 of *Patriotism: The Making and Unmaking of British National Identity,* ed. Raphael Samuel. London: Routledge, 1989, 144–57.

———. "Women and Work in Wartime Britain." In *The Upheaval of War: Family, Work and Welfare in Europe, 1914–1918,* ed. Richard Wall and Jay Winter. Cambridge: Cambridge University Press, 1988, 297–326.

———. "Women at the Woolwich Arsenal 1915–1919," *Oral History* 6 (Autumn 1978): 58–73.

Thompson, E. P. *The Making of the English Working Class.* 1963. Reprint. Penguin, 1980.

Tilly, Louise A., and Joan W. Scott. *Women, Work and Family.* New York and London: Methuen & Co., 1987.

Turner, C. "National Kitchens and National Health," *The Englishwoman* 39, no. 117 (September 1918): 97–101.

Tylee, Claire. *The Great War and Women's Consciousness: Images of Militarism and Womanhood in Women's Writings, 1914–64.* Iowa City: University of Iowa Press, 1990.

———. "'Maleness Run Riot'—The Great War and Women's Resistance to Militarism," *Women's Studies International Forum* 11, no. 3 (1988): 199–210.

Underhill, G. E. "British Rationing During The War," *Quarterly Review* 234 (October 1920): 280–300.

———. "The Food Problem 1914–1916," *Quarterly Review* 230 (July 1918): 145–65.

Usborne, H. M. *Women's Work in War Time: A Handbook of Employments.* London: T. Werner Laurie, 1917.

Valverde, Mariana. "The Love of Finery: Fashion and the Fallen Woman in Nineteenth-Century Social Discourse," *Victorian Studies* 32 (Winter 1989): 169–88.

Vellacott, Jo. "Feminist Consciousness and the First World War," *History Workshop Journal* 23 (Spring 1987): 81–101.

Vernon, H. M. *The Health and Efficiency of Munition Workers*. London: Oxford University Press, 1940.

Verschoyle, C. M. "The Street Again," *The Englishwoman* 32 (October 1916): 72–80.

Vicinus, Martha. *Independent Women: Work and Community for Single Women 1850–1920*. Chicago: University of Chicago Press, 1985.

Waites, Bernard. *A Class Society at War: England 1914–1918*. Leamington Spa: Berg, 1987.

Walbrook, H. M. "Women Police and Their Work," *Nineteenth Century* 85 (February 1919): 377–82.

Walby, Sylvia. *Patriarchy at Work: Patriarchal and Capitalist Relations in Employment*. Cambridge: Polity Press, 1986.

Walshe, Ellen. "A Munition-Makers' Canteen," *The Englishwoman* 28 (October 1915): 29–35.

Walvin, James. *Leisure and Society 1830–1950*. London: Longman, 1978.

Waters, Chris. *British Socialists and the Politics of Popular Culture 1884–1914*. Stanford: Stanford University Press, 1990.

Webb, Beatrice. *Health of Working Girls: A Handbook for Welfare Supervisors and Others*. London: Blackie and Son Ltd., 1917.

Wells, H. G. "The Woman and the War: What It Has Already Meant and What It Will Mean," *Ladies' Home Journal* (June 1916): 10, 59–62.

West, Rebecca. "Hands That War," *Daily Chronicle*, 1916. In *The Young Rebecca: Writings of Rebecca West 1911–1917*, ed. Jane Marcus. New York: Viking Press, 1982, 380–90.

Wheelwright, Julie. *Amazons and Military Maids: Women Who Dressed as Men in the Pursuit of Life, Liberty and Happiness*. London: Pandora, 1989.

Wilson, Trevor. *The Myriad Faces of War: Britain and the Great War 1914–1918*. Cambridge: Polity Press, 1986.

Winter, J. M. *The Great War and the British People*. Cambridge, Mass.: Harvard University Press, 1986.

Wolfe, Humbert. *Labour Supply and Regulation*. Oxford: Clarendon Press, 1923.

"Women in the Munitions Court," *The Englishwoman* 33 (March 1917): 213–21.

The Women Police Service. London: WPS, 1919.

The Women Police Service: An Account of Its Aims with a Report of Work Accomplished During the Year 1915–16. London: St. Clements Press, 1916.

The Women Police Service: A Report of Work Accomplished During the Year 1916–17. London: St. Clements Press, 1917.

The Women Police Service: A Report of Work Accomplished during the Year 1918–1919. N.p., n.d.

"Women's Employment—United Kingdom," *Encyclopaedia Britannica* 12th ed. Vol. 31–32 (1922), 1045–52.

Women's Industrial League. *Memorial to the Prime Minister on the Future Employment of Women in Industry and Mr. Lloyd George's Reply Thereto Constituting a New Charter for Women in Industry*. London: Women's Industrial League, 1918.

Women's Trade Union League. *Fortieth Annual Report . . . September, 1915*. Manchester, 1915.

———. *Forty-second Annual Report*. September 1917.

———. *Forty-third Annual Report*. 1918.

"Women's War Work—United Kingdom—Women's Land Army," *Encyclopaedia Britannica* 12th ed. Vol. 31–32 (1922), 1058.

The Women's Who's Who 1933. London: Shaw Publishing Co.

Women's Who's Who 1934–5. London: Shaw Publishing Co.

Woolf, Virginia. *Three Guineas*. 1938. Reprint. New York: Harcourt, Brace, Jovanovich, 1966.

Woollacott, Angela. "Sisters and Brothers in Arms: Family, Class and Gendering in World War I Britain." In *Gendering War Talk*, ed. Miriam Cooke and Angela Woollacott. Princeton: Princeton University Press, 1993, 128–47.

Yates, L. K. *The Woman's Part: A Record of Munitions Work*. New York: George H. Doran Co., 1918.

Yeo, Eileen and Stephen Yeo. "Ways of Seeing: Control and Leisure versus Class and Struggle." In *Popular Culture and Class Conflict 1590–1914: Explorations in the History of Labour and Leisure,* ed. Eileen and Stephen Yeo. Sussex: Harvester Press, 1981, 128–54.

YWCA. *Central Committee for Work among Girls in Military Centres*. Pamphlet 9, November 1914.

———. *Homes for Working Girls in London: The Work of the Year 1914*. London, n.d.

———. *Homes for Working Girls in London: The Work of the Year 1915*. London, n.d.

Index

Abortion, 148–50
Absenteeism, 68, 100
Adamson, Rhoda, 59
Addison, Christopher (Minister of Munitions), 61
Advisory Committee on Women's War Employment (Industrial), 48
Age, of women munitions workers, 37–38
Aintree National Amatol Factory, 76
Aircraft factories, 30
Air raids, 86–87
Allen, Mary, 124, 172, 175, 185
Amalgamated Society of Engineers (ASE), 92, 103, 112, 114, 181
Anderson, Adelaide, 60, 69, 80, 104
Armistice, 106
Armstrong's, 29
Asquith, Herbert Henry, 189
Austin Motor works, Birmingham, 32
Authority, women in positions of, 166–67, 166n.8. See also Women's war work: in professions

Barker, Lilian, 43, 151, 169–70, 184
Barker, Lottie, 4, 84
Barnbow National Factory, Leeds, 59, 62, 79, 146, 199
Beardmore's shipyard, Clydebank, 138, 202

Bedford, Madeline Ida, 125
Benevolent donations, of women munitions workers, 80, 124
Billeting of Civilians Act of May 1917, 49–50
Bineham, Lilian, 43, 100, 146, 199
Birth control, 147n.37, 149. See also Abortion; Infanticide
Birth rate, during World War I, 147–48
Braybon, Gail, 15n.35
British Women's Emigration Association (BWEA), 110
Brunner, Mond & Co., Silvertown, 85
Bryant, Grace, 21–22
Bryder, Linda, 60
Buchanan & Sons, Liverpool, 98

Campbell, Janet, 59
"Canary girls," 81, 193n.13, 205
Canteens, 63–65
Canute aircraft factory, 208
Cardonald National Projectile Factory, 65
Castle, Olive, 34
CE (compound explosive), 81
Central Control Board (Liquor Traffic), 63–64, 127
Chargehands, 166–67
Chilwell National Shell-Filling Factory, 4, 84
Chinn, Carl, 190

Christian evangelizing, 155–57
Churchill, Winston (Minister of
    Munitions), 77, 99
Cinema, 140–41
Class: differences among women, 2, 53–
    54, 162, 179–82; tensions among
    women, 4, 41–43, 158, 163–64,
    167, 168–70, 181–82. See also Cross-
    class interaction, among women;
    Feminists: class differences among;
    Middle-class women
Class identity, v. gender identity, 12, 166,
    182, 186–87, 216
Clubs, for women workers, 104, 155–60
Clydeside engineering and munitions
    works, 92
Communal kitchens, 63
Comradeship, among women workers,
    44–45, 138–39. See also Sisterhood
"Controlled establishments," private
    munitions works as, 90
Convalescent homes, for workers, 79–80
Cordite, 35, 81
Cosens, Monica, 52, 66, 200–201
Cost of living: rise in, early in the war,
    23–24; rise in, throughout the war,
    117–19
Creed's Munition Factory, Croydon,
    103
Crèches. See Nurseries
Cross-class interaction, among women, 2,
    13, 40–43, 162–64, 185–86. See also
    Class
Culleton, Claire, 213
Cycling, 48, 142

Dancing, 141–42
Deaths, among women munitions
    workers, 9–10, 211; from chemical
    poisoning, 80–84; from explosions,
    9n.21, 84–86
Defence of the Realm Regulations, 51
Demobilization, 89, 105–12; hostility
    toward women during, 105–6, 111–
    12; women's demonstrations against,
    106–7
Differences, among women munitions
    workers, 37, 58; age, 37–38; class,
    40–42, 162–63, 166–67, 179–82,
    185–87; country of origin, 38–39;
    racial, 39; regional, 39, 55; sexual, 39;
    tensions generated by, 43–44

"Dilution," 27, 30, 91–92, 91n.4, 94–95,
    116–17, 202; and Ministry of
    Munitions, 27, 180, 202
Divorce, 153–54. See also Marriage
Domestic Servants' Union, 185
Domestic service: changed attitudes
    toward, after war, 182–85;
    unpopularity of, 4, 5, 20
Doping, of airplanes, 33; "dope," 81
Drinking, 126–28, 143n.27; public
    charges of, 126–27

Emigration, of demobilized workers,
    110–11
Employment, of women: in munitions
    work, 25; in non-war-related
    occupations, 26; in paramilitary
    organizations, 26–27; postwar,
    111, 112n.89, 183–85; prewar,
    19–22
The Engineer, 95
Equal pay, lack of, 115–17, 122
Ethnic tension, among women workers,
    43–44
Experience, as category of historical
    analysis, 11–12, 11n.26
Explosions, in munitions factories, 84–
    88; deaths attributed to, 9n.21
Explosives, 35, 80–81

Fabian Women's Group, 121
Factory outings, 142–43
Fairey Aviation Company, 66
"Family wage," 120–22
Faversham, Kent, 192
Fawcett, Millicent Garrett, 165, 191
Feminists: class differences among, 165;
    views of war of, 164–66. See also
    Women's war work: feminist views of
Feminist scholarship, on gender and war,
    11, 13
Fiction: about women munitions
    workers, 8–9, 125, 205–6; read by
    women munitions workers, 203–6
Fights, among women workers, 43–44
First aid facilities, 73, 79
First Aid Nursing Yeomanry (FANY), 19,
    27
"Flappers," 4, 112, 144
Food rationing, 61–63
Football, 138
Friendship, among women. See

Comradeship, among women workers; Sisterhood
Fussell, Paul, 10

Gagnier, Regenia, 207
Gaiety, of women workers, 44–45, 138–39
Garden allotments, 63
Gender identity, v. class identity, 12, 166, 182, 186–87, 216
Gender significance: of public censure of women munitions workers' spending, 126, 133; of uniforms, 211–12; of women's clothes, 128–33; of women's munitions work, 2–3, 13, 192–201, 215–16; of women's war experience, 10, 207–16; of women's war work, 5–6
Georgetown National Filling Factory, Renfrewshire, 29, 47, 66, 138, 167, 198
Gilbert, Sandra, 204, 209–11
Girls' Friendly Society, 51, 55, 155–57
Greenwood and Batley Ltd., Leeds, 105, 150
Gretna, 22, 35, 46, 64, 68, 103–4, 174, 193
Gwynne's airplane engine factory, Chiswick, 32, 41, 142

Hamilton, Peggy, 129, 182
Harrison, Brian, 157
Health, 59–61, 65, 88, 215; and factory health checks, 73; and working conditions, 69–70; and working hours, 65–68. See also Health of Munition Workers Committee; Nutrition; TNT poisoning; Toxic jaundice
Health of Munition Workers Committee, 59, 67, 71–72, 75, 83
Hereford shell-filling factory, 43
Hirst, T. F., 93
History of the Ministry of Munitions, 18–19
Holton, Sandra Stanley, 189
Holton Heath Cordite Factory, 176
Home Office, 66, 126
Hostels, for munitions workers, 50–57
Housing, 48–50; hostels, 50–57; and rent control, 49
Household budgets, women's autonomy over, 123–24

Huddersfield national factory, 65
Hynes, Samuel, 14

Imperial War Museum, xiii, 30; Department of Sound Records of, 146, 202, 207
Industrial accidents, 79–80. See also Explosions, in munitions factories
Infanticide, 150–52
Institute of Personnel Management, 187
Institution of Mechanical Engineers, 95–96

Jaundice. See Toxic jaundice
Jones, Gareth Stedman, 130
Joyce, Patrick, 136, 160

King's Norton Club for women munitions workers, Abbey Wood, 141
Kynoch's munitions works, Stanford-le-hope, Essex, 106

Labor exchanges, 23, 24, 46, 49, 98, 108
Leaving certificates, 90, 97–99
Lee, Beatrice, 33, 108, 117, 208
Leisure, of women munitions workers, 135–43; beyond the factory, 139–43; in the factory, 136–39; historical significance of, 160–61
Leisure, working-class, 134–35
Liddington, Jill, 165
Lloyd George, David, 29, 63, 71, 107, 114
Lodgings, 48–50
London Association of Medical Women, 59
London Exhibition of Women's Work in Munition Production, 93
Lyddite, 81

Macarthur, Mary R., 102, 122, 143–44, 165, 168
Male experience of war, 10, 211
Marcus, Jane, 182, 210n.61
Marriage: ending in separation, 153–54; as portrayed in romance fiction, 205–6; rate of, during World War I, 153–54; women workers' attitudes toward 152–55. See also Divorce
Married women: and control of household budgets, 122–23; and job mobility, 120; prohibition against

Married women (*continued*)
    employment of, 20,145–46; and
    separation allowances, 119
Maternalism, 79
"Maternal nature," of women, 212–14
Maternity homes, 77
May, Amy, 44, 193n.13, 198
McIntyre, Elsie, 62, 167, 199
Medical officers, in munitions factories,
    76, 83
"Men's work," 30–33, 114–17
Middle- and upper-class women
    munitions workers, 180–82. *See also*
    Cosens, Monica; Hamilton, Peggy;
    Williams, Joan
Middle-class women, 2; recruitment of, as
    munitions workers, 40. *See also* Class
Midwives, 77
Miles, Lilian, 33, 48, 81–82, 141
Ministry of Munitions: exhibition of
    skilled work by women organized by,
    95; Intelligence and Record Section
    of, 30, 104; and private companies,
    29; providing housing for workers,
    50–51; recruitment of workers by, 38,
    40; and rent control, 49; role and
    policies of, 25, 30, 67–68, 85–86,
    90–94, 97, 107; and scientific
    management, 72; and TNT poisoning,
    82–83; welfare work of, 60, 94, 160
Munition Makers' Canteens Committee,
    64
Munitions, definition of, 24–25
Munitions factories, 27–30; accidents in,
    79–80; explosions in 84–88; strikes
    at, 104–5; welfare work in, 72–76;
    working conditions in, 69–70;
    working hours at, 65–68. *See also
    names of individual factories*
Munitions industries, 24–26; regulation
    of, 25
Munitions of War Act: of 1915, 47, 90,
    92, 97, 114; of 1917, 91
Munitions of War (Amendment) Act of
    1916, 90–91, 99, 114
Munitions tribunals, 90, 97–101, 116
Munition Wages (Bedford), 125
Music hall, 139–40

National Federation of Women Workers
    (NFWW), 70, 99, 101, 102–3, 116,
    186; and demobilization, 105, 108;
    and opposition to hostels, 54; and
    opposition to welfare supervisors, 168
National Organisation of Girls' Clubs,
    159
National projectile factories, 29
National shell-filling factories, 29–30
National Union of General Workers, 101,
    102–3, 186
National Union of Women's Suffrage
    Societies, 164, 173, 189
National Union of Women Workers
    (NUWW), 155, 159. *See also* Women
    patrols; Women Patrols Committee
Newman, Sir George, 64, 71
Nurseries, for munitions workers, 74, 77–
    79; postwar abolition of, 79
Nurses, 7
Nutrition, 60–61, 72; and communal
    kitchens, 63; and factory canteens, 65;
    and garden allotments, 63; and food
    rationing, 61–63

"On Her Their Lives Depend" (poster), 6
Oral history, 207–9
Order of the British Empire, 8, 87–88
Outwork, 34, 68
Overlookers, 166–67

Pankhurst, Sylvia, 118, 147–48, 165
Pemberton Billings aircraft factory,
    Southampton, 97, 141
Pembrey explosives factory, South Wales,
    35, 39, 69, 105, 174
Pirelli's wire-cable factory, Southampton,
    4, 117
Plumstead National Filling Factory, 203
Poisoning, 35, 80–84. *See also* TNT
    poisoning
Pregnant workers, 75–76, 119, 148–52
Public acclamation, 8
Public censure: gender significance of,
    126, 133; of women munitions
    workers' spending, 124–26, 128–33;
    of women's drinking, 126–28
"The Purple Poms," 141

Queen's Ferry, 35

Recreational activities: clubs for women
    workers, 155–60; entertainment,
    139–41; factory outings, 142; at

hostels, 56–57; rest huts, 155–56; social events, 137; sport, 137–38, 142
Rennles, Caroline, 8n.15, 86, 87, 181, 194, 197
Rent control, 49
Representation of the People Act of 1918, 188
Representations, of women munitions workers' lives, 8–9, 205–9
Respectability, 42, 42n.14
Rest huts, 155–59
Restoration of Pre-War Practices Act of 1919, 92, 101, 109
Roberts, Robert, 149, 190, 191–92
Rose, Sonya, 89
Rowntree, Seebohm, 71, 121
Royal Aircraft Factory, Farnborough, 30
Royal Naval Air Service aircraft factory, White City, 30
Rubin, Gerry, 101

Scarborough bag factory, 117
Scientific management, 66–68, 71–72, 71n.43
Scottish Filling Factory. See Georgetown National Filling Factory
Separation. See Marriage
Separation allowances, 119, 154
"Servant problem," 20
Sex Disqualification (Removal) Act of 1919, 188
Sexual harassment, 99, 202
Sexual morality and activity, 143–46, 148
Silvertown, explosion at, 85–86
Sisterhood, 44–45. See also Comradeship
Slades Green shell-filling factory, 87
Smith, Bonnie, 190
Smith, Harold, 115
Social activities. See Recreational activities
Society of Women Welders, 103, 109
Songs, sung by workers, 43, 44, 192–94, 193n.13
Southampton rolling mills, 76
Spending. See Household budgets, women's autonomy over; Public censure: of women munitions workers' spending
Special Arbitration Tribunal for Women's Wages, 115–16
Sport, for women munitions workers, 137–38
Standard of living: rise in, for women, 123–24; rise in, for working class, 120
Steedman, Carolyn, 130
Stephens, P. L., 96–97, 210
Strikes, by women, 104–5. See also Trade unionism, among women workers
Suffrage, 164–65, 164n.3, 172–73, 188–90; and women munitions workers, 189–90

Taylor, O. M., 33, 145–46, 196
Thom, Deborah, 200, 201
TNT poisoning, 73, 79, 80–84, 82n.80, 193–94, 205
"Tommy" ("Tommy Atkins"), 1, 6, 10, 15, 197, 201, 203
"Tommy's sister," 6–7, 10, 15, 37, 89, 197
Toxic jaundice, 81–84, 193–94; commercial exploitation of, 82
Trade unionism, among women workers, 101–4, 102n.44. See also Strikes, by women
Trade unionists, men: attitudes of toward women workers, 91–94, 101, 102n.46, 109, 181, 201–3
Trade unions: and "dilution," 91–92; and hostels for women workers, 54–55; and Restoration of Pre-War Practices Act, 92. See also names of individual unions
Training courses, for munitions workers, 92–94
Travel, to work, 46–48
Treasury Agreements, 92, 114
Treasury Conferences of March 1915, 92
Trousers, women in, 212
Tylee, Claire, 10, 210n.61

Unemployment: early in war, 23–24; at end of war, 105–8, 111; and Restoration of Pre-War Practices Act, 109; women's protests against, 106–7. See also Unemployment benefits
Unemployment benefits, 105–8
Uniforms, 132; gender significance of, 211–12

Valverde, Mariana, 131
Vicinus, Martha, 181
Vickers, 29, 51–52, 67, 122, 180

Voluntary Aid Detachments (VADs), 7, 19, 27, 214

Wages, 90–91, 113–17; effects on, of Ministry of Munitions, 113–16, 118–19
Waites, Bernard, 216
"War babies," 4, 147–48
War Cabinet Committee on Women in Industry, 18, 168, 191
Welfare Department of the Ministry of Munitions, 46–47, 50, 71–72, 76–80, 136, 167
Welfare supervisors, 70–76, 136–37, 148, 167–70; extramural, 49–50, 74–75
West, G. M., 35, 39, 40, 43, 69, 105
White and Poppe's factory, Coventry, 33, 63, 141
Williams, Joan, 32, 41, 47, 66, 102, 142–43
Winter, J. M., 60
Women: autonomy of, 1, 3, 190–92, 216; as breadwinners, 120–22; heterosexual relationships of, affected by war, 152; war experience of, 1; and World War I, historiographical debate about, 14–15, 15nn.35,37, 214–15. See also Married women; Middle- and upper-class women munitions workers; Middle-class women; Working-class women
Women drivers, 26, 33; women ambulance drivers, 7, 19, 210, 210n.62
Women factory inspectors, 68–70
Women in engineering: after war, 112; before war, 21
Women munitions workers: age range of, 37–38; demobilization of, 105–12; employers' attitudes toward, 94–96; disputes among, 43–44; gaiety among, 44–45, 138–39; mobility of, 46–48, 96–97; number of, 17–19, 30, 31; and pride in work, 45; relations of, with male coworkers, 197, 201–3; relations of, with men in armed forces, 197–201; and sense of group identity, 45; as symbol of modernity, 3; training of, 92–94; types of work performed, 31–36, 181; views of their own role in war, 192–

201, 207–9, 213–14. See also Health; Housing; Wages
Women patrols, 53, 176–78
Women Patrols Committee (of the NUWW), 157–58, 170–73, 176, 178–79
Women police, 53, 151
Women Police Service (WPS), 35, 124, 170–75, 178–79, 211; work of, for Ministry of Munitions, 173–74
Women Relief Munition Workers' Organisation, 41, 180
Women's Army Auxiliary Corps (WAAC), 7, 19, 26, 27
Women's clothes, cultural and gender significance of, 128–33
Women's Engineering Society, 109, 186
Women's experience of war, gender significance of, 10, 207–16
Women's International League for Peace and Freedom, 164
Women's Land Army, 19, 27, 211
Women's munitions work: areas of, 30–35; dangers of, 9–10, 33, 35; discomforts of, 4, 33–35; feminist views of, 11; gender significance of, 2–3, 13, 192–201, 215–16; historical significance of, 15, 189–92, 215–16; incentives for, 19–22, 194–96, 213; as liberating, 4, 110, 112, 190–92, 208–11, 215–16; as outwork, 34; pride in, 45; as war experience, 1–2, 7–11, 192–201
Women's Royal Air Force (WRAF), 27, 196
Women's Royal Naval Service (WRNS), 27, 196
Women's Social and Political Union (WSPU), 172
Women's Trade Union League (WTUL), 116, 23, 70, 102, 155, 186
Women's war work: gender significance of, 5–6; in professions, 26, 83, 162–64; and wartime work other than munitions, 26–27. See also Authority, women in positions of
Woolwich Advisory Committee on Women's Employment, 49
Woolwich Arsenal, 28–29; age range of workers at, 38; air raids on, 87; canteens at, 64, 65; class tension among women at, 182; comradeship

among women workers at, 44;
demobilized workers from, 107;
explosions at, 85, 86; hostels at, 53–
54, 56–57; munitions tribunals for
workers at, 100; outwork at, 34;
relations with male coworkers at, 197,
201, 203; sexual morality and sexual
activity at, 146; songs sung by
workers at, 193n.13; support for
wounded soldiers at, 199; TNT
poisoning at, 81; transport to, 47;
uniforms at, 132; unpopularity of
domestic service at, 184; welfare
supervisors at, 43, 73, 169; women
patrols at, 178; working hours at, 66
Workers' Union, 102–3, 185
Working Classes Cost of Living
Committee, 117–18, 120, 123–24
Working-class women: and benefits of
war, 5; and birth control, 146, 149;
and cross-class interactions, 12–13,
40–42, 162–66, 179, 181–82, 185–

87; and divorce, 154; and marriage,
154; and same-class interactions, 42–
43; status of, after war, 190
Working hours, 65–66; and absenteeism,
68; and health, 65–67; and
productivity, 67
World War I: British cultural memory of,
10–11; imaginative impact of, 14

Yorkshire Copper Works, Leeds, 108,
117, 208
YWCA: advocacy of, for women workers,
34, 70; canteen workers, 87; clubs
and rest huts, 44, 135, 155–57;
concern of, over war marriages, 153;
emigration work of, 110; hostels, 23,
51, 55–56, 77; publications for
women workers, 205, 207; split at
end of war, 56, 56n.65, 156

Zeppelins, 86–87

Compositor:	Terry Robinson & Co.
Text:	10/13 Galliard
Display:	Galliard
Printer and Binder:	Edwards Brothers, Inc.